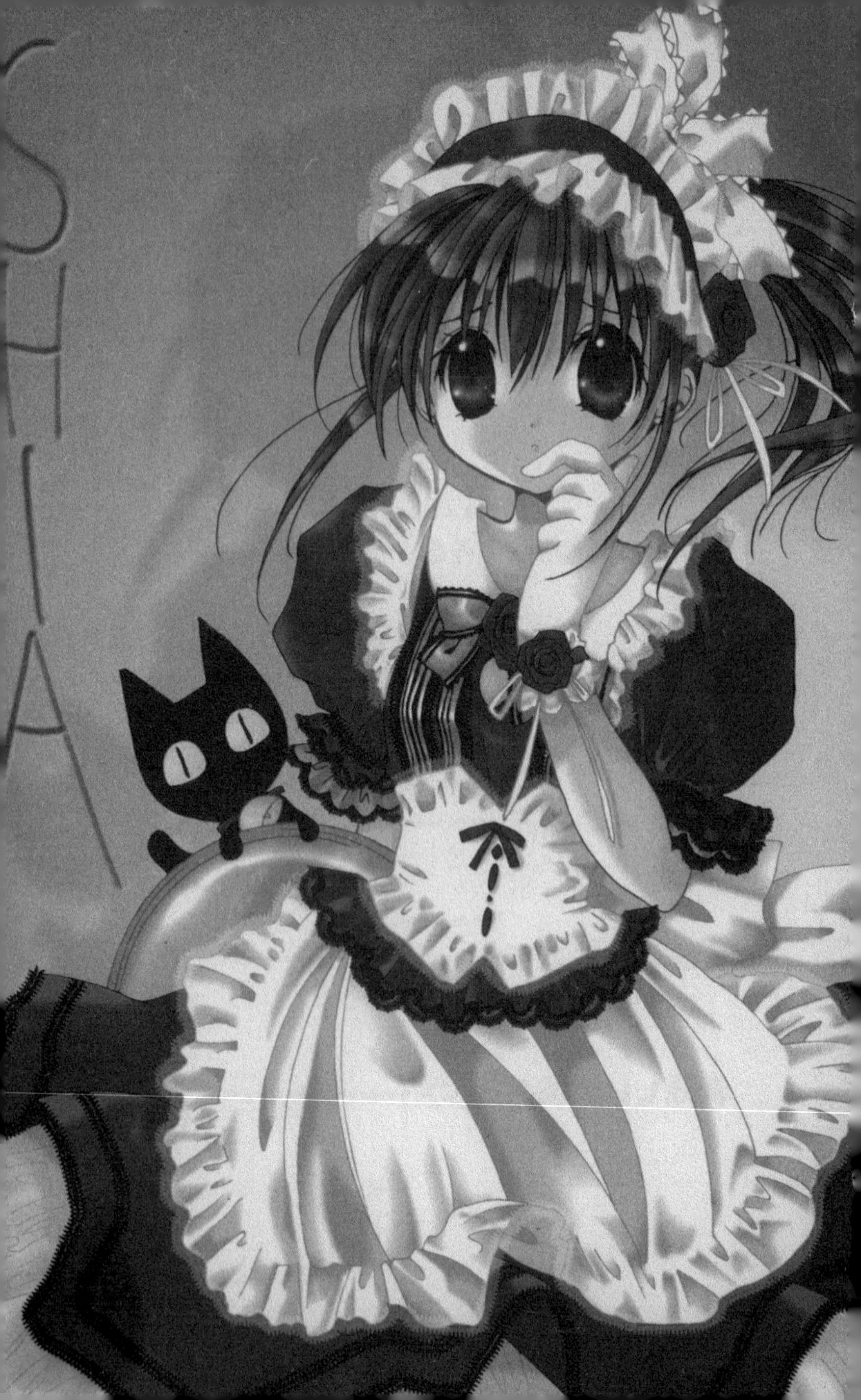

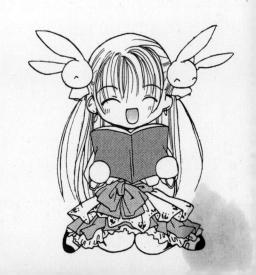

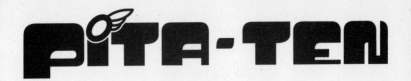

Volume 2

by
Koge-Donbo

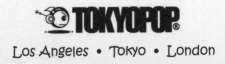

Los Angeles • Tokyo • London

Translator - Nan Rymer
English Adaptation - Adam Arnold
Copy Editors - Troy Lewter & Carol Fox
Retouch and Lettering - Abelardo Bigting
Cover Layout - Raymond Makowski
Graphic Designer - James Lee

Editor - Paul Morrissey
Managing Editor - Jill Freshney
Production Coordinator - Antonio DePietro
Production Managers - Jennifer Miller & Mutsumi Miyazaki
Art Director - Matt Alford
Editorial Director - Jeremy Ross
VP of Production - Ron Klamert
President & C.O.O. - John Parker
Publisher & C.E.O. - Stuart Levy

Email: editor@TOKYOPOP.com

Come visit us online at www.TOKYOPOP.com

A 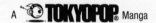 Manga

TOKYOPOP Inc.
5900 Wilshire Blvd. Suite 2000
Los Angeles, CA 90036

Pita-Ten Vol. 2

©2000 Koge-Donbo.
First published in Japan in 2000 by Media Works Inc., Tokyo, Japan.
English publication rights arranged through Media Works Inc.

English text copyright ©2004 TOKYOPOP Inc.

ISBN: 1-59182-628-4

First TOKYOPOP printing: March 2004

10 9 8 7 6 5 4 3 2 1

Printed in the USA

Contents

Lesson 8
How to Finish an Assignment 5

Lesson 9
How to Welcome a New Student: Part I 30

Lesson 10
How to Welcome a New Student: Part II 55

Lesson 11
How to Work a Bit of Mischief 87

Lesson 12
How to Cheer a Person Up 121

Lesson 13
How to Elegantly Eat Apples 245

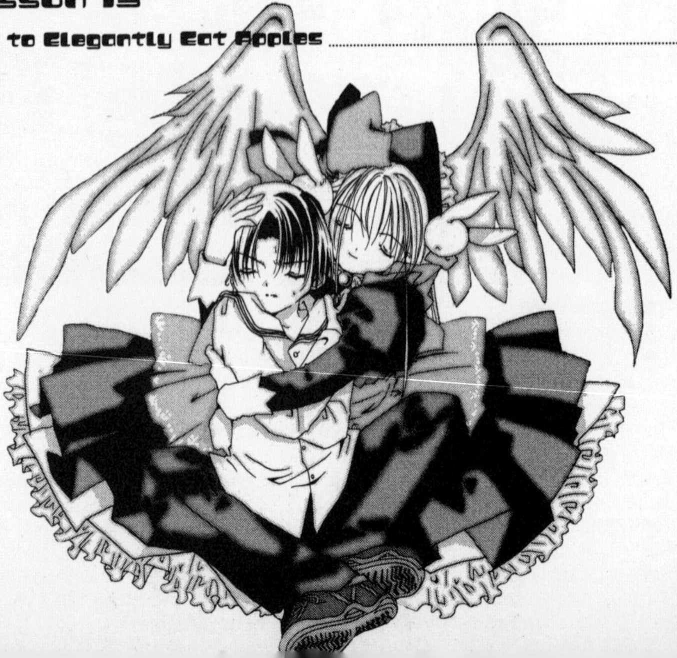

CHARACTERS

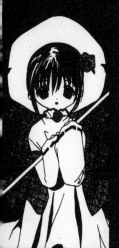

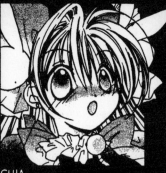

MISHA
This insanely perky girl is Kotarou's new next-door neighbor and her main passion in life is stalking and glomping Kotarou! Is she really an angel?

KOTAROU HIGUCHI
A calm and collected sixth grader who lives alone with his father. He's currently trying to study for his upcoming middle school entrance exams.

SHIA
A very polite and quiet girl who is great at cooking and cleaning. Little is known about her life before she became Misha's new roommate.

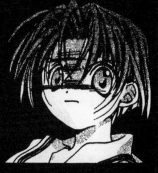

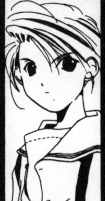

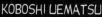

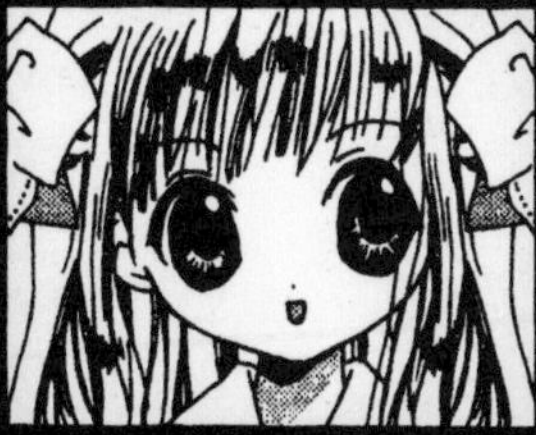

KOBOSHI UEMATSU
This semi-sweet loudmouth has the hots for Kotarou and can't stand the fact that Misha is honing in on her territory.

TAKASHI AYANOKOJI
Nicknamed Ten-chan, Takashi is nothing short of a ladies man. He's great at sports, is outgoing, and he never has to study!

The Story So Far:

A quiet elementary school student, Kotarou Higuchi is worse off than most kids. His mother died in a traffic accident and his workaholic father is never at home. This leaves Kotarou struggling to make it to school on time, cook his own meals, go shopping and keep up with his studies. Yet, his so-called normal life has thrown him a curve ball in the form of a mysterious girl named Misha who has not only moved in next door to him, but also started to attend the very same middle school as him! Out of loneliness and desperation, Misha decides to make it her life's work to chase after, "abuse" and latch on to Kotarou. But somehow, Kotarou adapts and life settles back down...that is, until *another* strange girl shows up. This time, it is Shia, a black-haired girl whose mere presence causes both Kotarou and Misha to receive pounding headaches amongst other supernatural side effects. Nonetheless, Shia's gentle demeanor and reserved personality manage to win the hearts of everyone but Kotarou, and she ultimately moves in as Misha's new roommate.

Lesson 8

How to Finish an Assignment

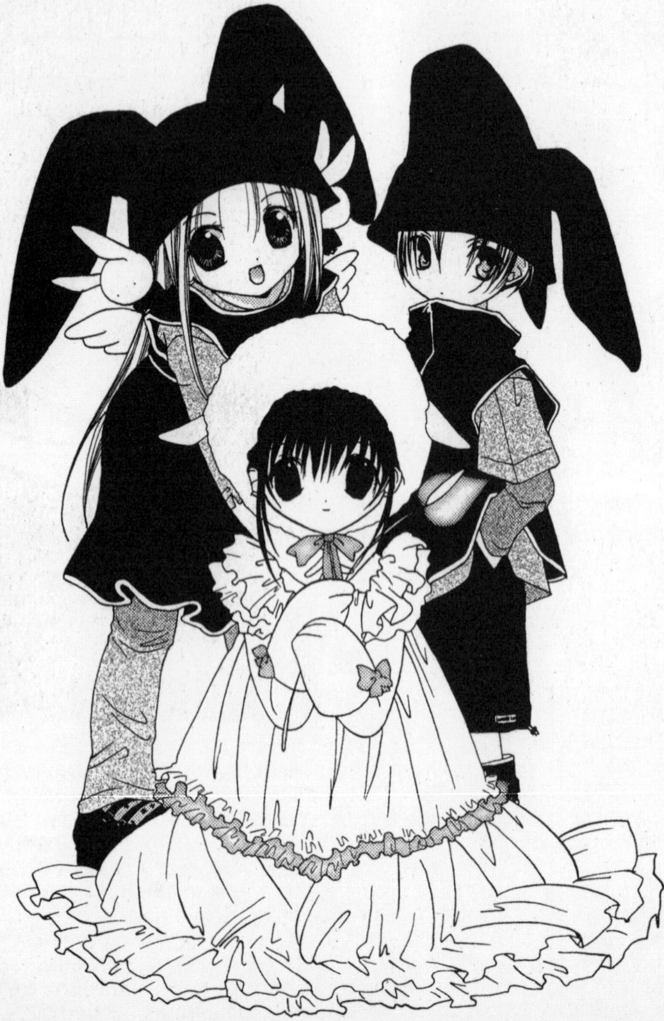

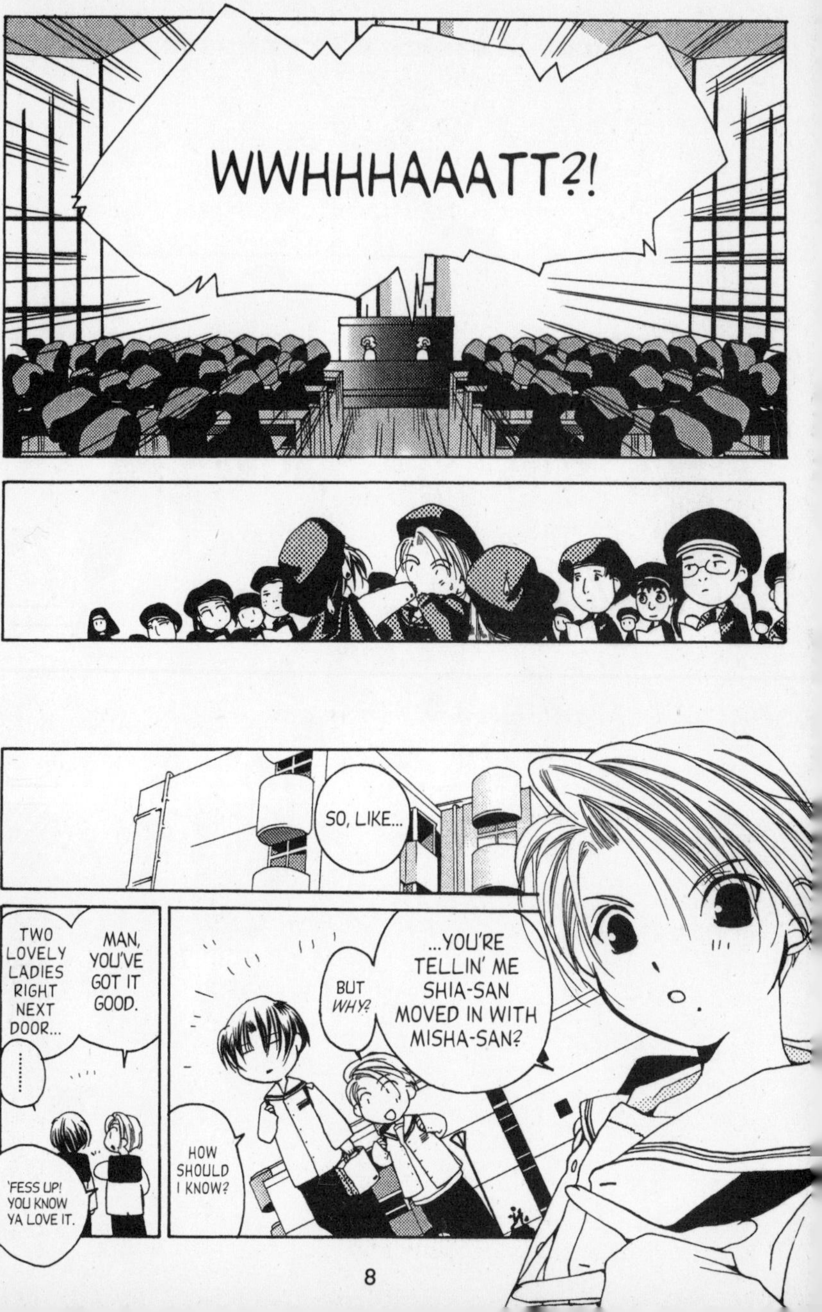
WWHHHAAATT?!
SO, LIKE...
...YOU'RE TELLIN' ME SHIA-SAN MOVED IN WITH MISHA-SAN?
BUT WHY?
HOW SHOULD I KNOW?
MAN, YOU'VE GOT IT GOOD.
TWO LOVELY LADIES RIGHT NEXT DOOR...
......
'FESS UP! YOU KNOW YA LOVE IT.

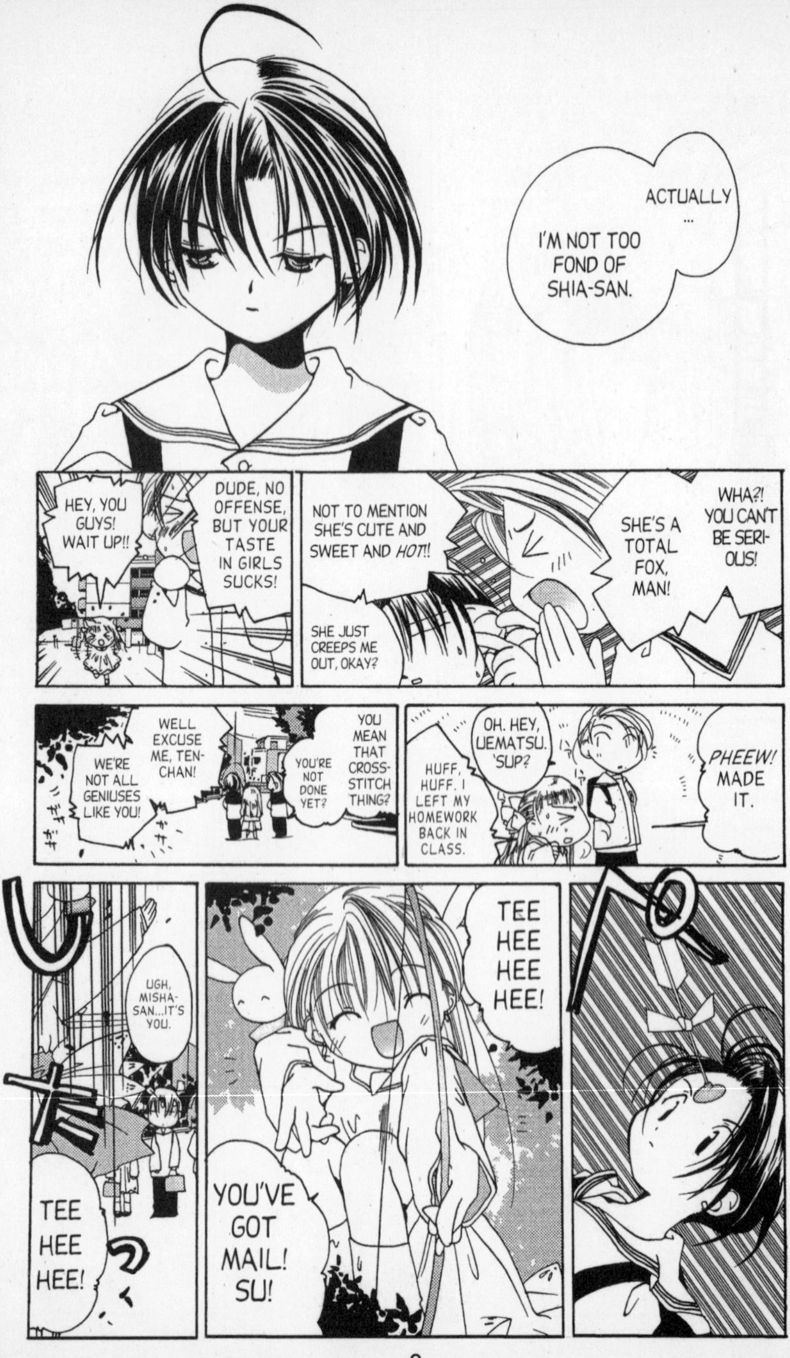
ACTUALLY ...
I'M NOT TOO FOND OF SHIA-SAN.
WHA?! YOU CAN'T BE SERI-OUS!
SHE'S A TOTAL FOX, MAN!
NOT TO MENTION SHE'S CUTE AND SWEET AND *HOT*!!
SHE JUST CREEPS ME OUT, OKAY?
DUDE, NO OFFENSE, BUT YOUR TASTE IN GIRLS SUCKS!
HEY, YOU GUYS! WAIT UP!!
PHEEW! MADE IT.
OH. HEY, UEMATSU. 'SUP?
HUFF, HUFF. I LEFT MY HOMEWORK BACK IN CLASS.
YOU MEAN THAT CROSS-STITCH THING?
YOU'RE NOT DONE YET?
WELL EXCUSE ME, TEN-CHAN!
WE'RE NOT ALL GENIUSES LIKE YOU!
TEE HEE HEE HEE!
YOU'VE GOT MAIL! SU!
UGH, MISHA-SAN...IT'S YOU.
TEE HEE HEE!

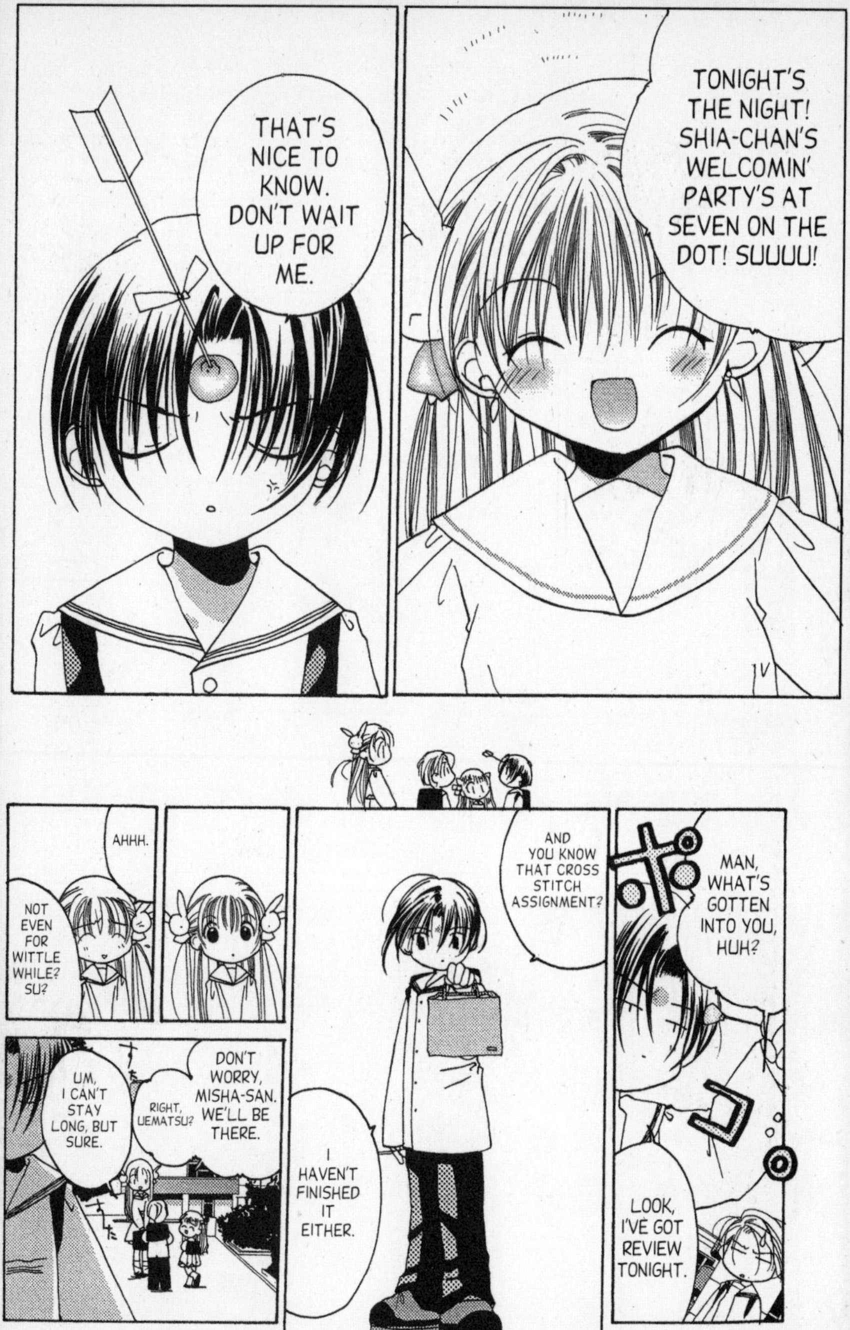

TONIGHT'S THE NIGHT! SHIA-CHAN'S WELCOMIN' PARTY'S AT SEVEN ON THE DOT! SUUUU!
THAT'S NICE TO KNOW. DON'T WAIT UP FOR ME.
MAN, WHAT'S GOTTEN INTO YOU, HUH?
LOOK, I'VE GOT REVIEW TONIGHT.
AND YOU KNOW THAT CROSS STITCH ASSIGNMENT?
I HAVEN'T FINISHED IT EITHER.
AHHH.
NOT EVEN FOR WITTLE WHILE? SU?
DON'T WORRY, MISHA-SAN. WE'LL BE THERE.
RIGHT, UEMATSU?
UM, I CAN'T STAY LONG, BUT SURE.

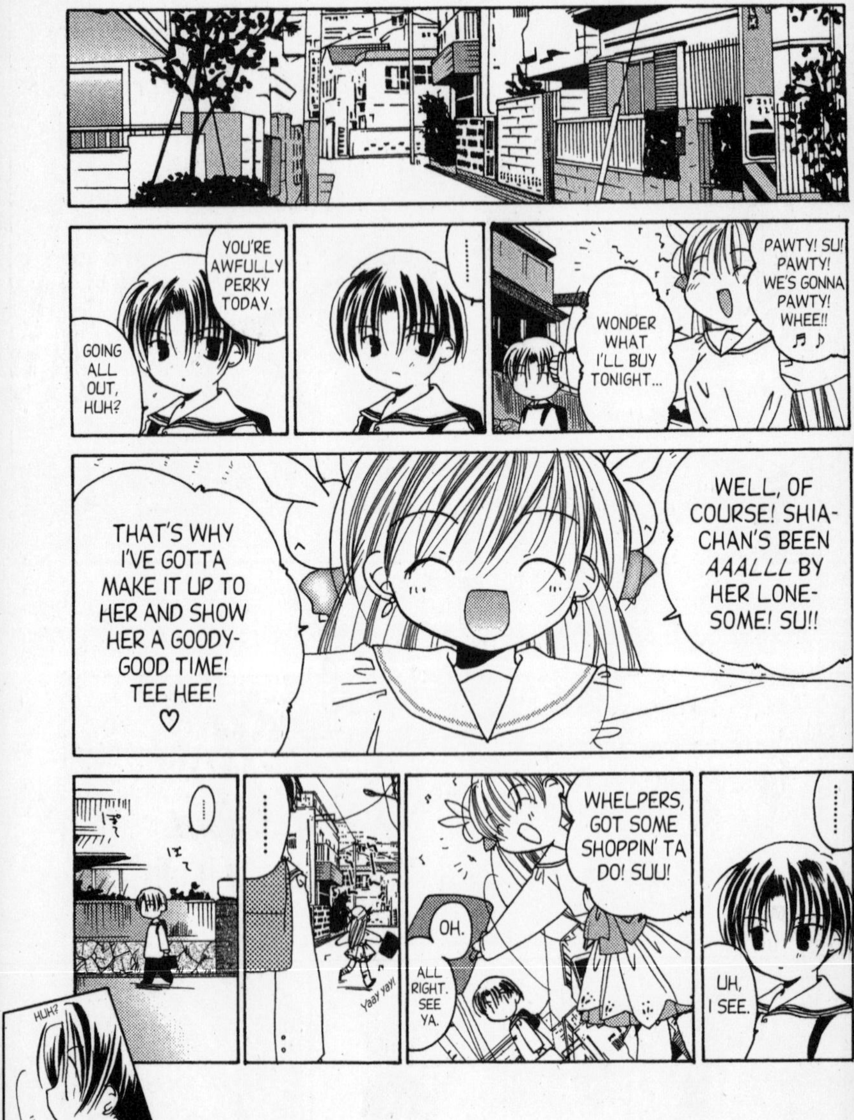
PAWTY! SU! PAWTY! WE'S GONNA PAWTY! WHEE!! ♬♪
WONDER WHAT I'LL BUY TONIGHT...
......
YOU'RE AWFULLY PERKY TODAY.
GOING ALL OUT, HUH?
WELL, OF COURSE! SHIA-CHAN'S BEEN *AAALLL* BY HER LONE-SOME! SU!!
THAT'S WHY I'VE GOTTA MAKE IT UP TO HER AND SHOW HER A GOODY-GOOD TIME! TEE HEE! ♡
......
UH, I SEE.
WHELPERS, GOT SOME SHOPPIN' TA DO! SUU!
OH.
ALL RIGHT. SEE YA.
....
Yaay yay!
......
HUH?

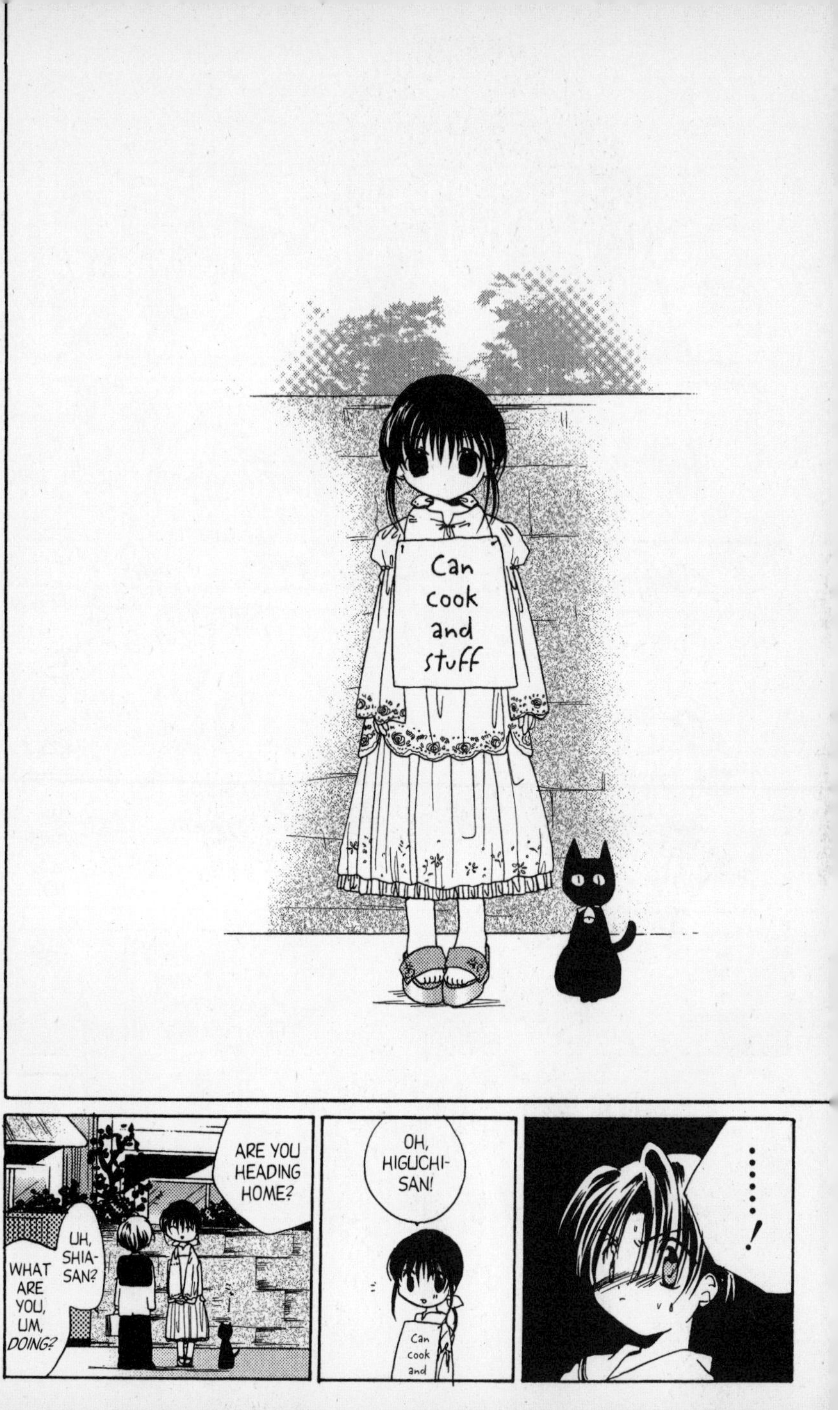
Can cook and stuff
......!
OH, HIGUCHI-SAN!
Can cook and
ARE YOU HEADING HOME?
UH, SHIA-SAN?
WHAT ARE YOU, UM, DOING?

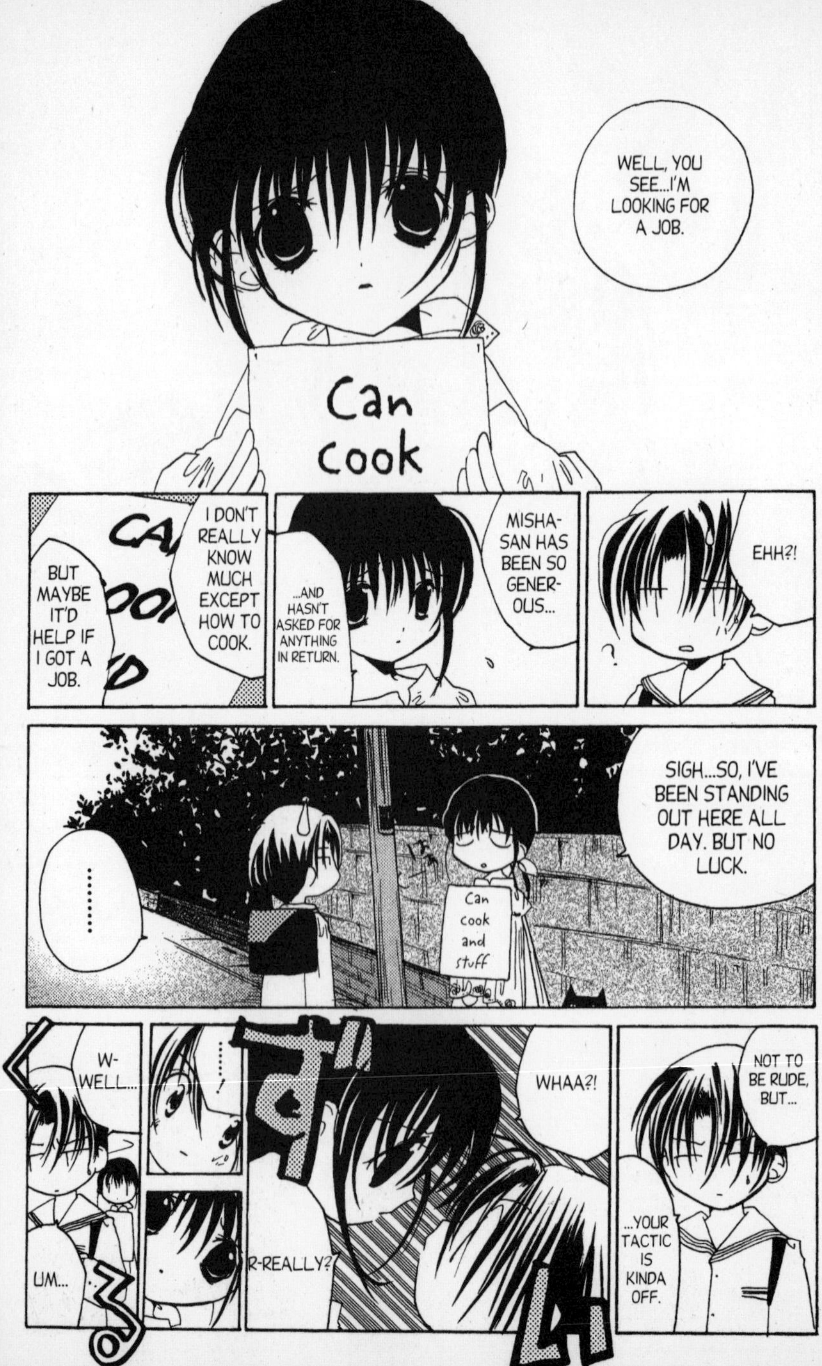
WELL, YOU SEE...I'M LOOKING FOR A JOB.
Can cook
EHH?!
MISHA-SAN HAS BEEN SO GENEROUS...
...AND HASN'T ASKED FOR ANYTHING IN RETURN.
I DON'T REALLY KNOW MUCH EXCEPT HOW TO COOK.
BUT MAYBE IT'D HELP IF I GOT A JOB.
SIGH...SO, I'VE BEEN STANDING OUT HERE ALL DAY. BUT NO LUCK.
Can cook and stuff
......
NOT TO BE RUDE, BUT...
...YOUR TACTIC IS KINDA OFF.
WHAA?!
......!
R-REALLY?
W-WELL...
UM...

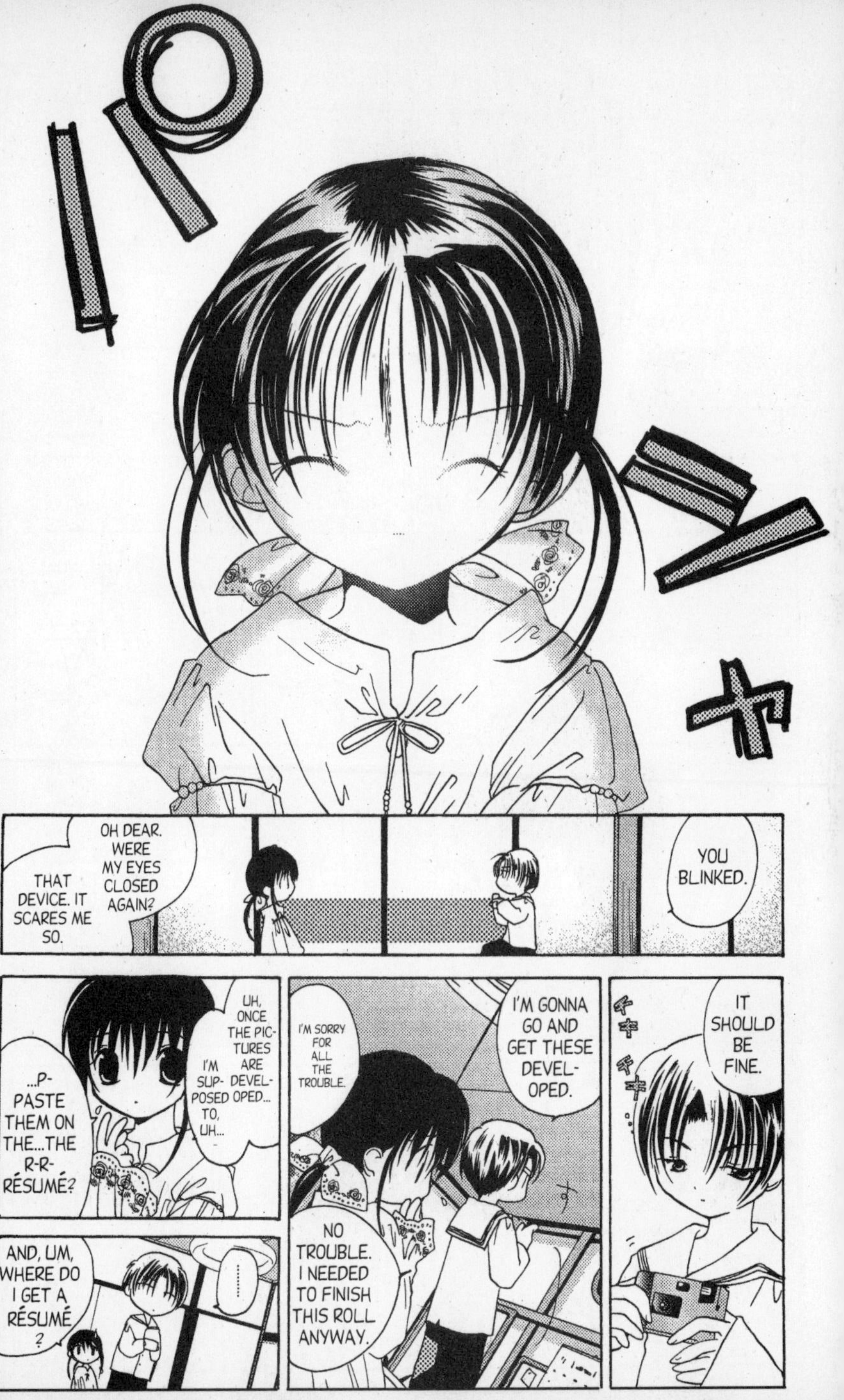
YOU BLINKED.
OH DEAR. WERE MY EYES CLOSED AGAIN?
THAT DEVICE. IT SCARES ME SO.
IT SHOULD BE FINE.
I'M GONNA GO AND GET THESE DEVEL-OPED.
I'M SORRY FOR ALL THE TROUBLE.
NO TROUBLE. I NEEDED TO FINISH THIS ROLL ANYWAY.
UH, ONCE THE PIC-TURES ARE DEVEL-OPED...
I'M SUP-POSED TO, UH...
...P-PASTE THEM ON THE...THE R-R-RÉSUMÉ?
......
AND, UM, WHERE DO I GET A RÉSUMÉ?

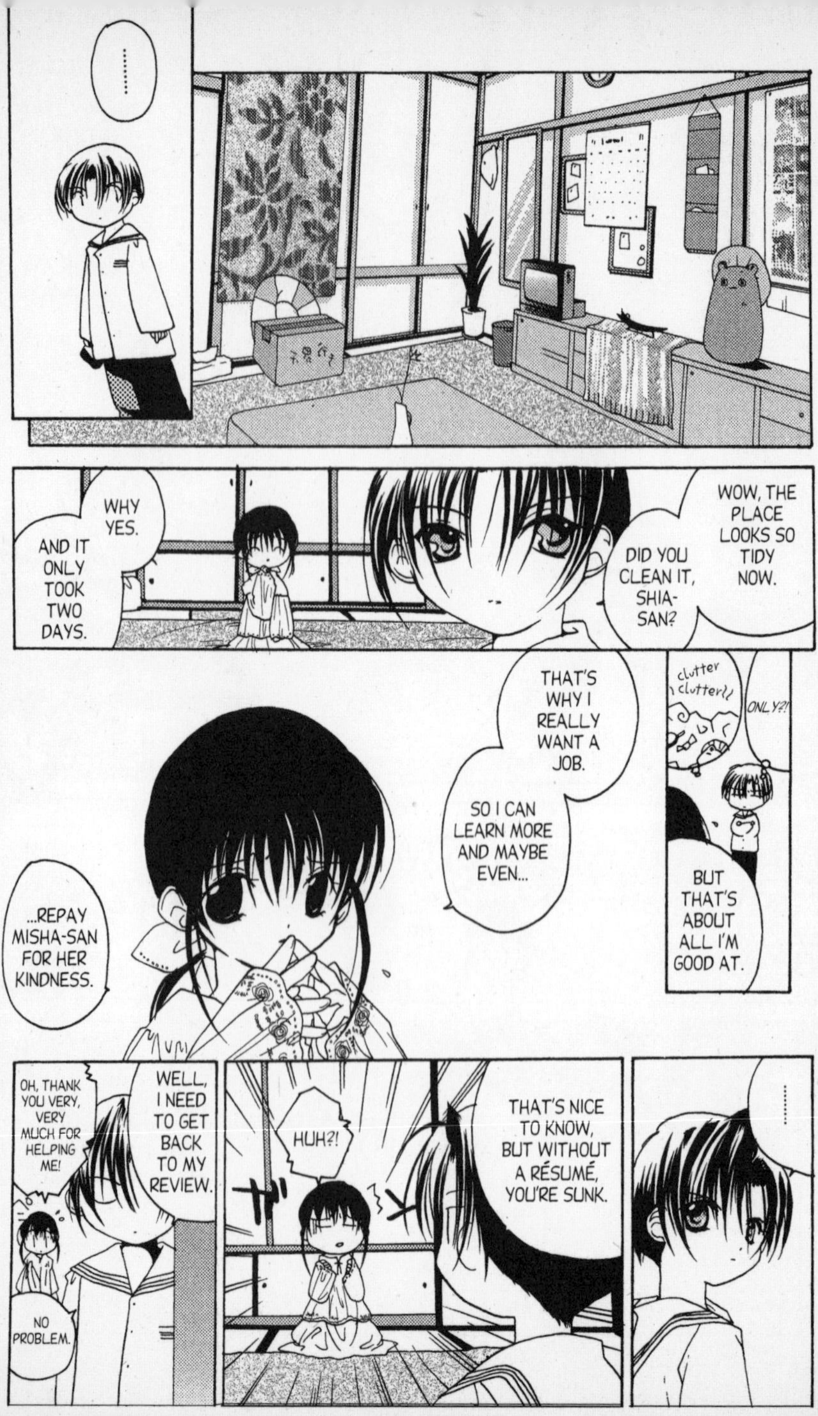

......
WOW, THE PLACE LOOKS SO TIDY NOW.
DID YOU CLEAN IT, SHIA-SAN?
WHY YES.
AND IT ONLY TOOK TWO DAYS.
ONLY?!
clutter clutter
BUT THAT'S ABOUT ALL I'M GOOD AT.
THAT'S WHY I REALLY WANT A JOB.
SO I CAN LEARN MORE AND MAYBE EVEN...
...REPAY MISHA-SAN FOR HER KINDNESS.
......
THAT'S NICE TO KNOW, BUT WITHOUT A RÉSUMÉ, YOU'RE SUNK.
HUH?!
WELL, I NEED TO GET BACK TO MY REVIEW.
OH, THANK YOU VERY, VERY MUCH FOR HELPING ME!
NO PROBLEM.

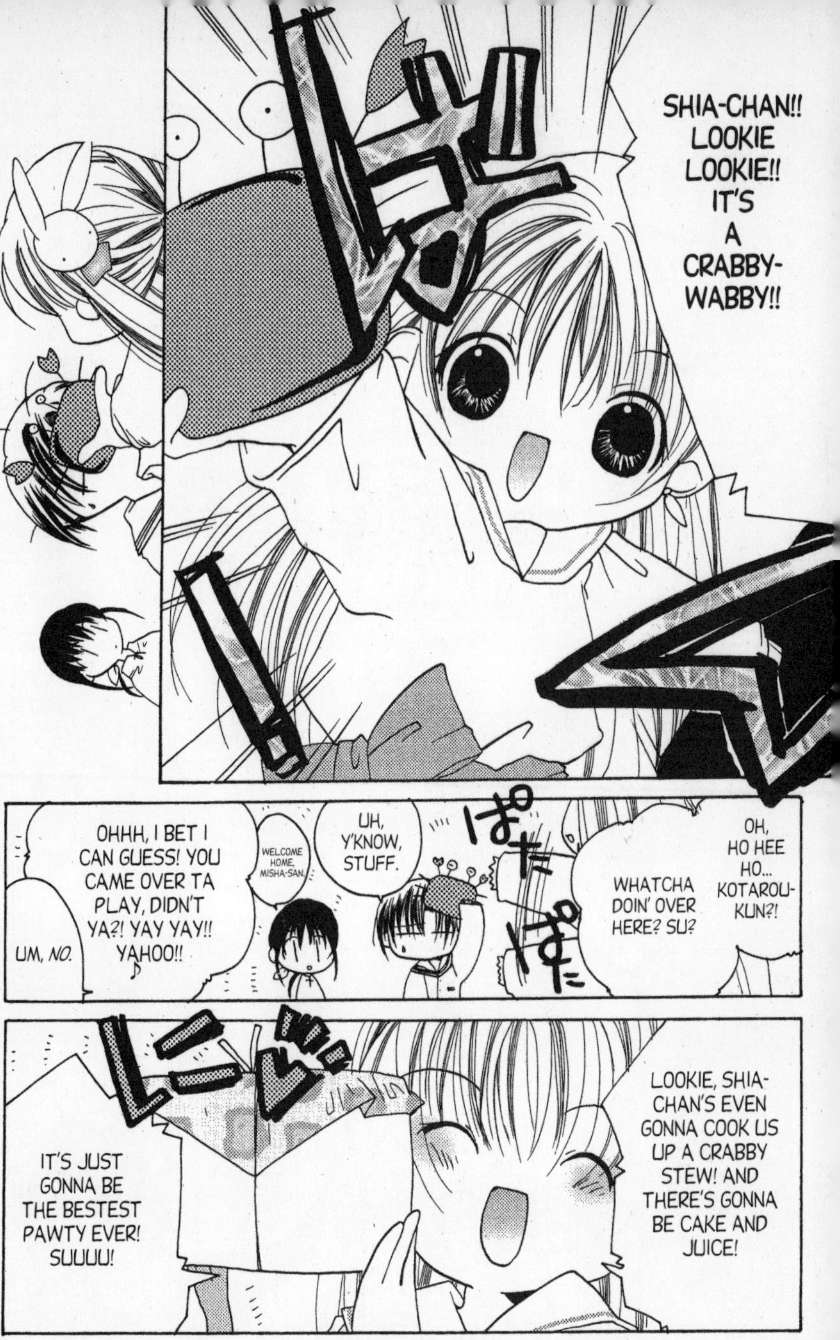
SHIA-CHAN!! LOOKIE LOOKIE!! IT'S A CRABBY-WABBY!!
OH, HO HEE HO... KOTAROU-KUN?!
WHATCHA DOIN' OVER HERE? SU?
UH, Y'KNOW, STUFF.
WELCOME HOME, MISHA-SAN.
OHHH, I BET I CAN GUESS! YOU CAME OVER TA PLAY, DIDN'T YA?! YAY YAY!! YAHOO!! ♪
UM, NO.
LOOKIE, SHIA-CHAN'S EVEN GONNA COOK US UP A CRABBY STEW! AND THERE'S GONNA BE CAKE AND JUICE!
IT'S JUST GONNA BE THE BESTEST PAWTY EVER! SUUUU!

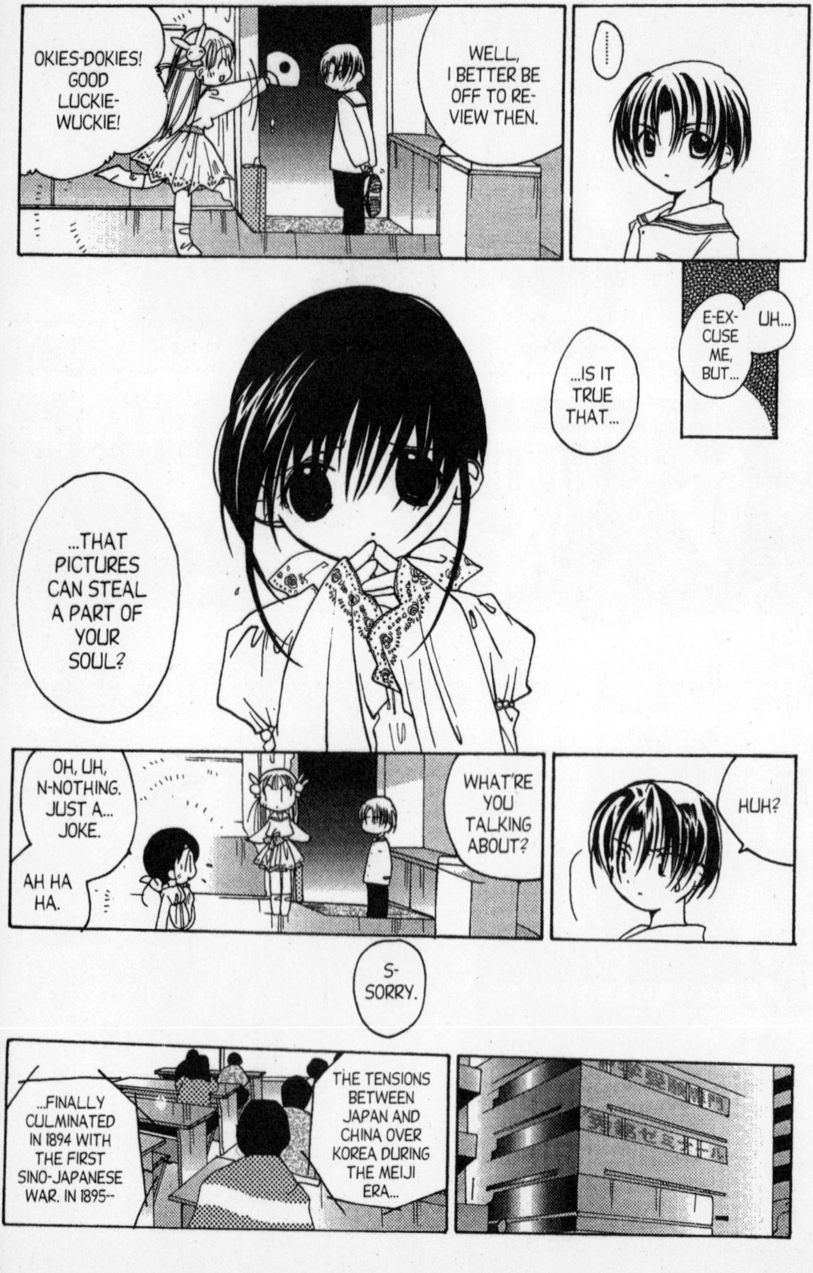
......
WELL, I BETTER BE OFF TO RE-VIEW THEN.
OKIES-DOKIES! GOOD LUCKIE-WUCKIE!
UH...
E-EX-CUSE ME, BUT...
...IS IT TRUE THAT...
...THAT PICTURES CAN STEAL A PART OF YOUR SOUL?
HUH?
WHAT'RE YOU TALKING ABOUT?
OH, UH, N-NOTHING. JUST A... JOKE.
AH HA HA.
S-SORRY.
THE TENSIONS BETWEEN JAPAN AND CHINA OVER KOREA DURING THE MEIJI ERA...
...FINALLY CULMINATED IN 1894 WITH THE FIRST SINO-JAPANESE WAR. IN 1895--

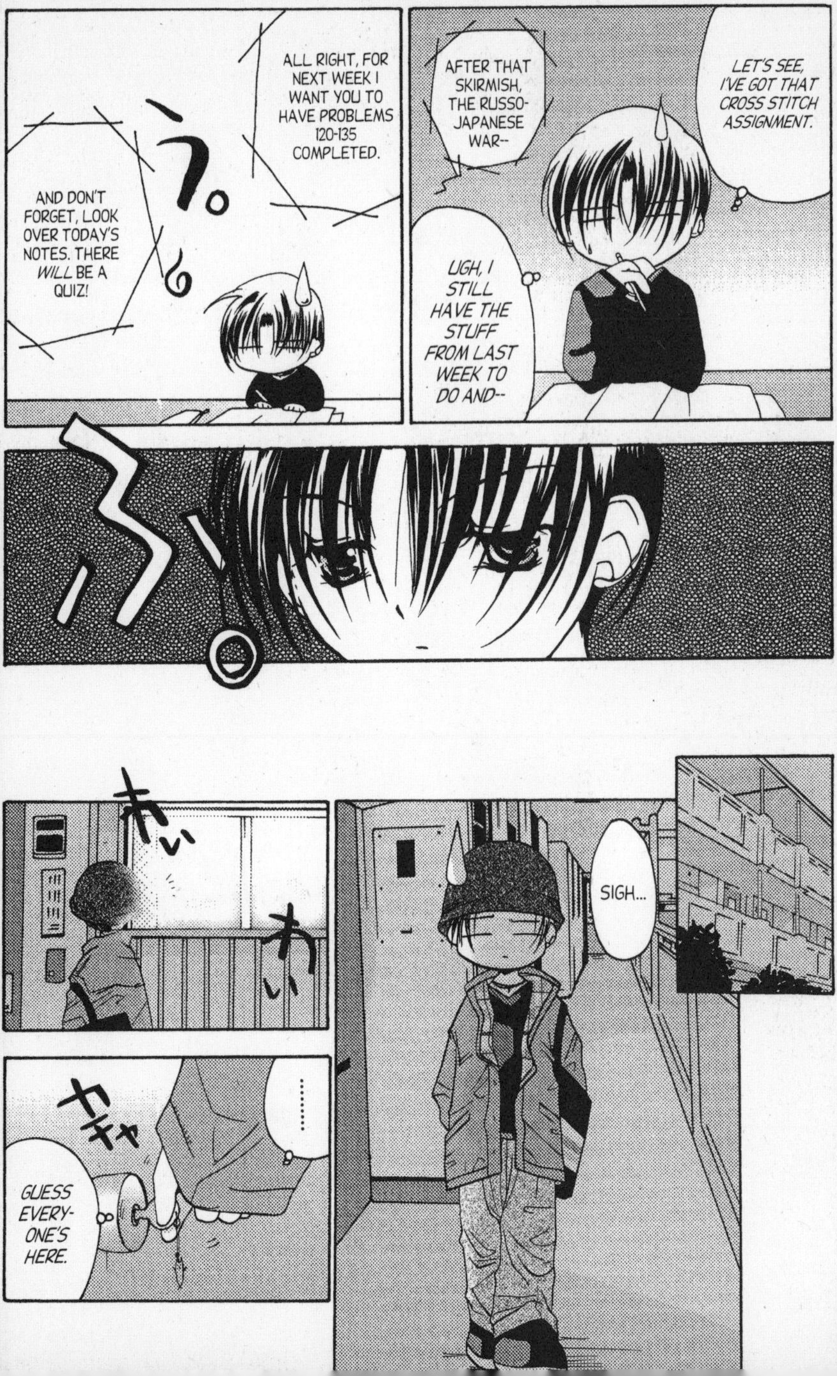
LET'S SEE, I'VE GOT THAT CROSS STITCH ASSIGNMENT.
AFTER THAT SKIRMISH, THE RUSSO-JAPANESE WAR--
UGH, I STILL HAVE THE STUFF FROM LAST WEEK TO DO AND--
ALL RIGHT, FOR NEXT WEEK I WANT YOU TO HAVE PROBLEMS 120-135 COMPLETED.
AND DON'T FORGET, LOOK OVER TODAY'S NOTES. THERE WILL BE A QUIZ!
SIGH...
....
GUESS EVERY-ONE'S HERE.

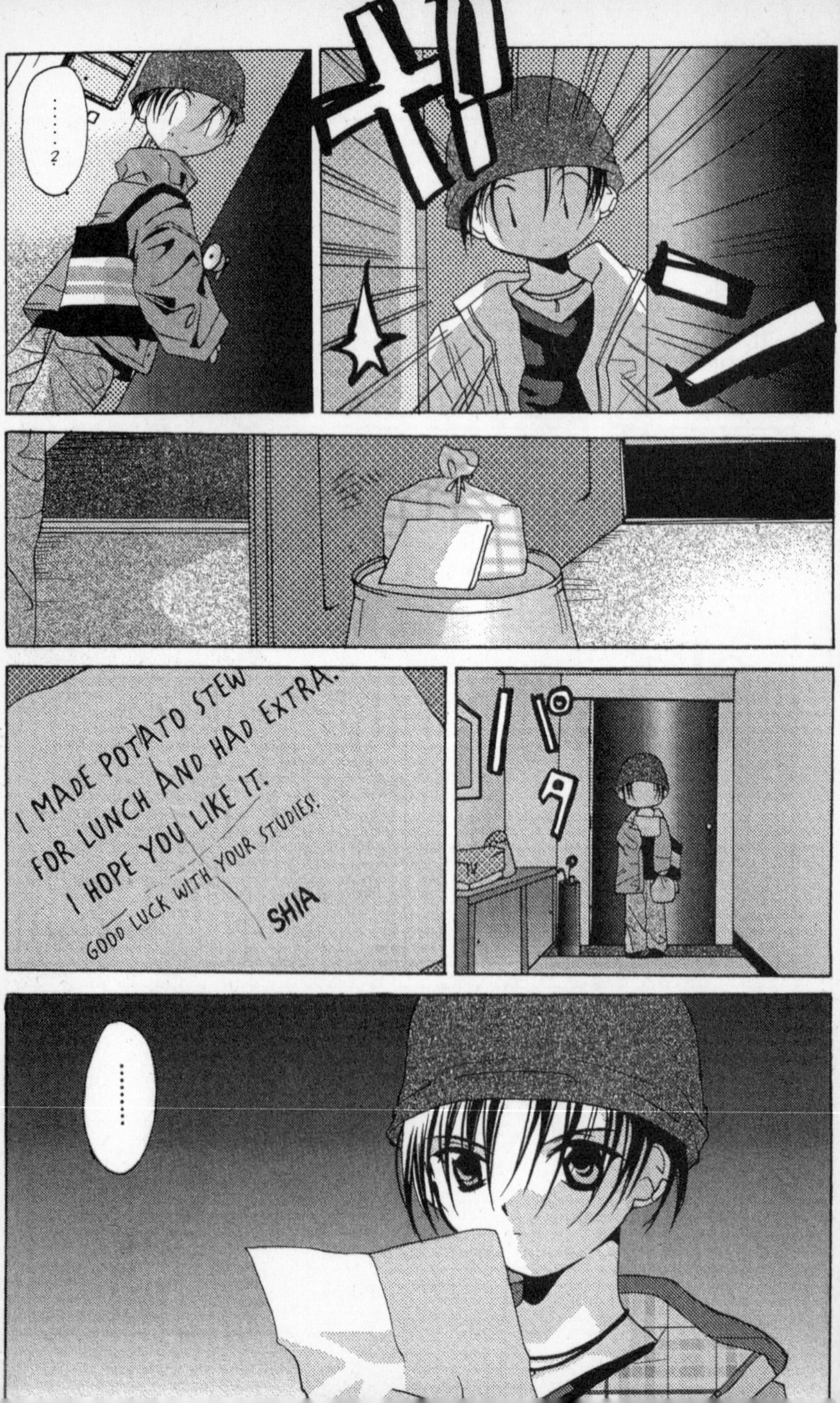
......?
パタ
I MADE POTATO STEW
FOR LUNCH AND HAD EXTRA.
I HOPE YOU LIKE IT.
GOOD LUCK WITH YOUR STUDIES!
SHIA
....

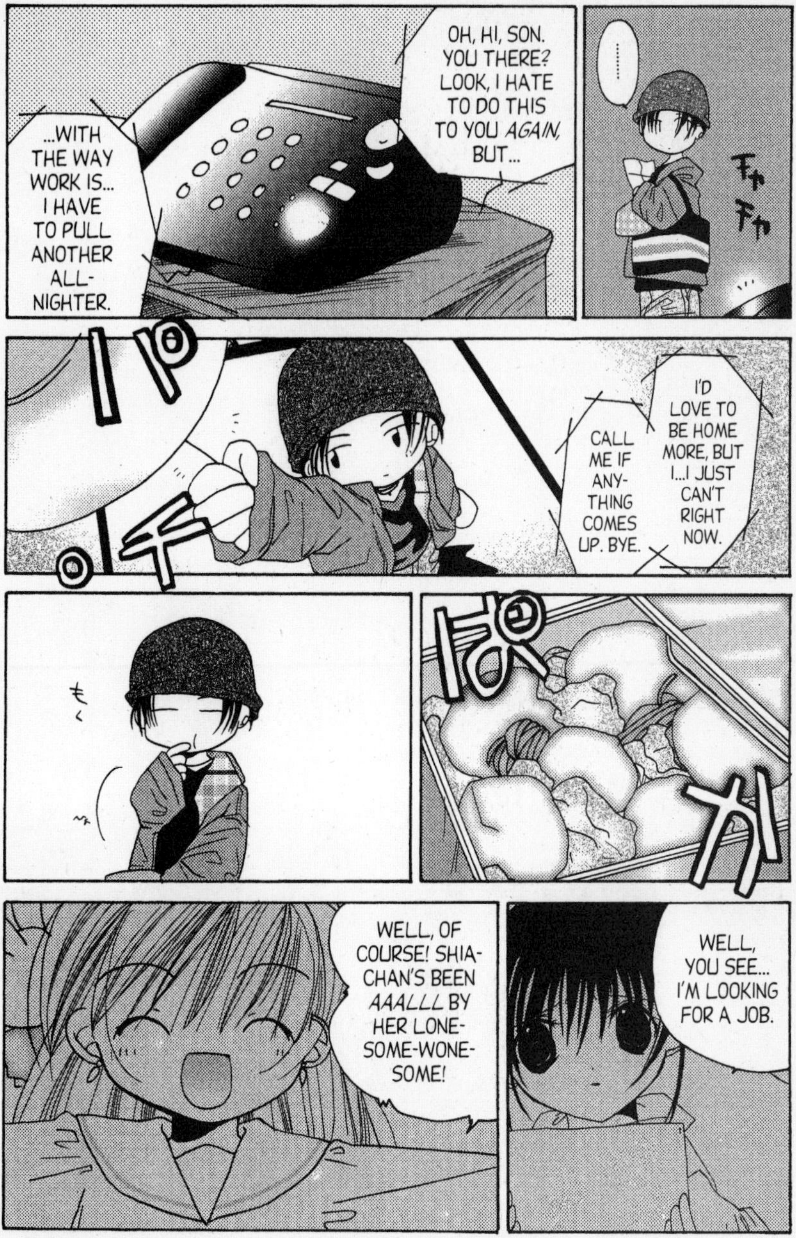
……
OH, HI, SON. YOU THERE? LOOK, I HATE TO DO THIS TO YOU *AGAIN,* BUT…
…WITH THE WAY WORK IS… I HAVE TO PULL ANOTHER ALL-NIGHTER.
I'D LOVE TO BE HOME MORE, BUT I…I JUST CAN'T RIGHT NOW.
CALL ME IF ANY-THING COMES UP. BYE.
WELL, YOU SEE… I'M LOOKING FOR A JOB.
WELL, OF COURSE! SHIA-CHAN'S BEEN *AAALLL* BY HER LONE-SOME-WONE-SOME!

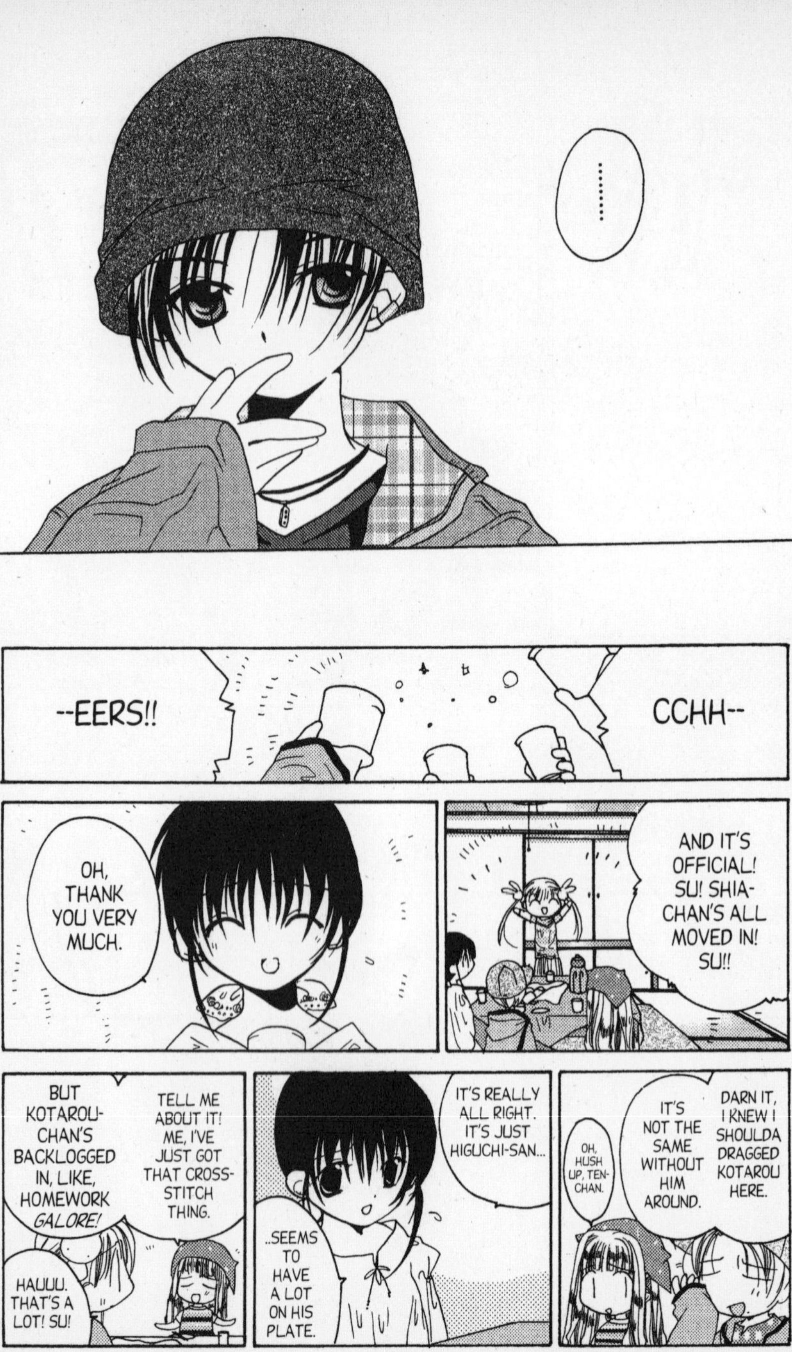
......
CCHH--
--EERS!!
AND IT'S OFFICIAL! SU! SHIA-CHAN'S ALL MOVED IN! SU!!
OH, THANK YOU VERY MUCH.
DARN IT, I KNEW I SHOULDA DRAGGED KOTAROU HERE.
IT'S NOT THE SAME WITHOUT HIM AROUND.
OH, HUSH UP, TEN-CHAN.
IT'S REALLY ALL RIGHT. IT'S JUST HIGUCHI-SAN...
..SEEMS TO HAVE A LOT ON HIS PLATE.
TELL ME ABOUT IT! ME, I'VE JUST GOT THAT CROSS-STITCH THING.
BUT KOTAROU-CHAN'S BACKLOGGED IN, LIKE, HOMEWORK *GALORE!*
HAUUU. THAT'S A LOT! SU!

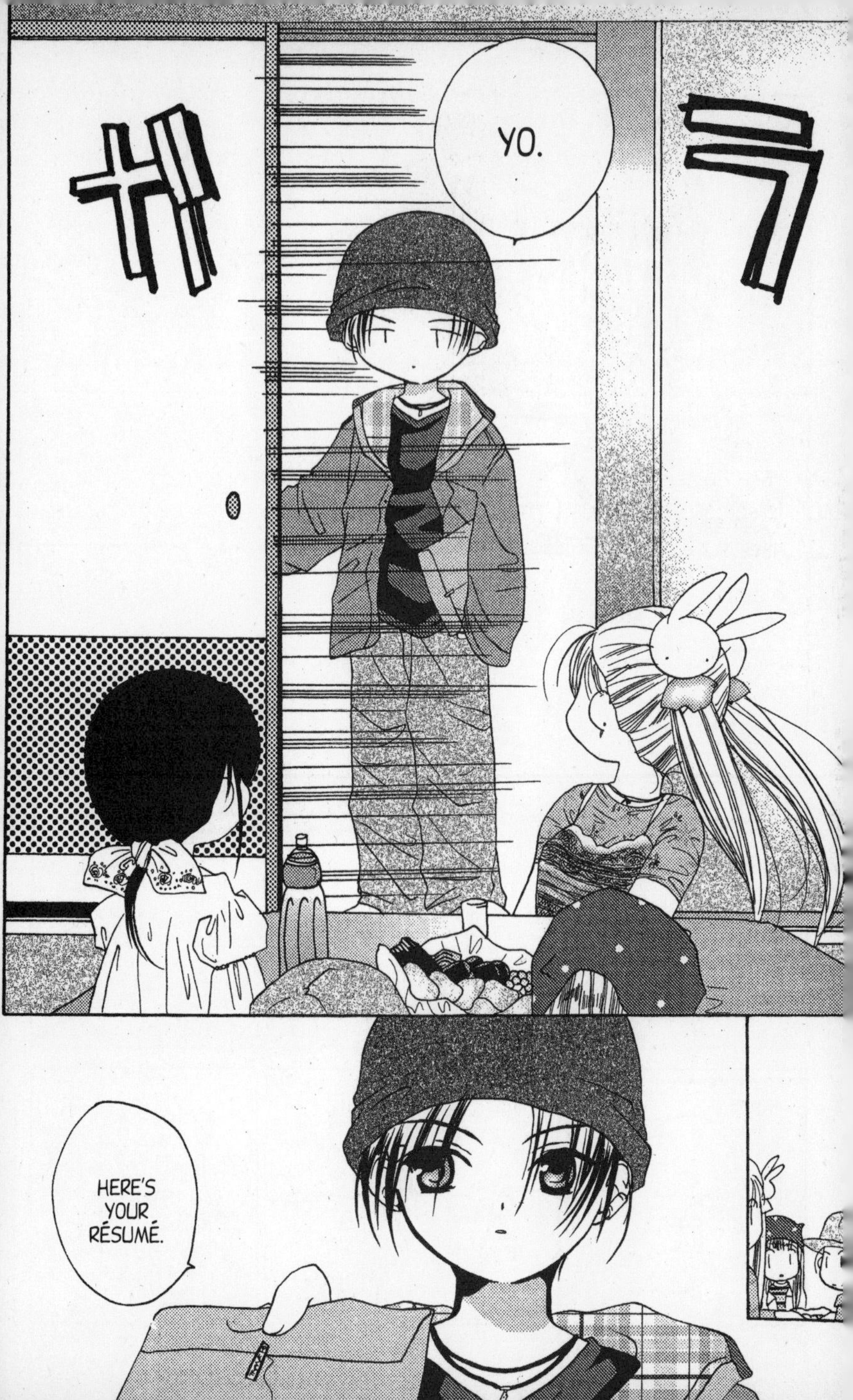
ガラ
YO.
HERE'S YOUR RÉSUMÉ.

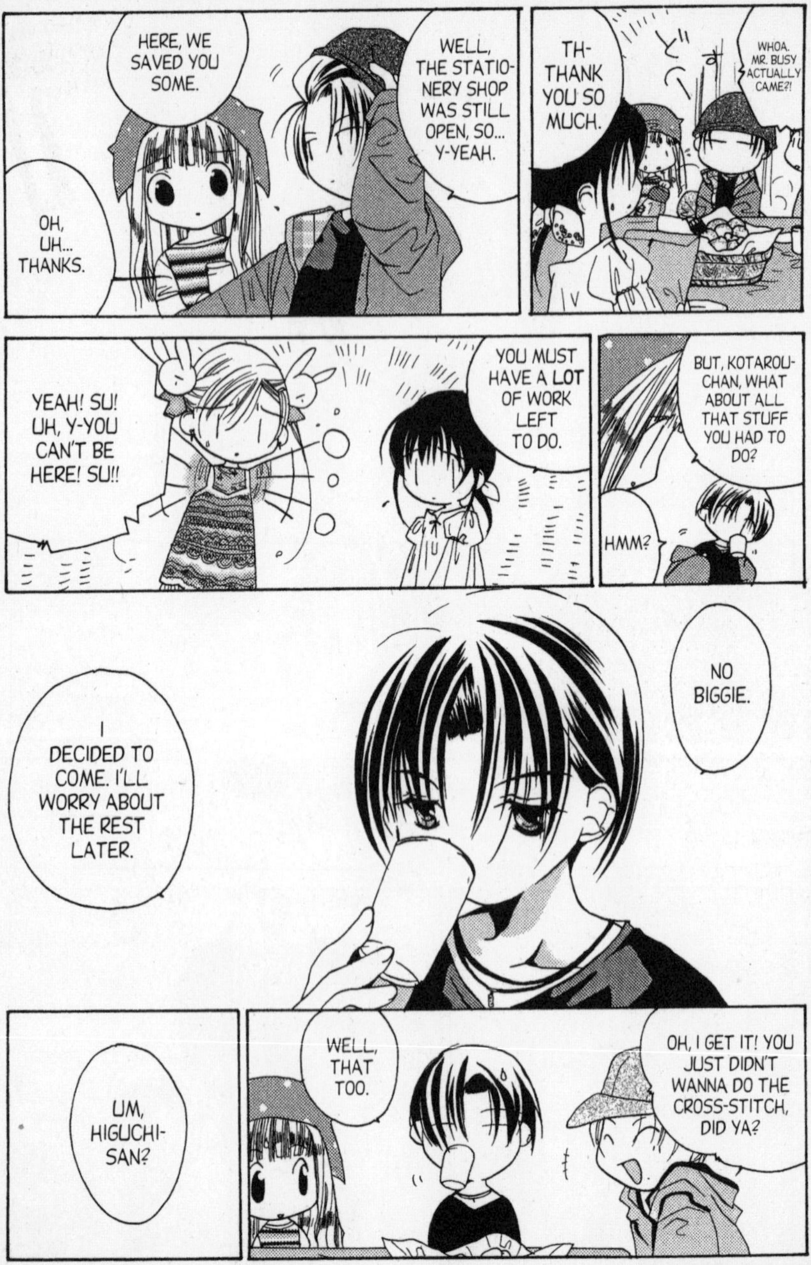
WHOA. MR. BUSY ACTUALLY CAME?!
TH- THANK YOU SO MUCH.
WELL, THE STATIO-NERY SHOP WAS STILL OPEN, SO... Y-YEAH.
HERE, WE SAVED YOU SOME.
OH, UH... THANKS.
BUT, KOTAROU-CHAN, WHAT ABOUT ALL THAT STUFF YOU HAD TO DO?
HMM?
YOU MUST HAVE A **LOT** OF WORK LEFT TO DO.
YEAH! SU! UH, Y-YOU CAN'T BE HERE! SU!!
NO BIGGIE.
I DECIDED TO COME. I'LL WORRY ABOUT THE REST LATER.
OH, I GET IT! YOU JUST DIDN'T WANNA DO THE CROSS-STITCH, DID YA?
WELL, THAT TOO.
UM, HIGUCHI-SAN?

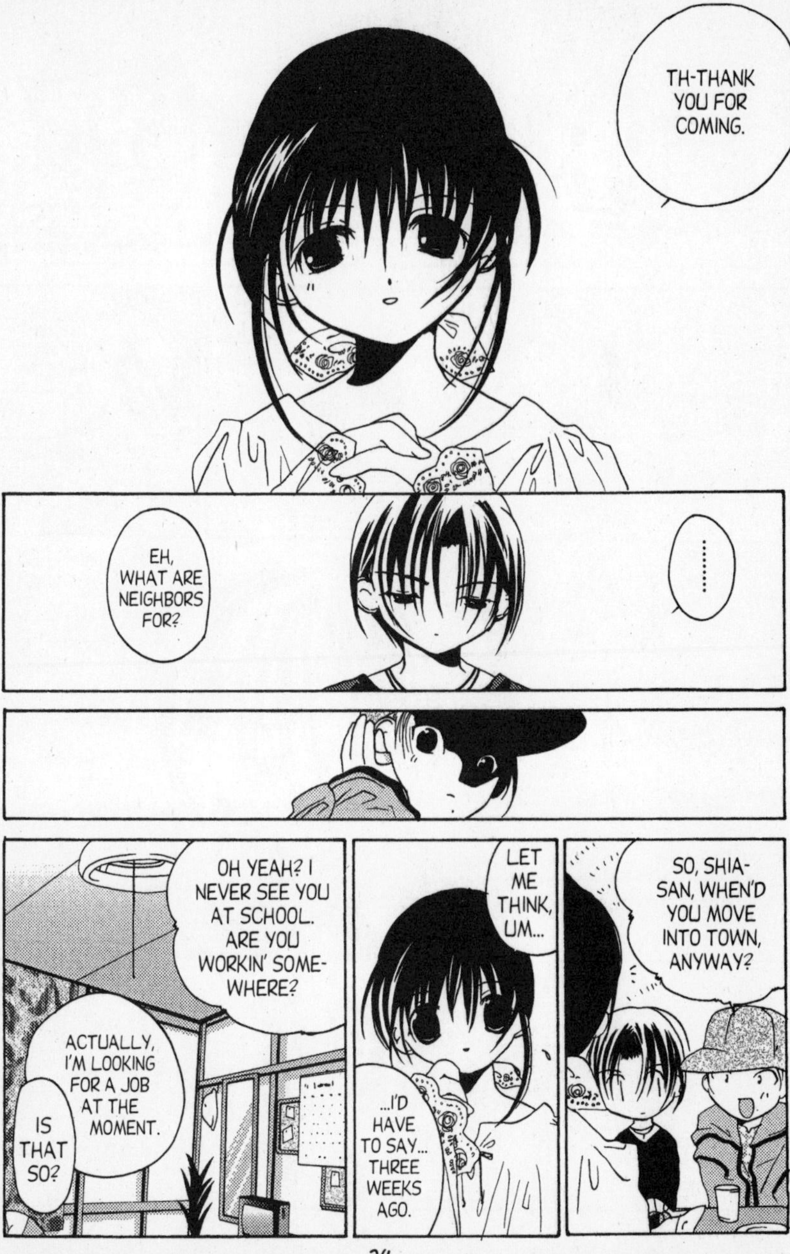

TH-THANK YOU FOR COMING.
......
EH, WHAT ARE NEIGHBORS FOR?
SO, SHIA-SAN, WHEN'D YOU MOVE INTO TOWN, ANYWAY?
LET ME THINK, UM...
...I'D HAVE TO SAY... THREE WEEKS AGO.
OH YEAH? I NEVER SEE YOU AT SCHOOL. ARE YOU WORKIN' SOMEWHERE?
ACTUALLY, I'M LOOKING FOR A JOB AT THE MOMENT.
IS THAT SO?

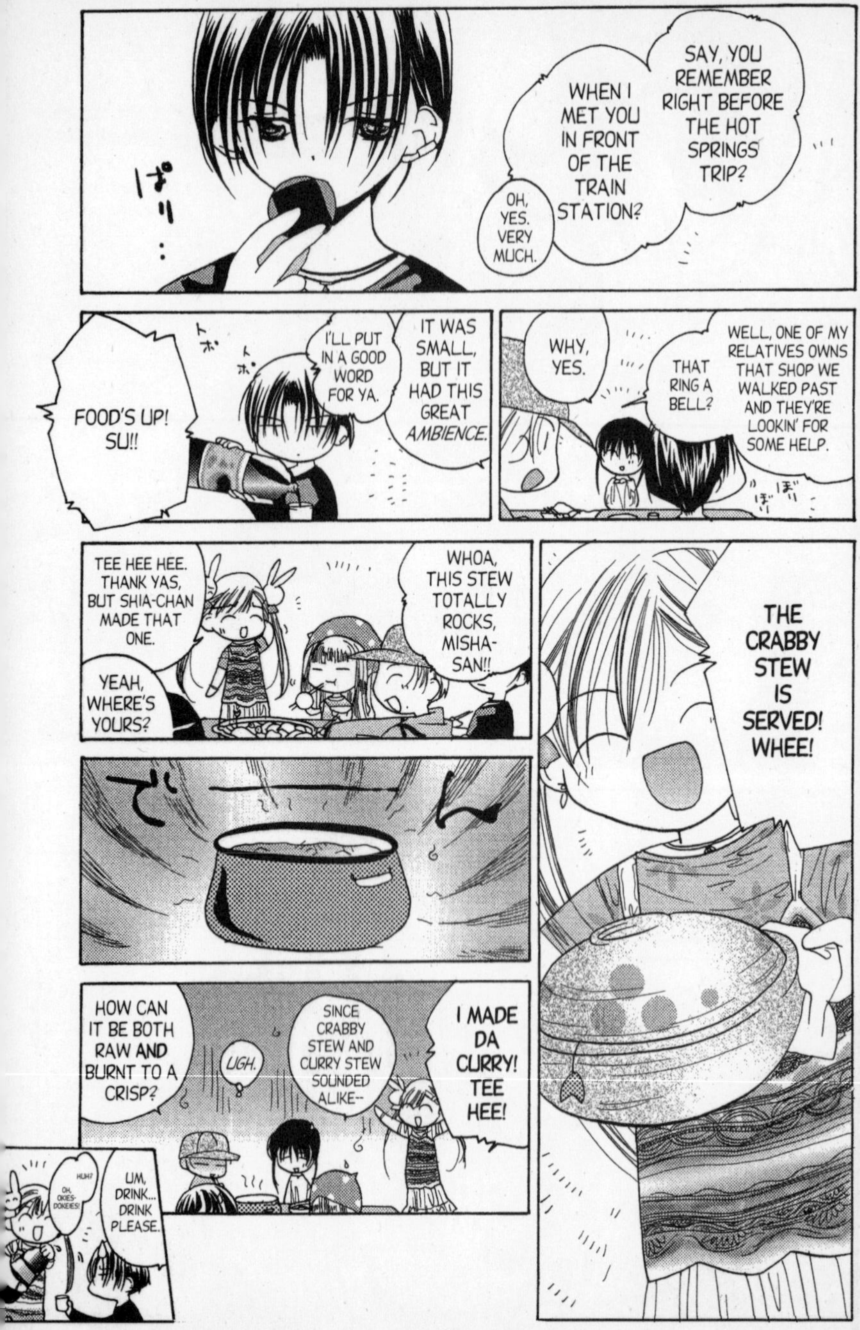
SAY, YOU REMEMBER RIGHT BEFORE THE HOT SPRINGS TRIP?
WHEN I MET YOU IN FRONT OF THE TRAIN STATION?
OH, YES. VERY MUCH.
ぱり…
WELL, ONE OF MY RELATIVES OWNS THAT SHOP WE WALKED PAST AND THEY'RE LOOKIN' FOR SOME HELP.
THAT RING A BELL?
WHY, YES.
ぼり ぼり
IT WAS SMALL, BUT IT HAD THIS GREAT *AMBIENCE*.
I'LL PUT IN A GOOD WORD FOR YA.
トポ トポ
FOOD'S UP! SU!!
THE CRABBY STEW IS SERVED! WHEE!
WHOA, THIS STEW TOTALLY ROCKS, MISHA-SAN!!
TEE HEE HEE. THANK YAS, BUT SHIA-CHAN MADE THAT ONE.
YEAH, WHERE'S YOURS?
でーーん
I MADE DA CURRY! TEE HEE!
SINCE CRABBY STEW AND CURRY STEW SOUNDED ALIKE--
UGH.
HOW CAN IT BE BOTH RAW AND BURNT TO A CRISP?
UM, DRINK... DRINK PLEASE.
HUH?
OH, OKIES-DOKEIES!

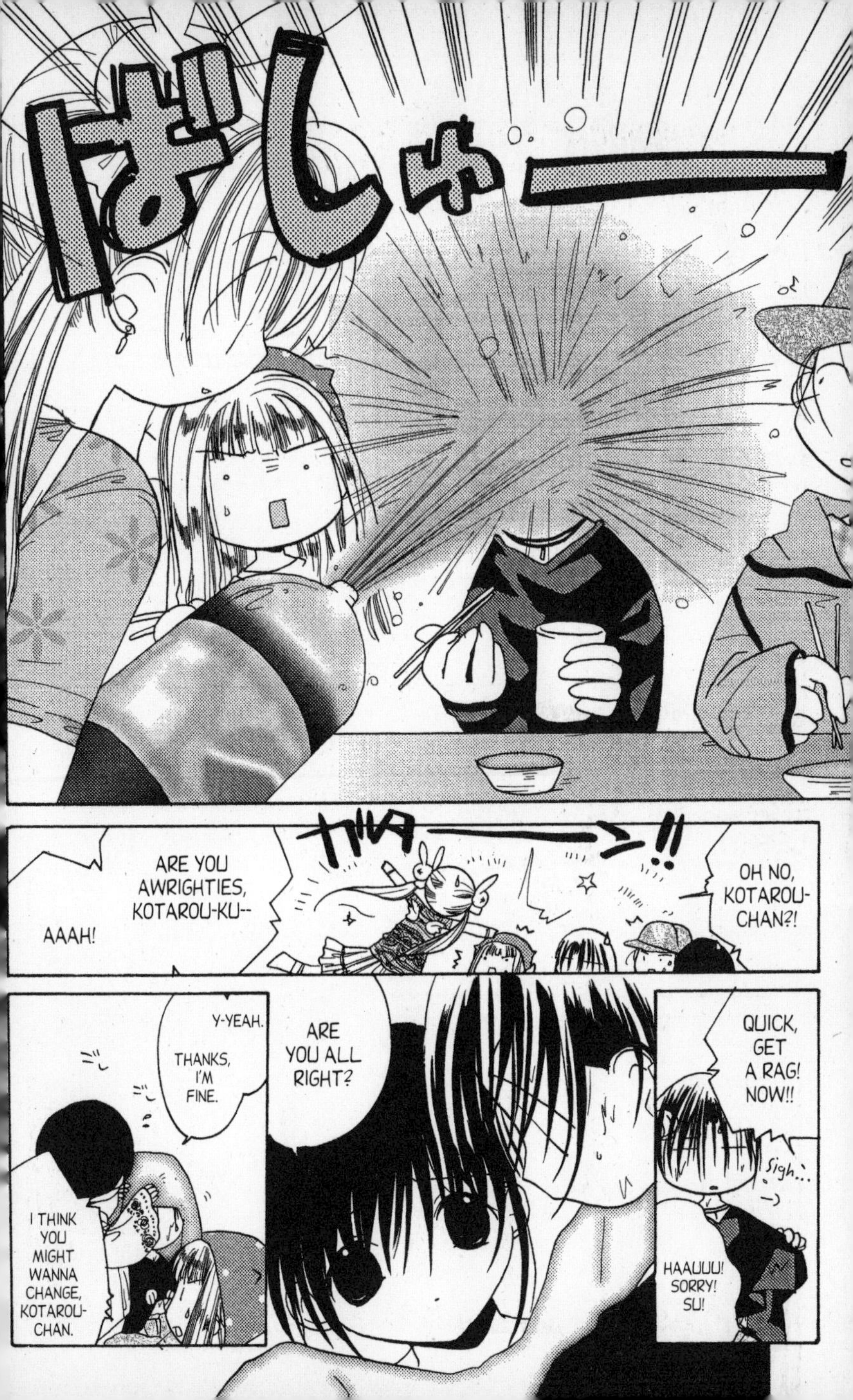
ぼしゅーー
OH NO, KOTAROU-CHAN?!
ガタ――ン!!
ARE YOU AWRIGHTIES, KOTAROU-KU--
AAAH!
QUICK, GET A RAG! NOW!!
Sigh...
HAAUUU! SORRY! SU!
ARE YOU ALL RIGHT?
Y-YEAH.
THANKS, I'M FINE.
I THINK YOU MIGHT WANNA CHANGE, KOTAROU-CHAN.

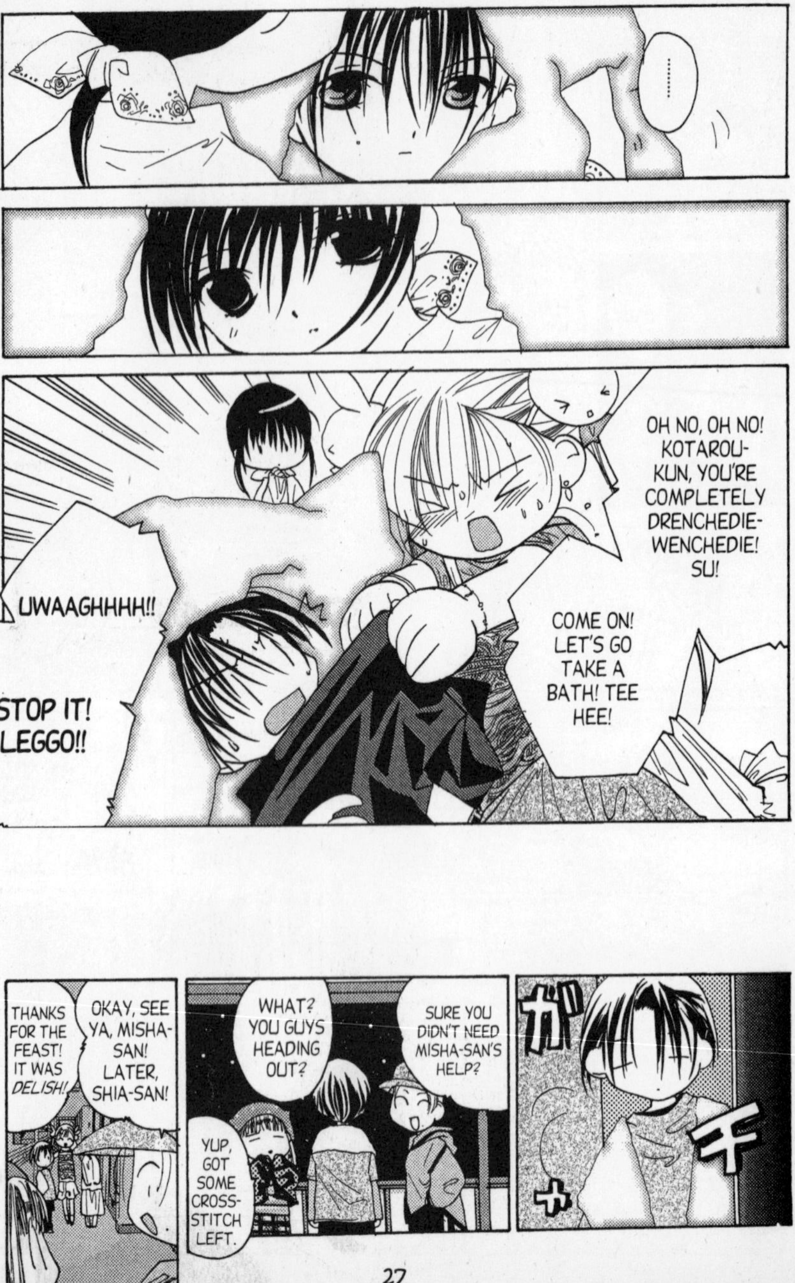
......
OH NO, OH NO! KOTAROU-KUN, YOU'RE COMPLETELY DRENCHEDIE-WENCHEDIE! SU!
COME ON! LET'S GO TAKE A BATH! TEE HEE!
UWAAGHHHH!!
STOP IT! LEGGO!!
ガチャ
SURE YOU DIDN'T NEED MISHA-SAN'S HELP?
WHAT? YOU GUYS HEADING OUT?
YUP, GOT SOME CROSS-STITCH LEFT.
OKAY, SEE YA, MISHA-SAN! LATER, SHIA-SAN!
THANKS FOR THE FEAST! IT WAS *DELISH!*

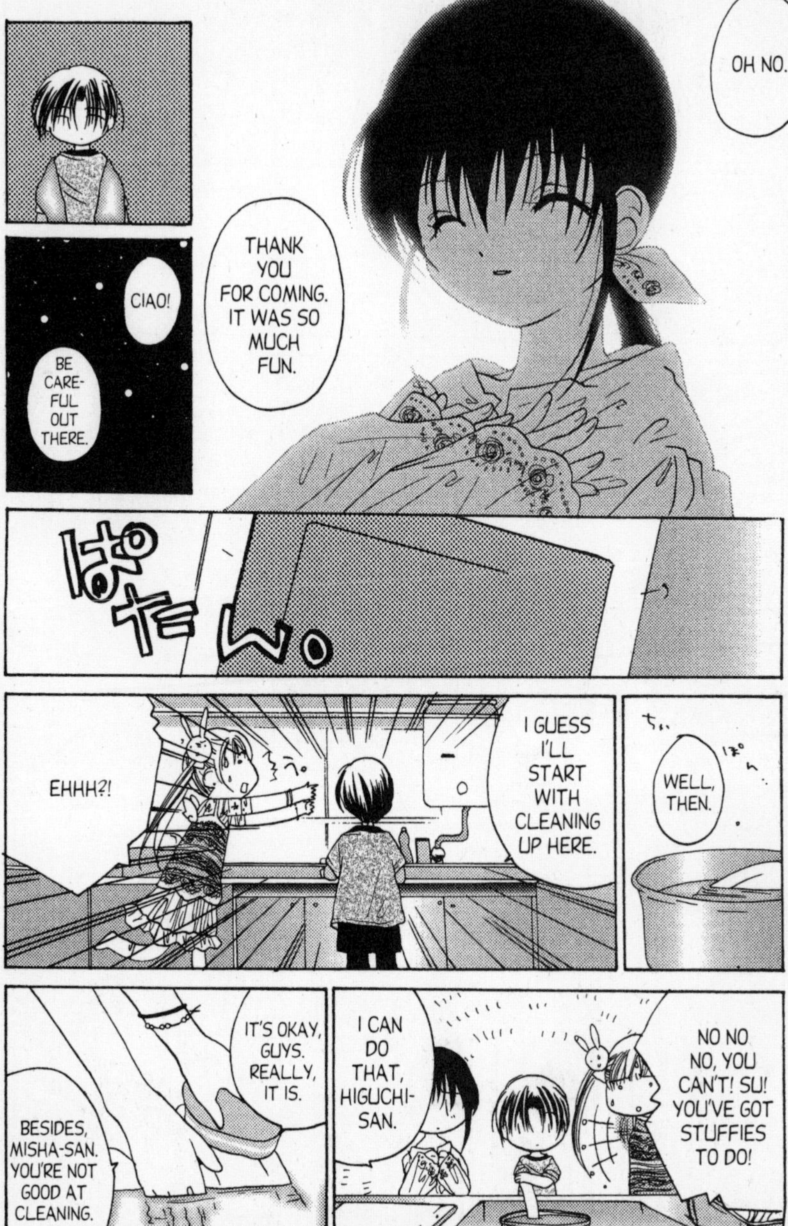
OH NO.
THANK YOU FOR COMING. IT WAS SO MUCH FUN.
CIAO!
BE CAREFUL OUT THERE.
ぱたん。
WELL, THEN.
I GUESS I'LL START WITH CLEANING UP HERE.
EHHH?!
NO NO NO, YOU CAN'T! SU! YOU'VE GOT STUFFIES TO DO!
I CAN DO THAT, HIGUCHI-SAN.
IT'S OKAY, GUYS. REALLY, IT IS.
BESIDES, MISHA-SAN. YOU'RE NOT GOOD AT CLEANING.

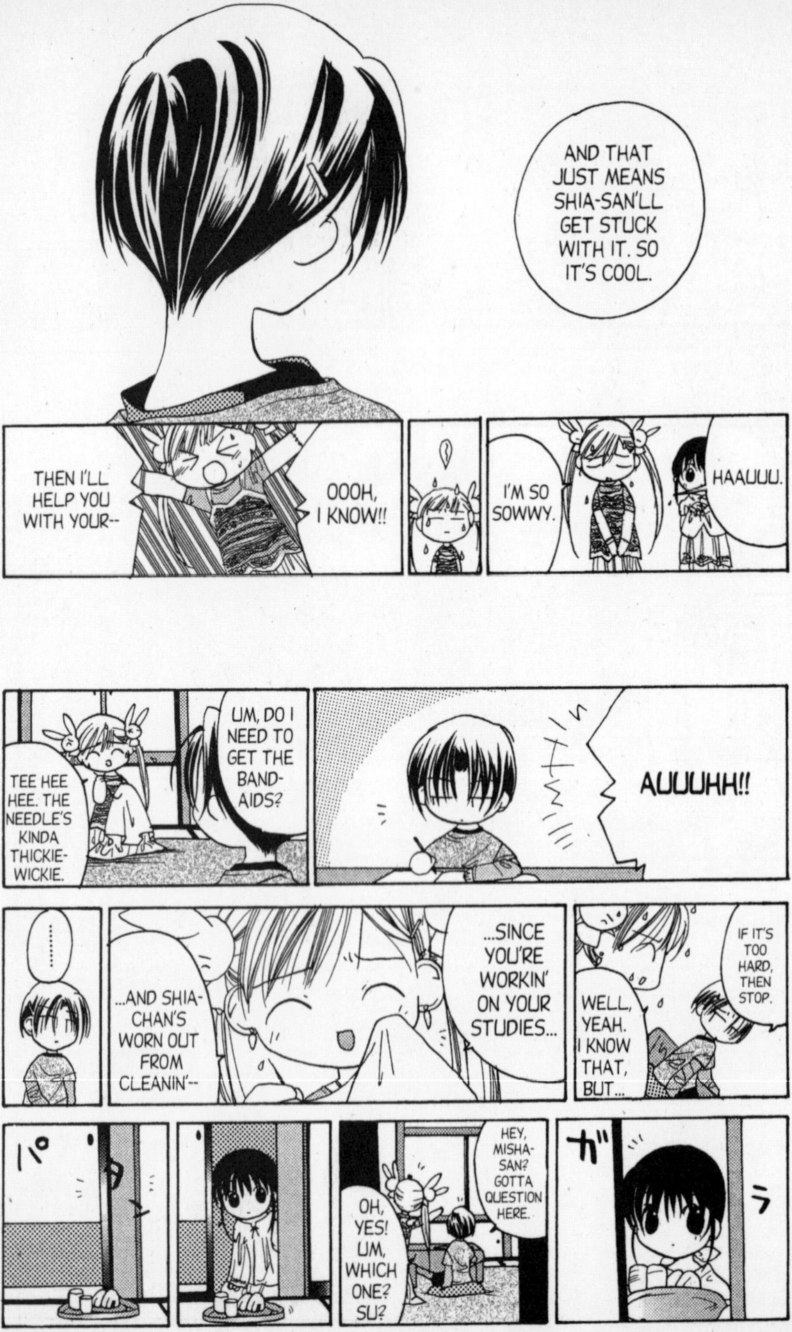
AND THAT JUST MEANS SHIA-SAN'LL GET STUCK WITH IT. SO IT'S COOL.
HAAUUU.
I'M SO SOWWY.
OOOH, I KNOW!!
THEN I'LL HELP YOU WITH YOUR--
AUUUHH!!
UM, DO I NEED TO GET THE BAND-AIDS?
TEE HEE HEE. THE NEEDLE'S KINDA THICKIE-WICKIE.
IF IT'S TOO HARD, THEN STOP.
WELL, YEAH. I KNOW THAT, BUT...
...SINCE YOU'RE WORKIN' ON YOUR STUDIES...
...AND SHIA-CHAN'S WORN OUT FROM CLEANIN'--
......
ガ
ラ
HEY, MISHA-SAN? GOTTA QUESTION HERE.
OH, YES! UM, WHICH ONE? SU?
パ
タ

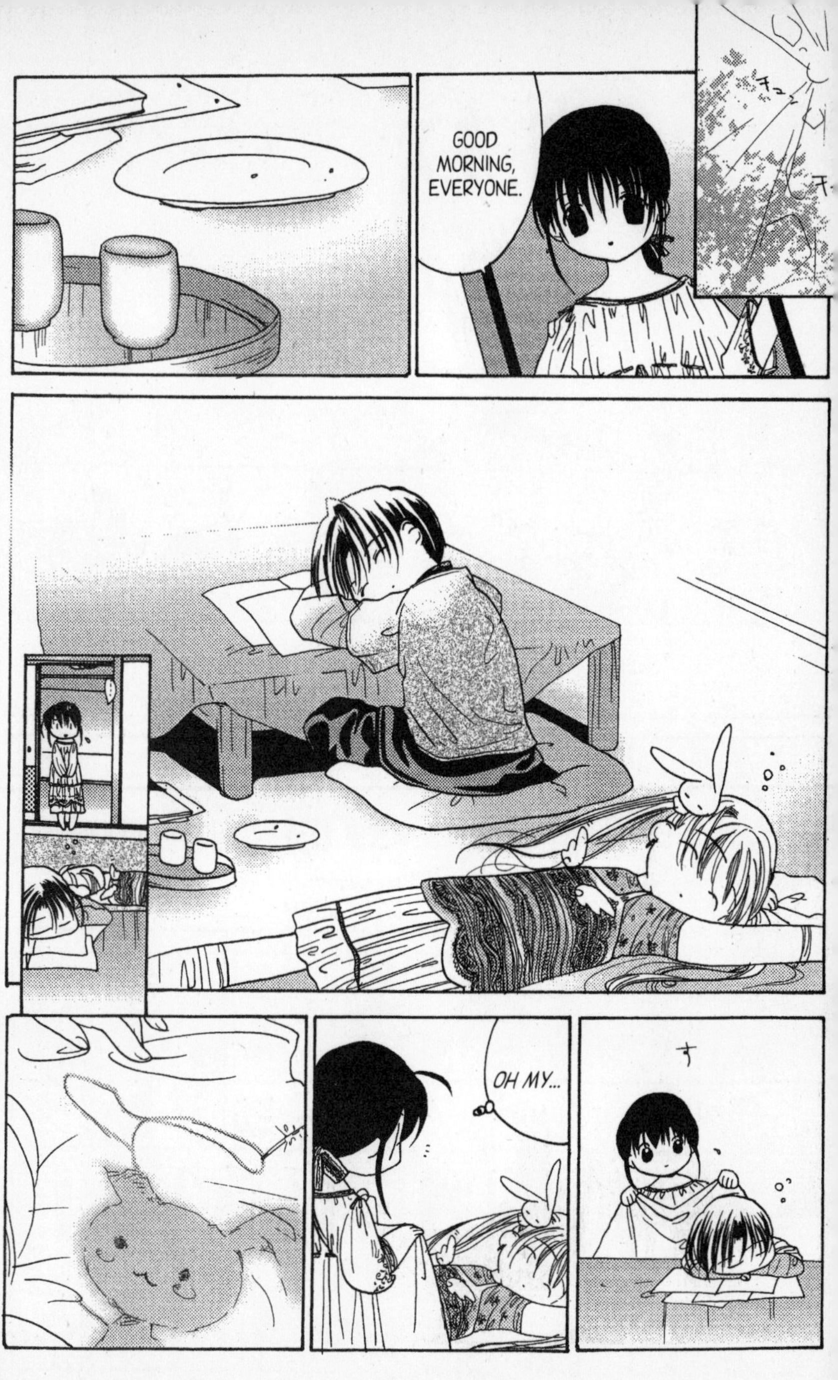
GOOD MORNING, EVERYONE.
OH MY...

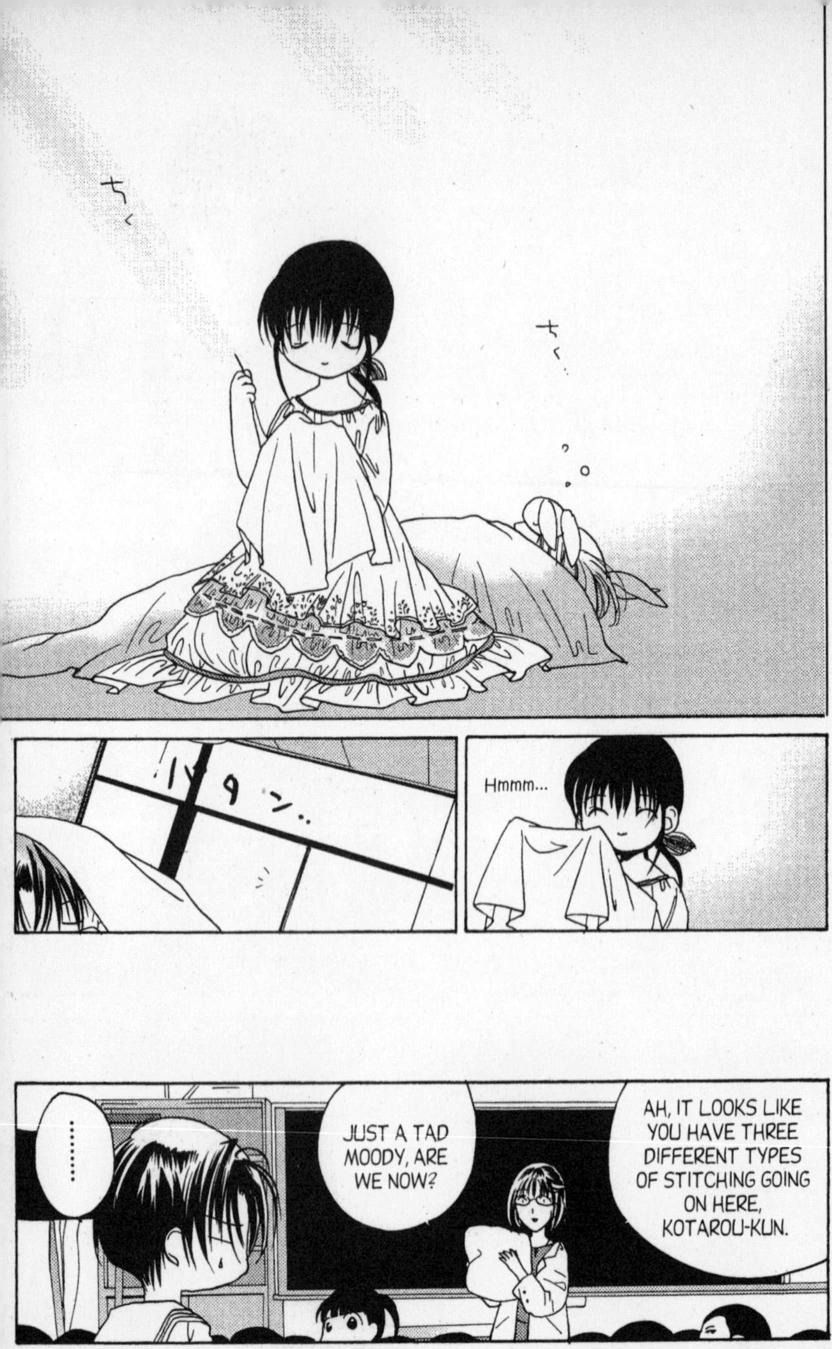
ちく
ちく..
Hmmm...
パタン..
AH, IT LOOKS LIKE YOU HAVE THREE DIFFERENT TYPES OF STITCHING GOING ON HERE, KOTAROU-KUN.
JUST A TAD MOODY, ARE WE NOW?
....

Lesson 9

How to Welcome a New Student: Part I

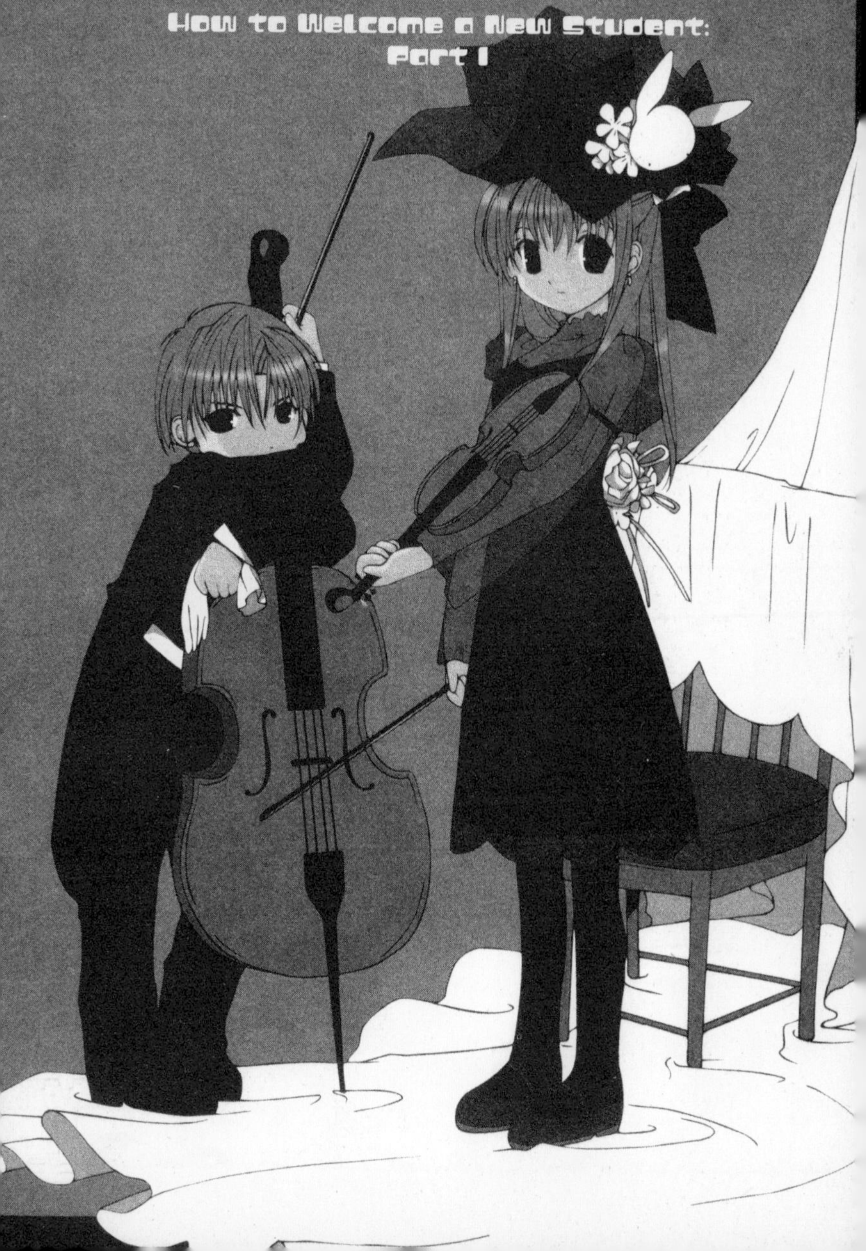

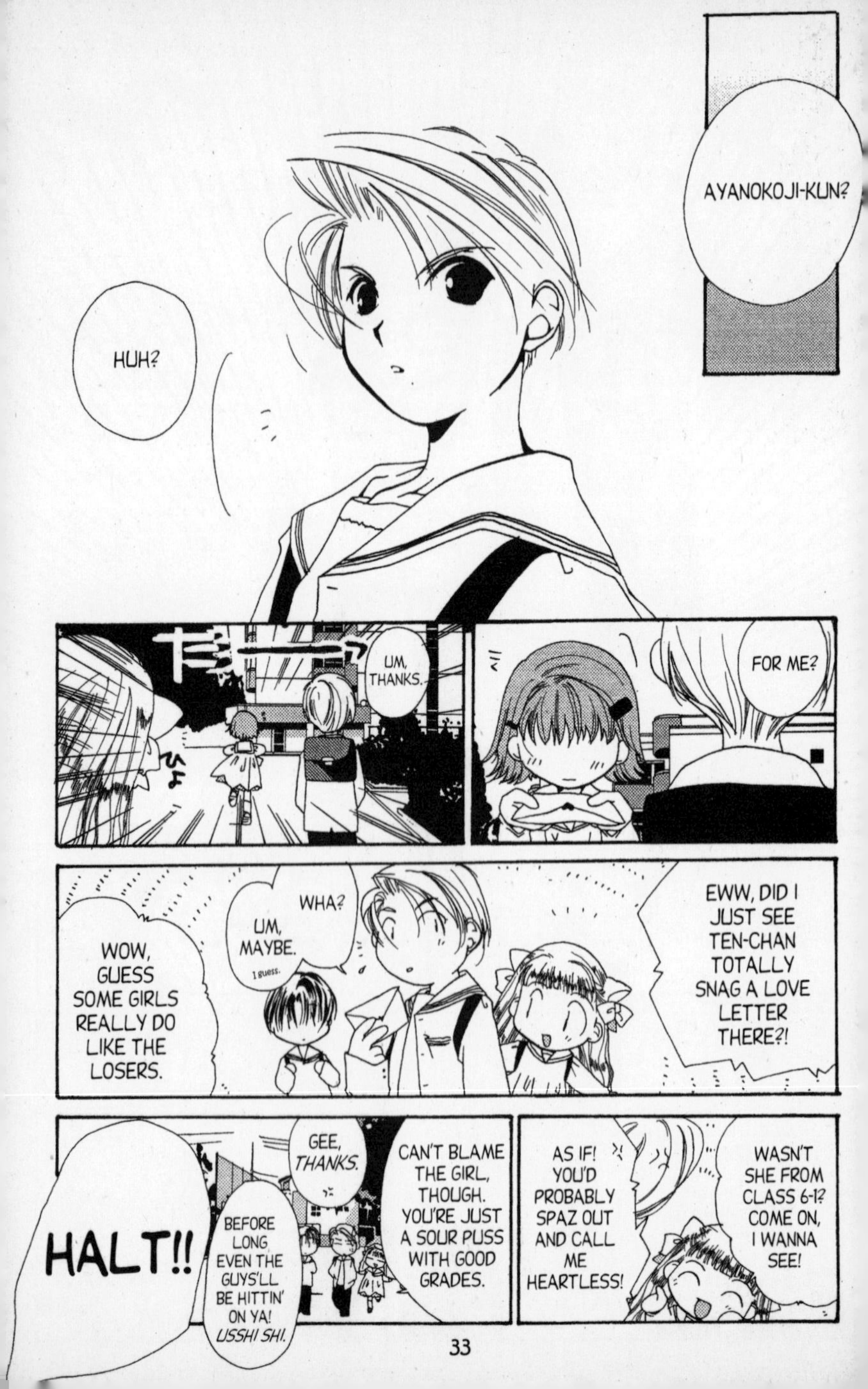
AYANOKOJI-KUN?
HUH?
FOR ME?
UM, THANKS.
EWW, DID I JUST SEE TEN-CHAN TOTALLY SNAG A LOVE LETTER THERE?!
WHA?
UM, MAYBE.
I guess.
WOW, GUESS SOME GIRLS REALLY DO LIKE THE LOSERS.
WASN'T SHE FROM CLASS 6-1? COME ON, I WANNA SEE!
AS IF! YOU'D PROBABLY SPAZ OUT AND CALL ME HEARTLESS!
CAN'T BLAME THE GIRL, THOUGH. YOU'RE JUST A SOUR PUSS WITH GOOD GRADES.
GEE, *THANKS.*
BEFORE LONG EVEN THE GUYS'LL BE HITTIN' ON YA! *USSHI SHI.*
HALT!!

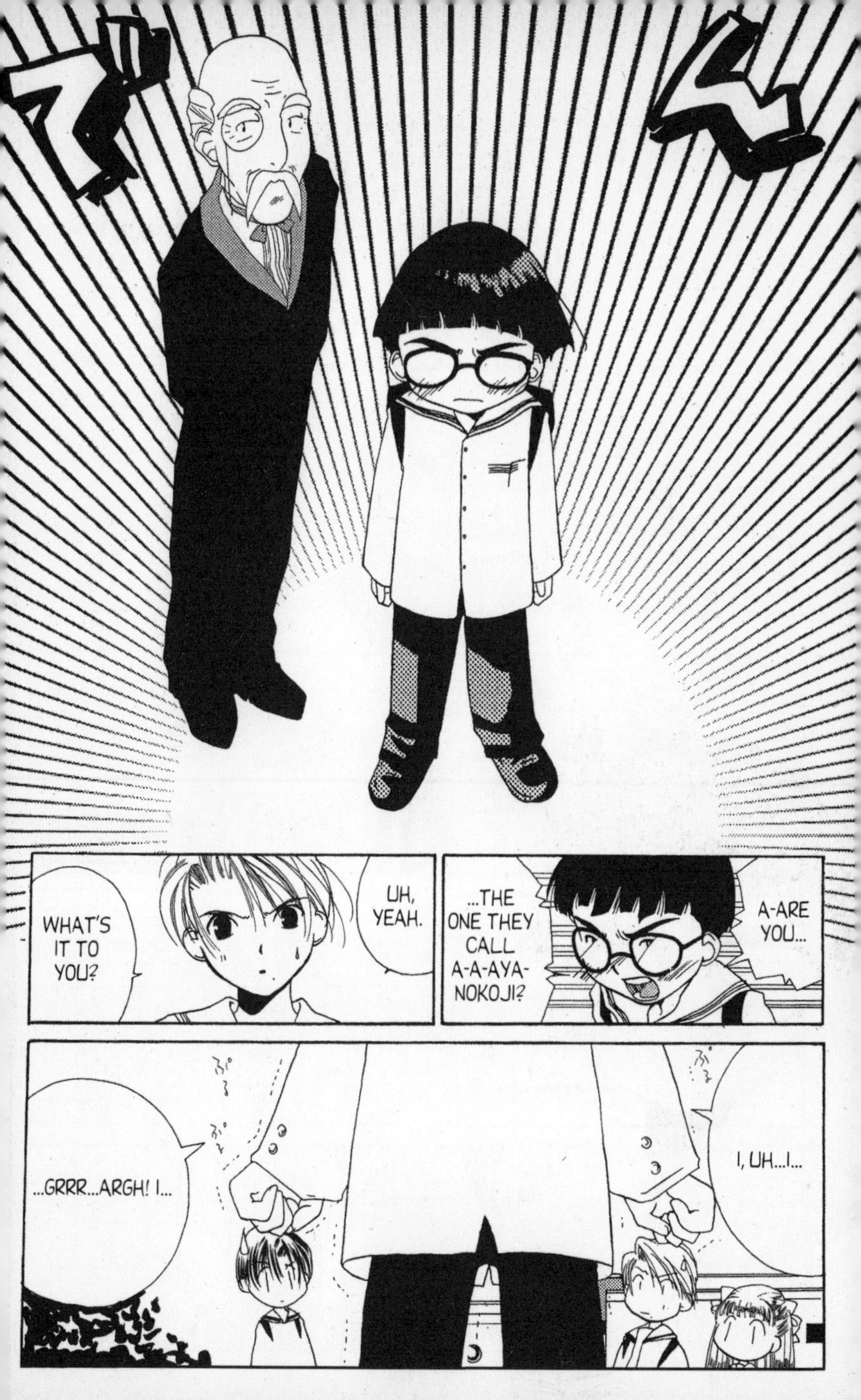
A-ARE YOU...
...THE ONE THEY CALL A-A-AYA-NOKOJI?
UH, YEAH.
WHAT'S IT TO YOU?
I, UH...I...
...GRRR...ARGH! I...

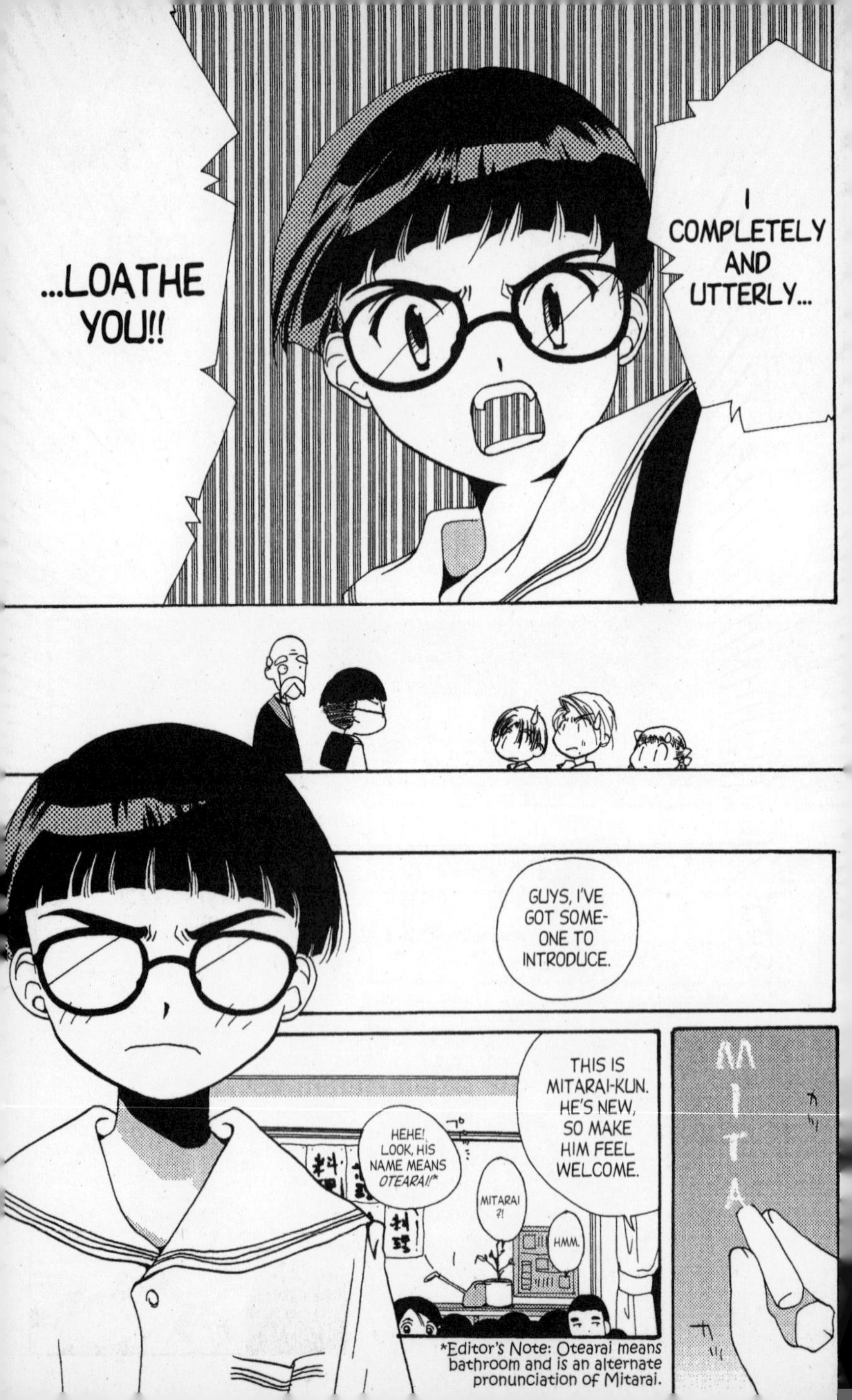
I COMPLETELY AND UTTERLY...
...LOATHE YOU!!
GUYS, I'VE GOT SOME-ONE TO INTRODUCE.
MITA
THIS IS MITARAI-KUN. HE'S NEW, SO MAKE HIM FEEL WELCOME.
HEHE! LOOK, HIS NAME MEANS *OTEARAI!**
MITARAI ?!
HMM.
*Editor's Note: Otearai means bathroom and is an alternate pronunciation of Mitarai.

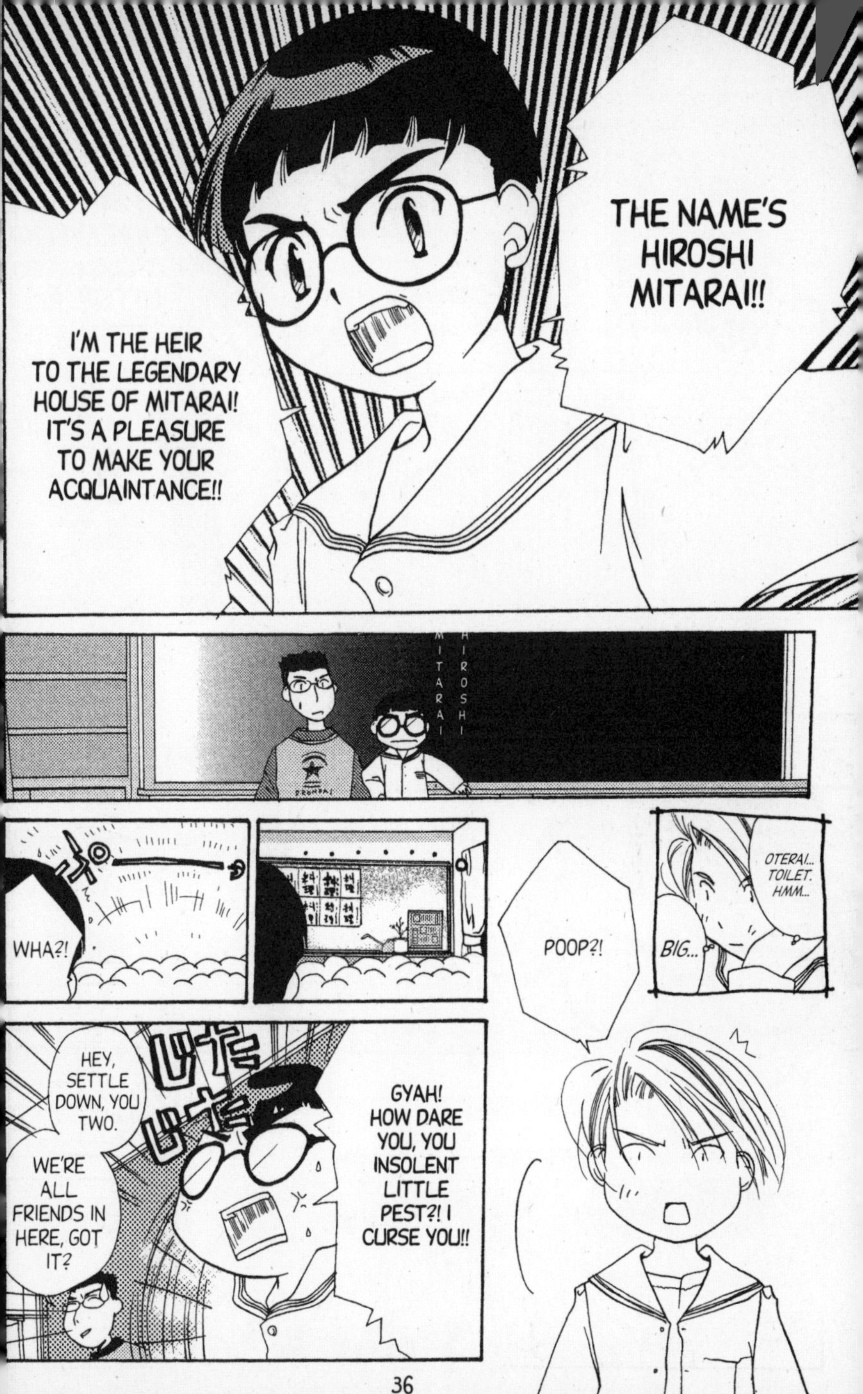
THE NAME'S HIROSHI MITARAI!!
I'M THE HEIR TO THE LEGENDARY HOUSE OF MITARAI! IT'S A PLEASURE TO MAKE YOUR ACQUAINTANCE!!
HIROSHI
MITARAI
OTERAI... TOILET. HMM...
BIG...
POOP?!
WHA?!
GYAH! HOW DARE YOU, YOU INSOLENT LITTLE PEST?! I CURSE YOU!!
HEY, SETTLE DOWN, YOU TWO.
WE'RE ALL FRIENDS IN HERE, GOT IT?

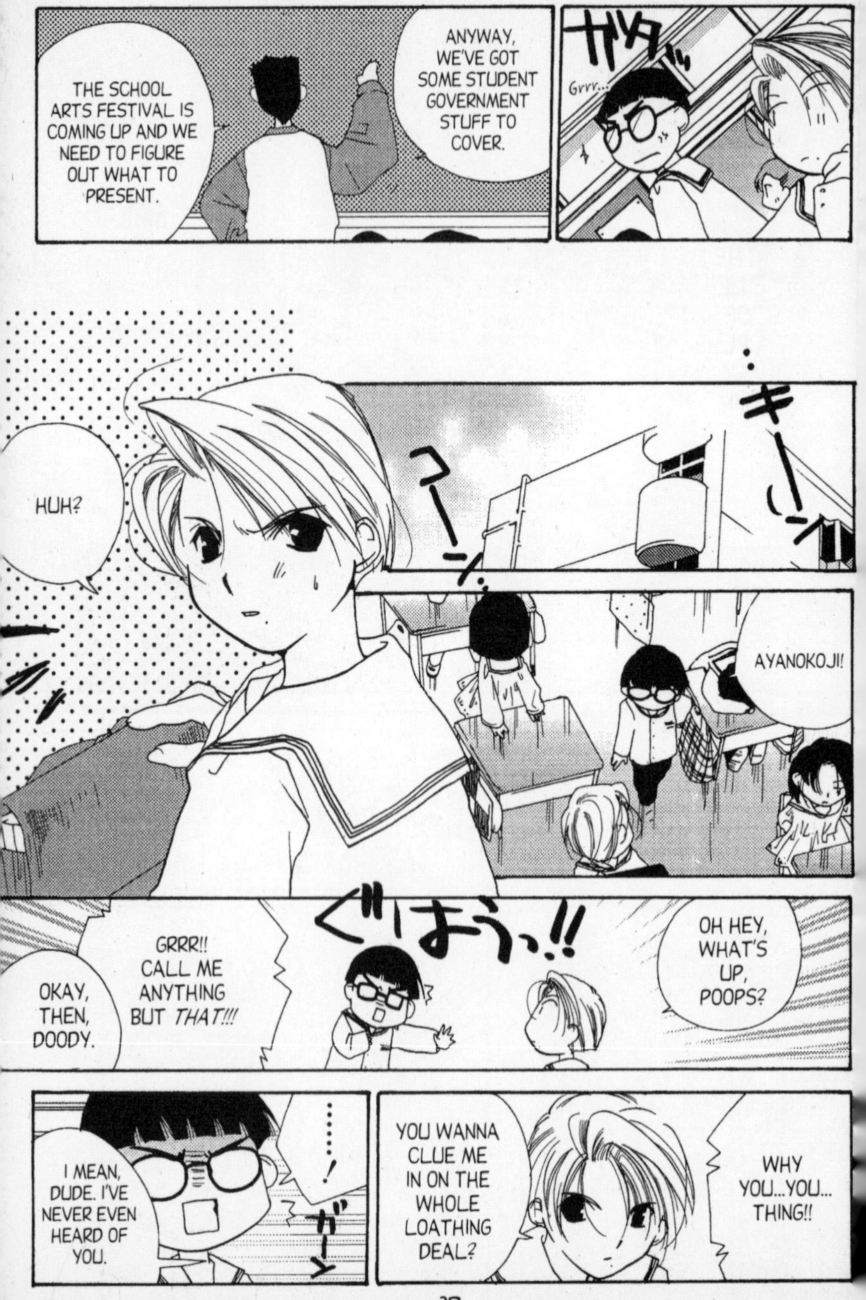
Grrr...
ANYWAY, WE'VE GOT SOME STUDENT GOVERNMENT STUFF TO COVER.
THE SCHOOL ARTS FESTIVAL IS COMING UP AND WE NEED TO FIGURE OUT WHAT TO PRESENT.
AYANOKOJI!
HUH?
OH HEY, WHAT'S UP, POOPS?
GRRR!! CALL ME ANYTHING BUT *THAT*!!!
OKAY, THEN, DOODY.
WHY YOU...YOU... THING!!
YOU WANNA CLUE ME IN ON THE WHOLE LOATHING DEAL?
......!
I MEAN, DUDE. I'VE NEVER EVEN HEARD OF YOU.

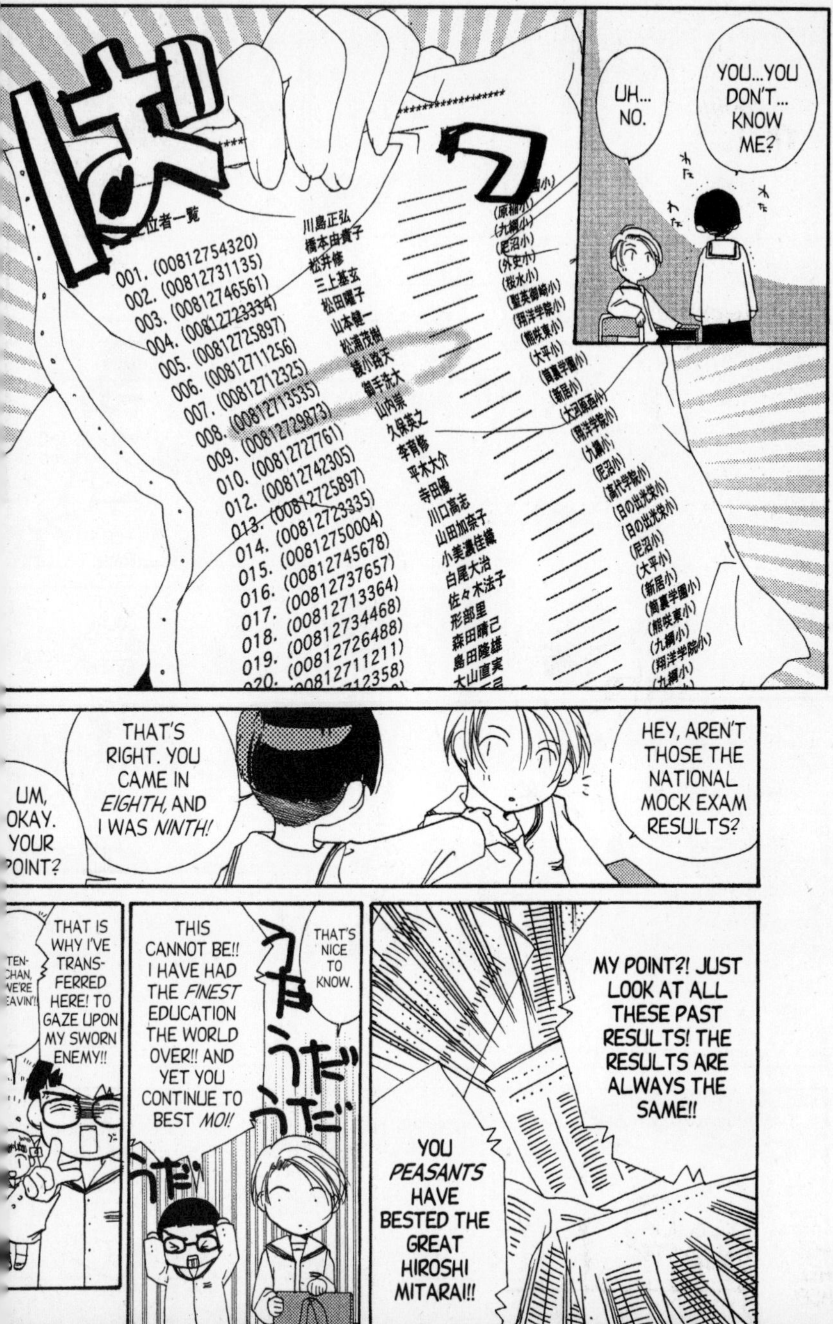
YOU...YOU DON'T... KNOW ME?
UH... NO.
ばっ
HEY, AREN'T THOSE THE NATIONAL MOCK EXAM RESULTS?
THAT'S RIGHT. YOU CAME IN *EIGHTH,* AND I WAS *NINTH!*
UM, OKAY. YOUR POINT?
MY POINT?! JUST LOOK AT ALL THESE PAST RESULTS! THE RESULTS ARE ALWAYS THE SAME!!
YOU *PEASANTS* HAVE BESTED THE GREAT HIROSHI MITARAI!!
THAT'S NICE TO KNOW.
THIS CANNOT BE!! I HAVE HAD THE *FINEST* EDUCATION THE WORLD OVER!! AND YET YOU CONTINUE TO BEST *MOI!!*
うだうだ
THAT IS WHY I'VE TRANS-FERRED HERE! TO GAZE UPON MY SWORN ENEMY!!
TEN-CHAN, WE'RE EAVIN'!!

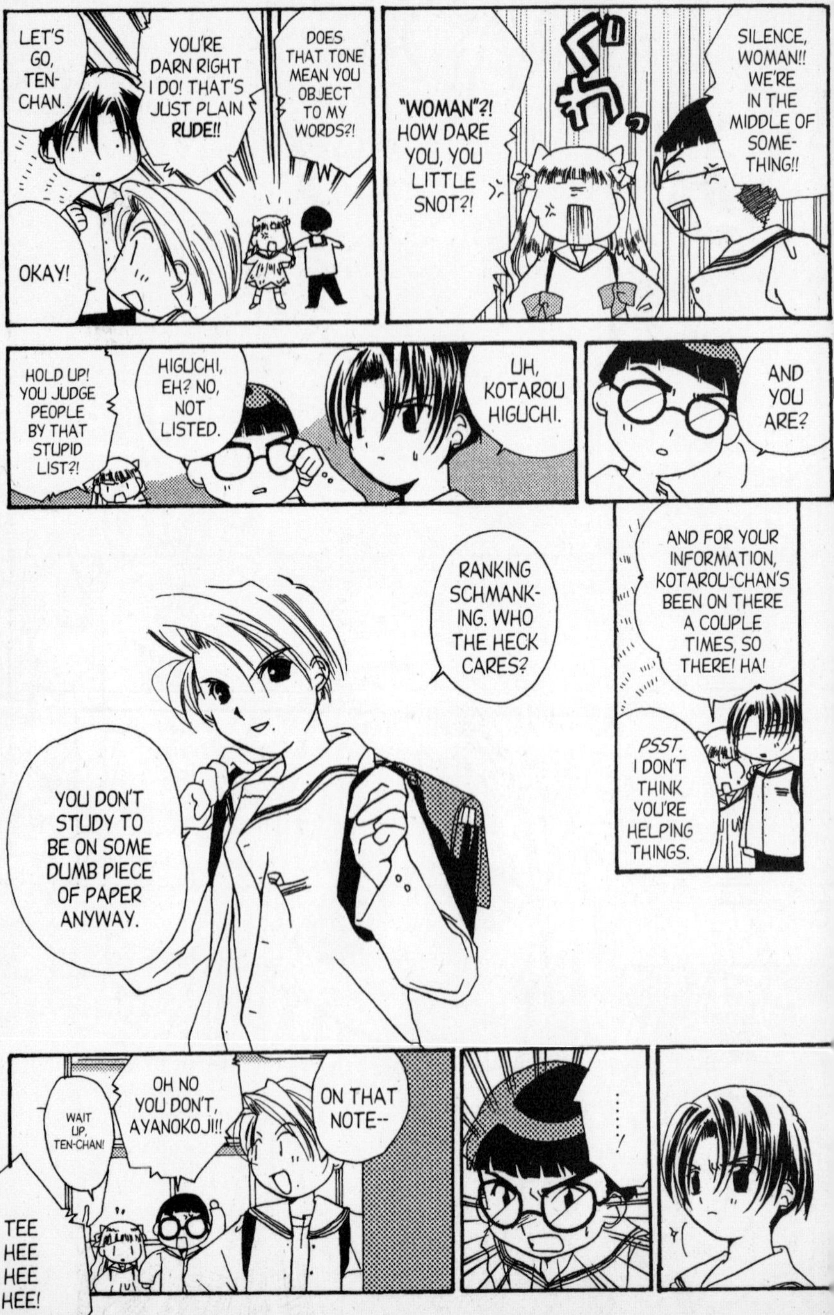
SILENCE, WOMAN!! WE'RE IN THE MIDDLE OF SOME-THING!!
"WOMAN"?! HOW DARE YOU, YOU LITTLE SNOT?!
DOES THAT TONE MEAN YOU OBJECT TO MY WORDS?!
YOU'RE DARN RIGHT I DO! THAT'S JUST PLAIN RUDE!!
LET'S GO, TEN-CHAN.
OKAY!
AND YOU ARE?
UH, KOTAROU HIGUCHI.
HIGUCHI, EH? NO, NOT LISTED.
HOLD UP! YOU JUDGE PEOPLE BY THAT STUPID LIST?!
AND FOR YOUR INFORMATION, KOTAROU-CHAN'S BEEN ON THERE A COUPLE TIMES, SO THERE! HA!
PSST. I DON'T THINK YOU'RE HELPING THINGS.
RANKING SCHMANK-ING. WHO THE HECK CARES?
YOU DON'T STUDY TO BE ON SOME DUMB PIECE OF PAPER ANYWAY.
......!
ON THAT NOTE--
OH NO YOU DON'T, AYANOKOJI!!
WAIT UP, TEN-CHAN!
TEE HEE HEE HEE!

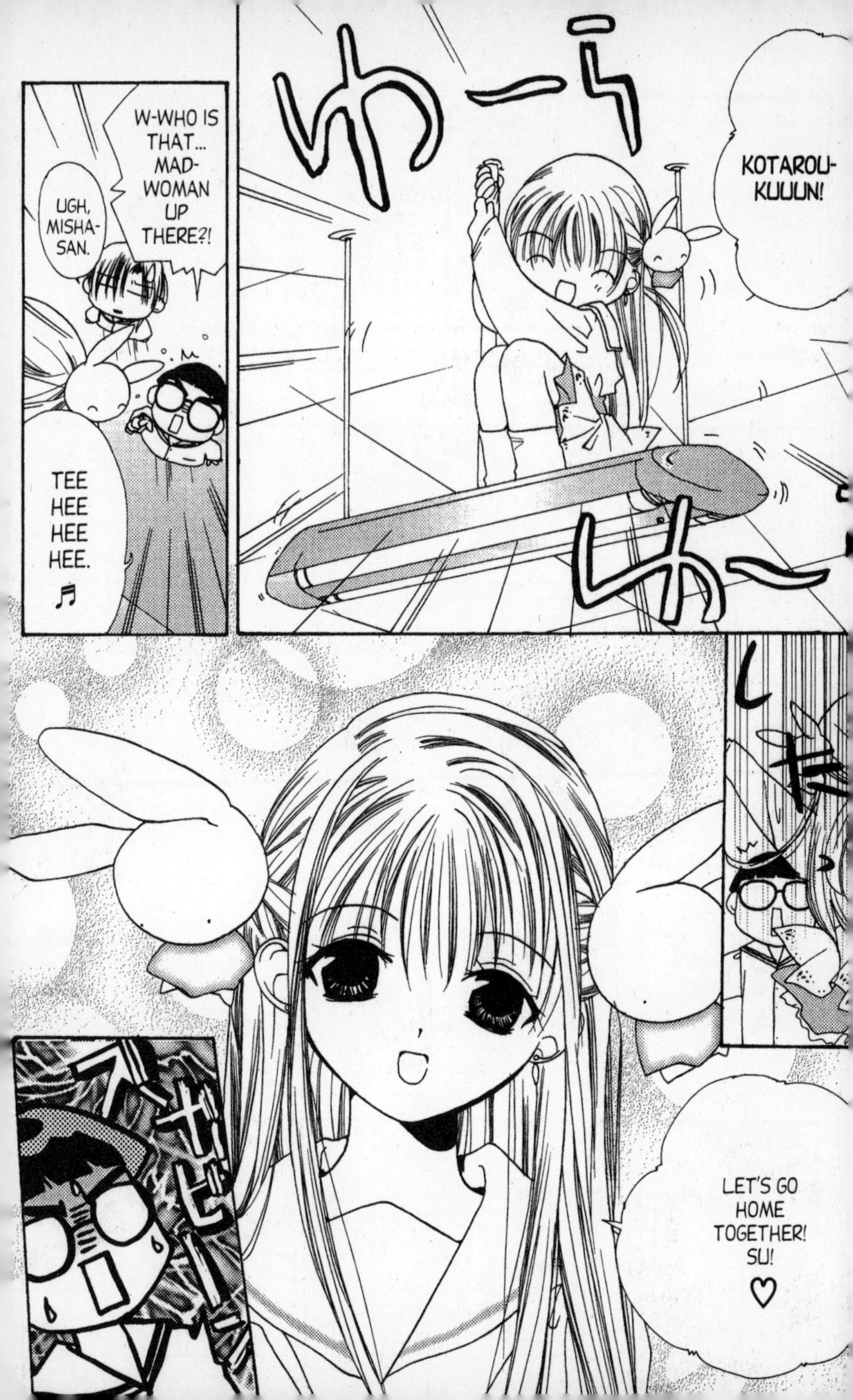
KOTAROU-KUUUN!
W-WHO IS THAT... MAD-WOMAN UP THERE?!
UGH, MISHA-SAN.
TEE HEE HEE HEE. ♬
LET'S GO HOME TOGETHER! SU! ♡

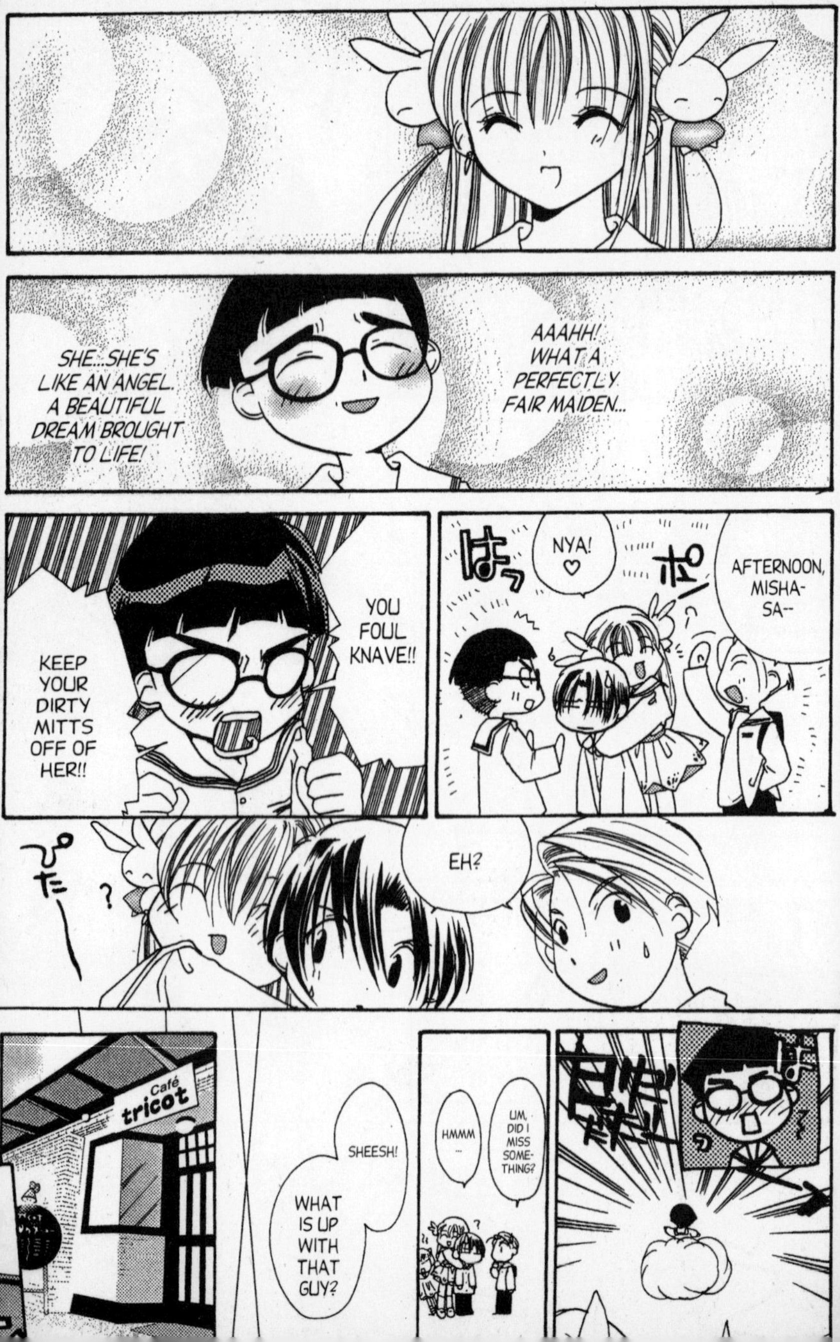
AAAHH! WHAT A PERFECTLY FAIR MAIDEN...
SHE...SHE'S LIKE AN ANGEL. A BEAUTIFUL DREAM BROUGHT TO LIFE!
AFTERNOON, MISHA-SA--
NYA! ♡
はっ
YOU FOUL KNAVE!!
KEEP YOUR DIRTY MITTS OFF OF HER!!
EH?
ぴたー
UM, DID I MISS SOME-THING?
HMMM...
SHEESH!
WHAT IS UP WITH THAT GUY?
Café tricot

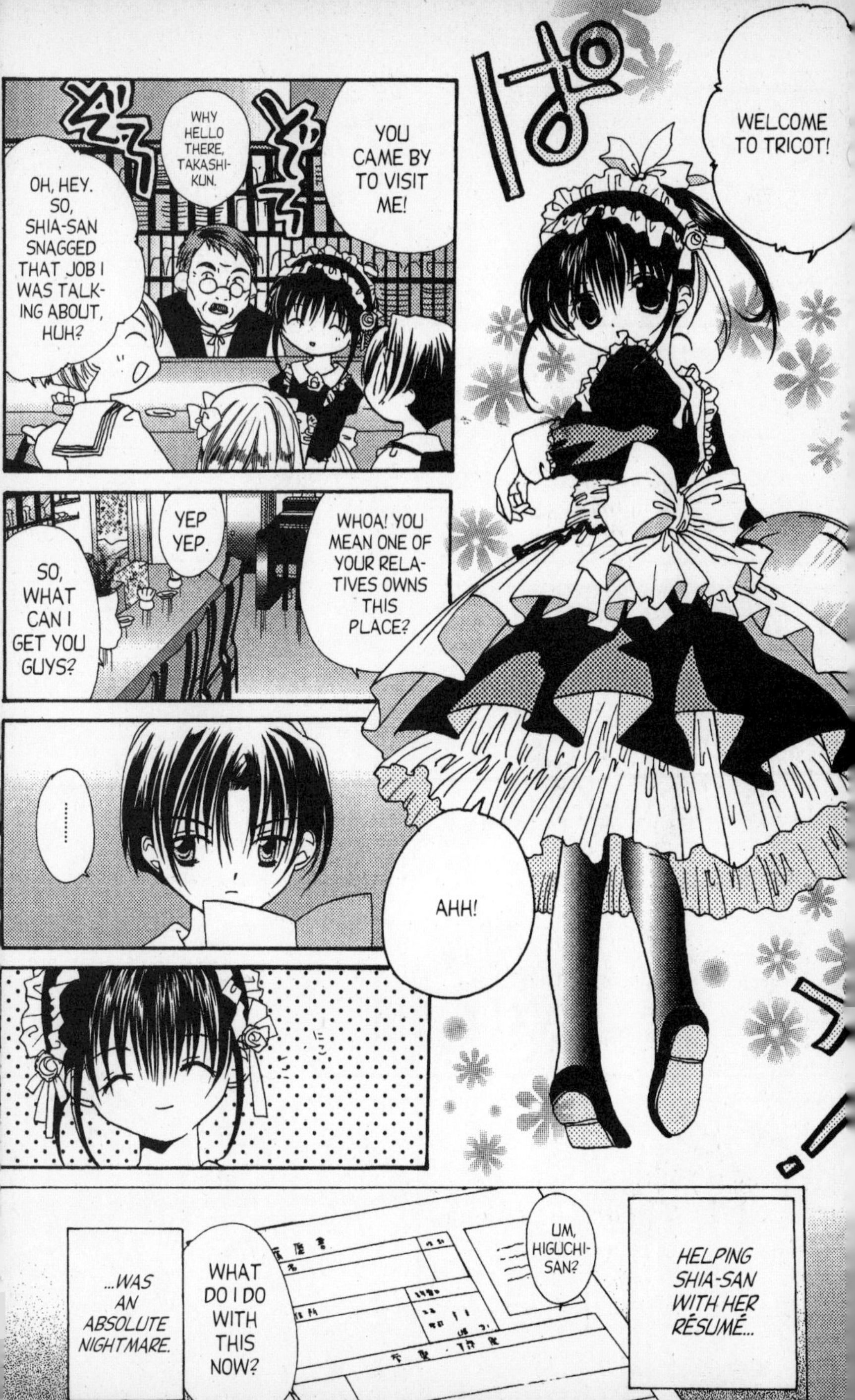
ぱ
WELCOME TO TRICOT!
AHH!
YOU CAME BY TO VISIT ME!
WHY HELLO THERE, TAKASHI-KUN.
OH, HEY. SO, SHIA-SAN SNAGGED THAT JOB I WAS TALKING ABOUT, HUH?
WHOA! YOU MEAN ONE OF YOUR RELATIVES OWNS THIS PLACE?
YEP YEP.
SO, WHAT CAN I GET YOU GUYS?
......
HELPING SHIA-SAN WITH HER RÉSUMÉ...
UM, HIGUCHI-SAN?
WHAT DO I DO WITH THIS NOW?
...WAS AN ABSOLUTE NIGHTMARE.

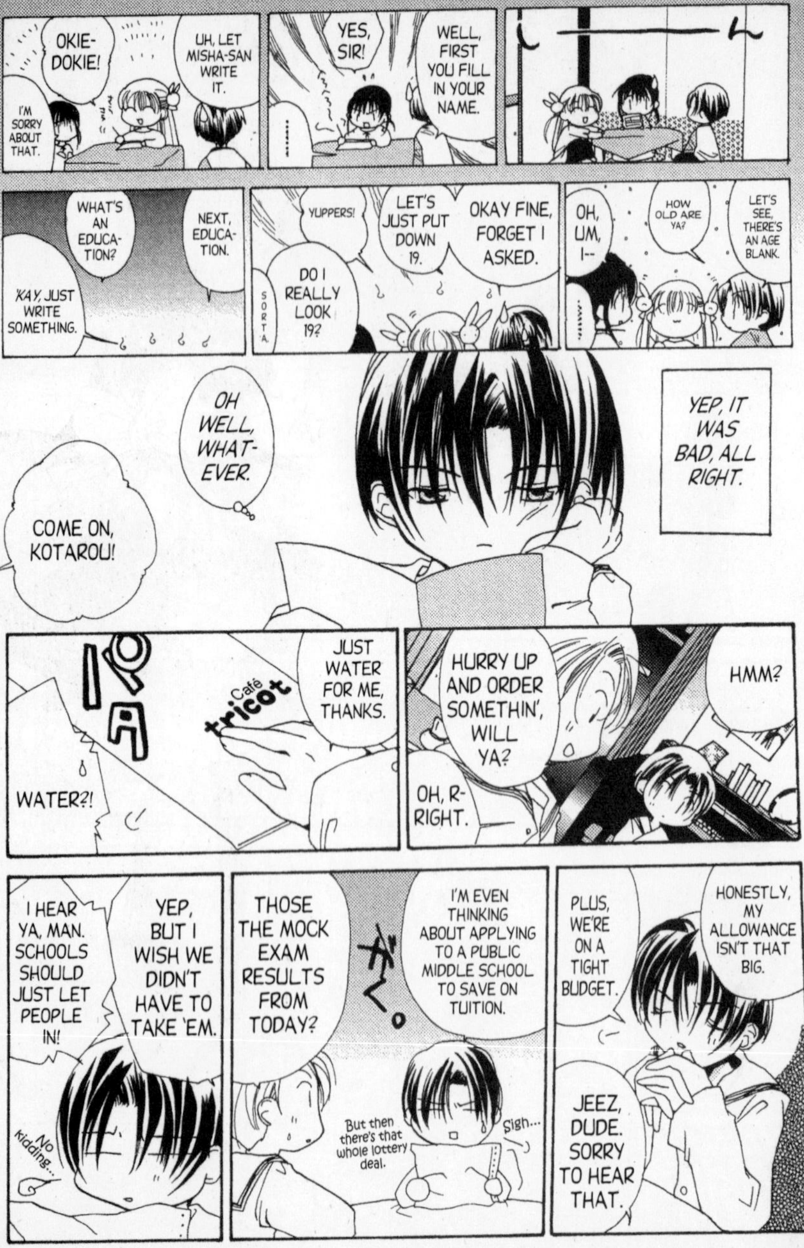
じーん
WELL, FIRST YOU FILL IN YOUR NAME.
YES, SIR!
......
UH, LET MISHA-SAN WRITE IT.
OKIE-DOKIE!
I'M SORRY ABOUT THAT.
LET'S SEE, THERE'S AN AGE BLANK.
HOW OLD ARE YA?
OH, UM, I--
......
OKAY FINE, FORGET I ASKED.
LET'S JUST PUT DOWN 19.
YUPPERS!
DO I REALLY LOOK 19?
SORTA.
NEXT, EDUCATION.
WHAT'S AN EDUCATION?
'KAY, JUST WRITE SOMETHING.
YEP, IT WAS BAD, ALL RIGHT.
OH WELL, WHATEVER.
COME ON, KOTAROU!
HMM?
HURRY UP AND ORDER SOMETHIN', WILL YA?
OH, R-RIGHT.
JUST WATER FOR ME, THANKS.
Café tricot
WATER?!
HONESTLY, MY ALLOWANCE ISN'T THAT BIG.
PLUS, WE'RE ON A TIGHT BUDGET.
JEEZ, DUDE. SORRY TO HEAR THAT.
I'M EVEN THINKING ABOUT APPLYING TO A PUBLIC MIDDLE SCHOOL TO SAVE ON TUITION.
THOSE THE MOCK EXAM RESULTS FROM TODAY?
ぎく。
Sigh...
But then there's that whole lottery deal.
YEP, BUT I WISH WE DIDN'T HAVE TO TAKE 'EM.
I HEAR YA, MAN. SCHOOLS SHOULD JUST LET PEOPLE IN!
No kidding...

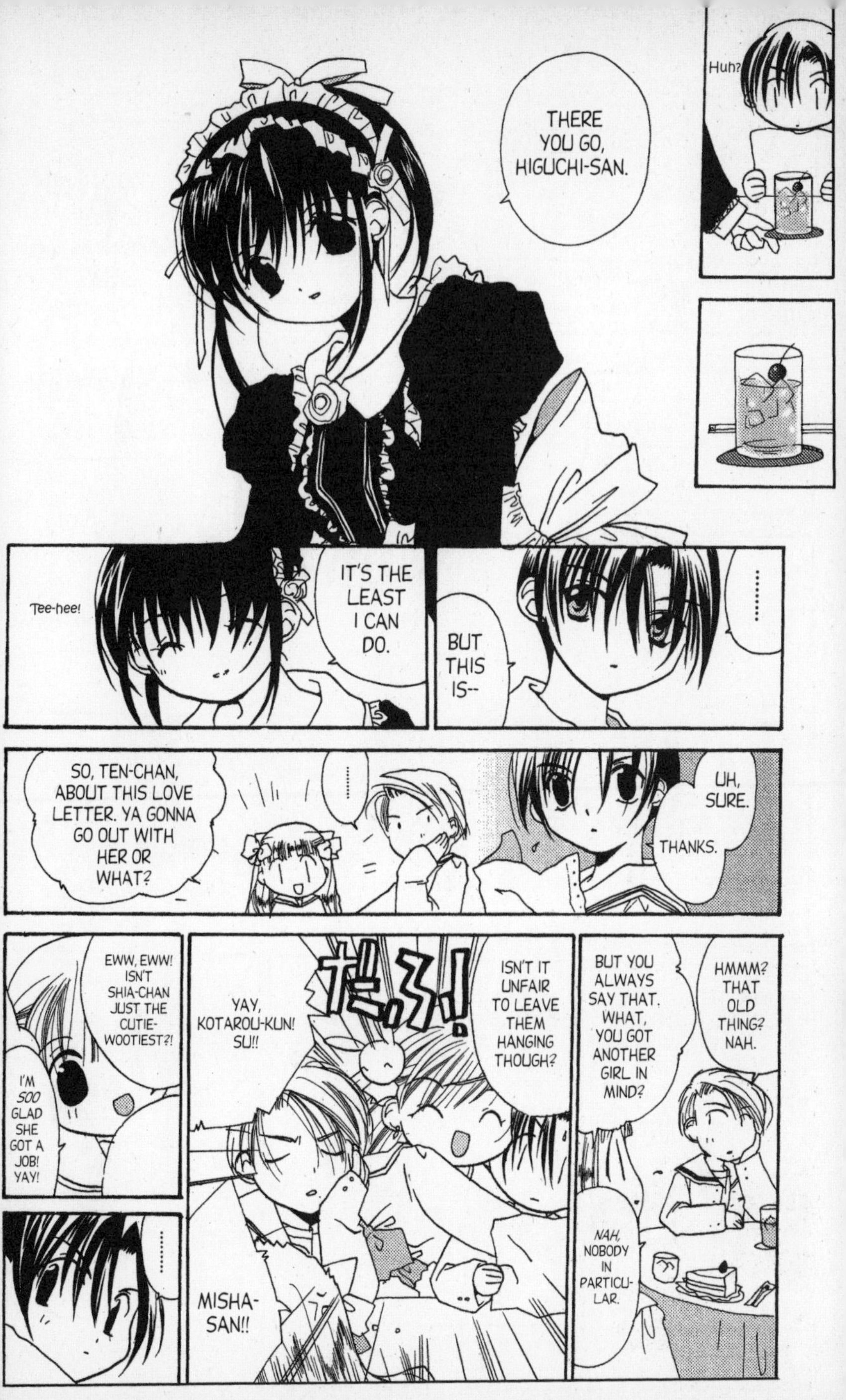
Huh?
THERE YOU GO, HIGUCHI-SAN.
......
BUT THIS IS--
IT'S THE LEAST I CAN DO.
Tee-hee!
UH, SURE.
THANKS.
......
SO, TEN-CHAN, ABOUT THIS LOVE LETTER. YA GONNA GO OUT WITH HER OR WHAT?
HMMM? THAT OLD THING? NAH.
BUT YOU ALWAYS SAY THAT. WHAT, YOU GOT ANOTHER GIRL IN MIND?
NAH, NOBODY IN PARTICU-LAR.
ISN'T IT UNFAIR TO LEAVE THEM HANGING THOUGH?
YAY, KOTAROU-KUN! SU!!
MISHA-SAN!!
EWW, EWW! ISN'T SHIA-CHAN JUST THE CUTIE-WOOTIEST?!
I'M *SOO* GLAD SHE GOT A JOB! YAY!
......

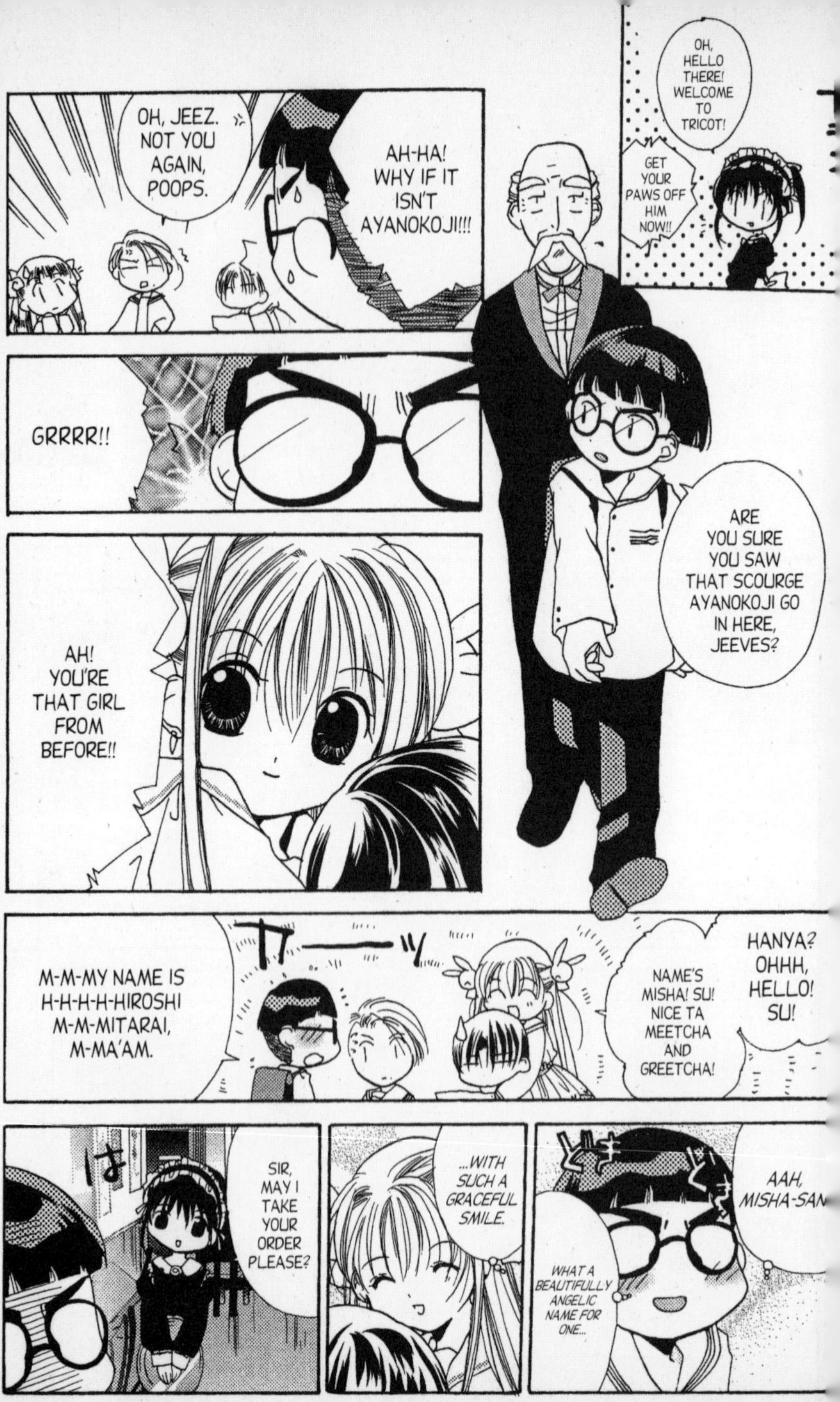
OH, HELLO THERE! WELCOME TO TRICOT!
GET YOUR PAWS OFF HIM NOW!!
ARE YOU SURE YOU SAW THAT SCOURGE AYANOKOJI GO IN HERE, JEEVES?
AH-HA! WHY IF IT ISN'T AYANOKOJI!!!
OH, JEEZ. NOT YOU AGAIN, POOPS.
GRRRR!!
AH! YOU'RE THAT GIRL FROM BEFORE!!
HANYA? OHHH, HELLO! SU!
NAME'S MISHA! SU! NICE TA MEETCHA AND GREETCHA!
カーーッ
M-M-MY NAME IS H-H-H-H-HIROSHI M-M-MITARAI, M-MA'AM.
どき どき
AAH, MISHA-SAN
WHAT A BEAUTIFULLY ANGELIC NAME FOR ONE...
...WITH SUCH A GRACEFUL SMILE.
は
SIR, MAY I TAKE YOUR ORDER PLEASE?

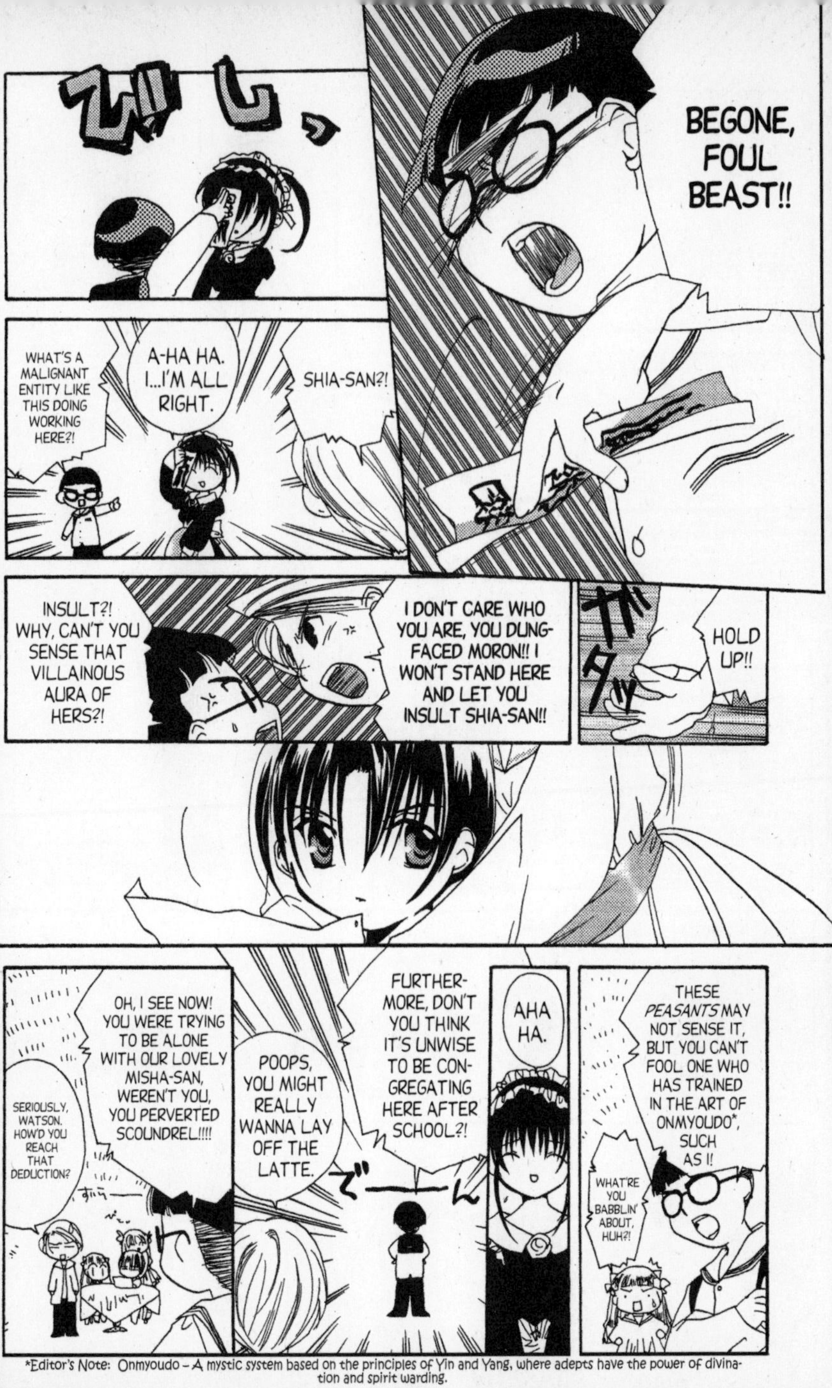
BEGONE, FOUL BEAST!!
びしっ
SHIA-SAN?!
A-HA HA. I...I'M ALL RIGHT.
WHAT'S A MALIGNANT ENTITY LIKE THIS DOING WORKING HERE?!
HOLD UP!!
ガタッ
I DON'T CARE WHO YOU ARE, YOU DUNG-FACED MORON!! I WON'T STAND HERE AND LET YOU INSULT SHIA-SAN!!
INSULT?! WHY, CAN'T YOU SENSE THAT VILLAINOUS AURA OF HERS?!
THESE *PEASANTS* MAY NOT SENSE IT, BUT YOU CAN'T FOOL ONE WHO HAS TRAINED IN THE ART OF ONMYOUDO*, SUCH AS I!
WHAT'RE YOU BABBLIN' ABOUT, HUH?!
AHA HA.
FURTHER-MORE, DON'T YOU THINK IT'S UNWISE TO BE CON-GREGATING HERE AFTER SCHOOL?!
POOPS, YOU MIGHT REALLY WANNA LAY OFF THE LATTE.
で――ん
OH, I SEE NOW! YOU WERE TRYING TO BE ALONE WITH OUR LOVELY MISHA-SAN, WEREN'T YOU, YOU PERVERTED SCOUNDREL!!!!
SERIOUSLY, WATSON. HOW'D YOU REACH THAT DEDUCTION?

*Editor's Note: Onmyoudo – A mystic system based on the principles of Yin and Yang, where adepts have the power of divination and spirit warding.

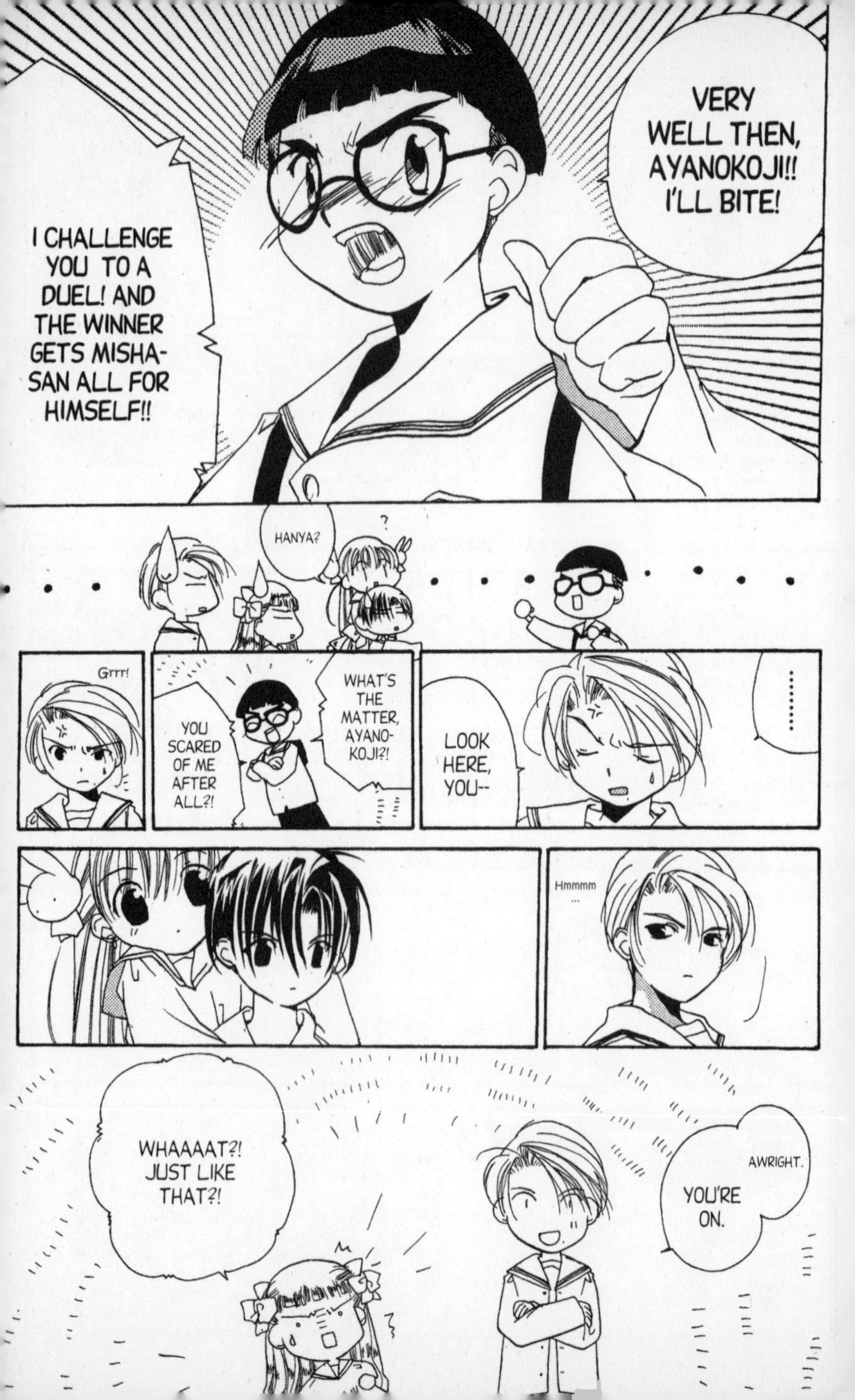
VERY WELL THEN, AYANOKOJI!! I'LL BITE!
I CHALLENGE YOU TO A DUEL! AND THE WINNER GETS MISHA-SAN ALL FOR HIMSELF!!
HANYA?
?
......
LOOK HERE, YOU--
WHAT'S THE MATTER, AYANOKOJI?!
YOU SCARED OF ME AFTER ALL?!
Grrr!
Hmmmm ...
AWRIGHT.
YOU'RE ON.
WHAAAAT?! JUST LIKE THAT?!

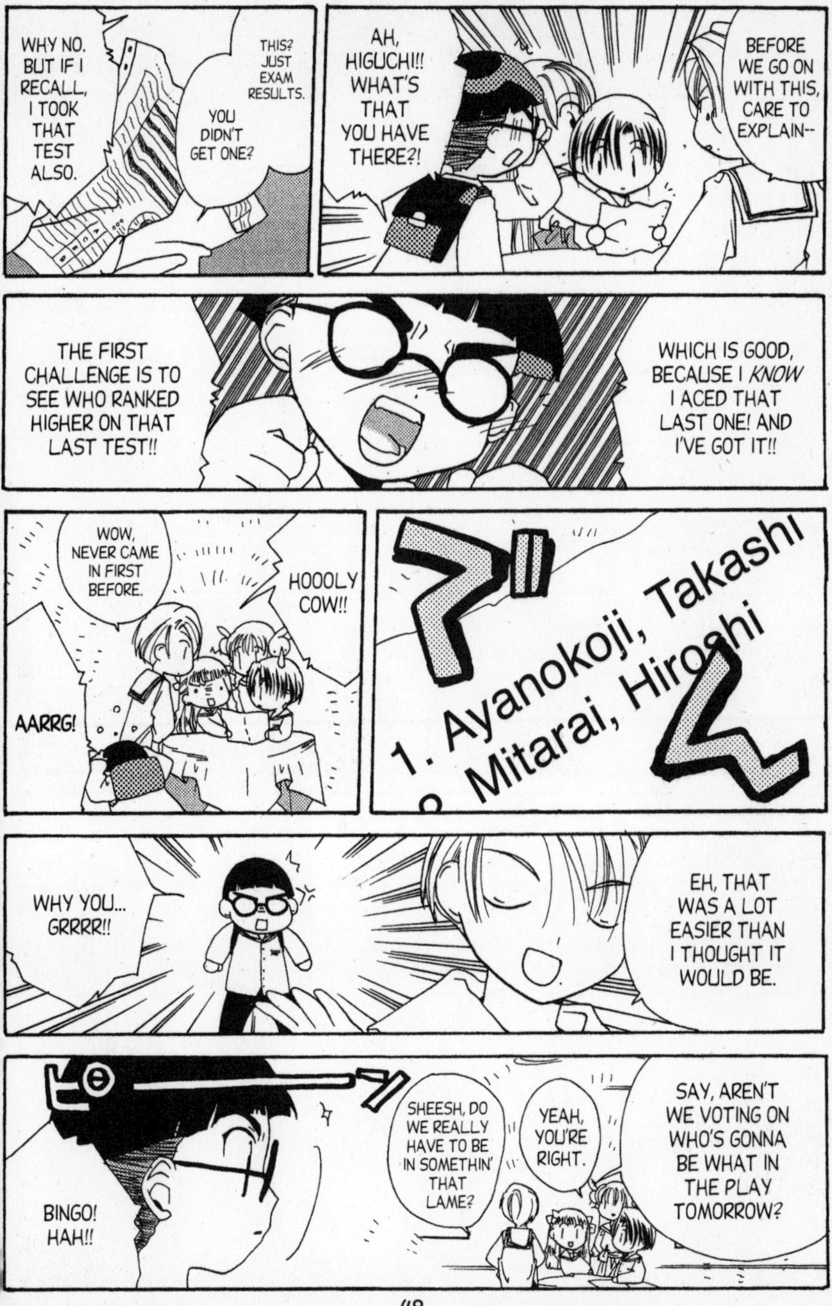
BEFORE WE GO ON WITH THIS, CARE TO EXPLAIN--
AH, HIGUCHI!! WHAT'S THAT YOU HAVE THERE?!
THIS? JUST EXAM RESULTS.
YOU DIDN'T GET ONE?
WHY NO. BUT IF I RECALL, I TOOK THAT TEST ALSO.
WHICH IS GOOD, BECAUSE I *KNOW* I ACED THAT LAST ONE! AND I'VE GOT IT!!
THE FIRST CHALLENGE IS TO SEE WHO RANKED HIGHER ON THAT LAST TEST!!
1. Ayanokoji, Takashi
Mitarai, Hiroshi
HOOOLY COW!!
WOW, NEVER CAME IN FIRST BEFORE.
AARRG!
EH, THAT WAS A LOT EASIER THAN I THOUGHT IT WOULD BE.
WHY YOU... GRRRR!!
SAY, AREN'T WE VOTING ON WHO'S GONNA BE WHAT IN THE PLAY TOMORROW?
YEAH, YOU'RE RIGHT.
SHEESH, DO WE REALLY HAVE TO BE IN SOMETHIN' THAT LAME?
BINGO! HAH!!

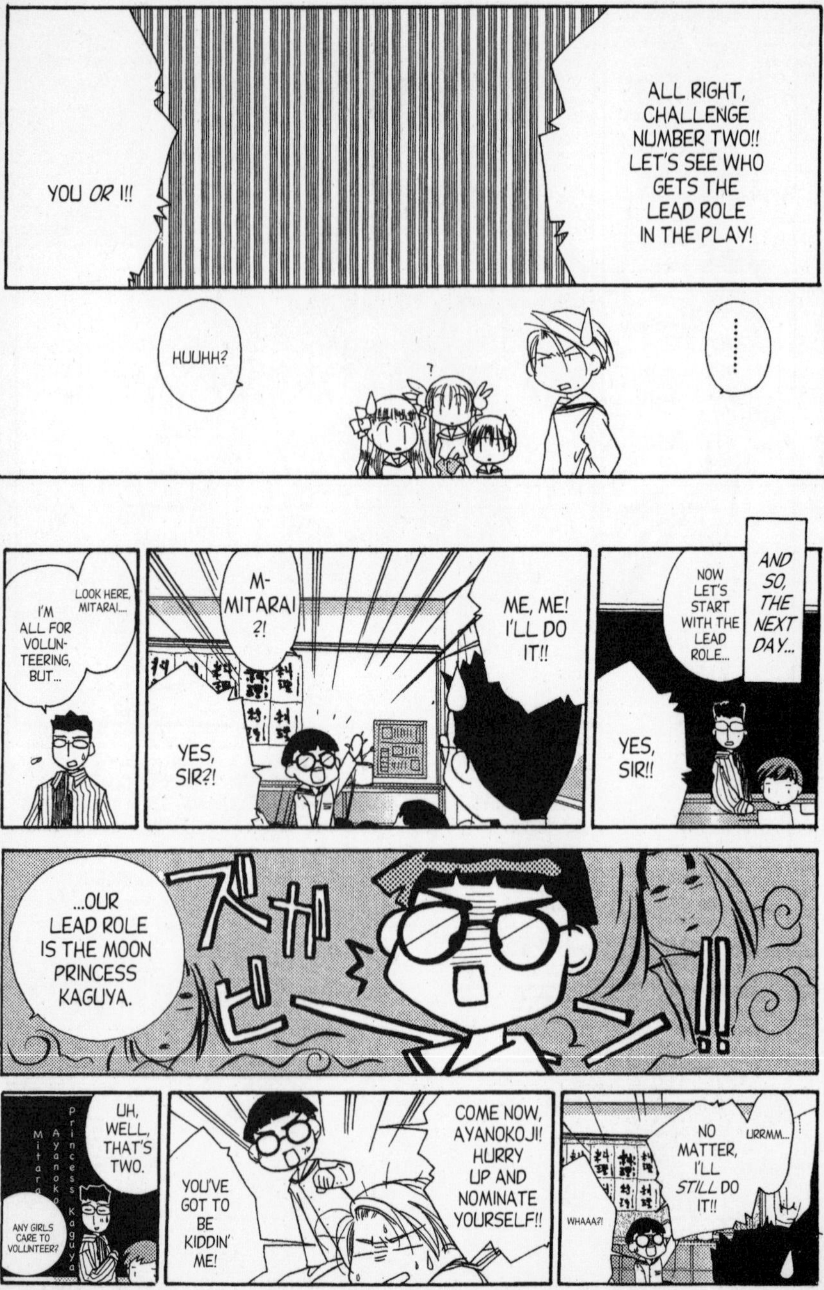
ALL RIGHT, CHALLENGE NUMBER TWO!! LET'S SEE WHO GETS THE LEAD ROLE IN THE PLAY!
YOU *OR* I!!
......
?
HUUHH?
AND SO, THE NEXT DAY...
NOW LET'S START WITH THE LEAD ROLE...
YES, SIR!!
ME, ME! I'LL DO IT!!
M-MITARAI?!
YES, SIR?!
LOOK HERE, MITARAI....
I'M ALL FOR VOLUNTEERING, BUT...
...OUR LEAD ROLE IS THE MOON PRINCESS KAGUYA.
ズガビーン!!
URRMM...
NO MATTER, I'LL *STILL* DO IT!!
WHAAA?!
COME NOW, AYANOKOJI! HURRY UP AND NOMINATE YOURSELF!!
YOU'VE GOT TO BE KIDDIN' ME!
UH, WELL, THAT'S TWO.
Princess Kaguya
Ayanokoji
Mitarai
ANY GIRLS CARE TO VOLUNTEER?

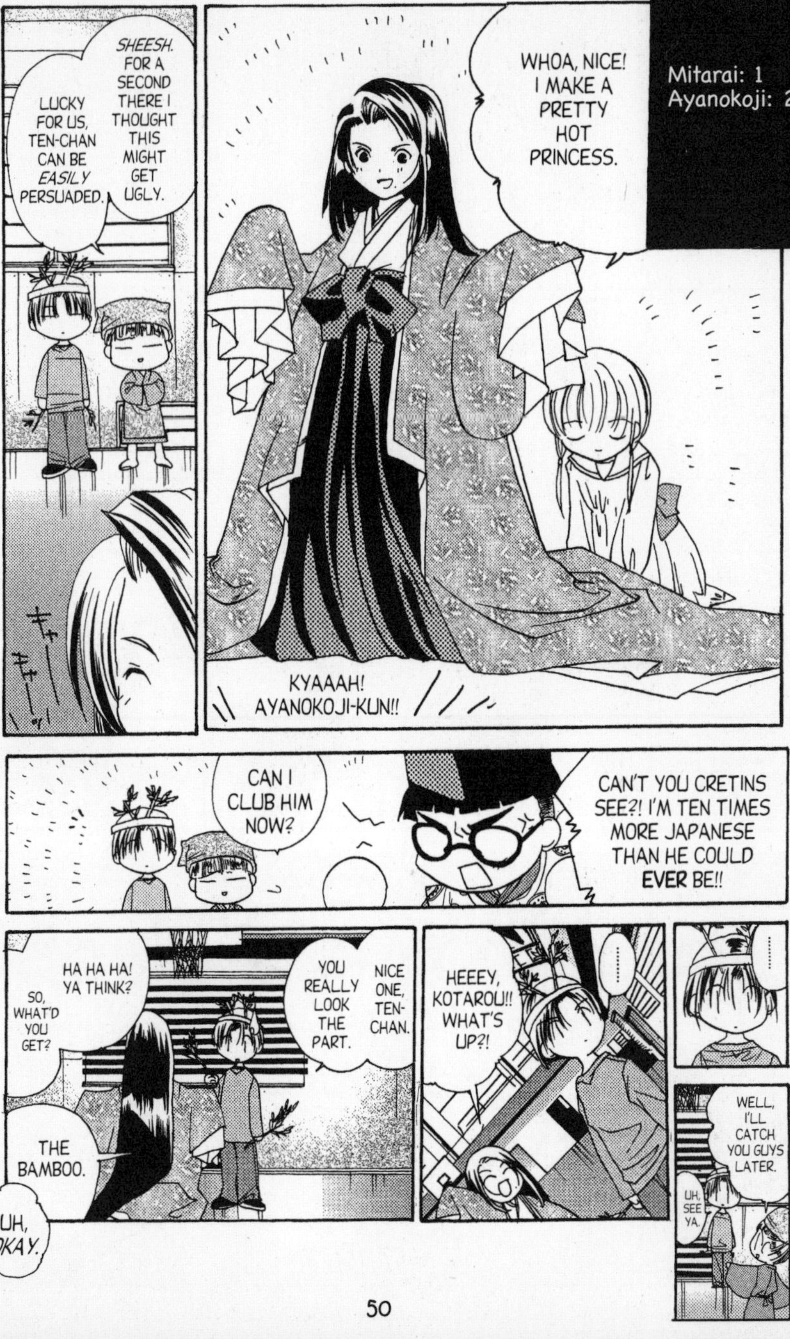
WHOA, NICE! I MAKE A PRETTY HOT PRINCESS.
KYAAAH! AYANOKOJI-KUN!!
SHEESH. FOR A SECOND THERE I THOUGHT THIS MIGHT GET UGLY.
LUCKY FOR US, TEN-CHAN CAN BE *EASILY* PERSUADED.
CAN'T YOU CRETINS SEE?! I'M TEN TIMES MORE JAPANESE THAN HE COULD **EVER** BE!!
CAN I CLUB HIM NOW?
......
WELL, I'LL CATCH YOU GUYS LATER.
UH, SEE YA.
......
HEEEY, KOTAROU!! WHAT'S UP?!
NICE ONE, TEN-CHAN.
YOU REALLY LOOK THE PART.
HA HA HA! YA THINK?
SO, WHAT'D YOU GET?
THE BAMBOO.
UH, *OKAY.*

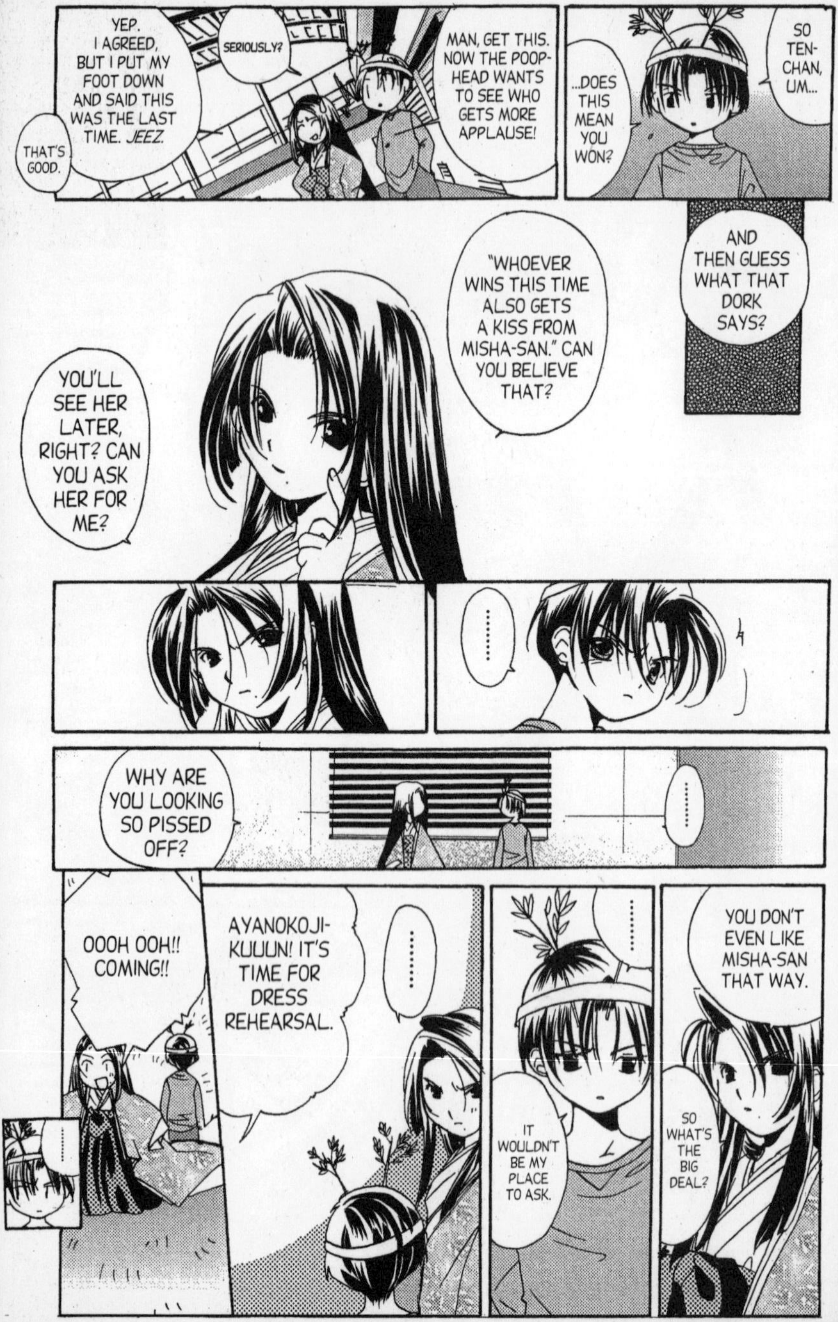
SO TEN-CHAN, UM...
...DOES THIS MEAN YOU WON?
MAN, GET THIS. NOW THE POOP-HEAD WANTS TO SEE WHO GETS MORE APPLAUSE!
SERIOUSLY?
YEP. I AGREED, BUT I PUT MY FOOT DOWN AND SAID THIS WAS THE LAST TIME. *JEEZ.*
THAT'S GOOD.
AND THEN GUESS WHAT THAT DORK SAYS?
"WHOEVER WINS THIS TIME ALSO GETS A KISS FROM MISHA-SAN." CAN YOU BELIEVE THAT?
YOU'LL SEE HER LATER, RIGHT? CAN YOU ASK HER FOR ME?
....
....
WHY ARE YOU LOOKING SO PISSED OFF?
YOU DON'T EVEN LIKE MISHA-SAN THAT WAY.
SO WHAT'S THE BIG DEAL?
....
IT WOULDN'T BE MY PLACE TO ASK.
....
AYANOKOJI-KUUUN! IT'S TIME FOR DRESS REHEARSAL.
OOOH OOH!! COMING!!
....

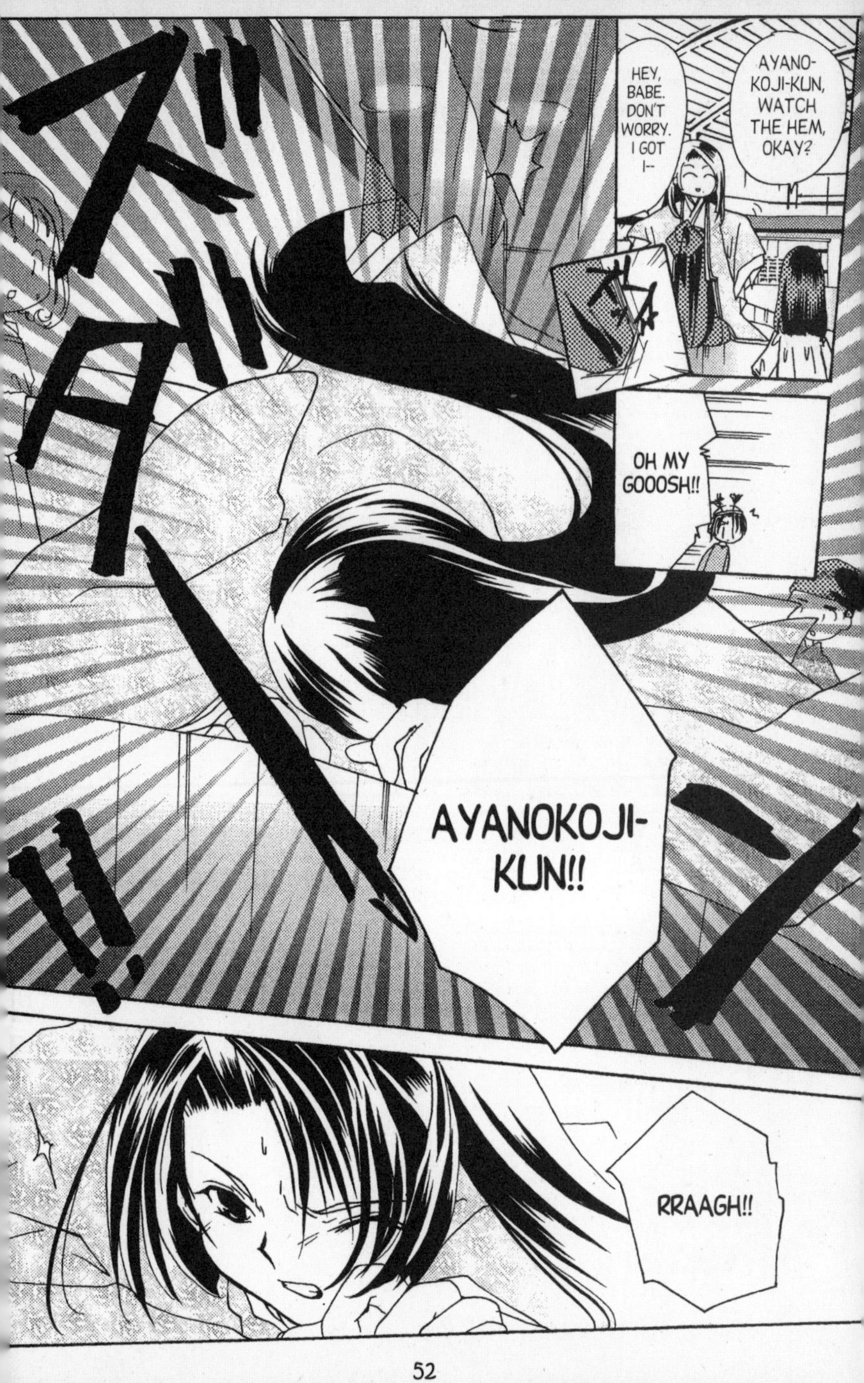
AYANO-KOJI-KUN, WATCH THE HEM, OKAY?
HEY, BABE. DON'T WORRY. I GOT I--
OH MY GOOOSH!!
AYANOKOJI-KUN!!
RRAAGH!!

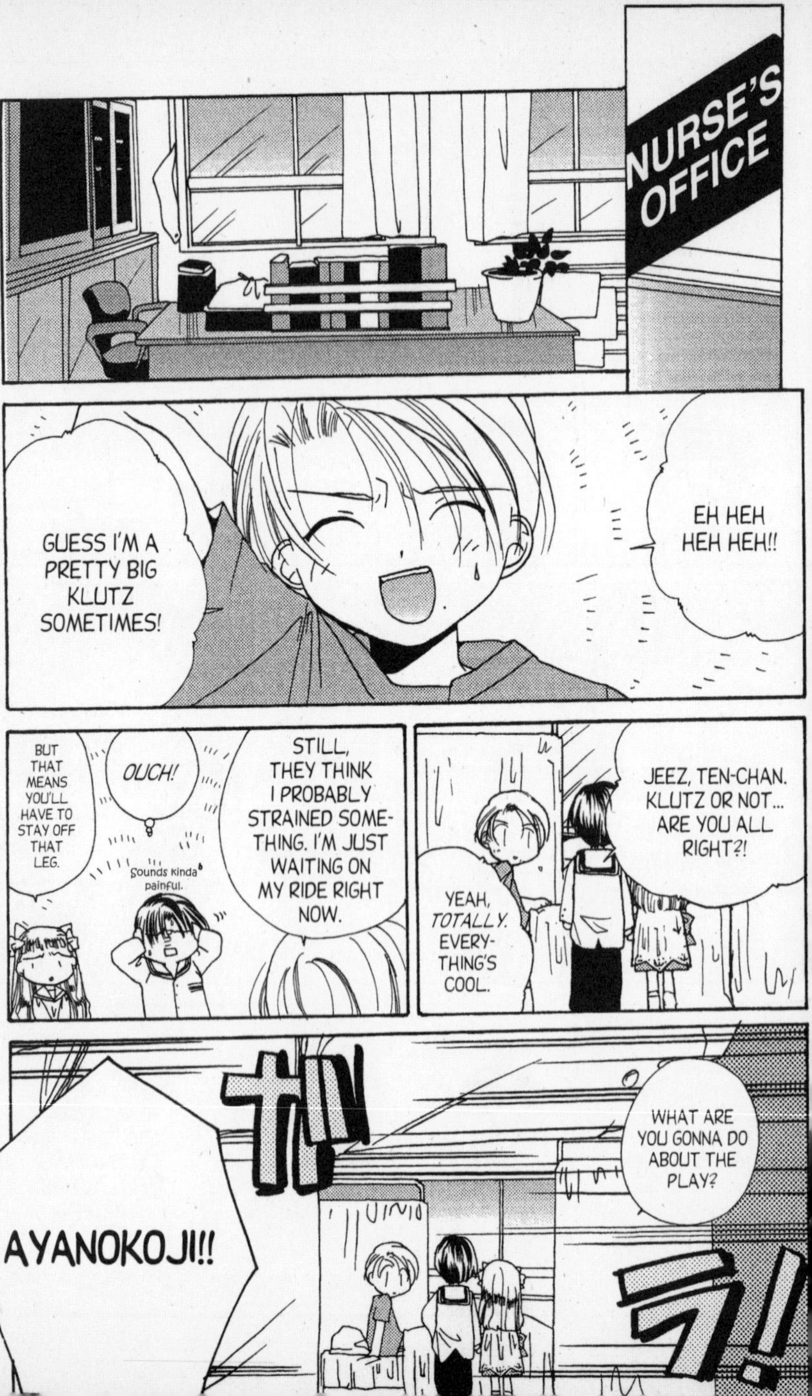

NURSE'S OFFICE
EH HEH HEH HEH!!
GUESS I'M A PRETTY BIG KLUTZ SOMETIMES!
JEEZ, TEN-CHAN. KLUTZ OR NOT... ARE YOU ALL RIGHT?!
YEAH, *TOTALLY.* EVERY-THING'S COOL.
STILL, THEY THINK I PROBABLY STRAINED SOME-THING. I'M JUST WAITING ON MY RIDE RIGHT NOW.
OUCH!
BUT THAT MEANS YOU'LL HAVE TO STAY OFF THAT LEG.
Sounds kinda painful.
WHAT ARE YOU GONNA DO ABOUT THE PLAY?
ガラ!!
AYANOKOJI!!!

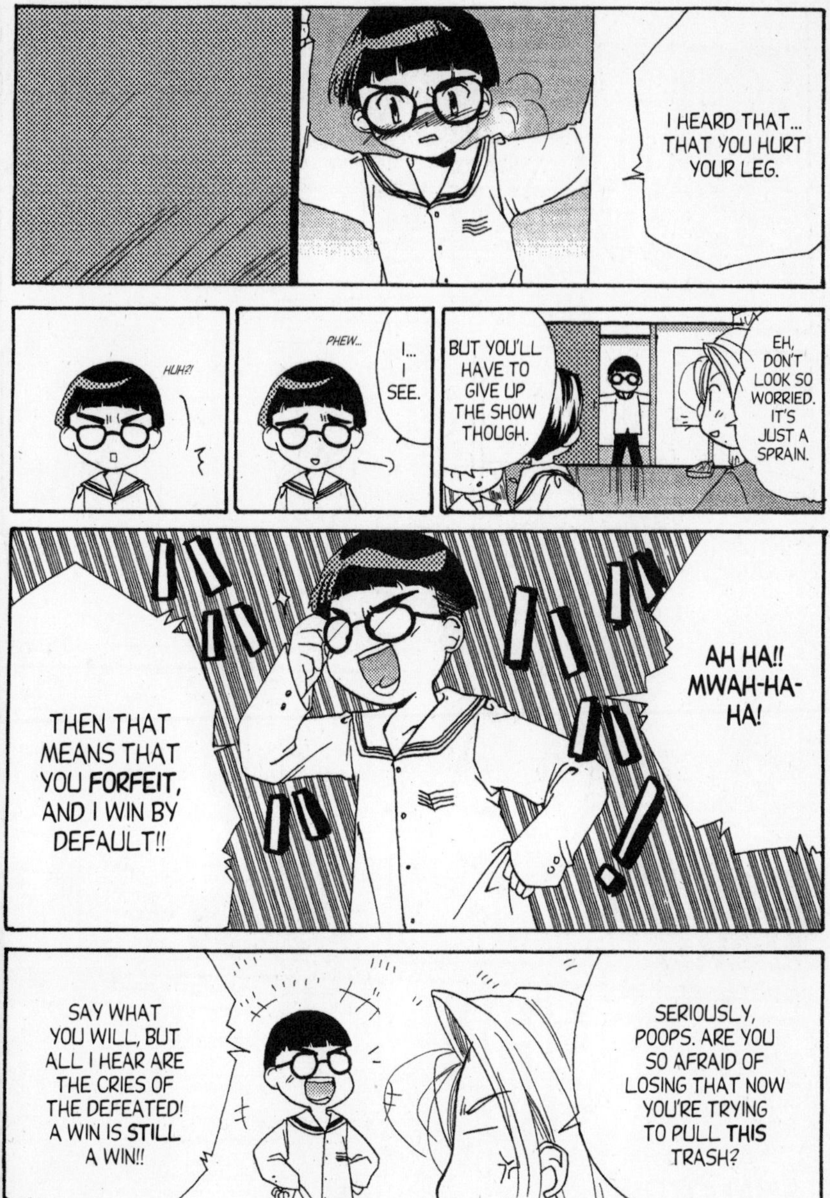
I HEARD THAT... THAT YOU HURT YOUR LEG.
EH, DON'T LOOK SO WORRIED. IT'S JUST A SPRAIN.
BUT YOU'LL HAVE TO GIVE UP THE SHOW THOUGH.
PHEW...
I... I SEE.
HUH?!
AH HA!! MWAH-HA-HA!
THEN THAT MEANS THAT YOU **FORFEIT**, AND I WIN BY DEFAULT!!
SERIOUSLY, POOPS. ARE YOU SO AFRAID OF LOSING THAT NOW YOU'RE TRYING TO PULL **THIS** TRASH?
SAY WHAT YOU WILL, BUT ALL I HEAR ARE THE CRIES OF THE DEFEATED! A WIN IS **STILL** A WIN!!

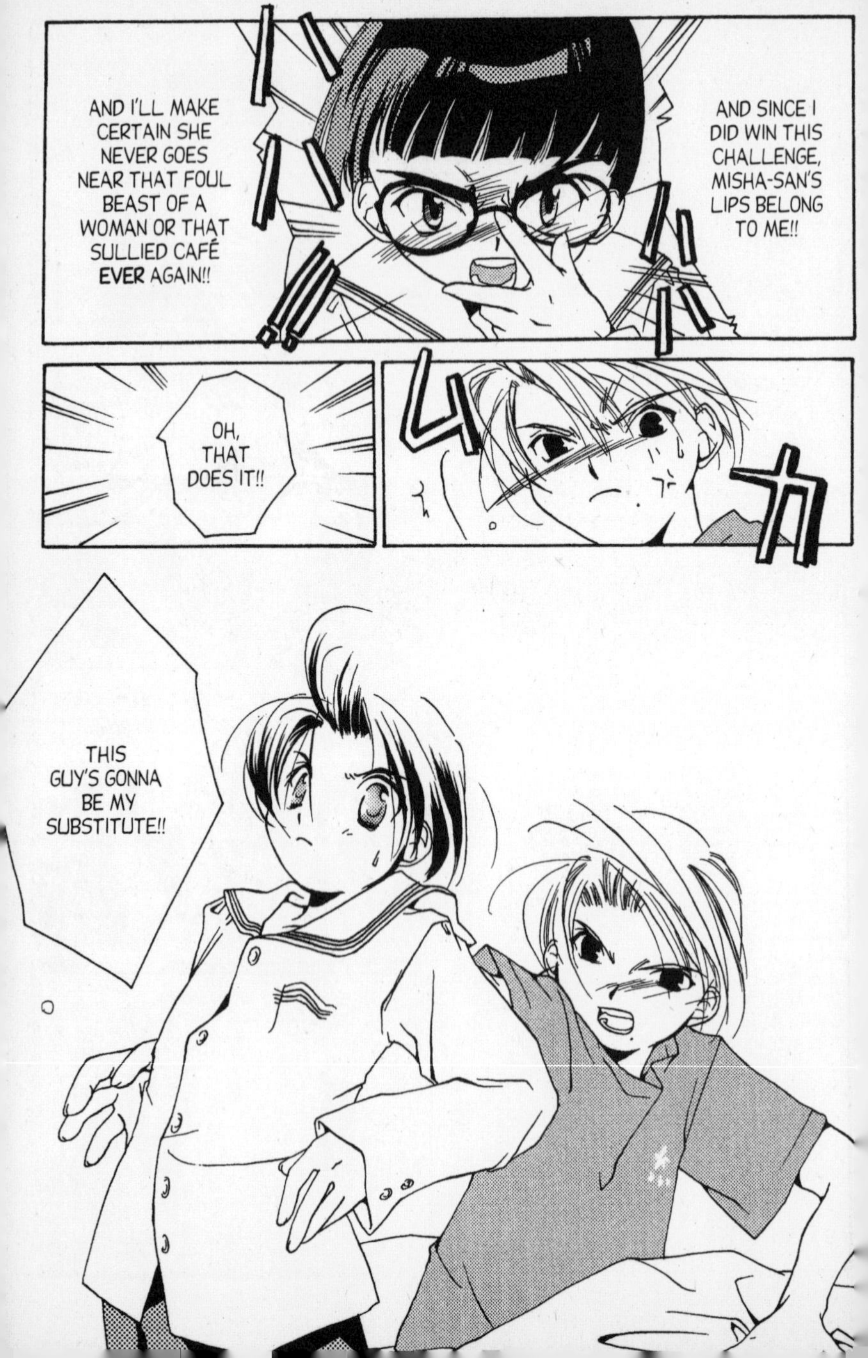
AND SINCE I DID WIN THIS CHALLENGE, MISHA-SAN'S LIPS BELONG TO ME!!
AND I'LL MAKE CERTAIN SHE NEVER GOES NEAR THAT FOUL BEAST OF A WOMAN OR THAT SULLIED CAFÉ **EVER** AGAIN!!
ムカ
OH, THAT DOES IT!!
THIS GUY'S GONNA BE MY SUBSTITUTE!!

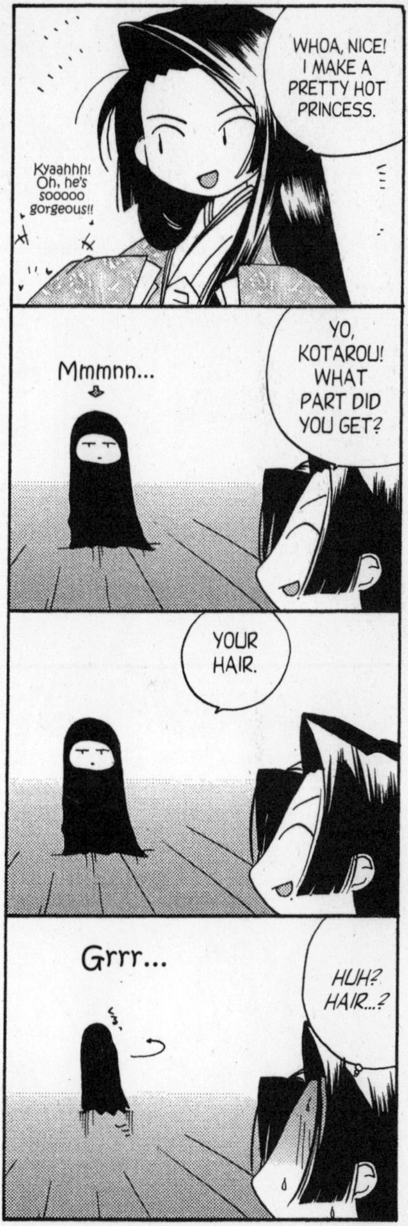
WHOA, NICE! I MAKE A PRETTY HOT PRINCESS.
Kyaahhh! Oh, he's sooooo gorgeous!!
YO, KOTAROU! WHAT PART DID YOU GET?
Mmmnn...
YOUR HAIR.
HUH? HAIR...?
Grrr...

Lesson 10

How to Welcome a New Student Part 2

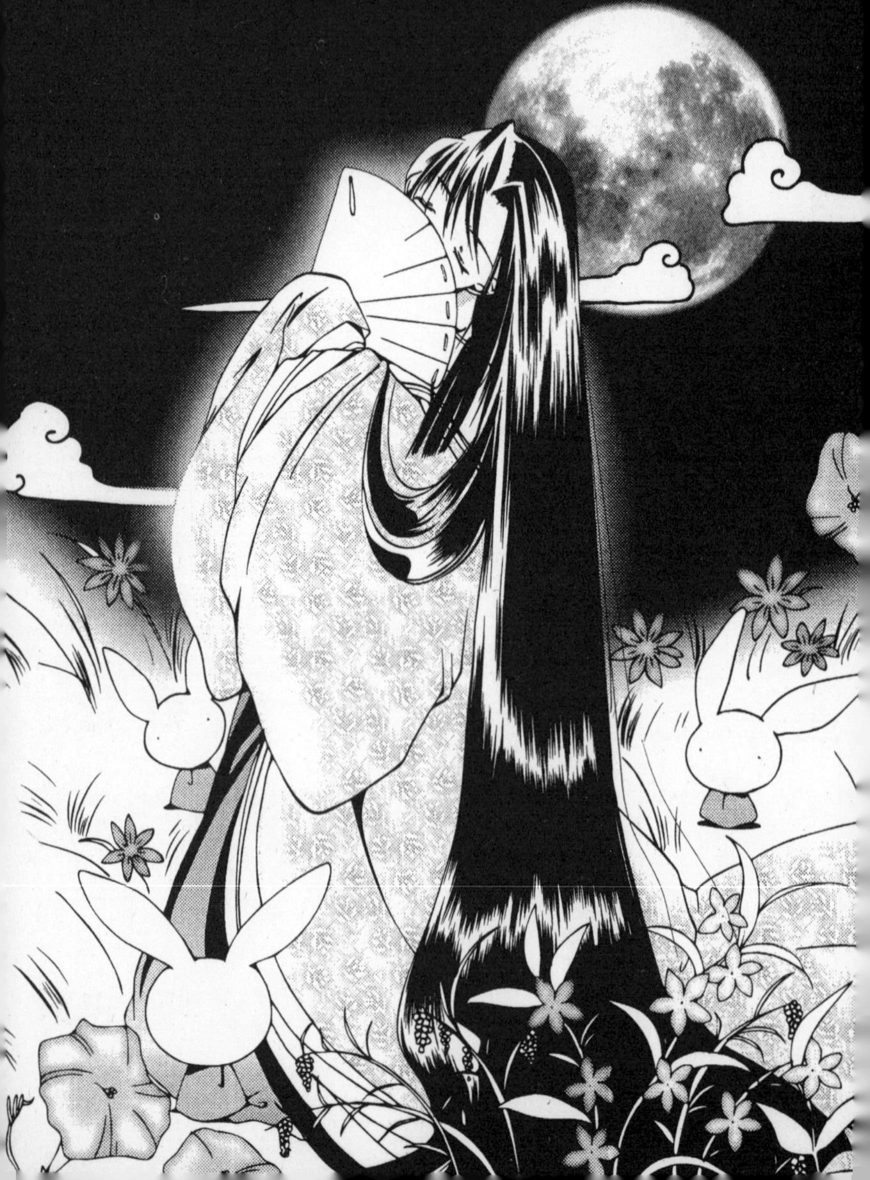

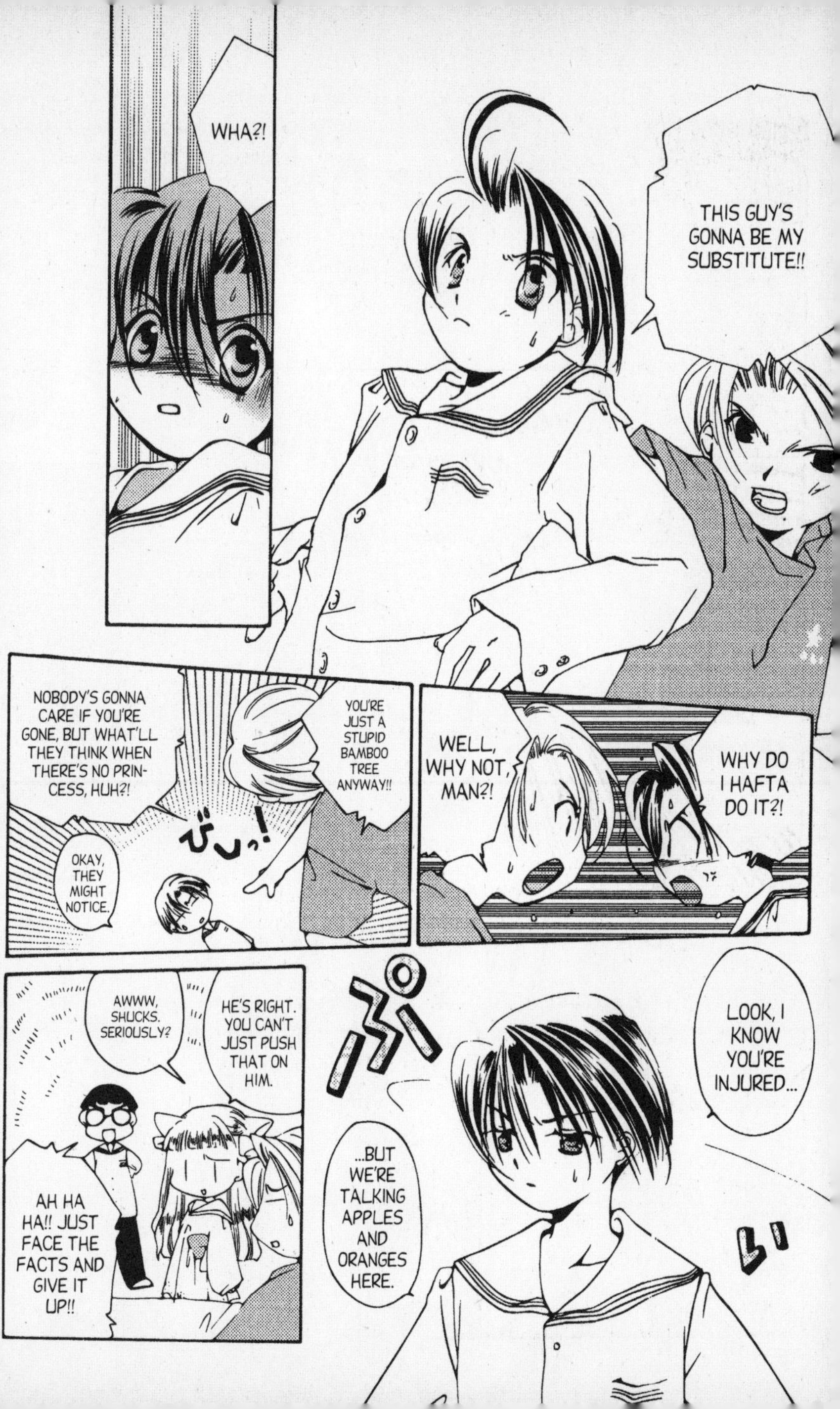
THIS GUY'S GONNA BE MY SUBSTITUTE!!
WHA?!
WHY DO I HAFTA DO IT?!
WELL, WHY NOT, MAN?!
YOU'RE JUST A STUPID BAMBOO TREE ANYWAY!!
NOBODY'S GONNA CARE IF YOU'RE GONE, BUT WHAT'LL THEY THINK WHEN THERE'S NO PRIN-CESS, HUH?!
びしっ!
OKAY, THEY MIGHT NOTICE.
ぷ
LOOK, I KNOW YOU'RE INJURED...
...BUT WE'RE TALKING APPLES AND ORANGES HERE.
HE'S RIGHT. YOU CAN'T JUST PUSH THAT ON HIM.
AWWW, SHUCKS. SERIOUSLY?
AH HA HA!! JUST FACE THE FACTS AND GIVE IT UP!!

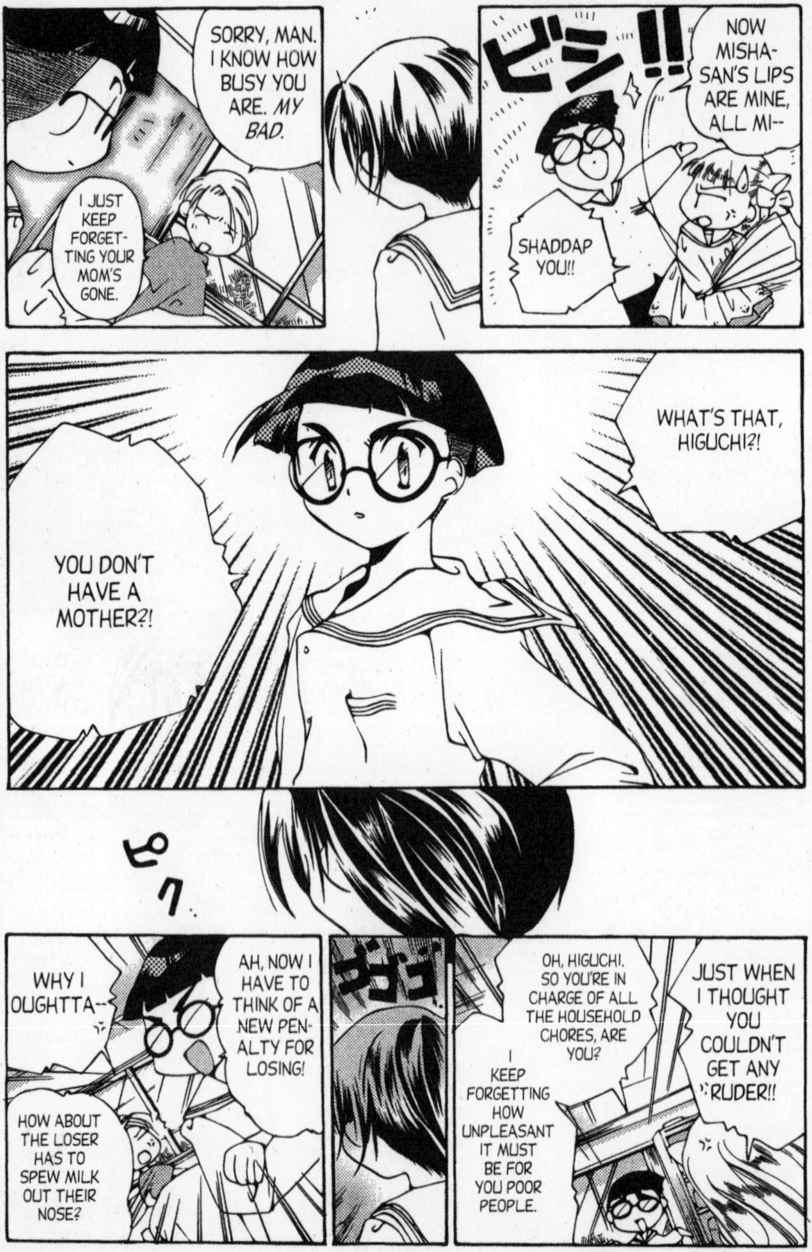
ビシ!!
NOW MISHA-SAN'S LIPS ARE MINE, ALL MI--
SHADDAP YOU!!
SORRY, MAN. I KNOW HOW BUSY YOU ARE. *MY BAD.*
I JUST KEEP FORGETTING YOUR MOM'S GONE.
WHAT'S THAT, HIGUCHI?!
YOU DON'T HAVE A MOTHER?!
ピク
JUST WHEN I THOUGHT YOU COULDN'T GET ANY RUDER!!
OH, HIGUCHI. SO YOU'RE IN CHARGE OF ALL THE HOUSEHOLD CHORES, ARE YOU?
I KEEP FORGETTING HOW UNPLEASANT IT MUST BE FOR YOU POOR PEOPLE.
ゴゴゴ
AH, NOW I HAVE TO THINK OF A NEW PENALTY FOR LOSING!
WHY I OUGHTTA--
HOW ABOUT THE LOSER HAS TO SPEW MILK OUT THEIR NOSE?

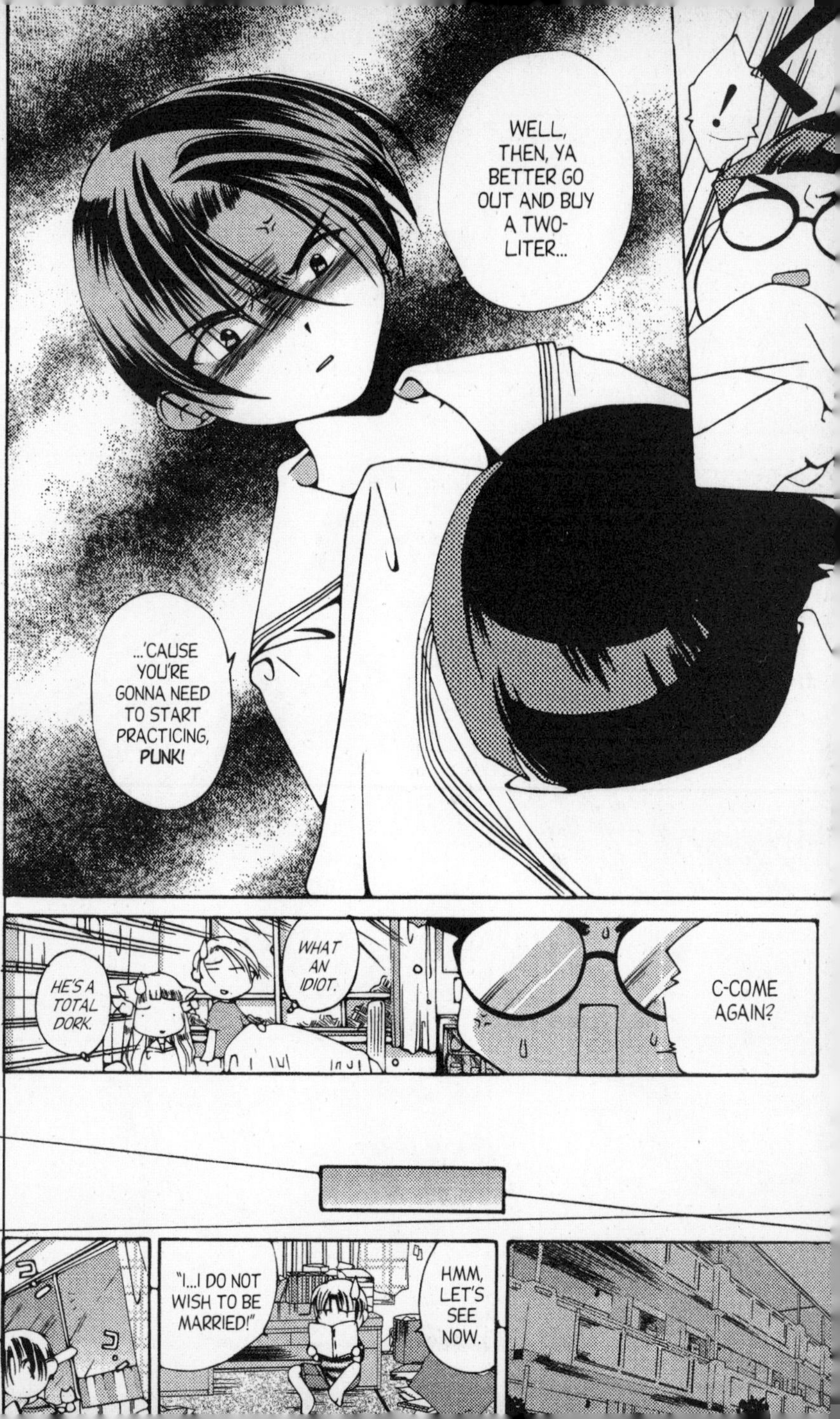
!
WELL, THEN, YA BETTER GO OUT AND BUY A TWO-LITER...
...'CAUSE YOU'RE GONNA NEED TO START PRACTICING, **PUNK!**
C-COME AGAIN?
WHAT AN IDIOT.
HE'S A TOTAL DORK.
HMM, LET'S SEE NOW.
"I...I DO NOT WISH TO BE MARRIED!"

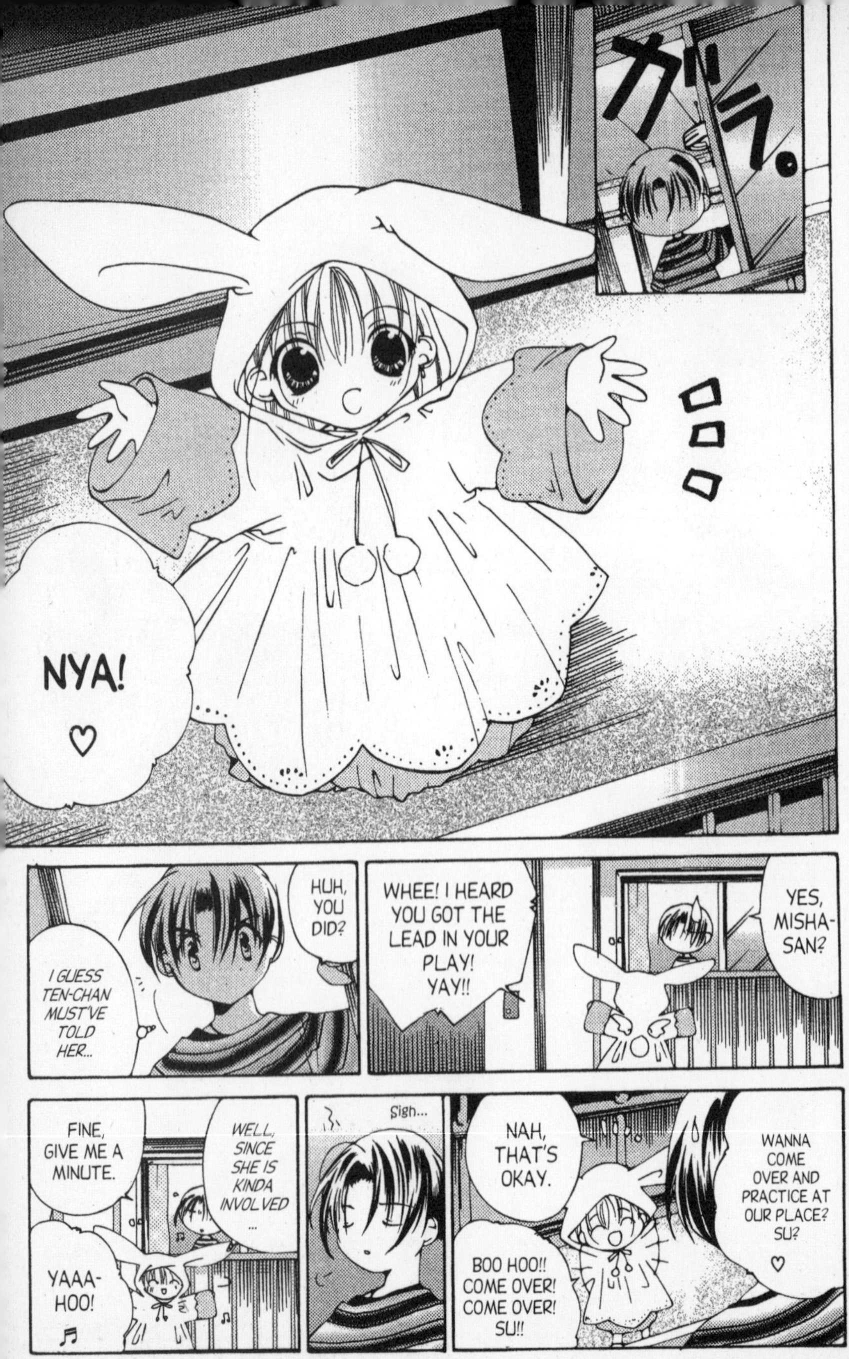
ガラ。
NYA! ♡
YES, MISHA-SAN?
WHEE! I HEARD YOU GOT THE LEAD IN YOUR PLAY! YAY!!
HUH, YOU DID?
I GUESS TEN-CHAN MUST'VE TOLD HER...
WANNA COME OVER AND PRACTICE AT OUR PLACE? SU? ♡
NAH, THAT'S OKAY.
BOO HOO!! COME OVER! COME OVER! SU!!
Sigh...
WELL, SINCE SHE IS KINDA INVOLVED...
FINE, GIVE ME A MINUTE.
YAAA-HOO! ♫

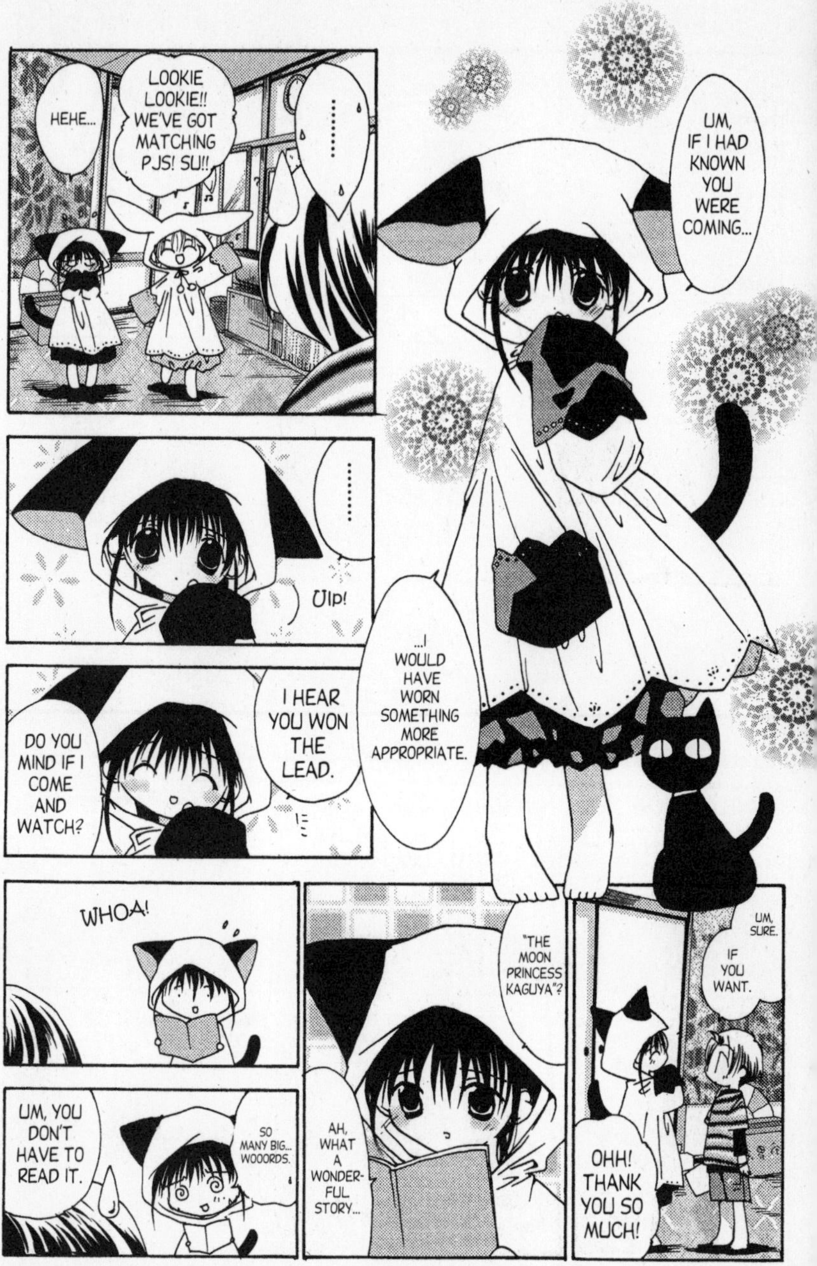
UM, IF I HAD KNOWN YOU WERE COMING...
...I WOULD HAVE WORN SOMETHING MORE APPROPRIATE.
....
LOOKIE LOOKIE!! WE'VE GOT MATCHING PJS! SU!!
HEHE...
....
UIP!
I HEAR YOU WON THE LEAD.
DO YOU MIND IF I COME AND WATCH?
UM, SURE.
IF YOU WANT.
OHH! THANK YOU SO MUCH!
"THE MOON PRINCESS KAGUYA"?
AH, WHAT A WONDERFUL STORY...
WHOA!
SO MANY BIG... WOOORDS.
UM, YOU DON'T HAVE TO READ IT.

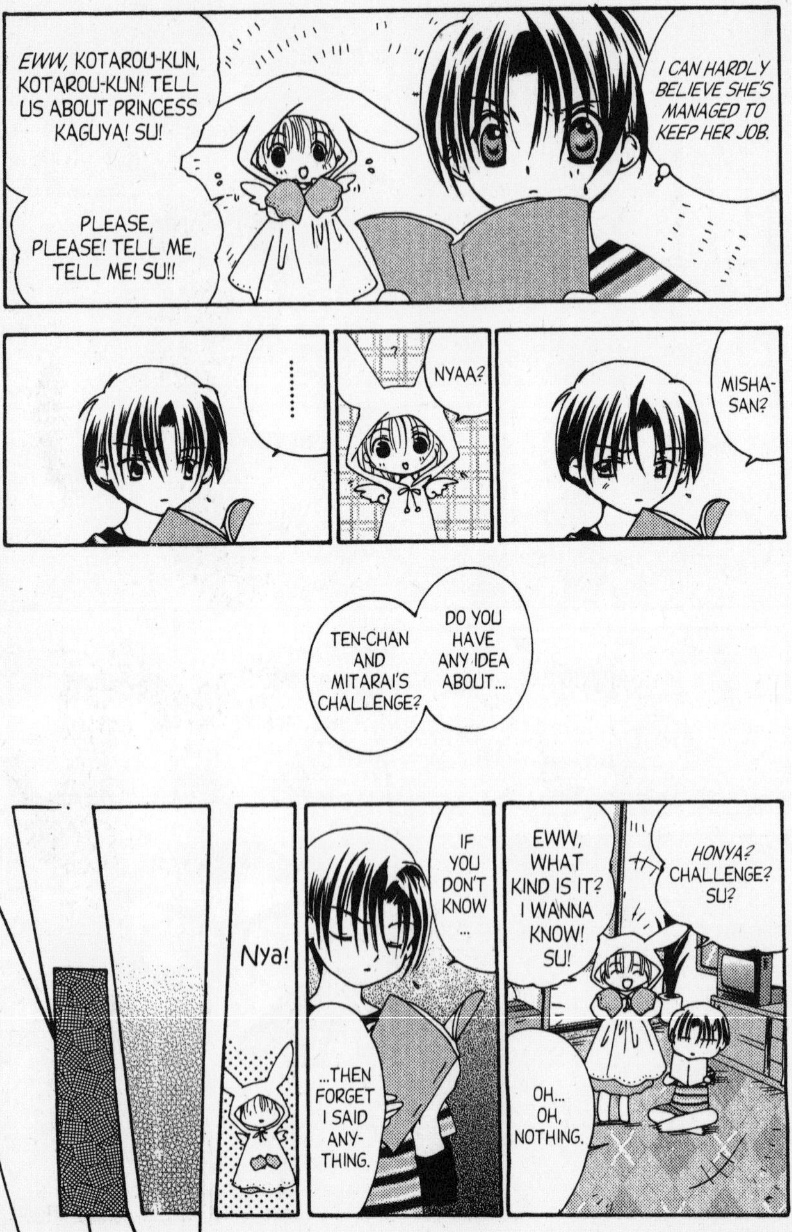
I CAN HARDLY BELIEVE SHE'S MANAGED TO KEEP HER JOB.
EWW, KOTAROU-KUN, KOTAROU-KUN! TELL US ABOUT PRINCESS KAGUYA! SU!
PLEASE, PLEASE! TELL ME, TELL ME! SU!!
MISHA-SAN?
NYAA?
......
DO YOU HAVE ANY IDEA ABOUT...
TEN-CHAN AND MITARAI'S CHALLENGE?
HONYA? CHALLENGE? SU?
EWW, WHAT KIND IS IT? I WANNA KNOW! SU!
OH... OH, NOTHING.
IF YOU DON'T KNOW ...
...THEN FORGET I SAID ANYTHING.
Nya!

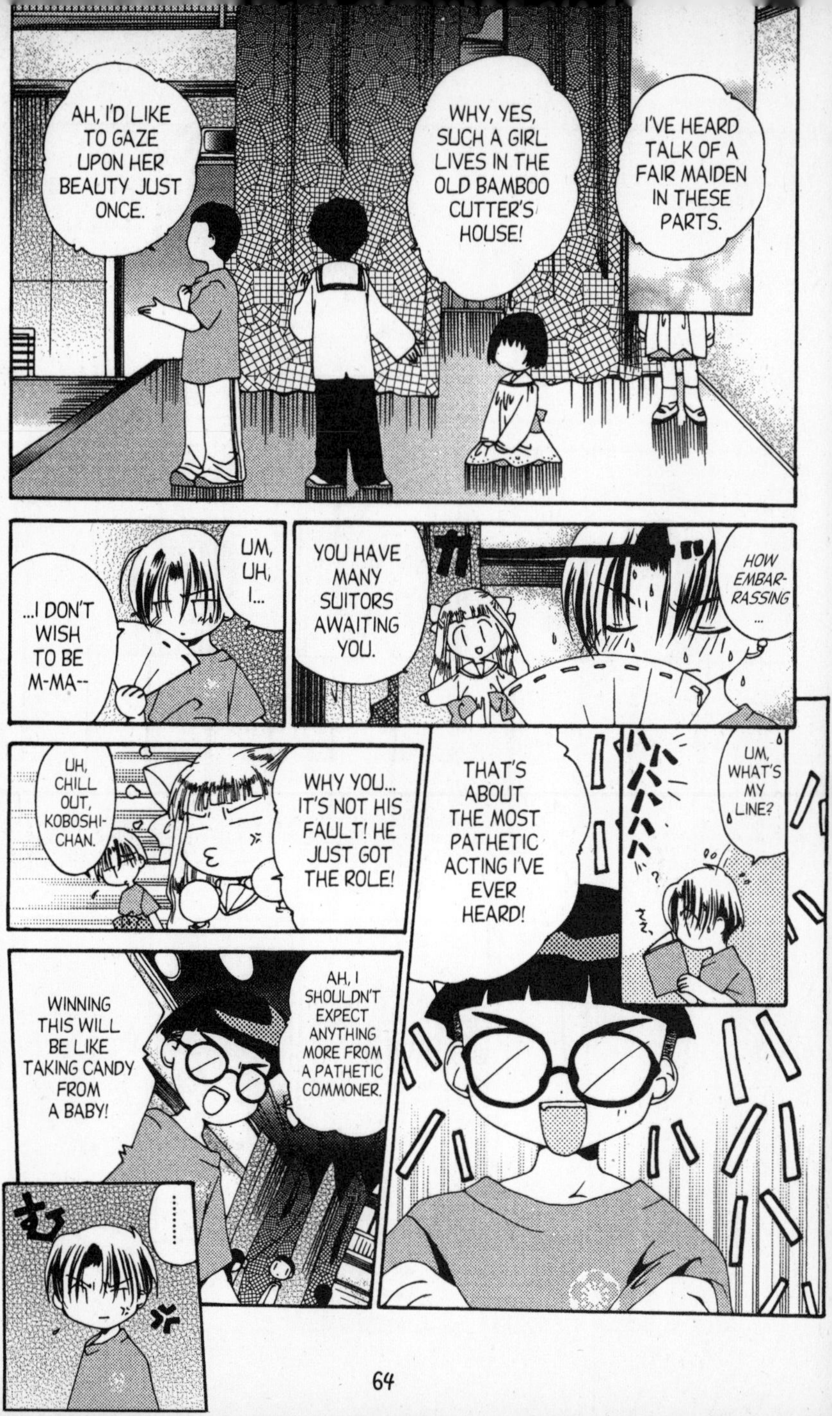
I'VE HEARD TALK OF A FAIR MAIDEN IN THESE PARTS.
WHY, YES, SUCH A GIRL LIVES IN THE OLD BAMBOO CUTTER'S HOUSE!
AH, I'D LIKE TO GAZE UPON HER BEAUTY JUST ONCE.
HOW EMBARRASSING ...
YOU HAVE MANY SUITORS AWAITING YOU.
UM, UH, I...
...I DON'T WISH TO BE M-MA--
UM, WHAT'S MY LINE?
THAT'S ABOUT THE MOST PATHETIC ACTING I'VE EVER HEARD!
WHY YOU... IT'S NOT HIS FAULT! HE JUST GOT THE ROLE!
UH, CHILL OUT, KOBOSHI-CHAN.
AH, I SHOULDN'T EXPECT ANYTHING MORE FROM A PATHETIC COMMONER.
WINNING THIS WILL BE LIKE TAKING CANDY FROM A BABY!
....

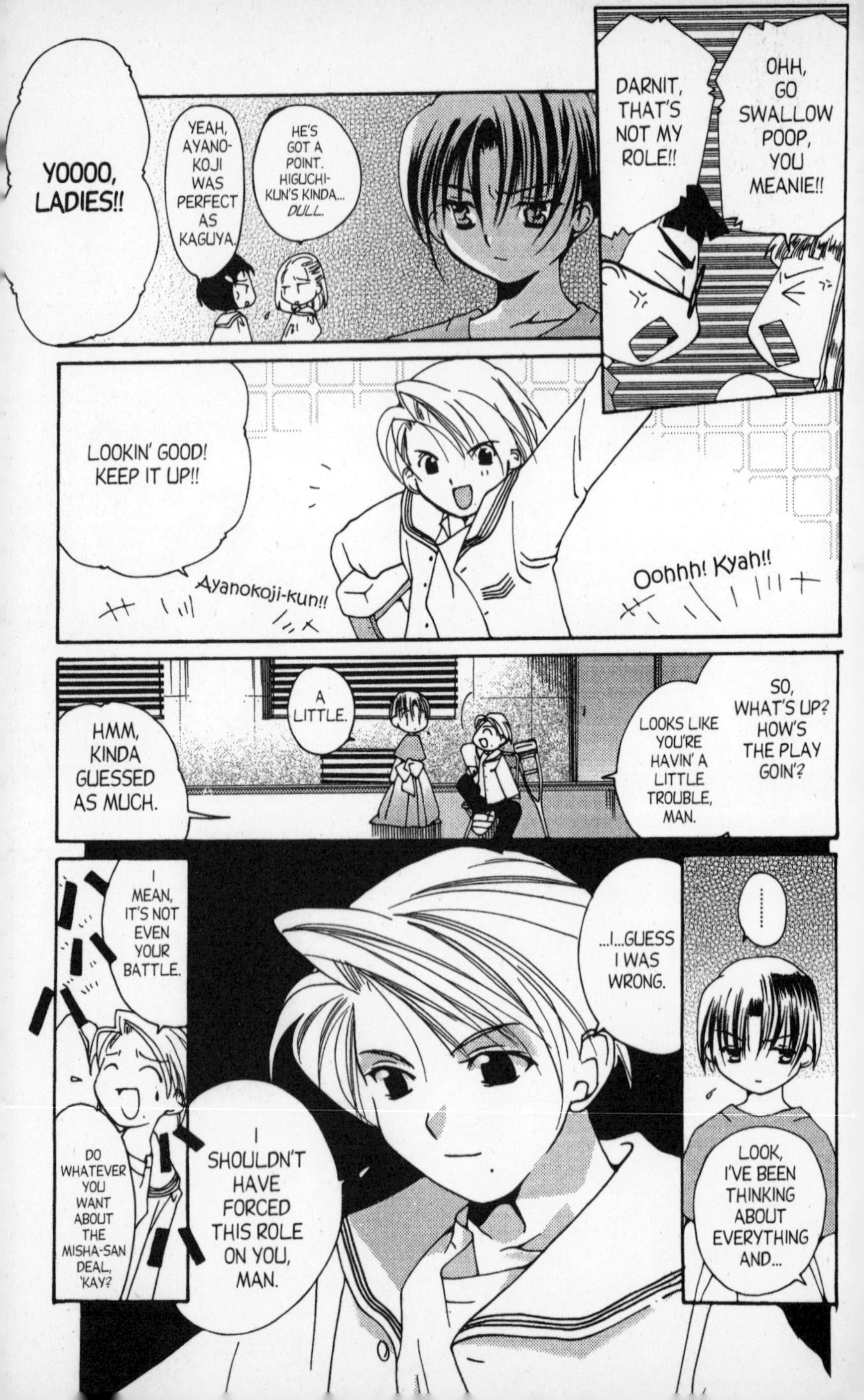
OHH, GO SWALLOW POOP, YOU MEANIE!!
DARNIT, THAT'S NOT MY ROLE!!
HE'S GOT A POINT. HIGUCHI-KUN'S KINDA... *DULL*.
YEAH, AYANO-KOJI WAS PERFECT AS KAGUYA.
YOOOO, LADIES!!
LOOKIN' GOOD! KEEP IT UP!!
Oohhh! Kyah!!
Ayanokoji-kun!!
SO, WHAT'S UP? HOW'S THE PLAY GOIN'?
LOOKS LIKE YOU'RE HAVIN' A LITTLE TROUBLE, MAN.
A LITTLE.
HMM, KINDA GUESSED AS MUCH.
......
LOOK, I'VE BEEN THINKING ABOUT EVERYTHING AND...
...I...GUESS I WAS WRONG.
I SHOULDN'T HAVE FORCED THIS ROLE ON YOU, MAN.
I MEAN, IT'S NOT EVEN YOUR BATTLE.
DO WHATEVER YOU WANT ABOUT THE MISHA-SAN DEAL, 'KAY?

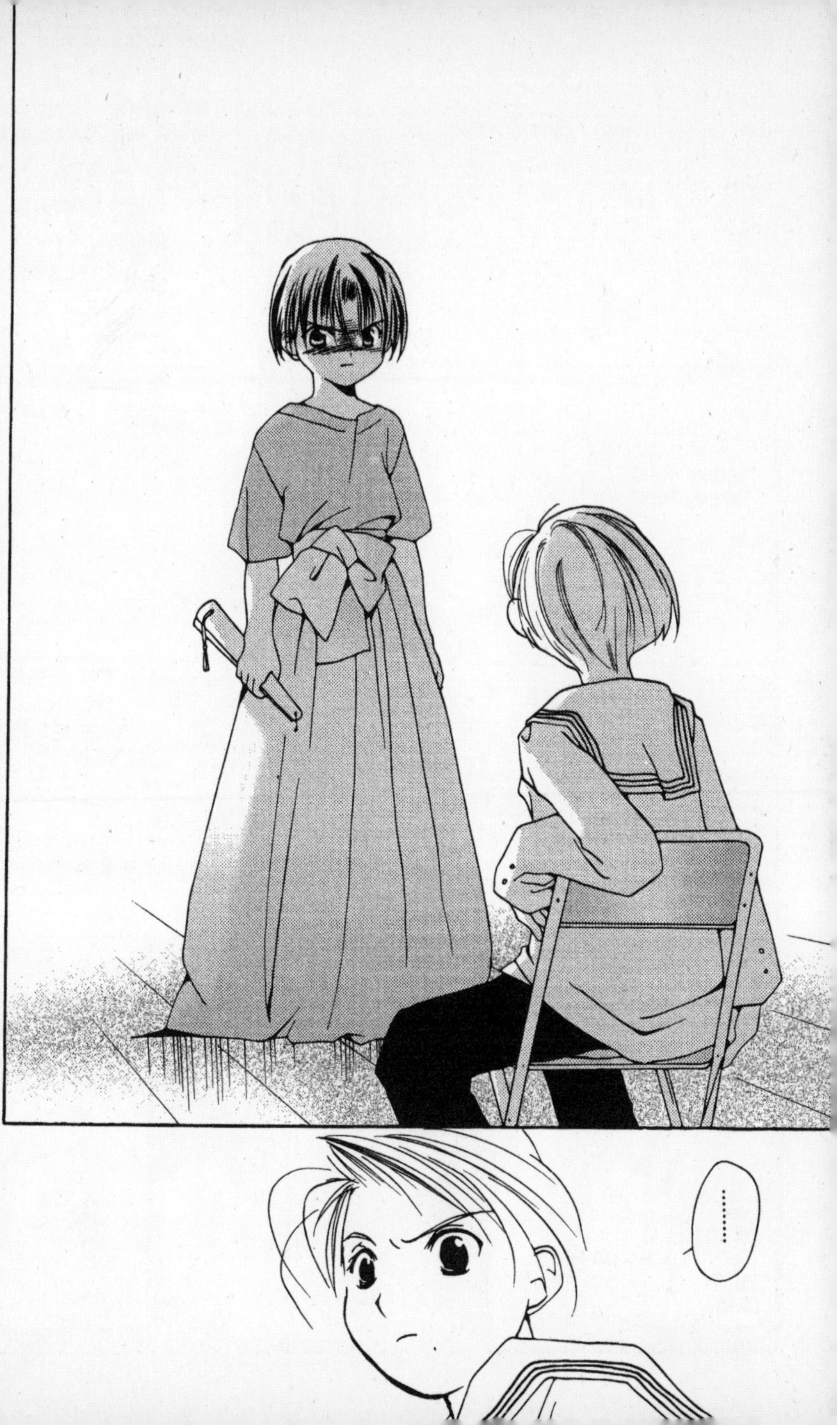
......

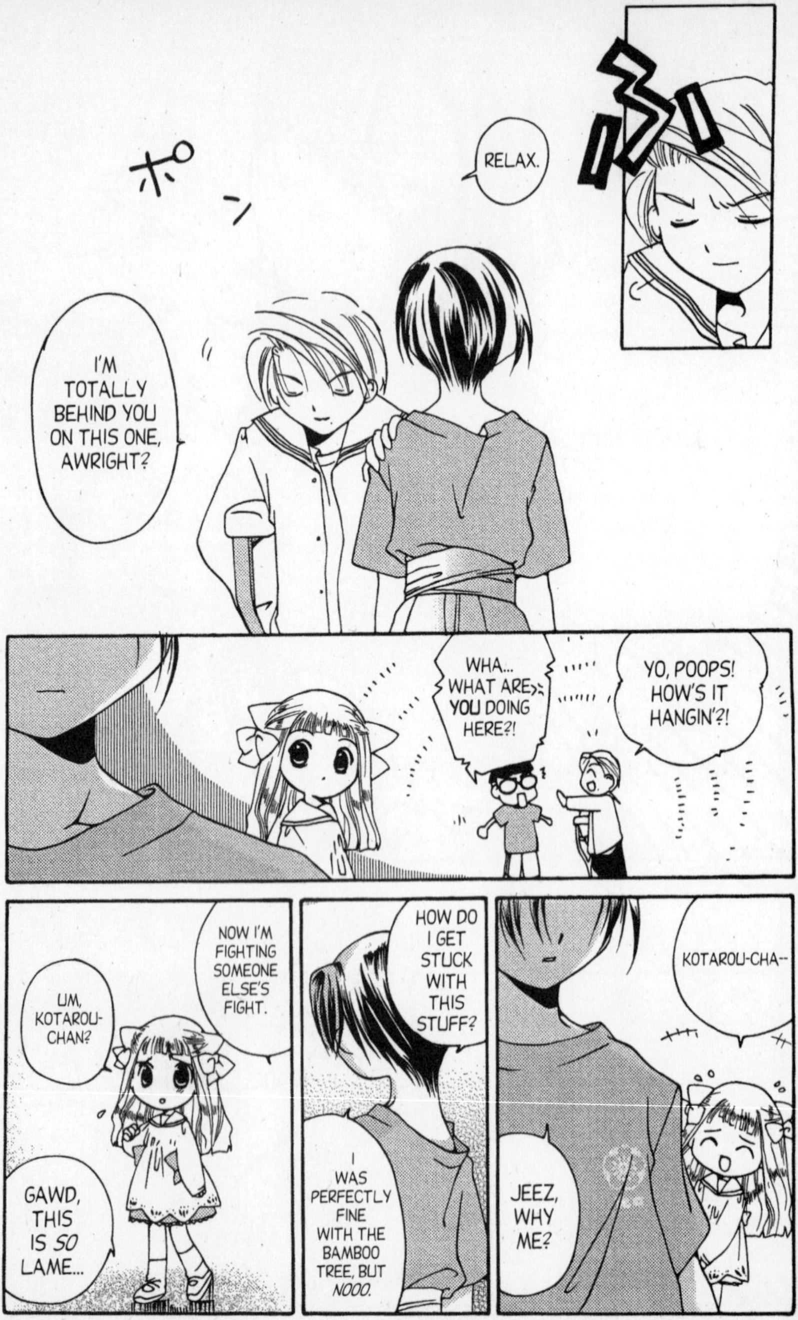
ポン
RELAX.
I'M TOTALLY BEHIND YOU ON THIS ONE, AWRIGHT?
YO, POOPS! HOW'S IT HANGIN'?!
WHA... WHAT ARE **YOU** DOING HERE?!
KOTAROU-CHA--
JEEZ, WHY ME?
HOW DO I GET STUCK WITH THIS STUFF?
I WAS PERFECTLY FINE WITH THE BAMBOO TREE, BUT *NOOO.*
NOW I'M FIGHTING SOMEONE ELSE'S FIGHT.
UM, KOTAROU-CHAN?
GAWD, THIS IS *SO* LAME...

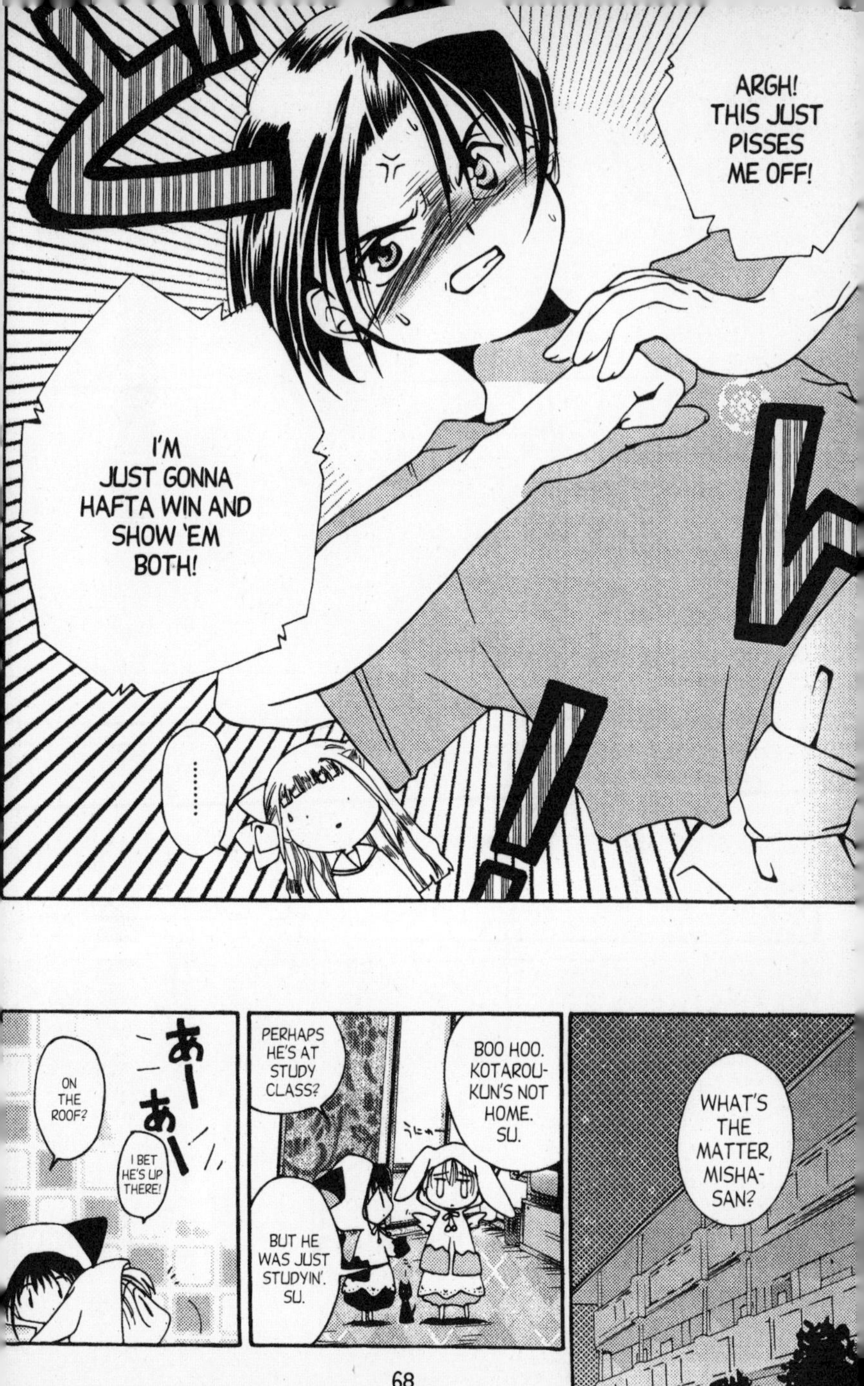
ARGH! THIS JUST PISSES ME OFF!
I'M JUST GONNA HAFTA WIN AND SHOW 'EM BOTH!
......
WHAT'S THE MATTER, MISHA-SAN?
BOO HOO. KOTAROU-KUN'S NOT HOME. SU.
PERHAPS HE'S AT STUDY CLASS?
BUT HE WAS JUST STUDYIN'. SU.
あーあー
ON THE ROOF?
I BET HE'S UP THERE!

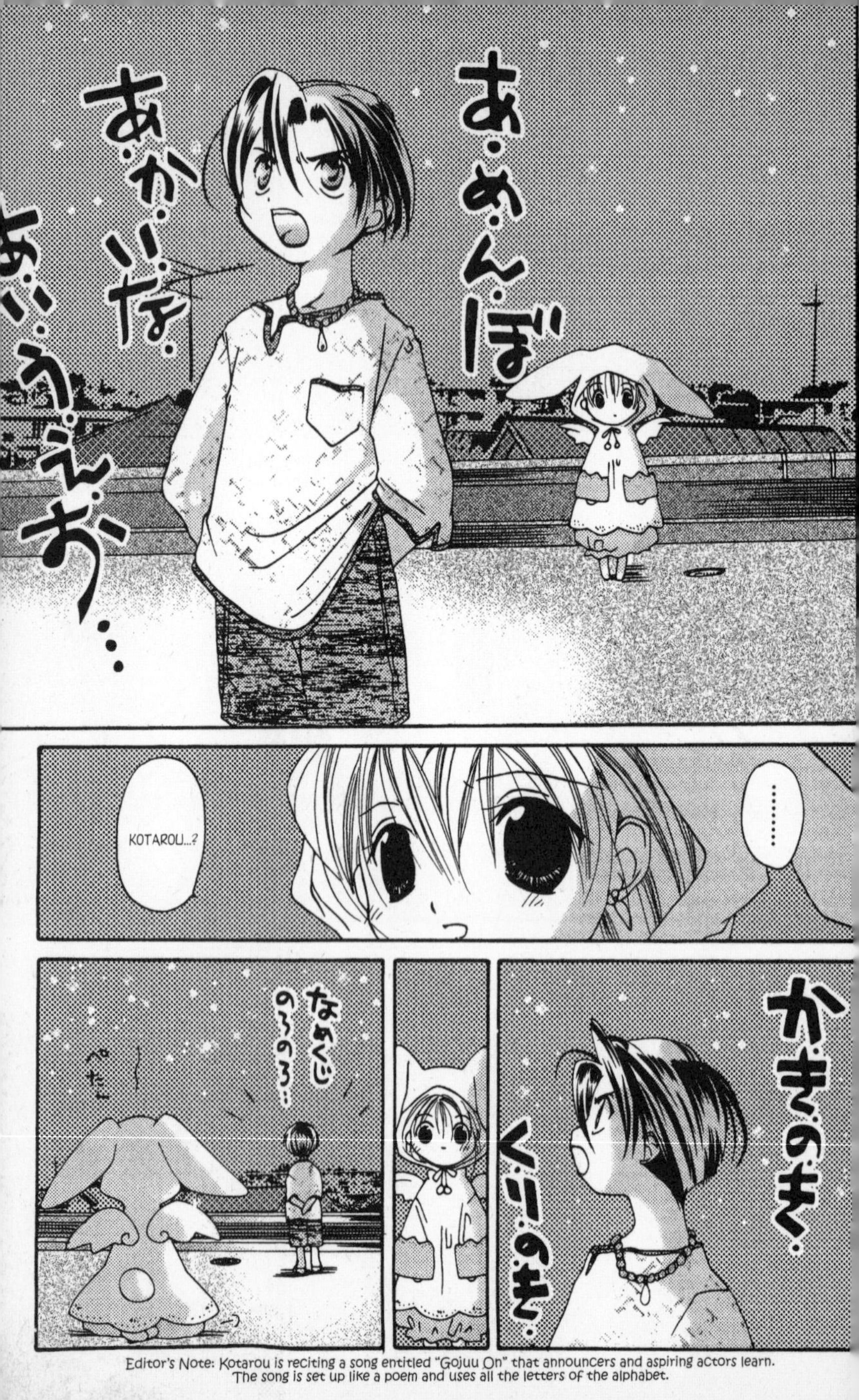

あ・め・ん・ぼ
あ・か・い・な・
あ・い・う・え・お〜…
……
KOTAROU...?
かきのき・
くりのき・
なめくじ
のろのろ…
ぺた

Editor's Note: Kotarou is reciting a song entitled "Gojuu On" that announcers and aspiring actors learn. The song is set up like a poem and uses all the letters of the alphabet.

Editor's Note: Kotarou is STILL reciting "Gojuu On."

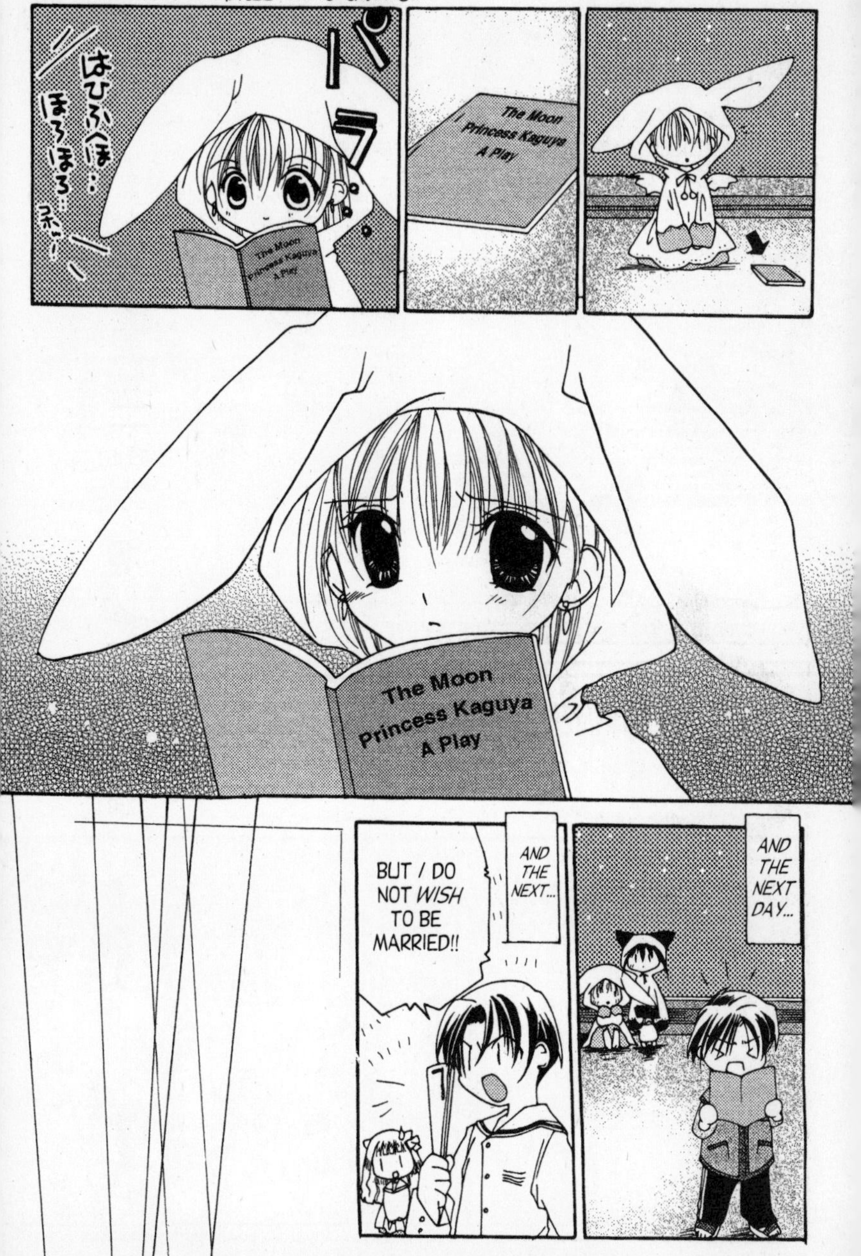
The Moon Princess Kaguya A Play
The Moon Princess Kaguya A Play
パラ
ぱぴぷぺぽ‥
ぽろぽろ‥
The Moon Princess Kaguya A Play
The Moon Princess Kaguya A Play
AND THE NEXT DAY...
AND THE NEXT...
BUT I DO NOT WISH TO BE MARRIED!!

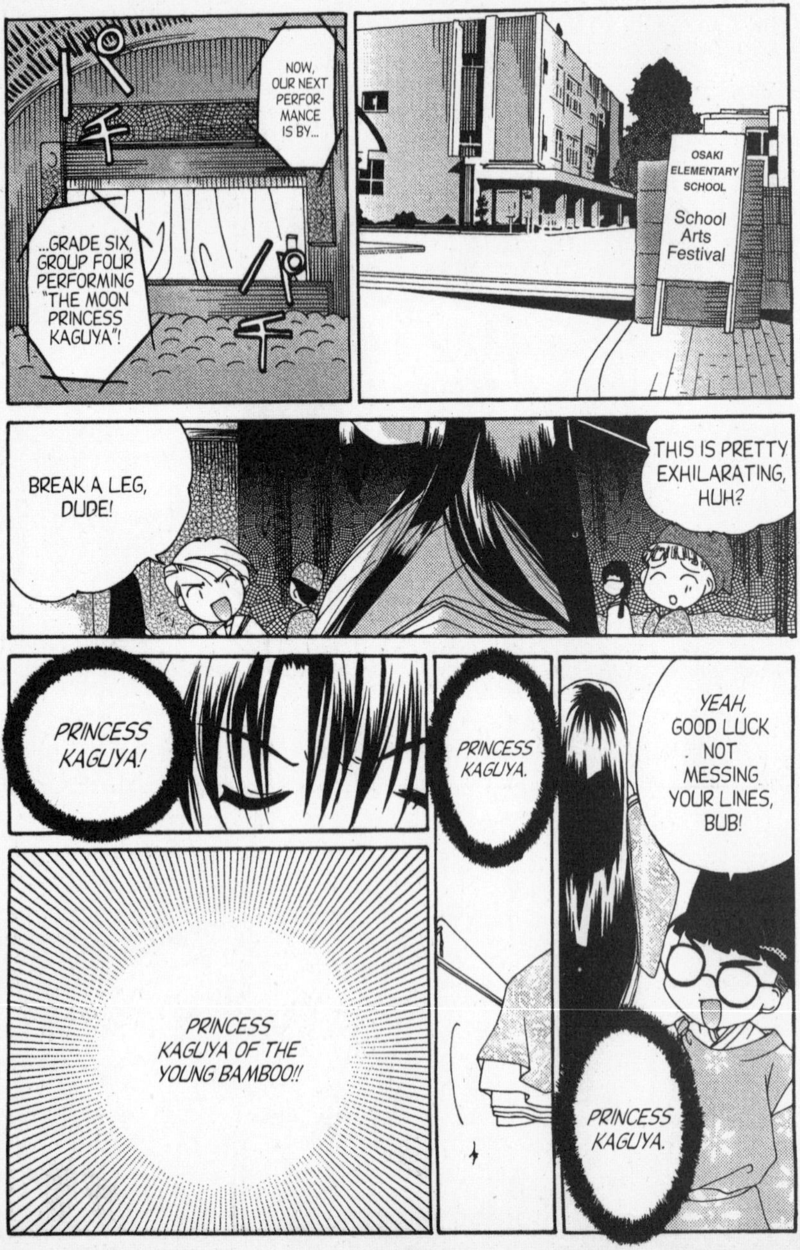

OSAKI ELEMENTARY SCHOOL
School Arts Festival
NOW, OUR NEXT PERFORMANCE IS BY...
パチ
パチ
...GRADE SIX, GROUP FOUR PERFORMING "THE MOON PRINCESS KAGUYA"!
THIS IS PRETTY EXHILARATING, HUH?
BREAK A LEG, DUDE!
YEAH, GOOD LUCK NOT MESSING YOUR LINES, BUB!
PRINCESS KAGUYA.
PRINCESS KAGUYA.
PRINCESS KAGUYA!
PRINCESS KAGUYA OF THE YOUNG BAMBOO!!

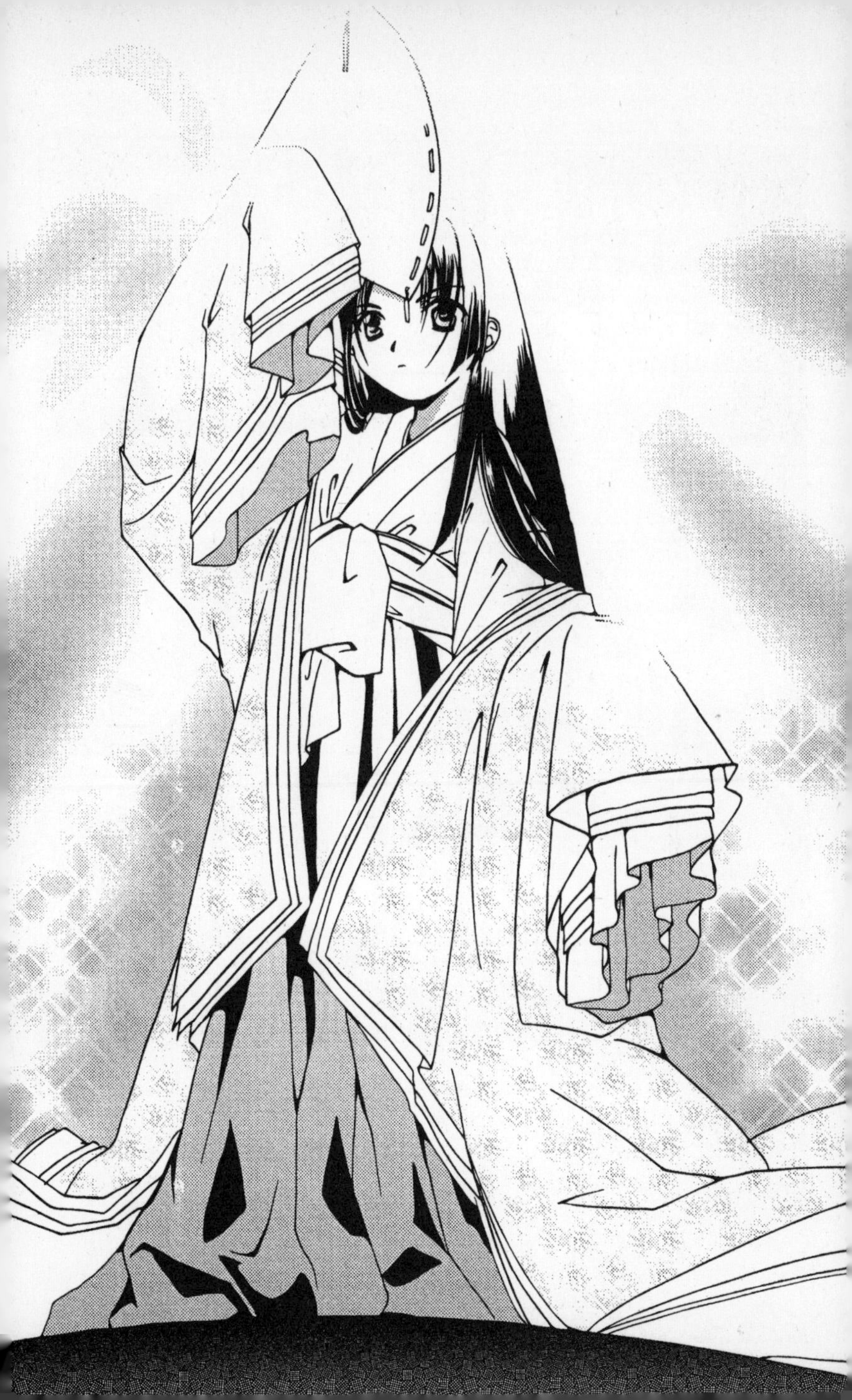

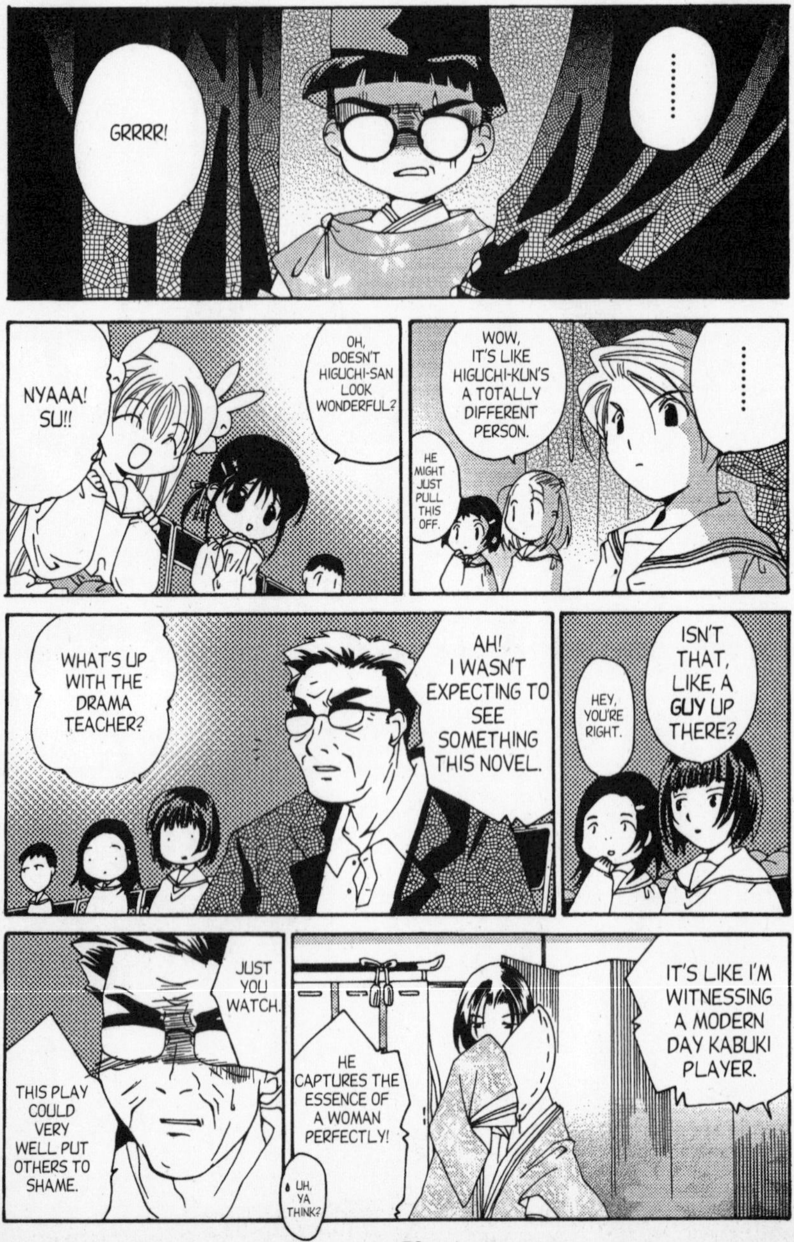
......
GRRRR!
......
WOW, IT'S LIKE HIGUCHI-KUN'S A TOTALLY DIFFERENT PERSON.
HE MIGHT JUST PULL THIS OFF.
OH, DOESN'T HIGUCHI-SAN LOOK WONDERFUL?
NYAAA! SU!!
ISN'T THAT, LIKE, A **GUY** UP THERE?
HEY, YOU'RE RIGHT.
AH! I WASN'T EXPECTING TO SEE SOMETHING THIS NOVEL.
WHAT'S UP WITH THE DRAMA TEACHER?
IT'S LIKE I'M WITNESSING A MODERN DAY KABUKI PLAYER.
HE CAPTURES THE ESSENCE OF A WOMAN PERFECTLY!
UH, YA THINK?
JUST YOU WATCH.
THIS PLAY COULD VERY WELL PUT OTHERS TO SHAME.

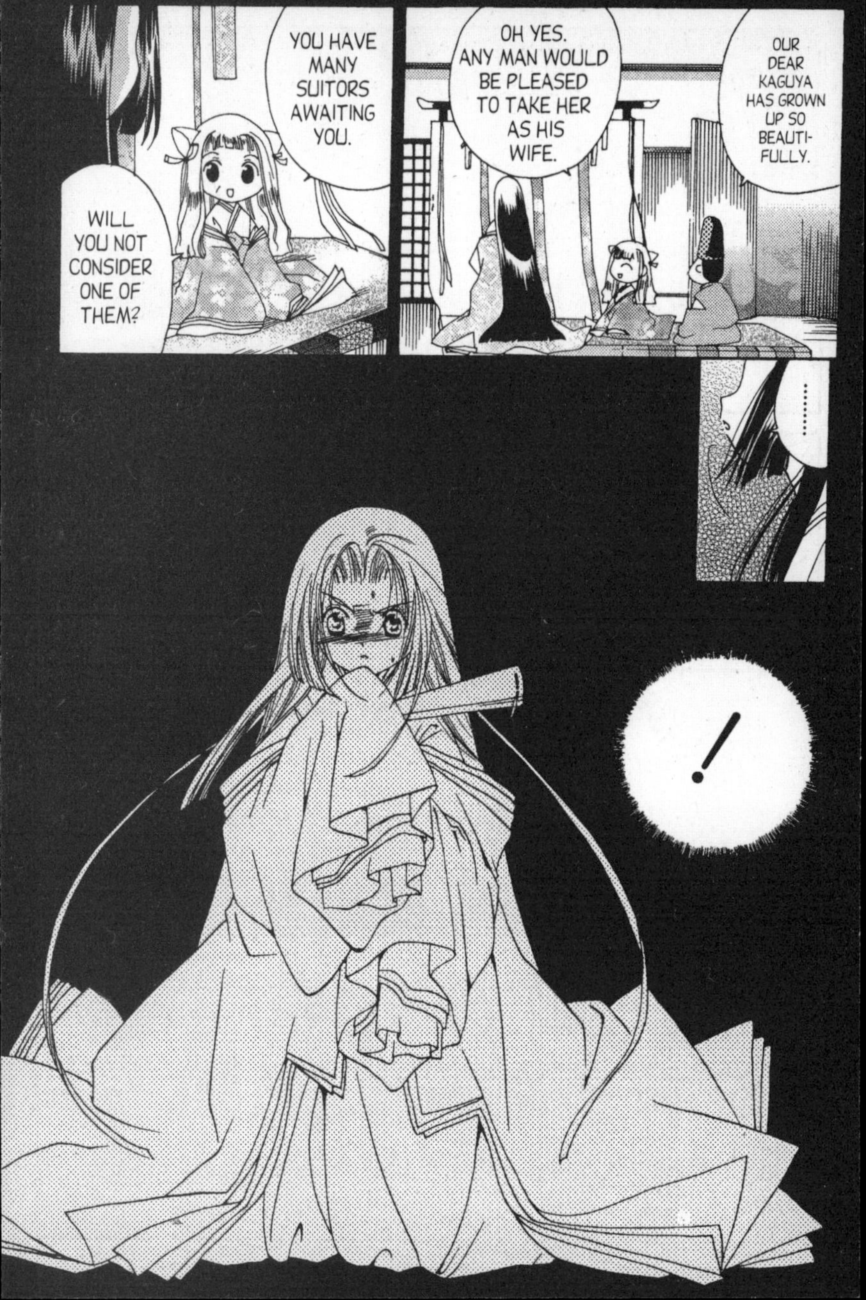
OUR DEAR KAGUYA HAS GROWN UP SO BEAUTIFULLY.
OH YES. ANY MAN WOULD BE PLEASED TO TAKE HER AS HIS WIFE.
YOU HAVE MANY SUITORS AWAITING YOU.
WILL YOU NOT CONSIDER ONE OF THEM?
......
!

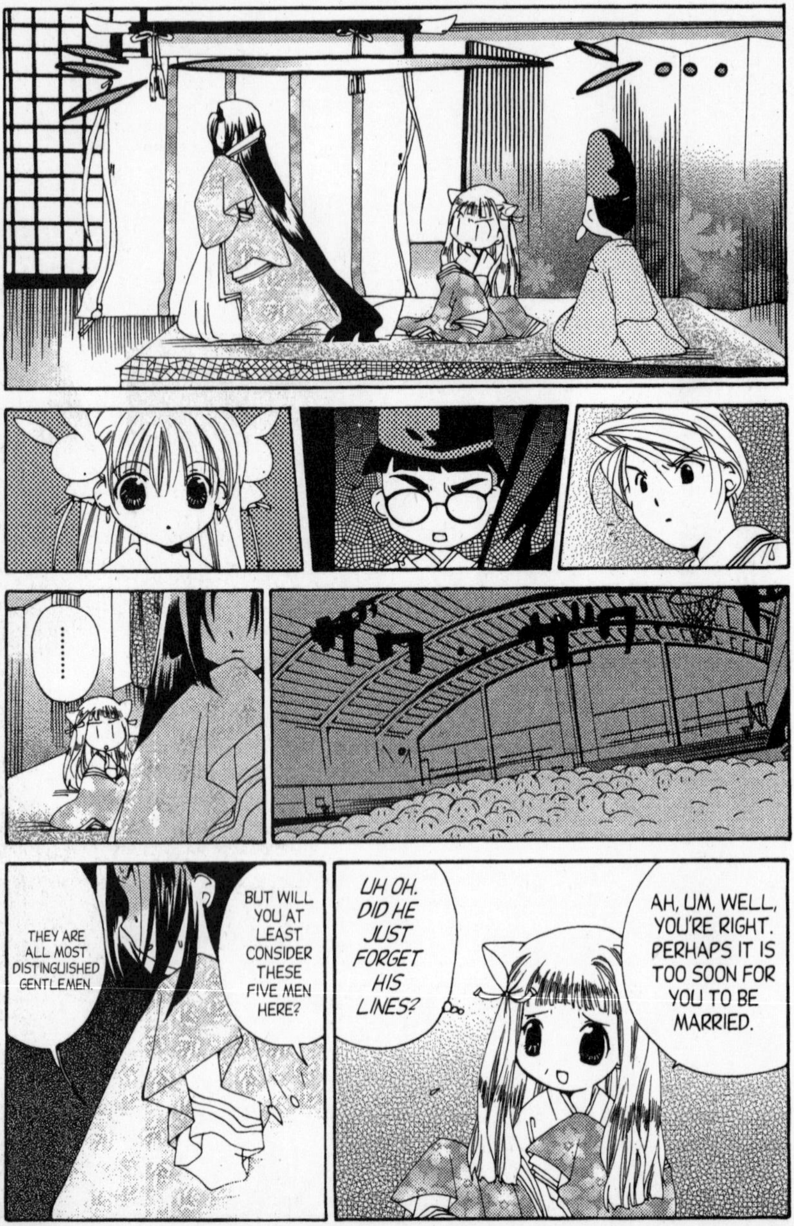
ザワ‥ザワ
....
AH, UM, WELL, YOU'RE RIGHT. PERHAPS IT IS TOO SOON FOR YOU TO BE MARRIED.
UH OH. DID HE JUST FORGET HIS LINES?
BUT WILL YOU AT LEAST CONSIDER THESE FIVE MEN HERE?
THEY ARE ALL MOST DISTINGUISHED GENTLEMEN.

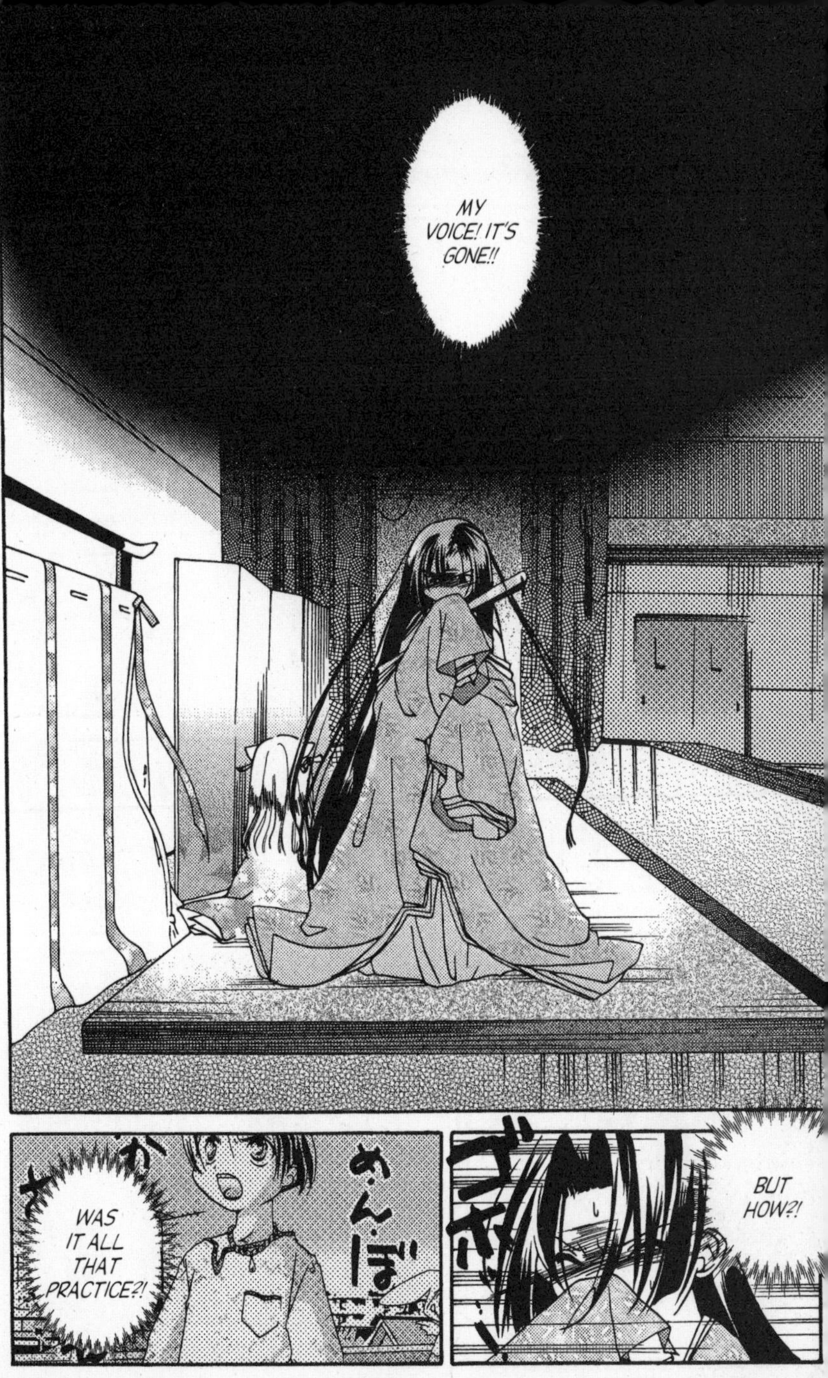
MY VOICE! IT'S GONE!!
BUT HOW?!
WAS IT ALL THAT PRACTICE?!

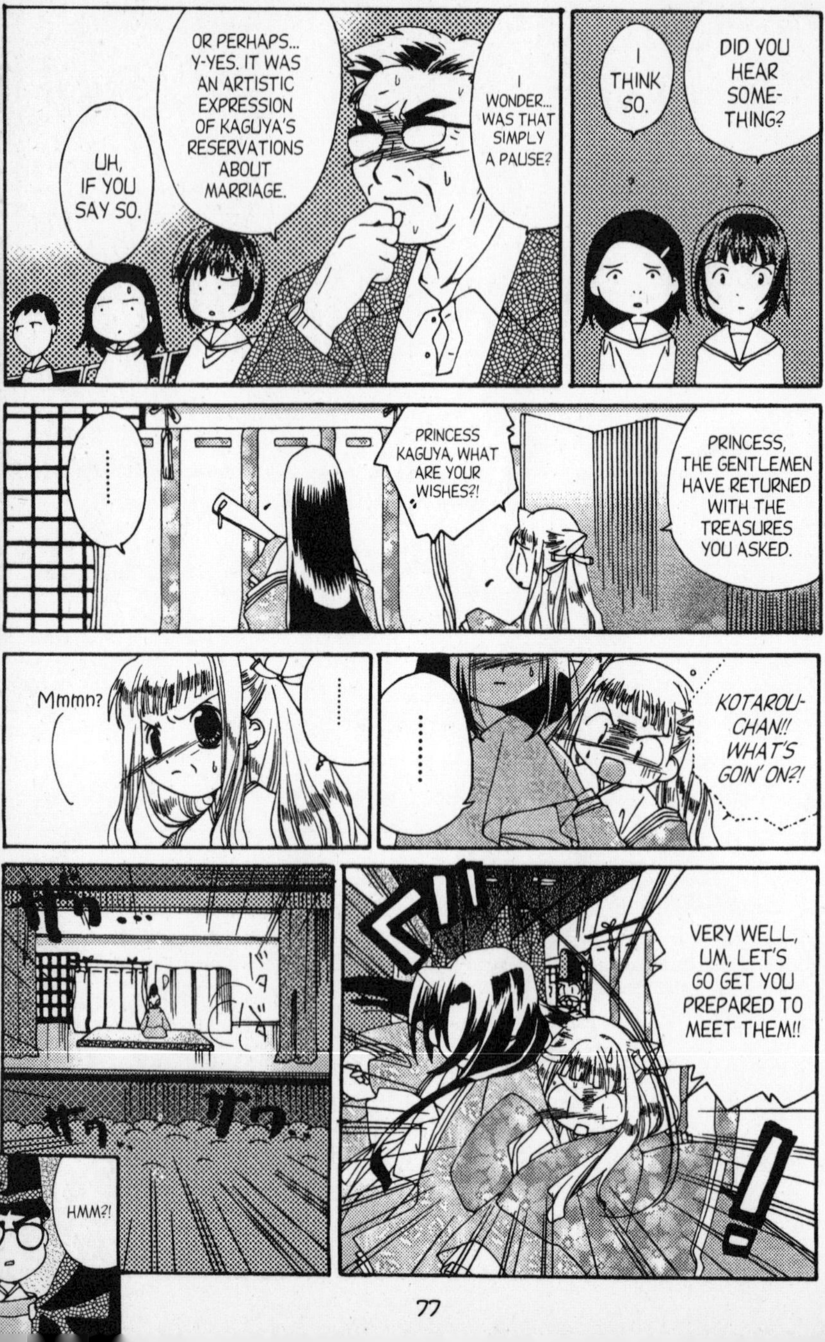
DID YOU HEAR SOME-THING?
I THINK SO.
I WONDER... WAS THAT SIMPLY A PAUSE?
OR PERHAPS... Y-YES. IT WAS AN ARTISTIC EXPRESSION OF KAGUYA'S RESERVATIONS ABOUT MARRIAGE.
UH, IF YOU SAY SO.
PRINCESS, THE GENTLEMEN HAVE RETURNED WITH THE TREASURES YOU ASKED.
PRINCESS KAGUYA, WHAT ARE YOUR WISHES?!
....
KOTAROU-CHAN!! WHAT'S GOIN' ON?!
....
....
Mmmn?
VERY WELL, UM, LET'S GO GET YOU PREPARED TO MEET THEM!!
!
HMM?!

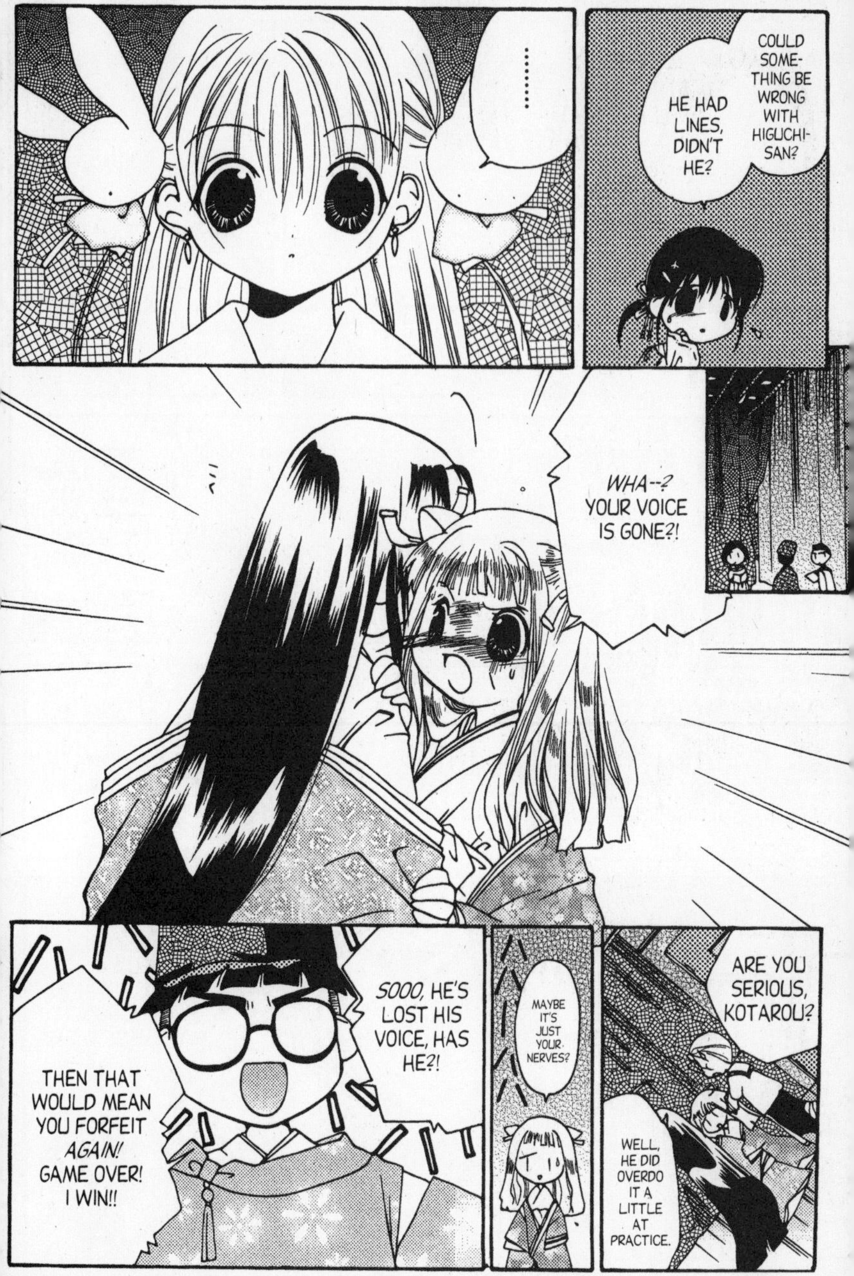
COULD SOMETHING BE WRONG WITH HIGUCHI-SAN?
HE HAD LINES, DIDN'T HE?
......
WHA--? YOUR VOICE IS GONE?!
ARE YOU SERIOUS, KOTAROU?
WELL, HE DID OVERDO IT A LITTLE AT PRACTICE.
MAYBE IT'S JUST YOUR NERVES?
SOOO, HE'S LOST HIS VOICE, HAS HE?!
THEN THAT WOULD MEAN YOU FORFEIT AGAIN! GAME OVER! I WIN!!

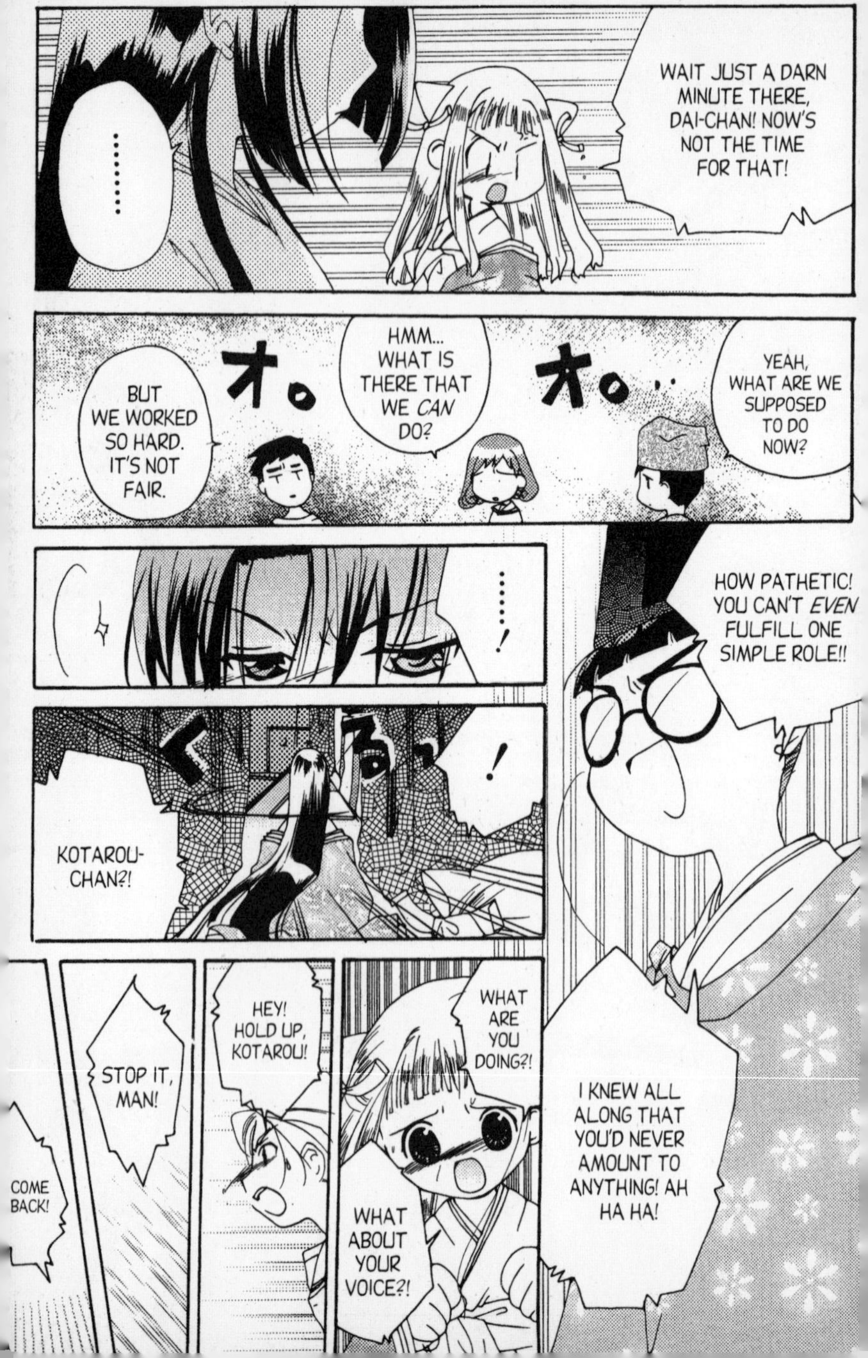
WAIT JUST A DARN MINUTE THERE, DAI-CHAN! NOW'S NOT THE TIME FOR THAT!
……
YEAH, WHAT ARE WE SUPPOSED TO DO NOW?
HMM... WHAT IS THERE THAT WE *CAN* DO?
BUT WE WORKED SO HARD. IT'S NOT FAIR.
HOW PATHETIC! YOU CAN'T *EVEN* FULFILL ONE SIMPLE ROLE!!
I KNEW ALL ALONG THAT YOU'D NEVER AMOUNT TO ANYTHING! AH HA HA!
……!
KOTAROU-CHAN?!
WHAT ARE YOU DOING?!
WHAT ABOUT YOUR VOICE?!
HEY! HOLD UP, KOTAROU!
STOP IT, MAN!
COME BACK!

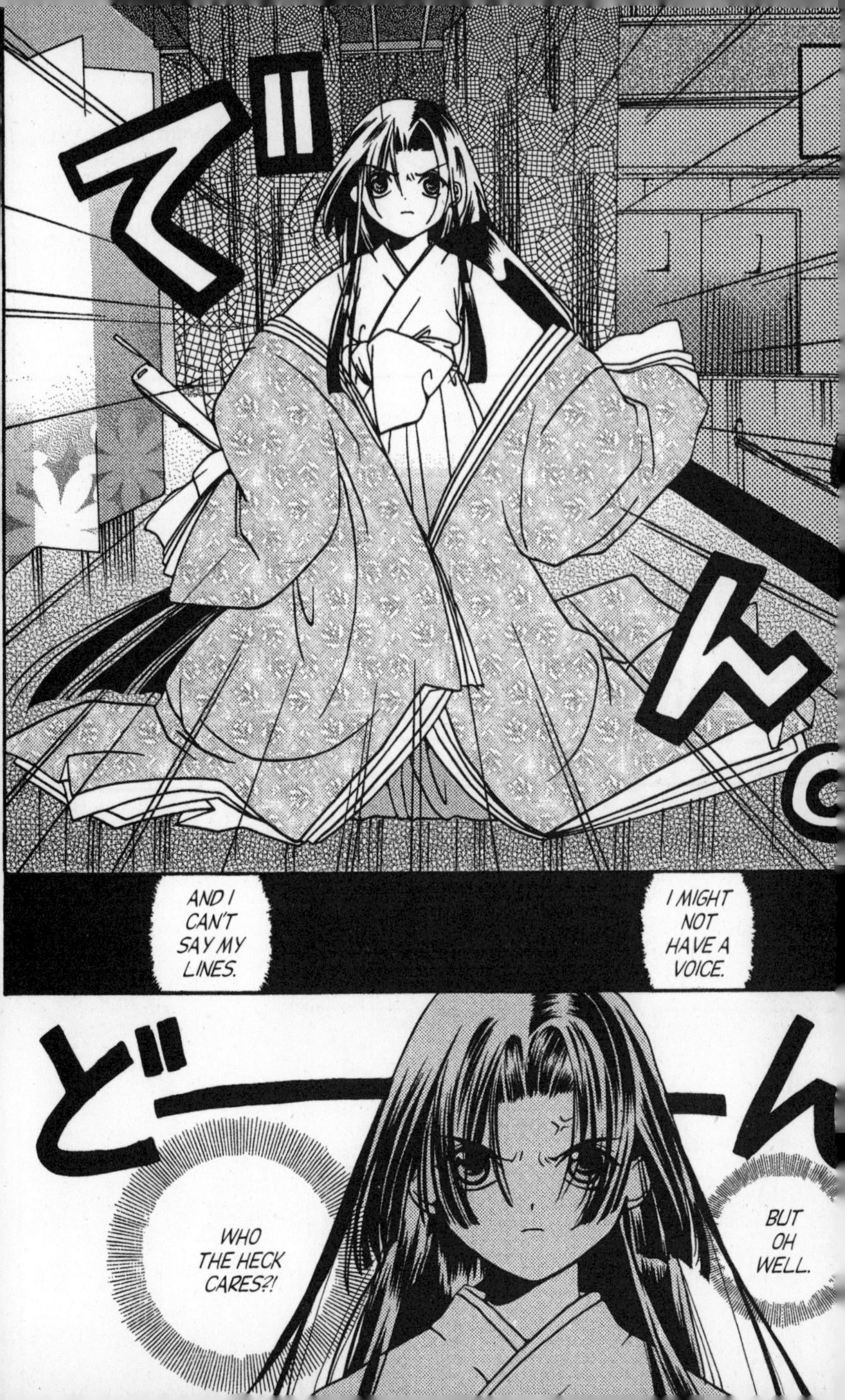

でーん
I MIGHT NOT HAVE A VOICE.
AND I CAN'T SAY MY LINES.
どーーん
BUT OH WELL.
WHO THE HECK CARES?!

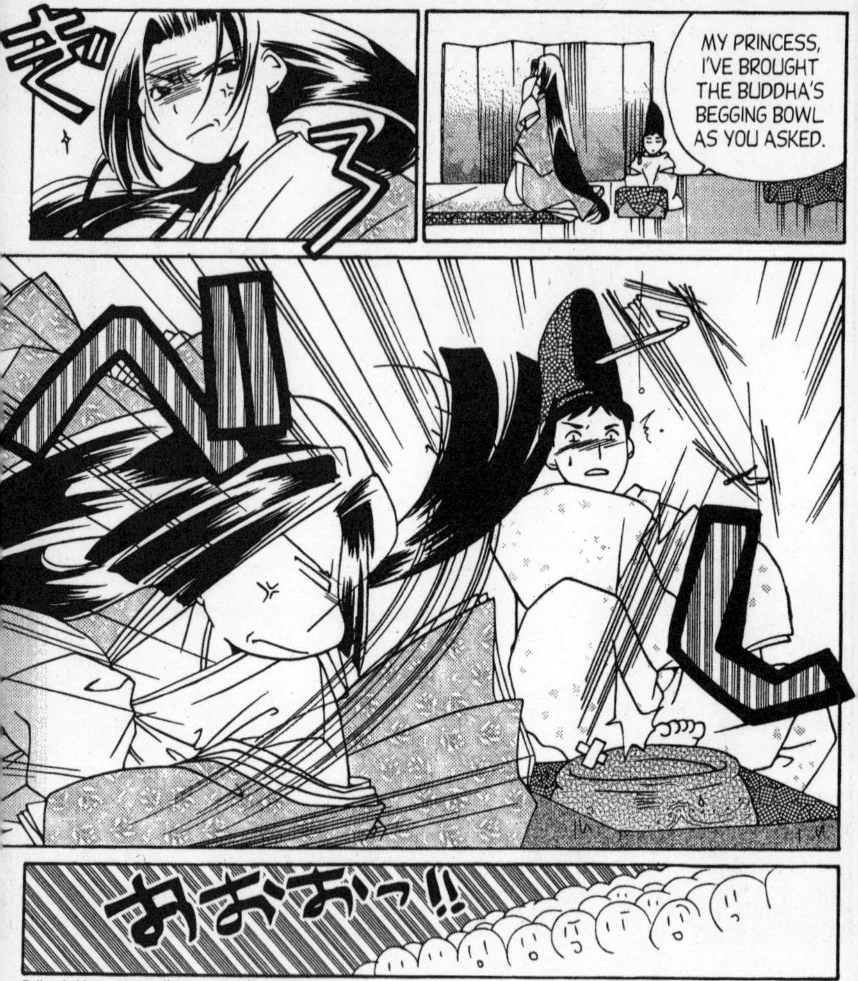
MY PRINCESS, I'VE BROUGHT THE BUDDHA'S BEGGING BOWL AS YOU ASKED.
ぎく
おおおっ!!

Editor's Note: The audience collectively gasps!

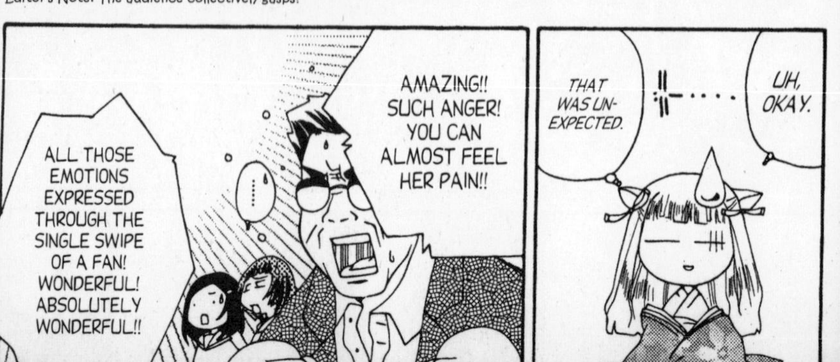
UH, OKAY.
THAT WAS UN-EXPECTED.
AMAZING!! SUCH ANGER! YOU CAN ALMOST FEEL HER PAIN!!
ALL THOSE EMOTIONS EXPRESSED THROUGH THE SINGLE SWIPE OF A FAN! WONDERFUL! ABSOLUTELY WONDERFUL!!

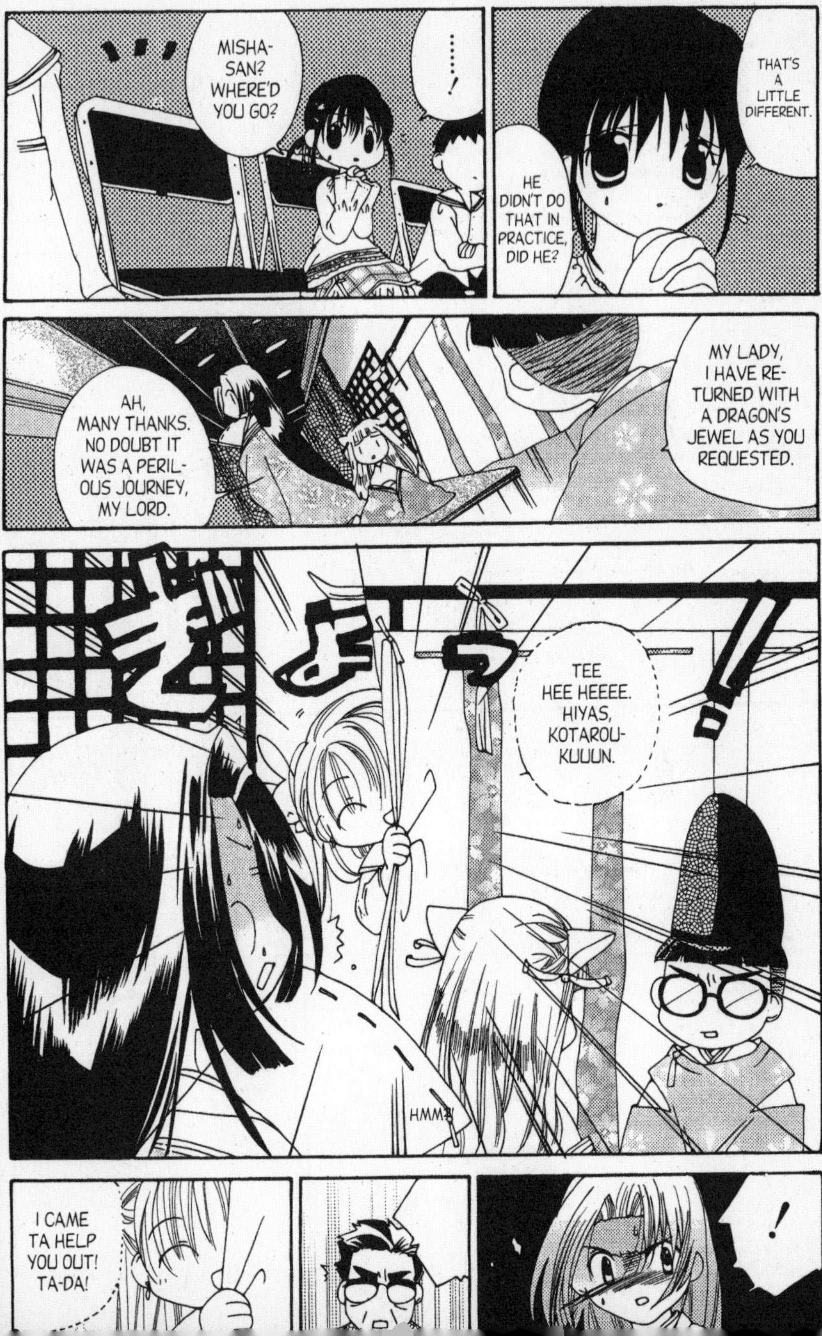
THAT'S A LITTLE DIFFERENT.
HE DIDN'T DO THAT IN PRACTICE, DID HE?
......!
MISHA-SAN? WHERE'D YOU GO?
MY LADY, I HAVE RE-TURNED WITH A DRAGON'S JEWEL AS YOU REQUESTED.
AH, MANY THANKS. NO DOUBT IT WAS A PERIL-OUS JOURNEY, MY LORD.
!
TEE HEE HEEEE. HIYAS, KOTAROU-KUUUN.
HMM?!
!
I CAME TA HELP YOU OUT! TA-DA!

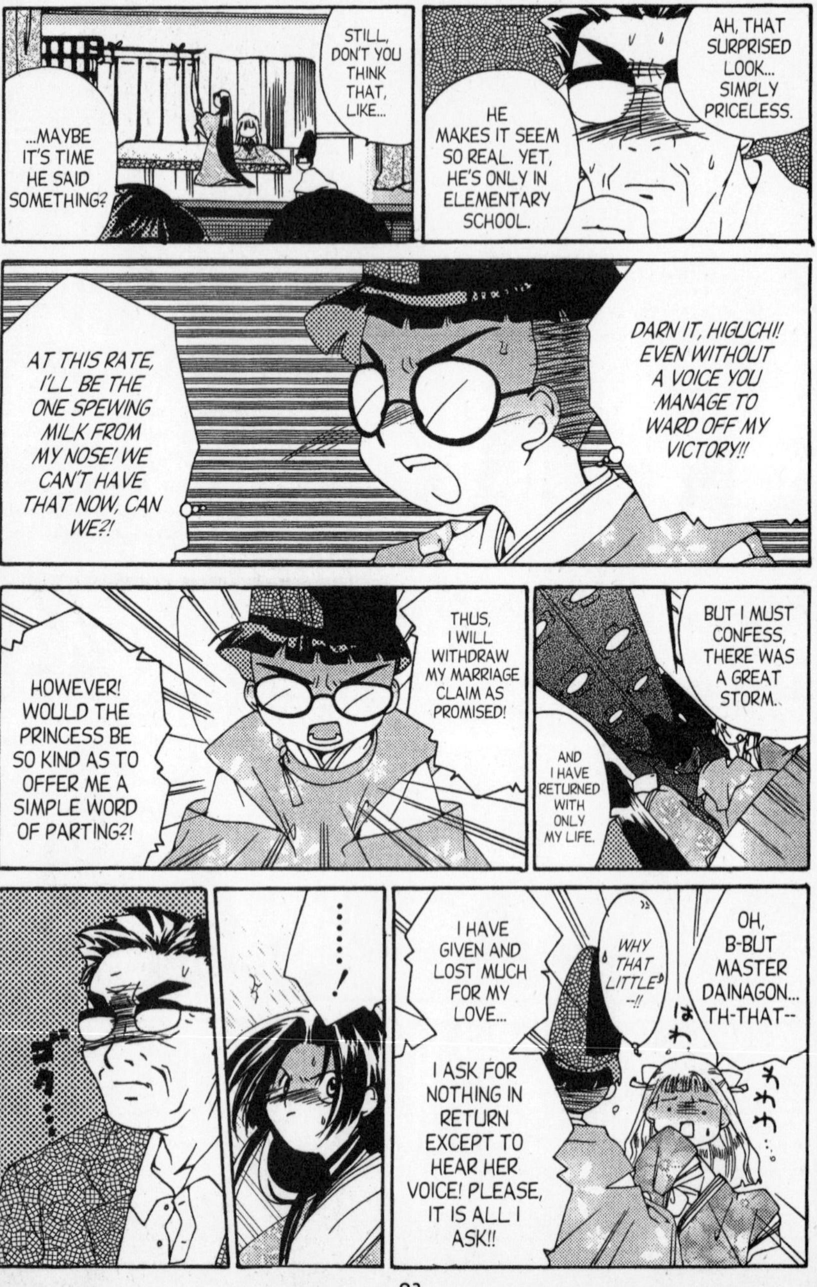
AH, THAT SURPRISED LOOK... SIMPLY PRICELESS.
HE MAKES IT SEEM SO REAL. YET, HE'S ONLY IN ELEMENTARY SCHOOL.
STILL, DON'T YOU THINK THAT, LIKE...
...MAYBE IT'S TIME HE SAID SOMETHING?
DARN IT, HIGUCHI! EVEN WITHOUT A VOICE YOU MANAGE TO WARD OFF MY VICTORY!!
AT THIS RATE, I'LL BE THE ONE SPEWING MILK FROM MY NOSE! WE CAN'T HAVE THAT NOW, CAN WE?!
BUT I MUST CONFESS, THERE WAS A GREAT STORM..
AND I HAVE RETURNED WITH ONLY MY LIFE.
THUS, I WILL WITHDRAW MY MARRIAGE CLAIM AS PROMISED!
HOWEVER! WOULD THE PRINCESS BE SO KIND AS TO OFFER ME A SIMPLE WORD OF PARTING?!
OH, B-BUT MASTER DAINAGON... TH-THAT--
WHY THAT LITTLE--!!
I HAVE GIVEN AND LOST MUCH FOR MY LOVE...
I ASK FOR NOTHING IN RETURN EXCEPT TO HEAR HER VOICE! PLEASE, IT IS ALL I ASK!!
......!

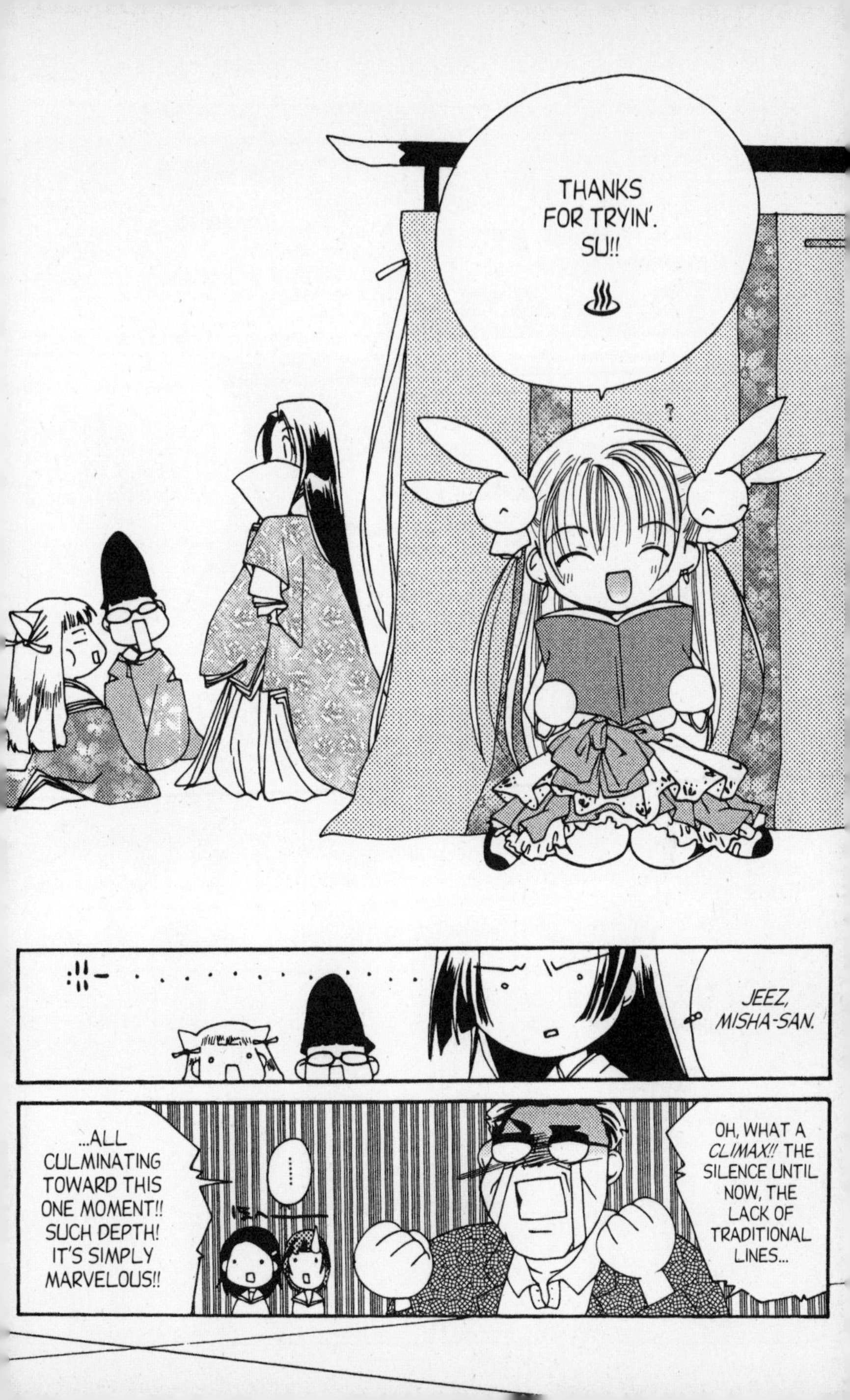
THANKS FOR TRYIN'. SU!!
?
JEEZ, MISHA-SAN.
OH, WHAT A CLIMAX!! THE SILENCE UNTIL NOW, THE LACK OF TRADITIONAL LINES...
...ALL CULMINATING TOWARD THIS ONE MOMENT!! SUCH DEPTH! IT'S SIMPLY MARVELOUS!!
......

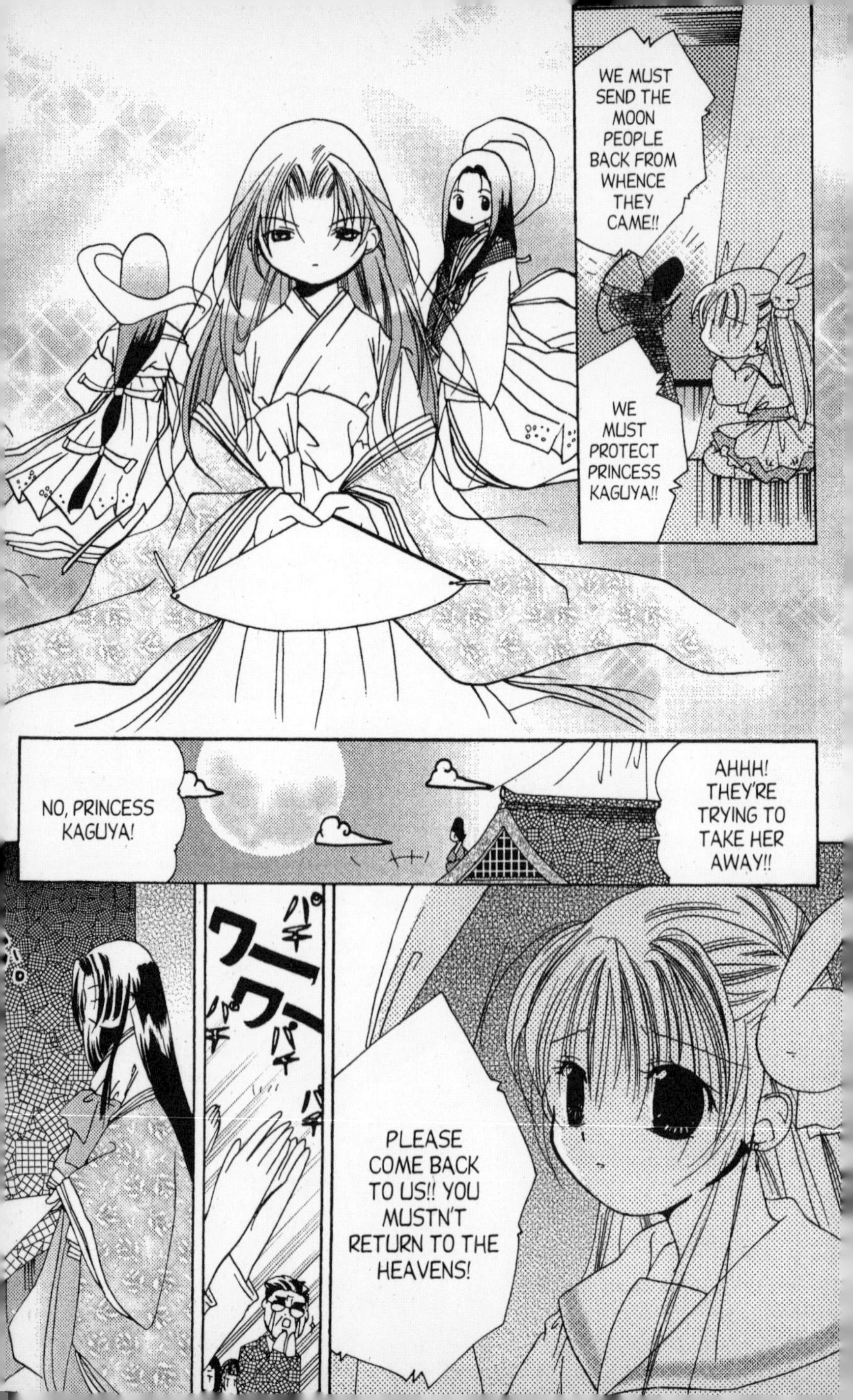
WE MUST SEND THE MOON PEOPLE BACK FROM WHENCE THEY CAME!!
WE MUST PROTECT PRINCESS KAGUYA!!
AHHH! THEY'RE TRYING TO TAKE HER AWAY!!
NO, PRINCESS KAGUYA!
PLEASE COME BACK TO US!! YOU MUSTN'T RETURN TO THE HEAVENS!
ワーワー
パチパチ

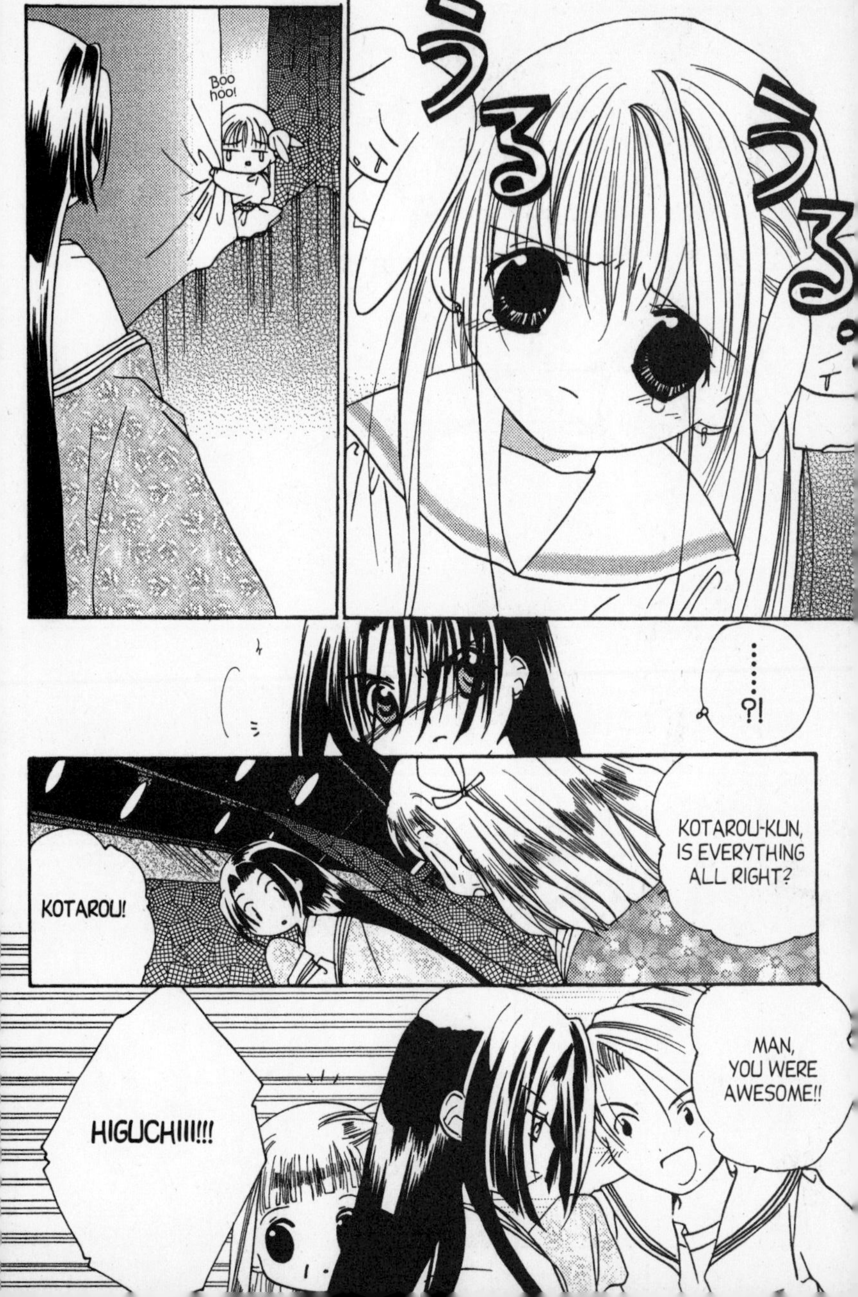
うるうる。
Boo hoo!
……?!
KOTAROU-KUN, IS EVERYTHING ALL RIGHT?
KOTAROU!
MAN, YOU WERE AWESOME!!
HIGUCHIIII!!!

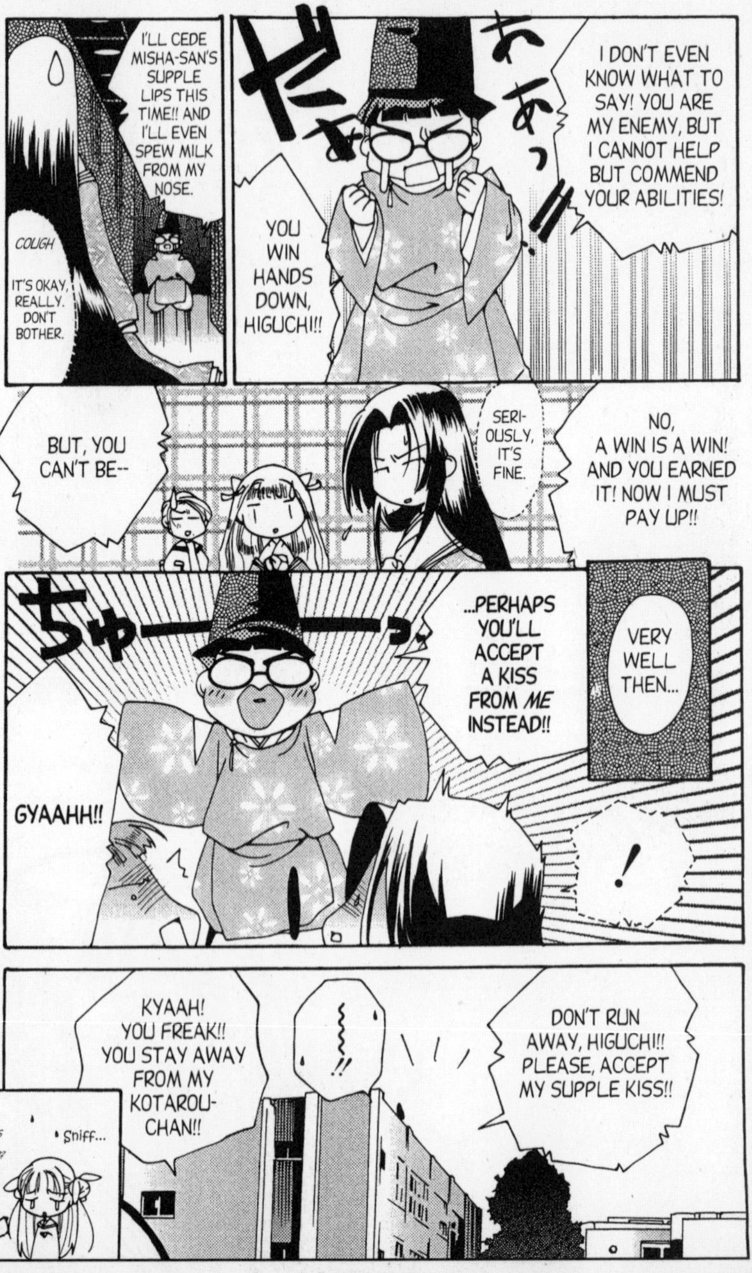
I DON'T EVEN KNOW WHAT TO SAY! YOU ARE MY ENEMY, BUT I CANNOT HELP BUT COMMEND YOUR ABILITIES!
YOU WIN HANDS DOWN, HIGUCHI!!
I'LL CEDE MISHA-SAN'S SUPPLE LIPS THIS TIME!! AND I'LL EVEN SPEW MILK FROM MY NOSE.
COUGH
IT'S OKAY, REALLY. DON'T BOTHER.
NO, A WIN IS A WIN! AND YOU EARNED IT! NOW I MUST PAY UP!!
SERIOUSLY, IT'S FINE.
BUT, YOU CAN'T BE--
VERY WELL THEN...
...PERHAPS YOU'LL ACCEPT A KISS FROM *ME* INSTEAD!!
ちゅーーーっ
!
GYAAHH!!
DON'T RUN AWAY, HIGUCHI!! PLEASE, ACCEPT MY SUPPLE KISS!!
~~~!!
KYAAH! YOU FREAK!! YOU STAY AWAY FROM MY KOTAROU-CHAN!!
Sniff...
WHAT'S THE MATTER?
~~~

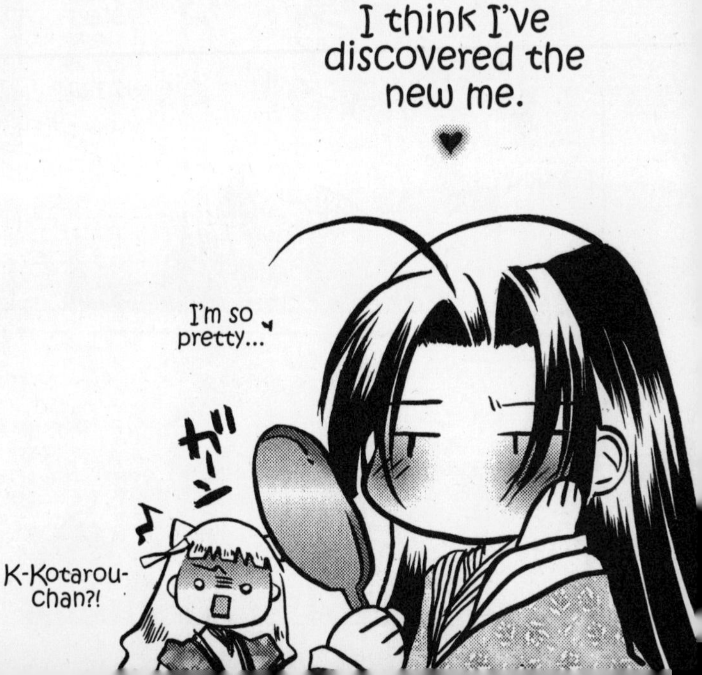
I think I've discovered the new me. ♥
I'm so pretty...♥
ガーン
K-Kotarou-chan?!

Lesson 11
How to Work a Bit of Mischief

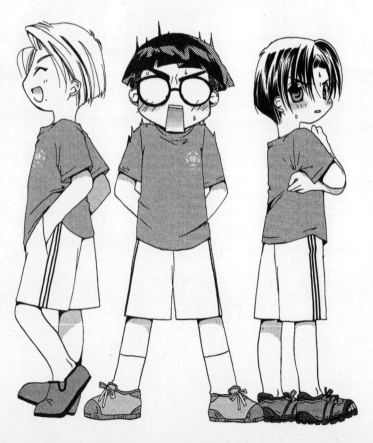

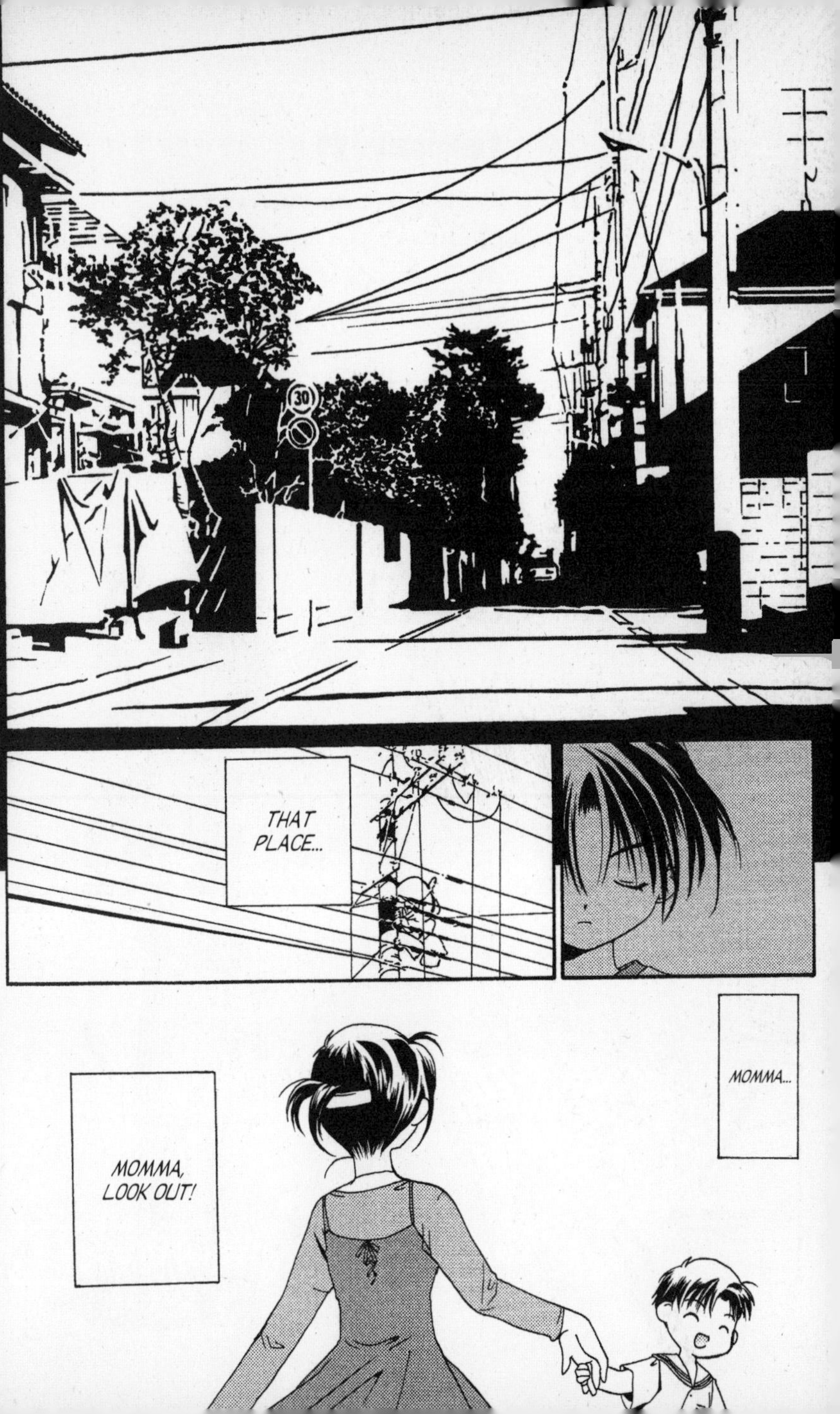
THAT PLACE...
MOMMA...
MOMMA, LOOK OUT!

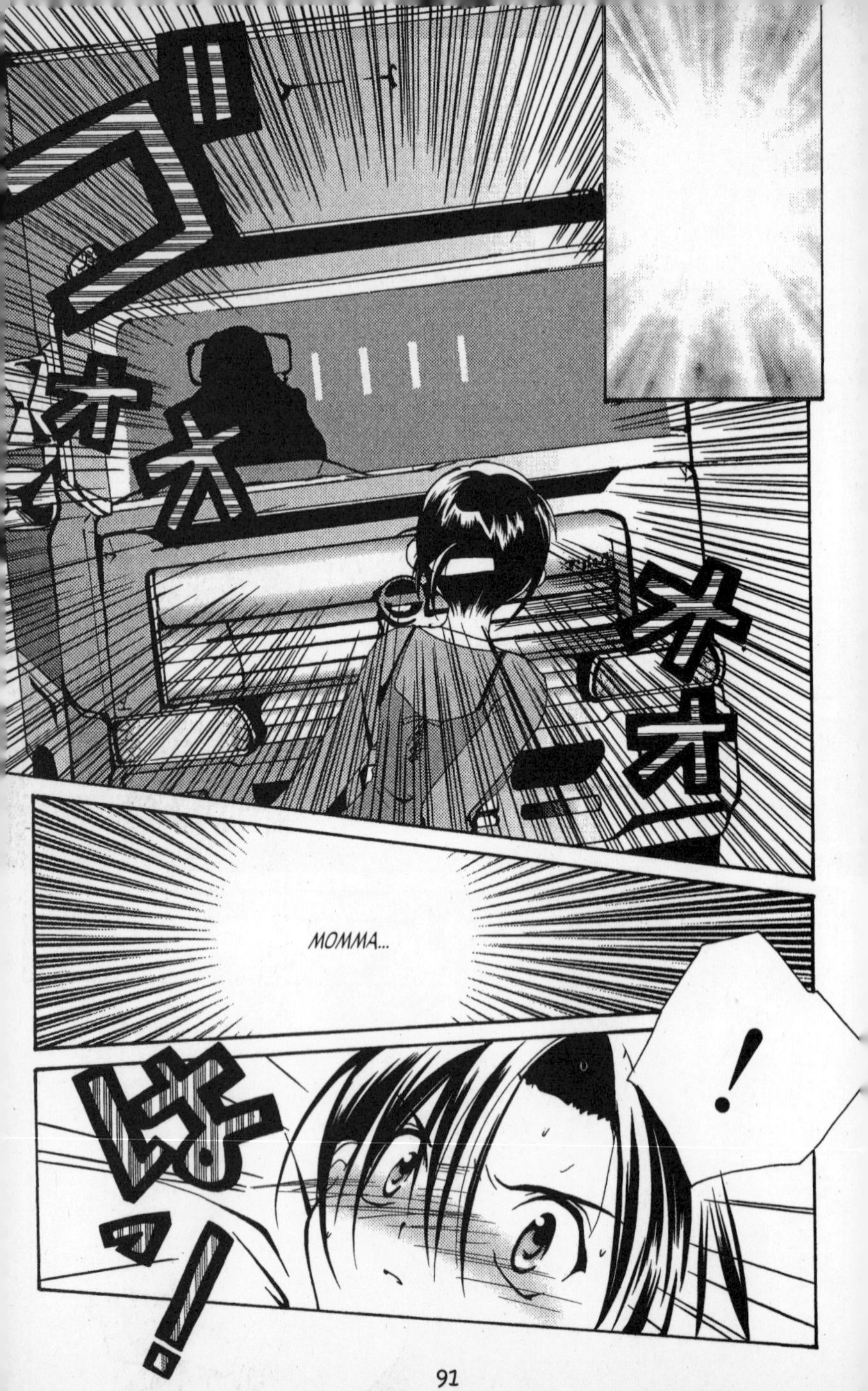
MOMMA...
!

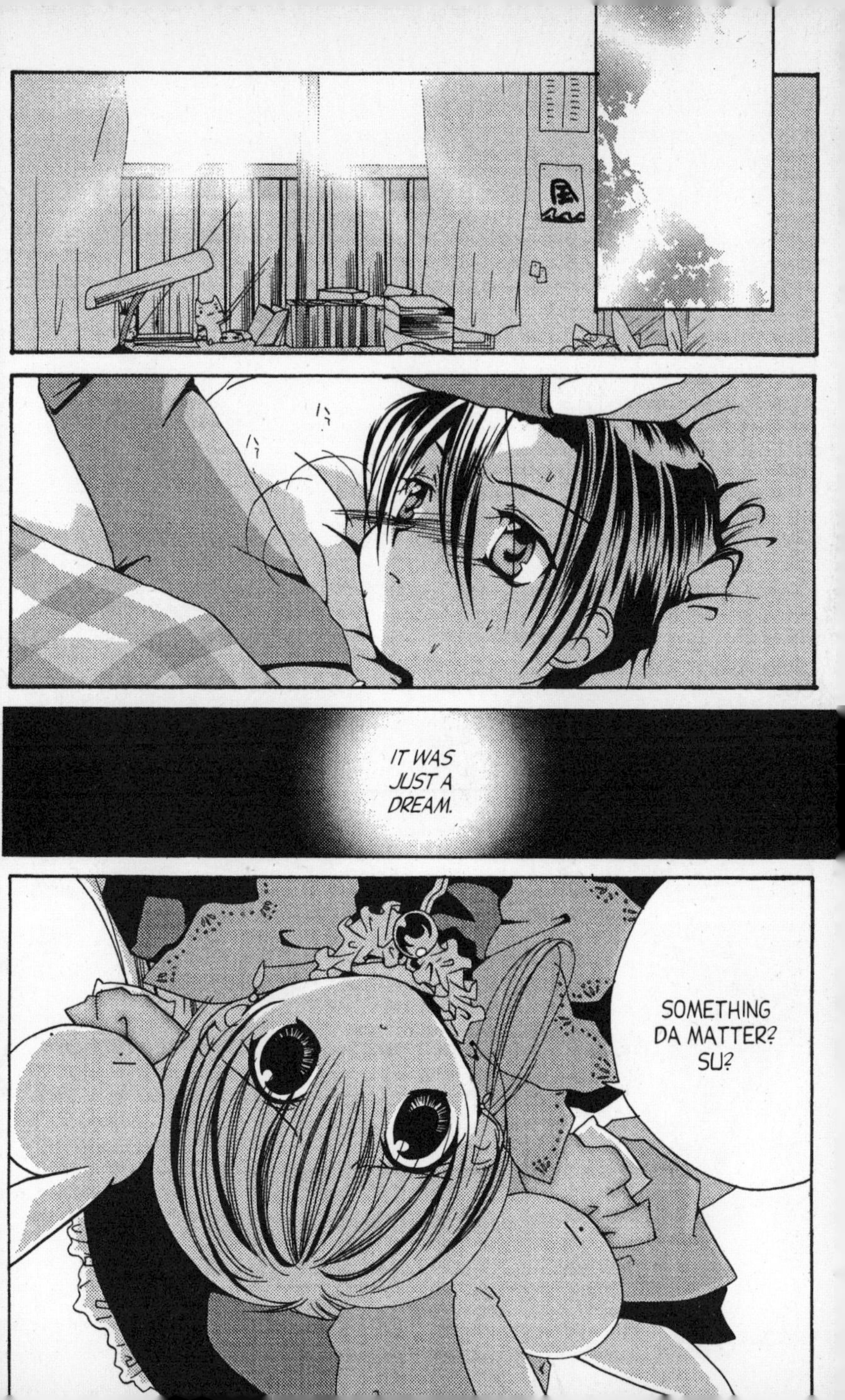
IT WAS JUST A DREAM.
SOMETHING DA MATTER? SU?

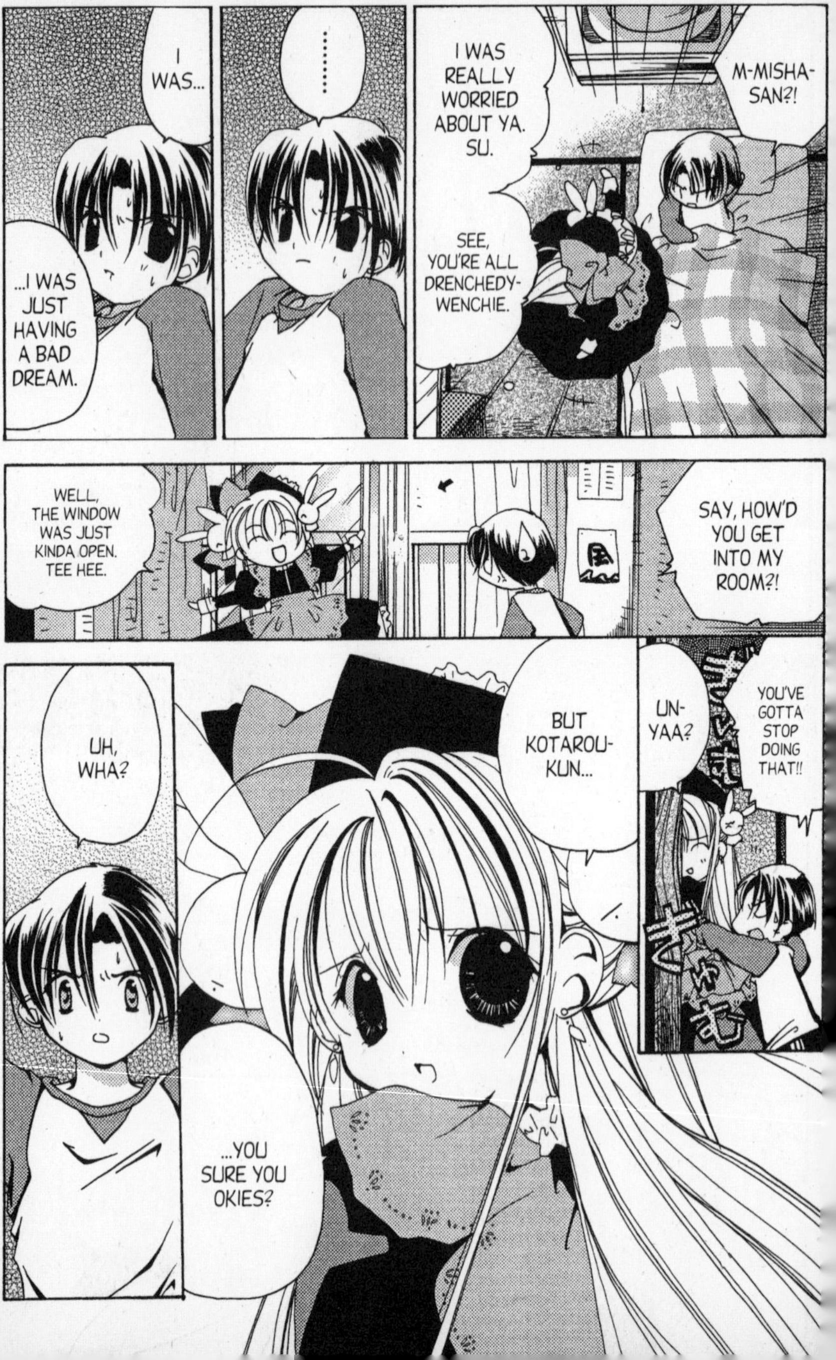
M-MISHA-SAN?!
I WAS REALLY WORRIED ABOUT YA. SU.
SEE, YOU'RE ALL DRENCHEDY-WENCHIE.
......
I WAS...
...I WAS JUST HAVING A BAD DREAM.
SAY, HOW'D YOU GET INTO MY ROOM?!
WELL, THE WINDOW WAS JUST KINDA OPEN. TEE HEE.
YOU'VE GOTTA STOP DOING THAT!!
UN-YAA?
BUT KOTAROU-KUN...
UH, WHA?
...YOU SURE YOU OKIES?

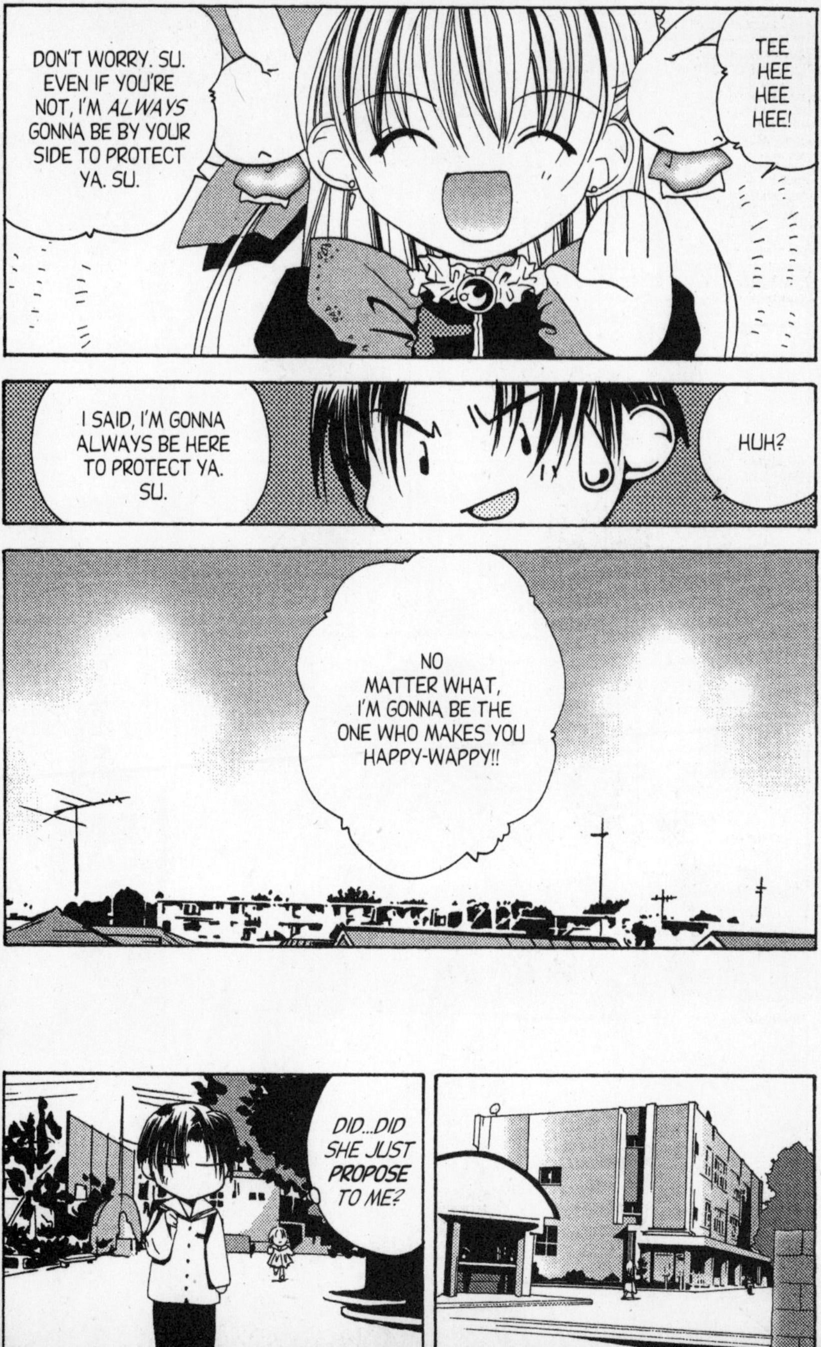
TEE HEE HEE HEE!
DON'T WORRY. SU. EVEN IF YOU'RE NOT, I'M *ALWAYS* GONNA BE BY YOUR SIDE TO PROTECT YA. SU.
HUH?
I SAID, I'M GONNA ALWAYS BE HERE TO PROTECT YA. SU.
NO MATTER WHAT, I'M GONNA BE THE ONE WHO MAKES YOU HAPPY-WAPPY!!
DID...DID SHE JUST PROPOSE TO ME?

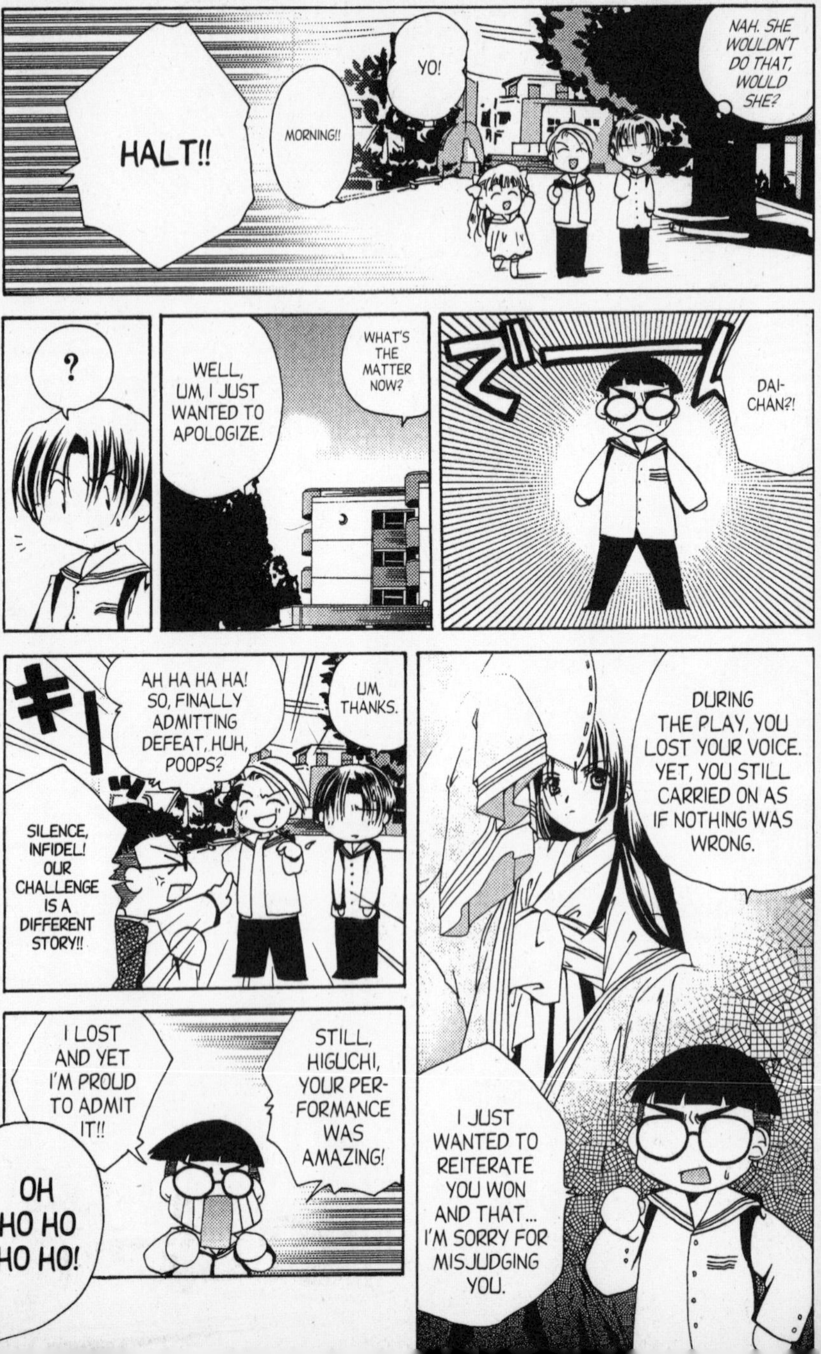
NAH. SHE WOULDN'T DO THAT, WOULD SHE?
YO!
MORNING!!
HALT!!
DAI-CHAN?!
WHAT'S THE MATTER NOW?
WELL, UM, I JUST WANTED TO APOLOGIZE.
?
DURING THE PLAY, YOU LOST YOUR VOICE. YET, YOU STILL CARRIED ON AS IF NOTHING WAS WRONG.
I JUST WANTED TO REITERATE YOU WON AND THAT... I'M SORRY FOR MISJUDGING YOU.
UM, THANKS.
AH HA HA HA! SO, FINALLY ADMITTING DEFEAT, HUH, POOPS?
SILENCE, INFIDEL! OUR CHALLENGE IS A DIFFERENT STORY!!
STILL, HIGUCHI, YOUR PERFORMANCE WAS AMAZING!
I LOST AND YET I'M PROUD TO ADMIT IT!!
OH HO HO HO HO!

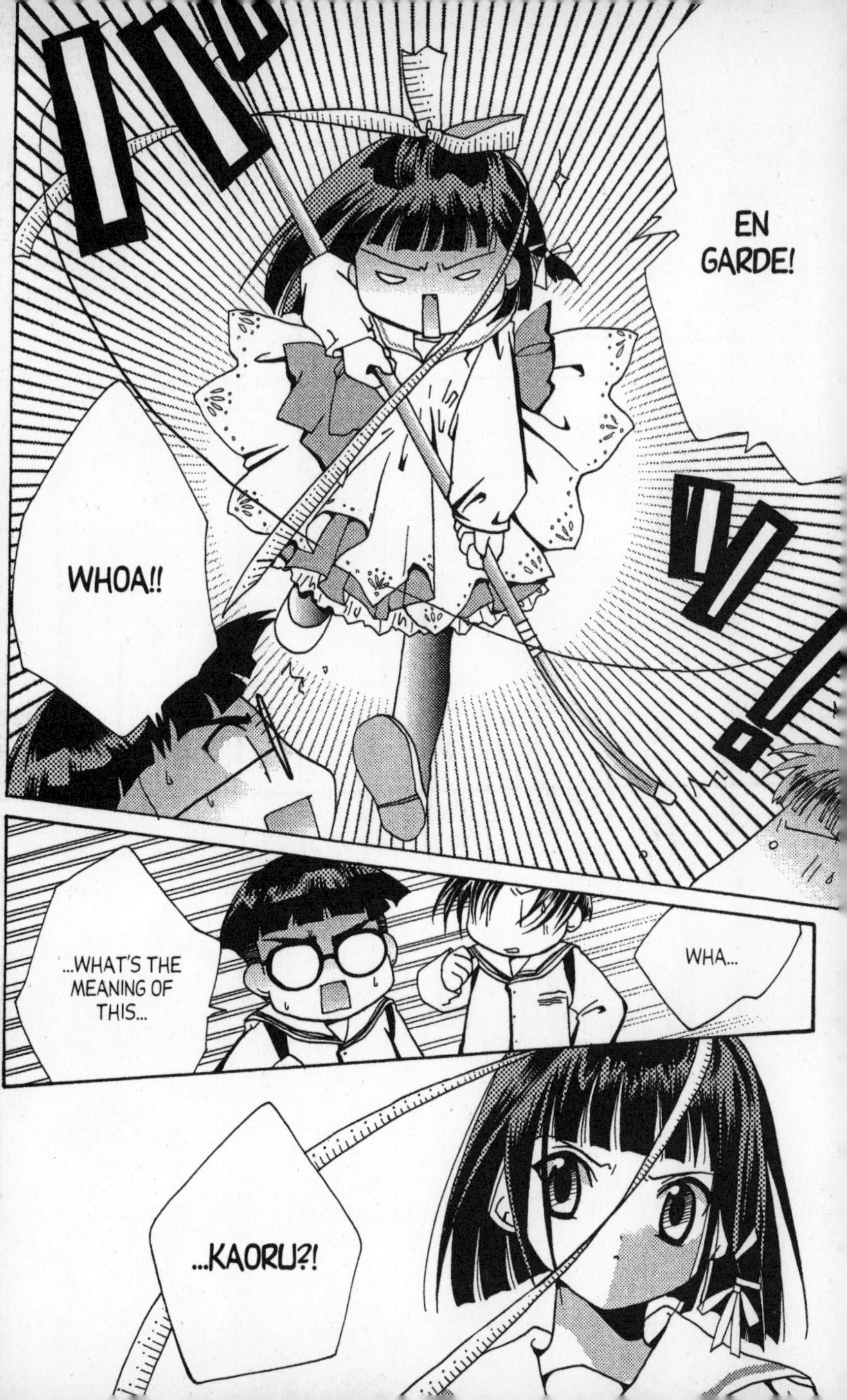
EN GARDE!
WHOA!!
WHA...
...WHAT'S THE MEANING OF THIS...
...KAORU?!

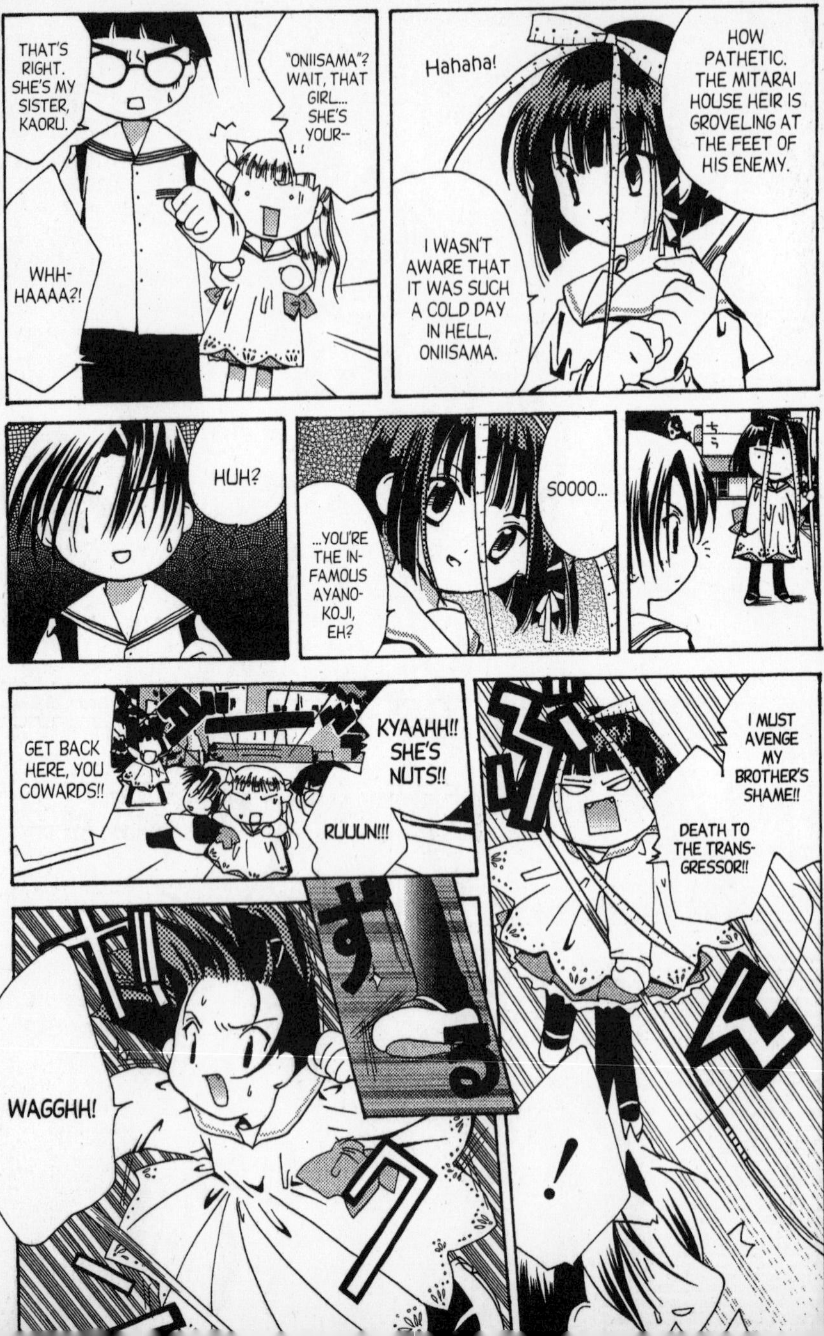

HOW PATHETIC. THE MITARAI HOUSE HEIR IS GROVELING AT THE FEET OF HIS ENEMY.
Hahaha!
I WASN'T AWARE THAT IT WAS SUCH A COLD DAY IN HELL, ONIISAMA.
"ONIISAMA"? WAIT, THAT GIRL... SHE'S YOUR--
THAT'S RIGHT. SHE'S MY SISTER, KAORU.
WHH-HAAAA?!
SOOOO...
...YOU'RE THE IN-FAMOUS AYANO-KOJI, EH?
HUH?
I MUST AVENGE MY BROTHER'S SHAME!!
DEATH TO THE TRANS-GRESSOR!!
KYAAHH!! SHE'S NUTS!!
RUUUN!!!
GET BACK HERE, YOU COWARDS!!
ずる
WAGGHH!
!

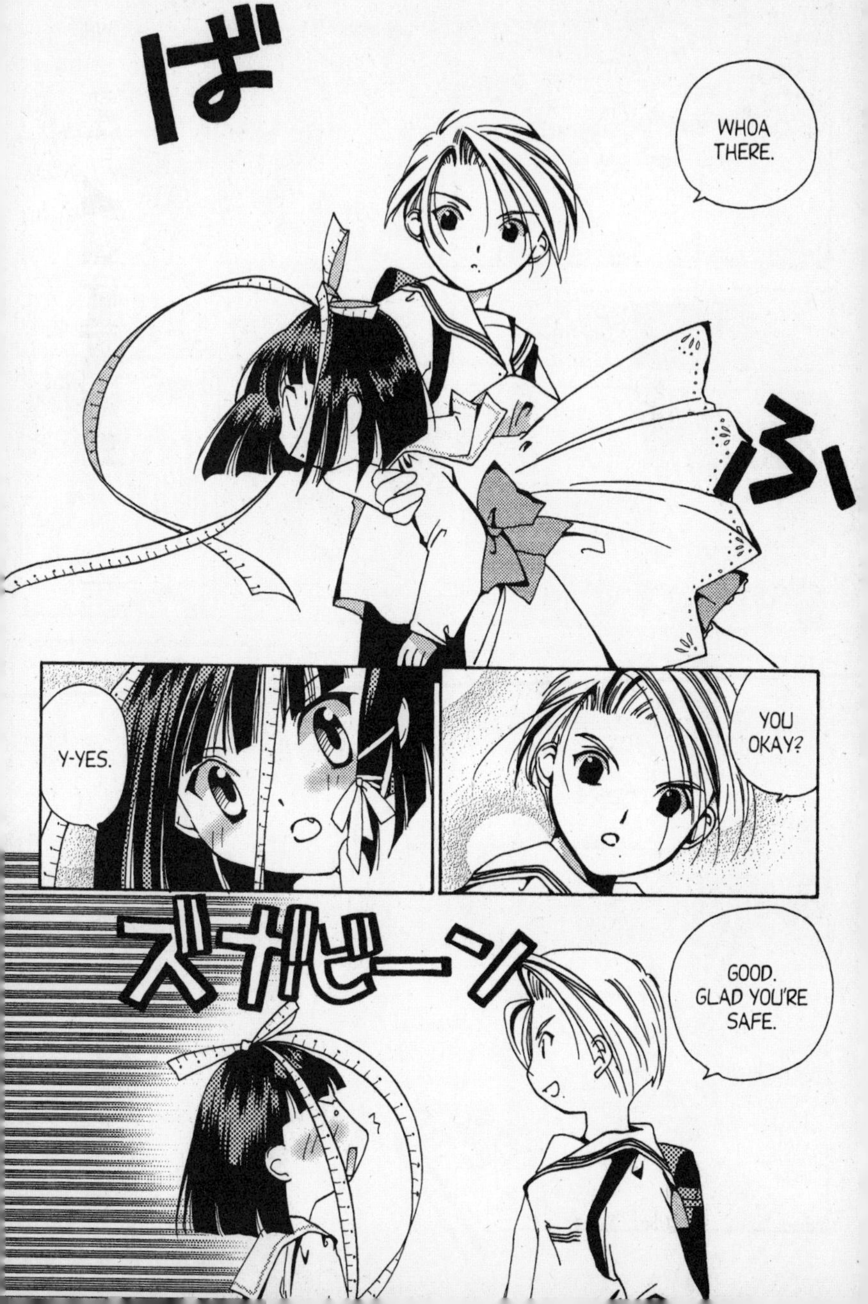
WHOA THERE.
ば
ふ
YOU OKAY?
Y-YES.
GOOD. GLAD YOU'RE SAFE.

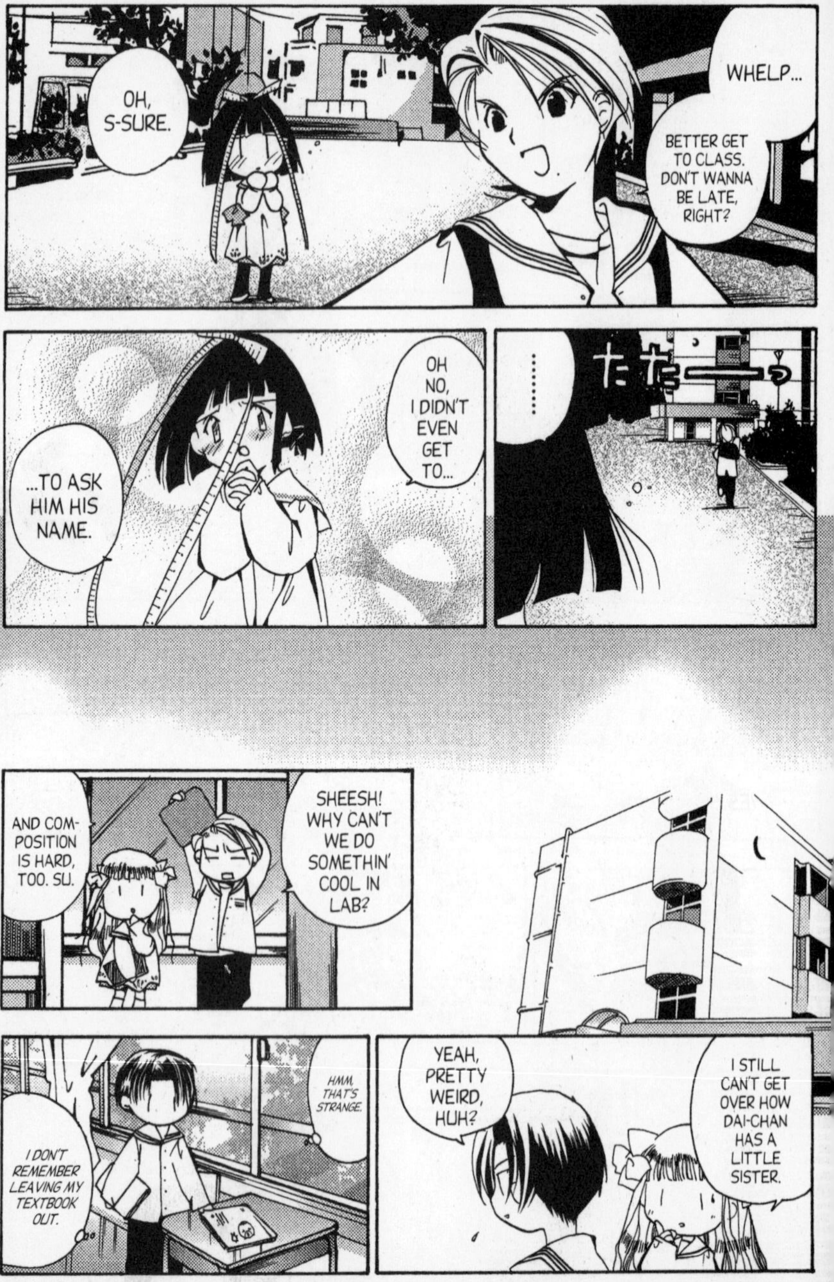

WHELP...
BETTER GET TO CLASS. DON'T WANNA BE LATE, RIGHT?
OH, S-SURE.
......
OH NO, I DIDN'T EVEN GET TO...
...TO ASK HIM HIS NAME.
SHEESH! WHY CAN'T WE DO SOMETHIN' COOL IN LAB?
AND COM-POSITION IS HARD, TOO. SU.
I STILL CAN'T GET OVER HOW DAI-CHAN HAS A LITTLE SISTER.
YEAH, PRETTY WEIRD, HUH?
HMM, THAT'S STRANGE.
I DON'T REMEMBER LEAVING MY TEXTBOOK OUT.

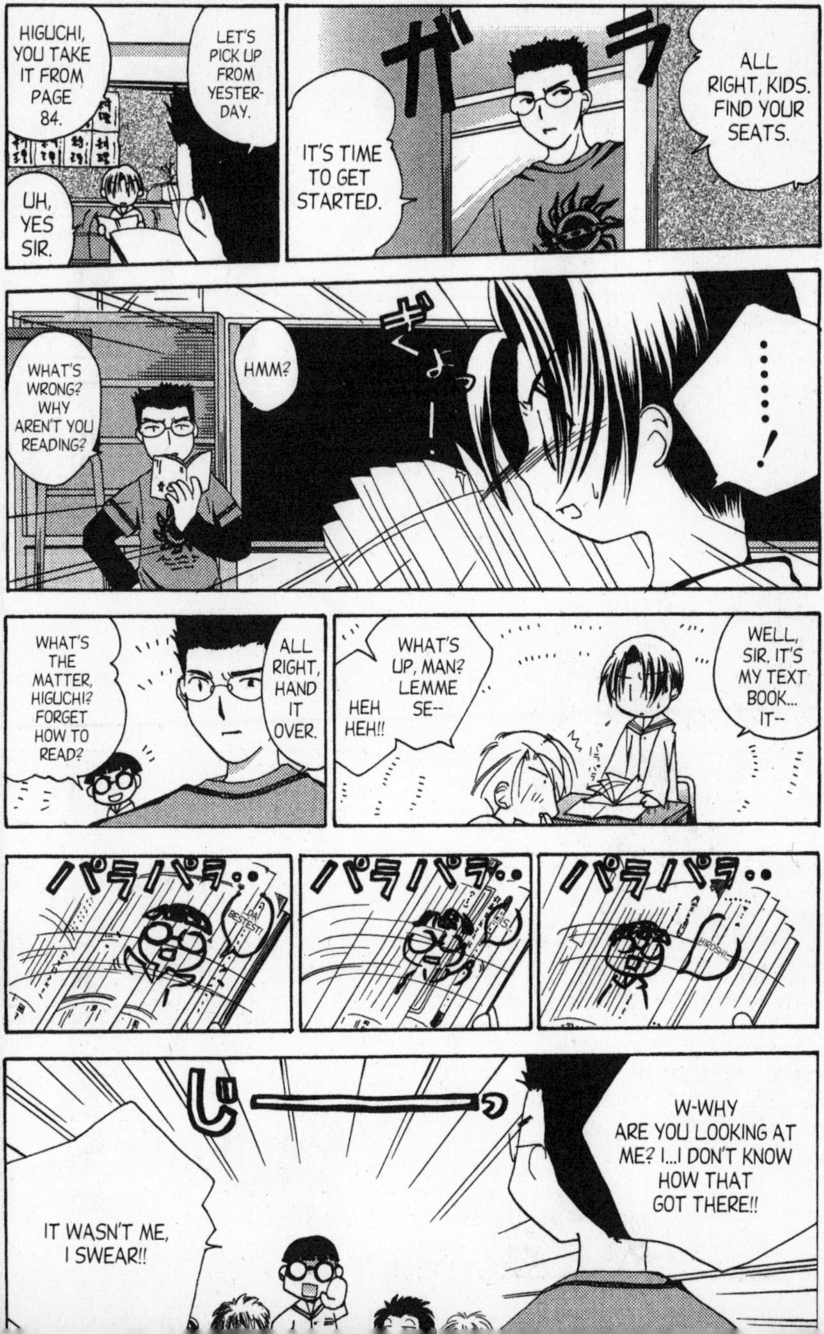
ガラ
ALL RIGHT, KIDS. FIND YOUR SEATS.
IT'S TIME TO GET STARTED.
LET'S PICK UP FROM YESTER-DAY.
HIGUCHI, YOU TAKE IT FROM PAGE 84.
UH, YES SIR.
......!
HMM?
WHAT'S WRONG? WHY AREN'T YOU READING?
WELL, SIR. IT'S MY TEXT BOOK... IT--
WHAT'S UP, MAN? LEMME SE--
HEH HEH!!
ALL RIGHT, HAND IT OVER.
WHAT'S THE MATTER, HIGUCHI? FORGET HOW TO READ?
パラパラ..
HIROSHI...
パラパラ..
IS!
パラパラ..
...DAI BESTEST!
じーっ
W-WHY ARE YOU LOOKING AT ME? I...I DON'T KNOW HOW THAT GOT THERE!!
IT WASN'T ME, I SWEAR!!

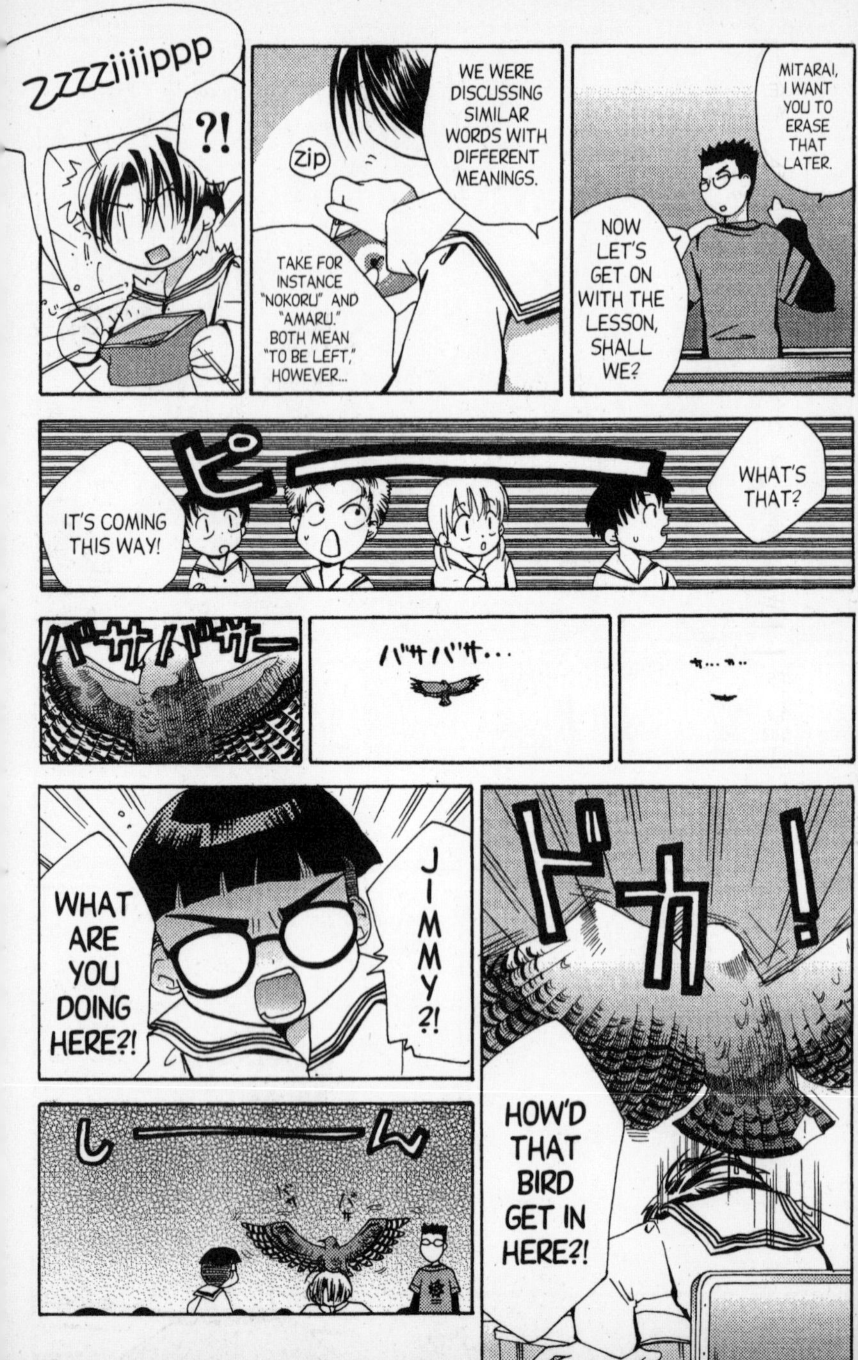
MITARAI, I WANT YOU TO ERASE THAT LATER.
NOW LET'S GET ON WITH THE LESSON, SHALL WE?
WE WERE DISCUSSING SIMILAR WORDS WITH DIFFERENT MEANINGS.
Zip
TAKE FOR INSTANCE "NOKORU" AND "AMARU." BOTH MEAN "TO BE LEFT," HOWEVER...
Zzzziiiippp
?!
WHAT'S THAT?
ピー
IT'S COMING THIS WAY!
バサバサ…
ドカ!
HOW'D THAT BIRD GET IN HERE?!
JIMMY?!
WHAT ARE YOU DOING HERE?!
しーん

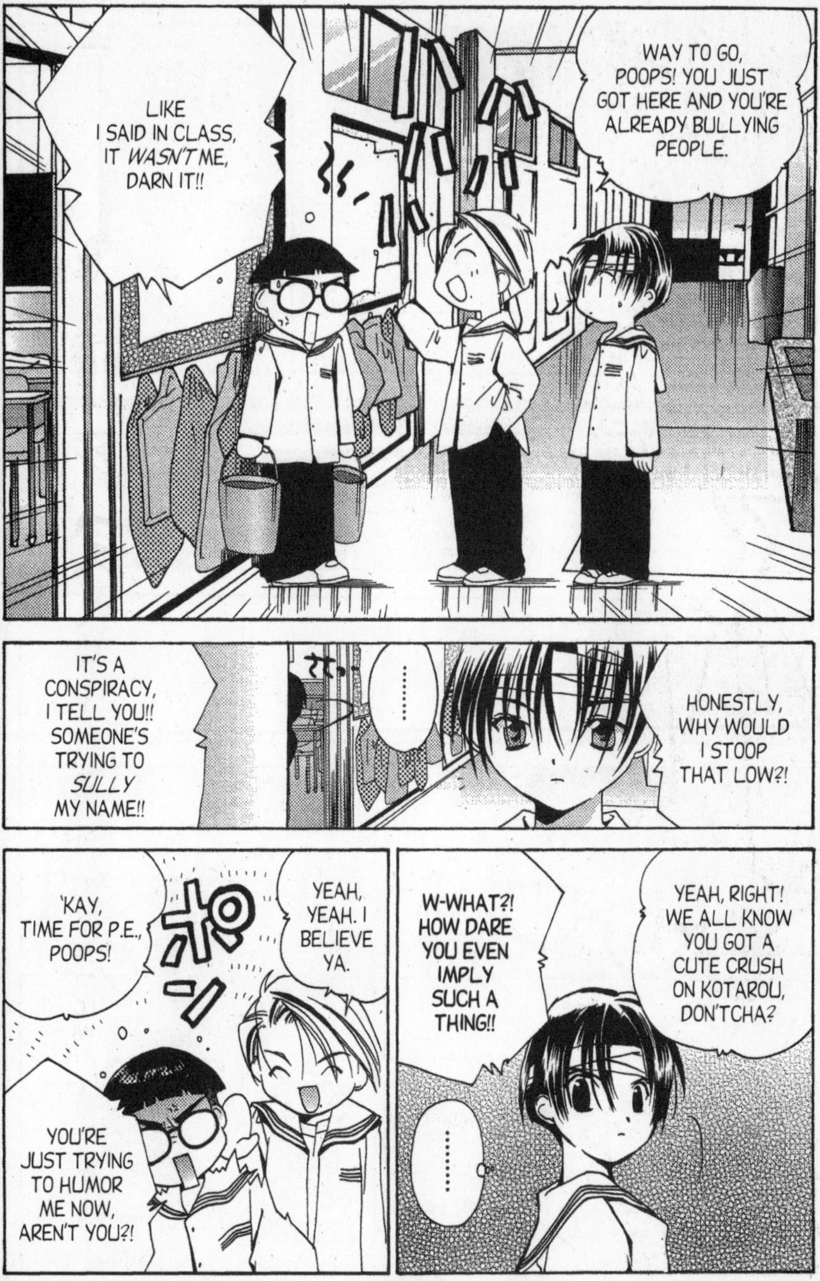
WAY TO GO, POOPS! YOU JUST GOT HERE AND YOU'RE ALREADY BULLYING PEOPLE.
LIKE I SAID IN CLASS, IT *WASN'T* ME, DARN IT!!
HONESTLY, WHY WOULD I STOOP THAT LOW?!
......
IT'S A CONSPIRACY, I TELL YOU!! SOMEONE'S TRYING TO *SULLY* MY NAME!!
YEAH, RIGHT! WE ALL KNOW YOU GOT A CUTE CRUSH ON KOTAROU, DON'TCHA?
W-WHAT?! HOW DARE YOU EVEN IMPLY SUCH A THING!!
......
YEAH, YEAH. I BELIEVE YA.
'KAY, TIME FOR P.E., POOPS!
YOU'RE JUST TRYING TO HUMOR ME NOW, AREN'T YOU?!

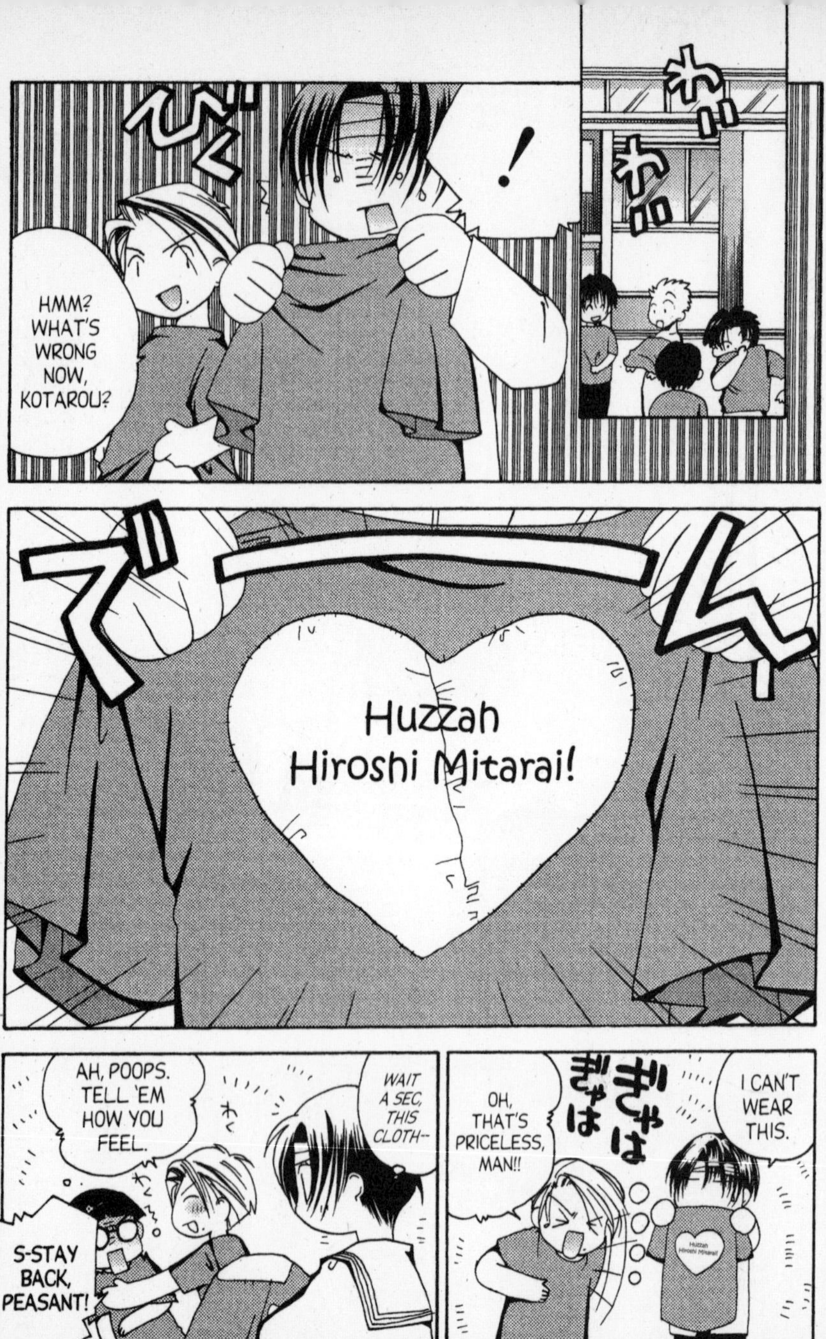

わいわい
びく
!
HMM? WHAT'S WRONG NOW, KOTAROU?
ずーん
Huzzah Hiroshi Mitarai!
I CAN'T WEAR THIS.
ぎゃは ぎゃは
OH, THAT'S PRICELESS, MAN!!
Huzzah Hiroshi Mitarai!
WAIT A SEC, THIS CLOTH--
AH, POOPS. TELL 'EM HOW YOU FEEL.
わくわく
S-STAY BACK, PEASANT!

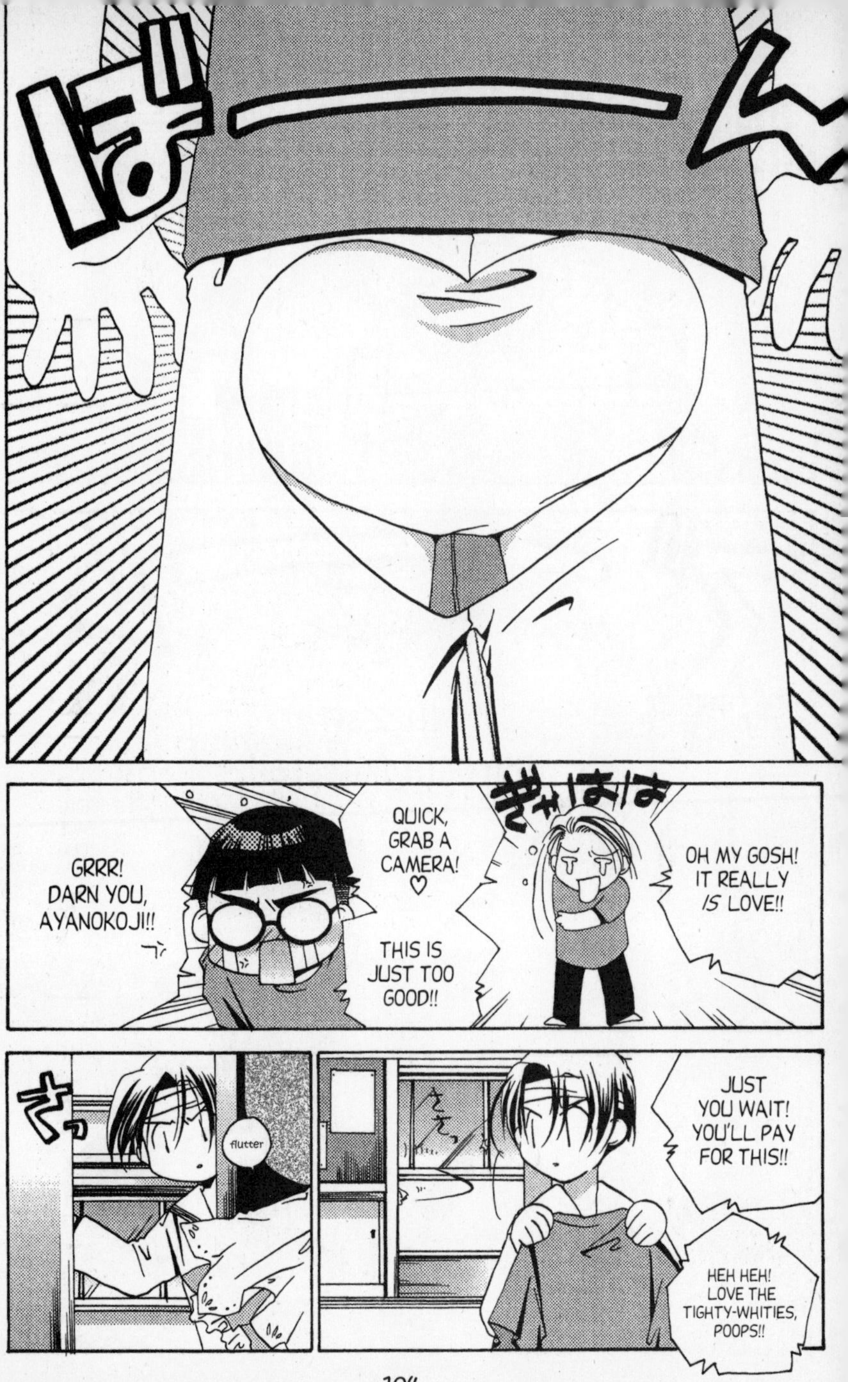
ぼーーん
OH MY GOSH! IT REALLY *IS* LOVE!!
ぎゃはは
QUICK, GRAB A CAMERA! ♡
THIS IS JUST TOO GOOD!!
GRRR! DARN YOU, AYANOKOJI!!
JUST YOU WAIT! YOU'LL PAY FOR THIS!!
HEH HEH! LOVE THE TIGHTY-WHITIES, POOPS!!
flutter
さっ

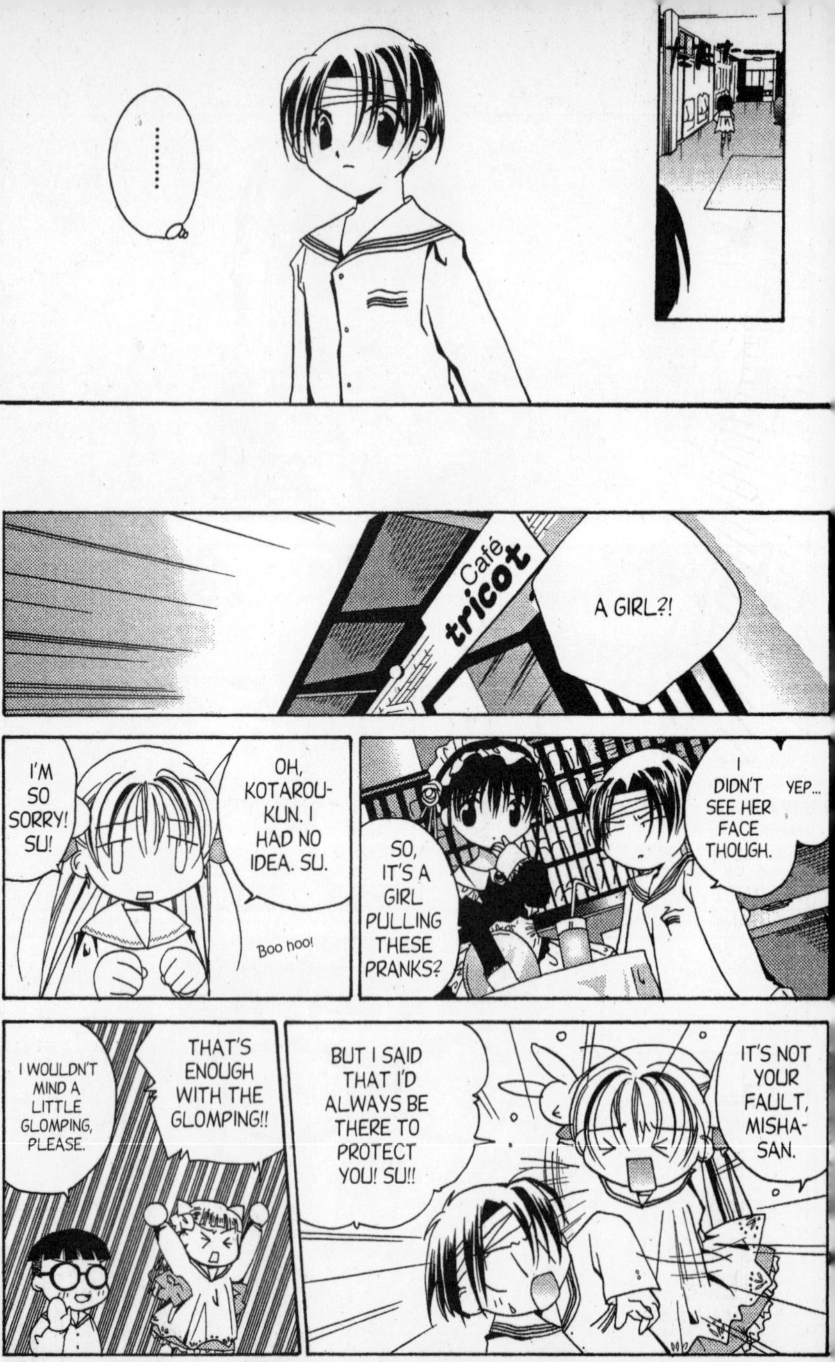
......
A GIRL?!
Café tricot
I DIDN'T SEE HER FACE THOUGH.
YEP...
SO, IT'S A GIRL PULLING THESE PRANKS?
OH, KOTAROU-KUN. I HAD NO IDEA. SU.
I'M SO SORRY! SU!
Boo hoo!
IT'S NOT YOUR FAULT, MISHA-SAN.
BUT I SAID THAT I'D ALWAYS BE THERE TO PROTECT YOU! SU!!
THAT'S ENOUGH WITH THE GLOMPING!!
I WOULDN'T MIND A LITTLE GLOMPING, PLEASE.

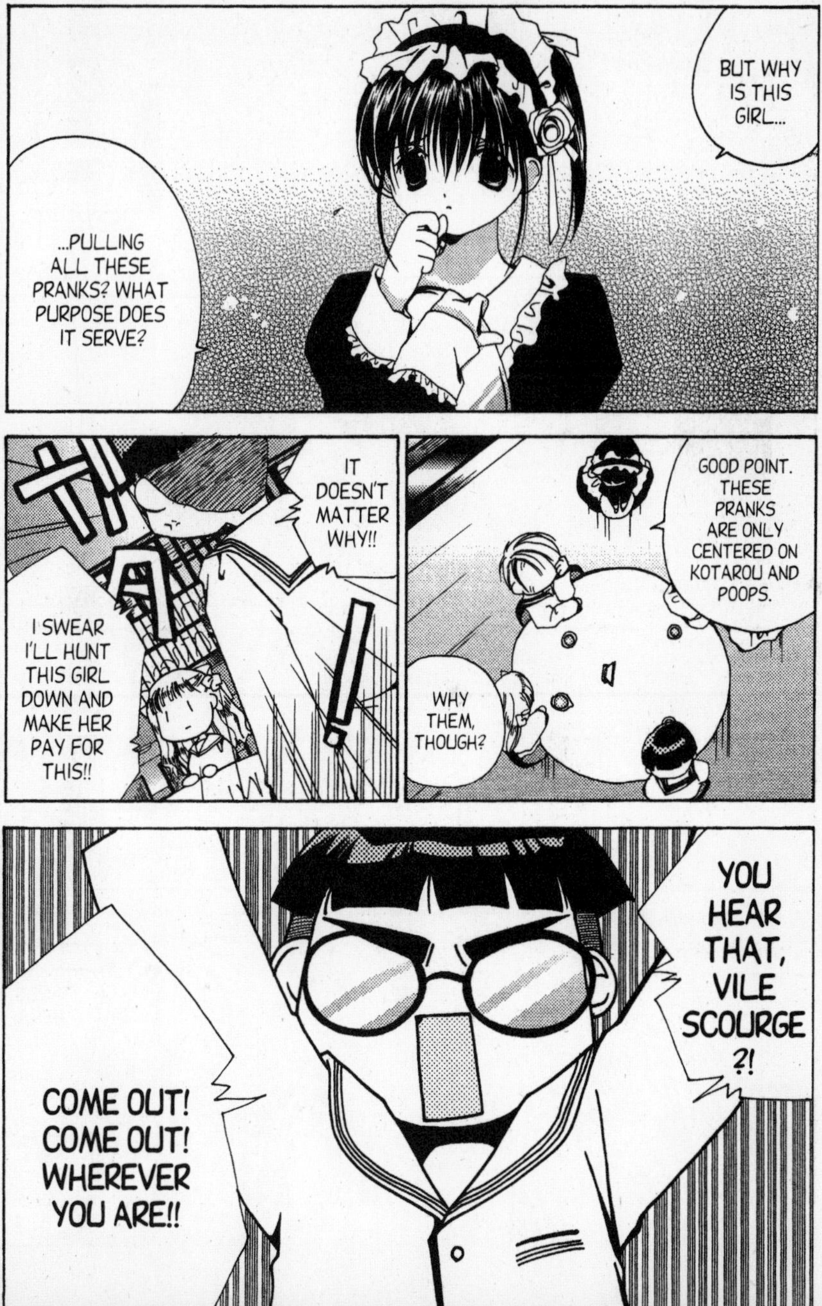
BUT WHY IS THIS GIRL...
...PULLING ALL THESE PRANKS? WHAT PURPOSE DOES IT SERVE?
GOOD POINT. THESE PRANKS ARE ONLY CENTERED ON KOTAROU AND POOPS.
WHY THEM, THOUGH?
IT DOESN'T MATTER WHY!!
I SWEAR I'LL HUNT THIS GIRL DOWN AND MAKE HER PAY FOR THIS!!
YOU HEAR THAT, VILE SCOURGE?!
COME OUT! COME OUT! WHEREVER YOU ARE!!

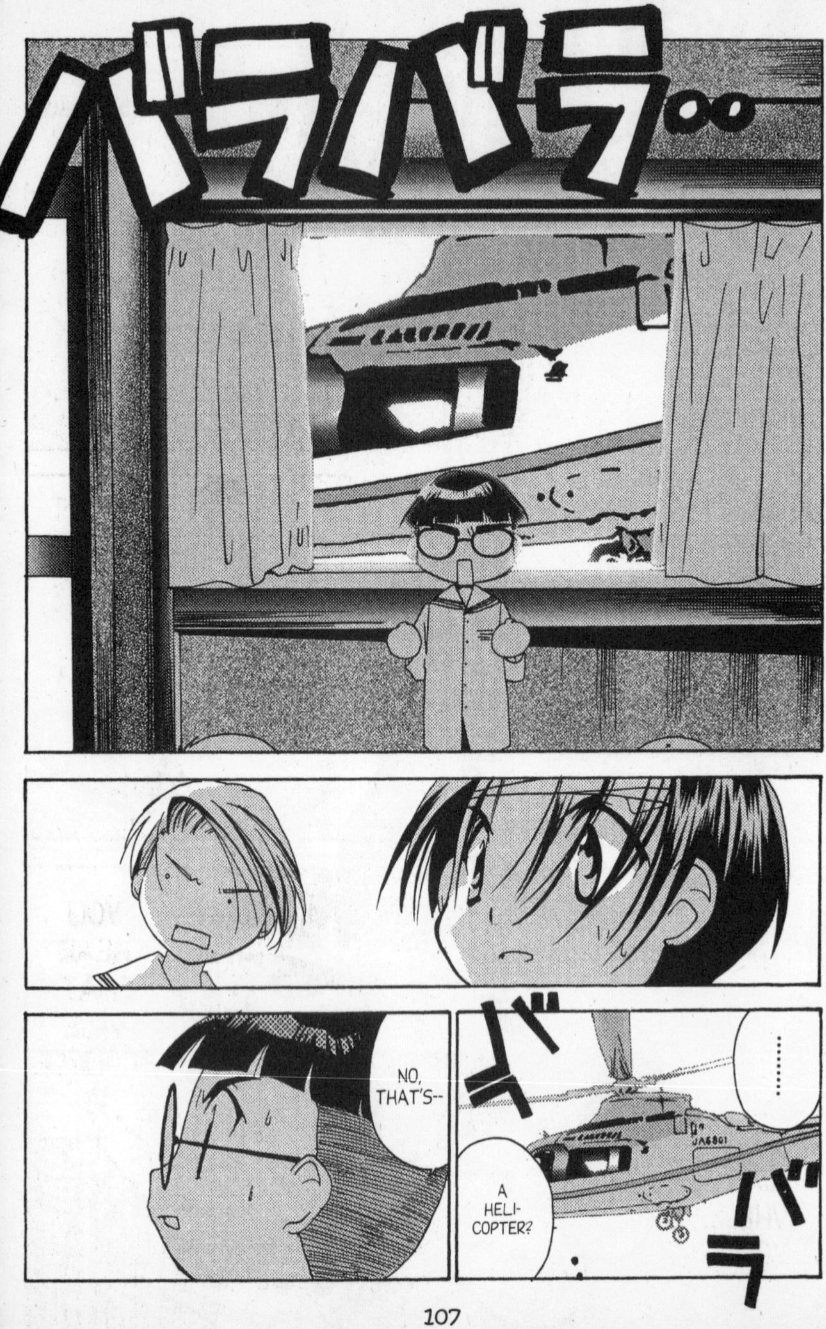
バラバラ
……
A HELI-COPTER?
バ
バラ
NO, THAT'S--

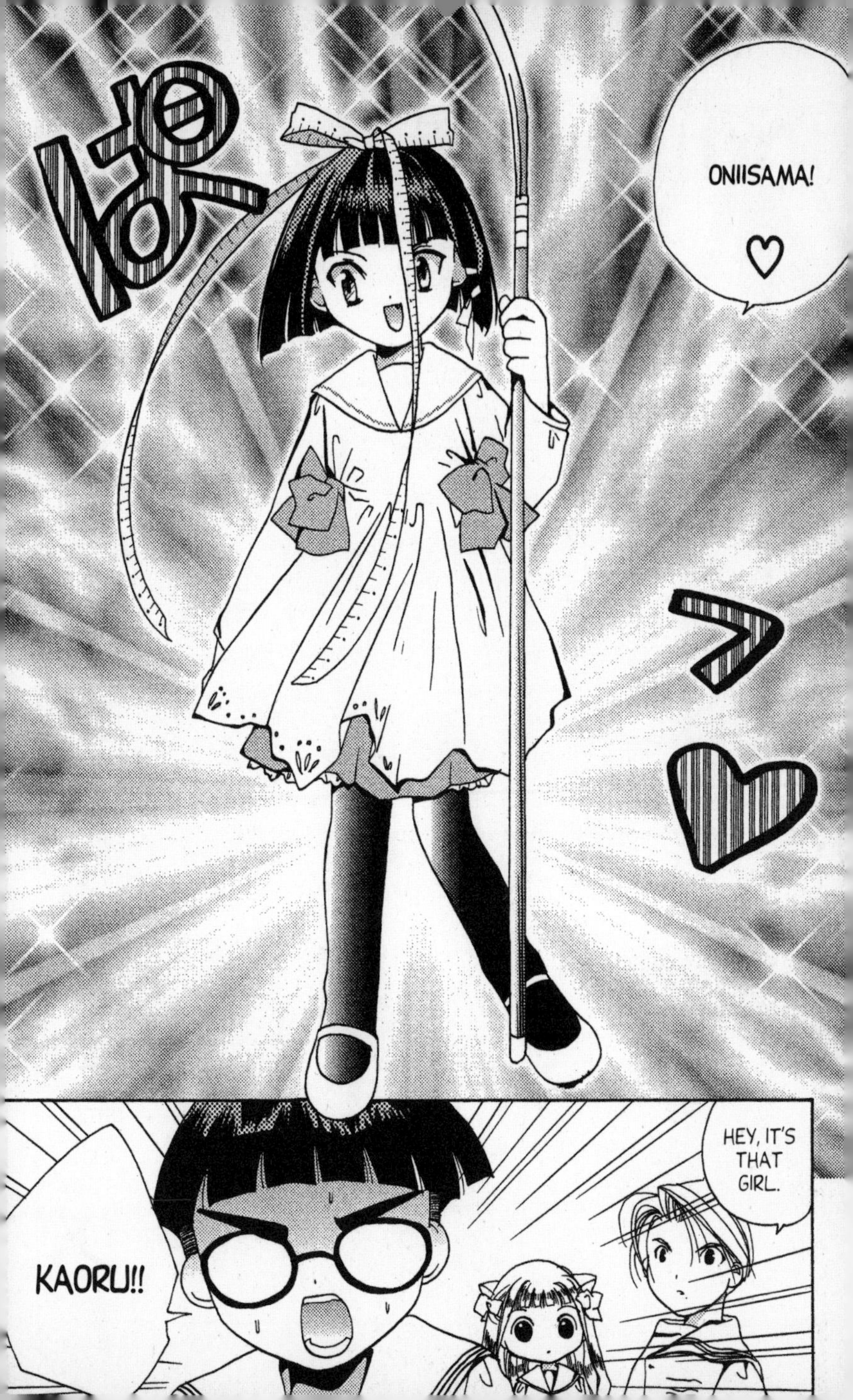
ONIISAMA! ♡
HEY, IT'S THAT GIRL.
KAORU!!

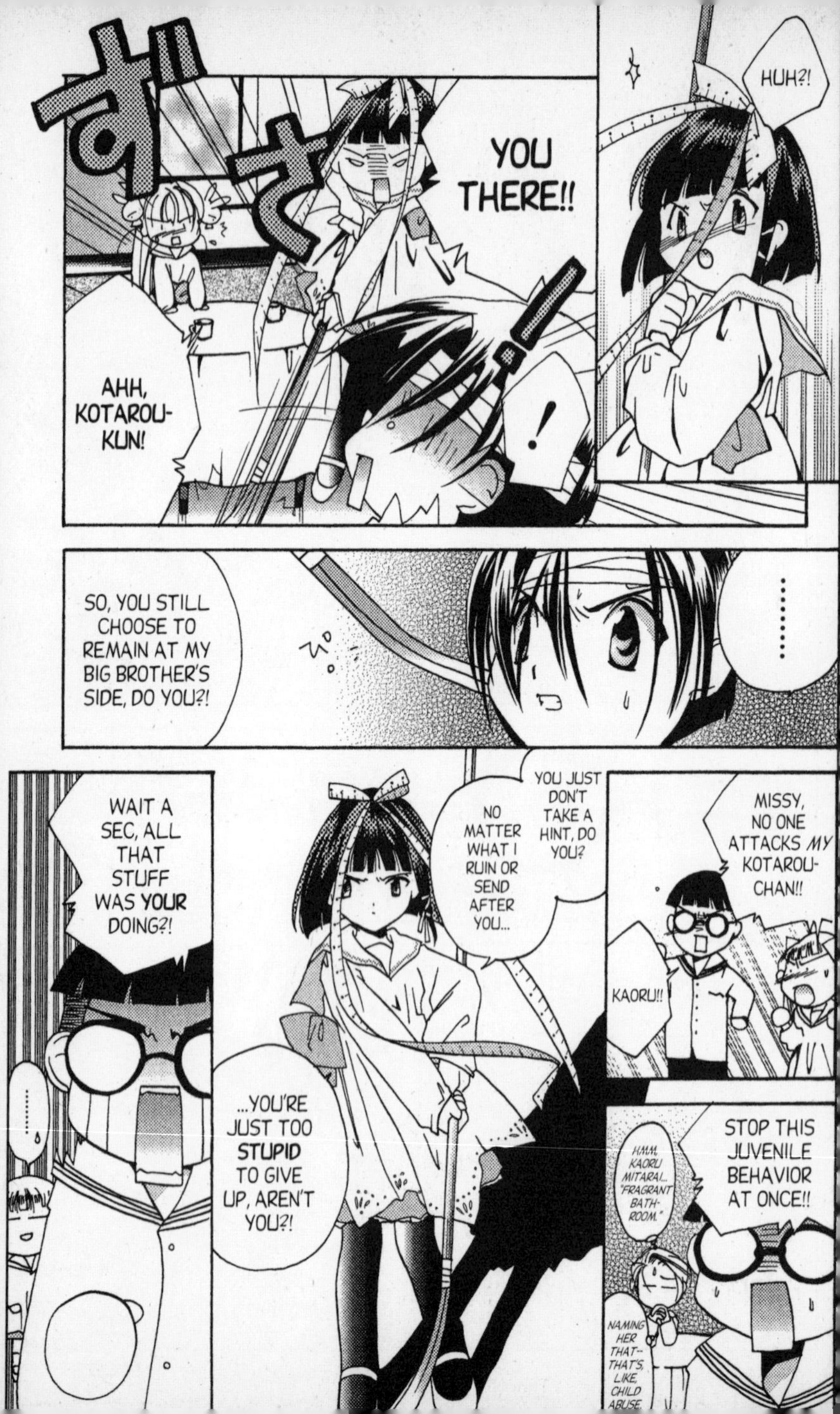
HUH?!
ずさ
YOU THERE!!
AHH, KOTAROU-KUN!
!
......
SO, YOU STILL CHOOSE TO REMAIN AT MY BIG BROTHER'S SIDE, DO YOU?!
MISSY, NO ONE ATTACKS MY KOTAROU-CHAN!!
KAORU!!
STOP THIS JUVENILE BEHAVIOR AT ONCE!!
HMM, KAORU MITARAI... "FRAGRANT BATH-ROOM."
NAMING HER THAT-- THAT'S, LIKE, CHILD ABUSE.
YOU JUST DON'T TAKE A HINT, DO YOU?
NO MATTER WHAT I RUIN OR SEND AFTER YOU...
...YOU'RE JUST TOO STUPID TO GIVE UP, AREN'T YOU?!
WAIT A SEC, ALL THAT STUFF WAS YOUR DOING?!
......

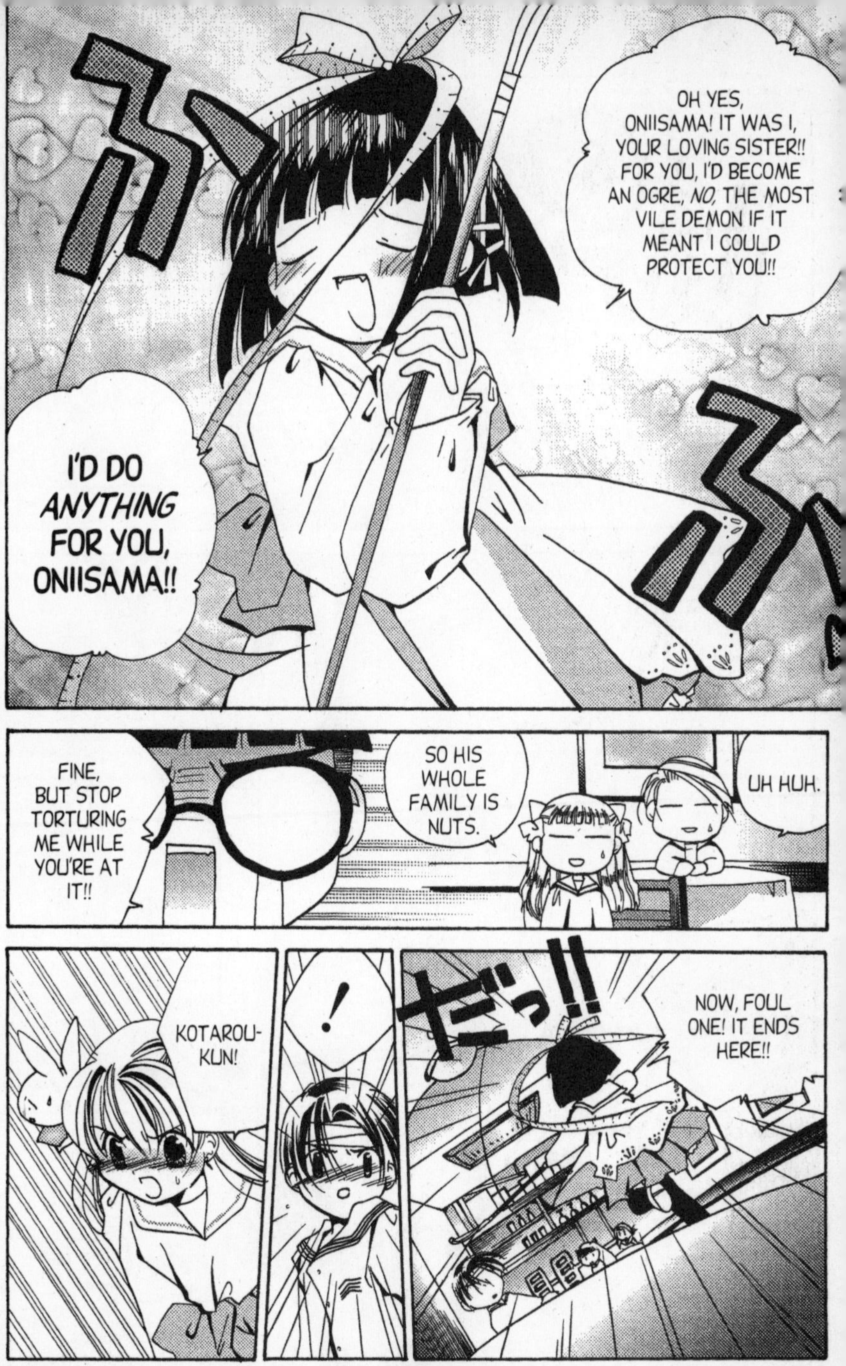
OH YES, ONIISAMA! IT WAS I, YOUR LOVING SISTER!! FOR YOU, I'D BECOME AN OGRE, *NO,* THE MOST VILE DEMON IF IT MEANT I COULD PROTECT YOU!!
I'D DO *ANYTHING* FOR YOU, ONIISAMA!!
UH HUH.
SO HIS WHOLE FAMILY IS NUTS.
FINE, BUT STOP TORTURING ME WHILE YOU'RE AT IT!!
NOW, FOUL ONE! IT ENDS HERE!!
だっ!!
!
KOTAROU-KUN!

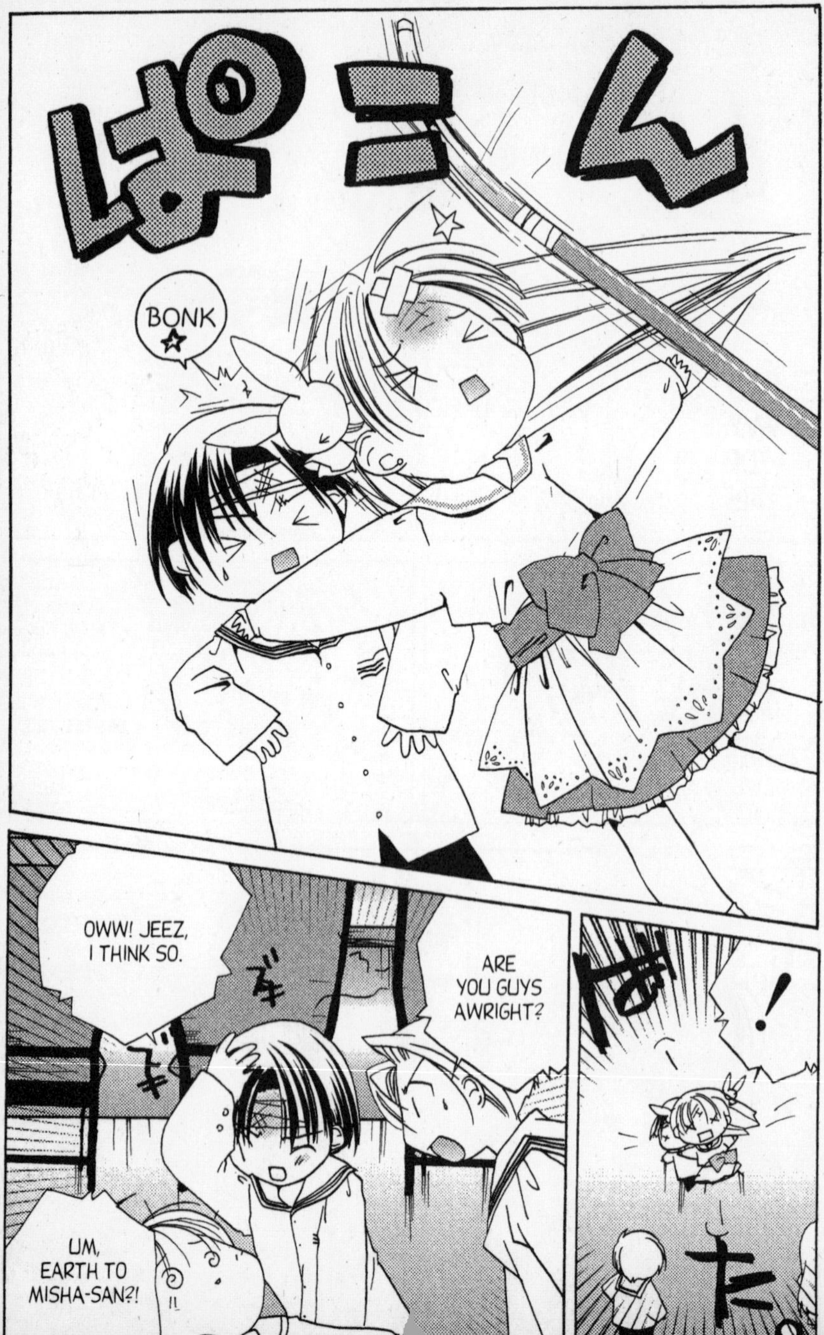
ぱこん
BONK ☆
あ
!
た。
ARE YOU GUYS AWRIGHT?
OWW! JEEZ, I THINK SO.
ズキ
ズキ
UM, EARTH TO MISHA-SAN?!

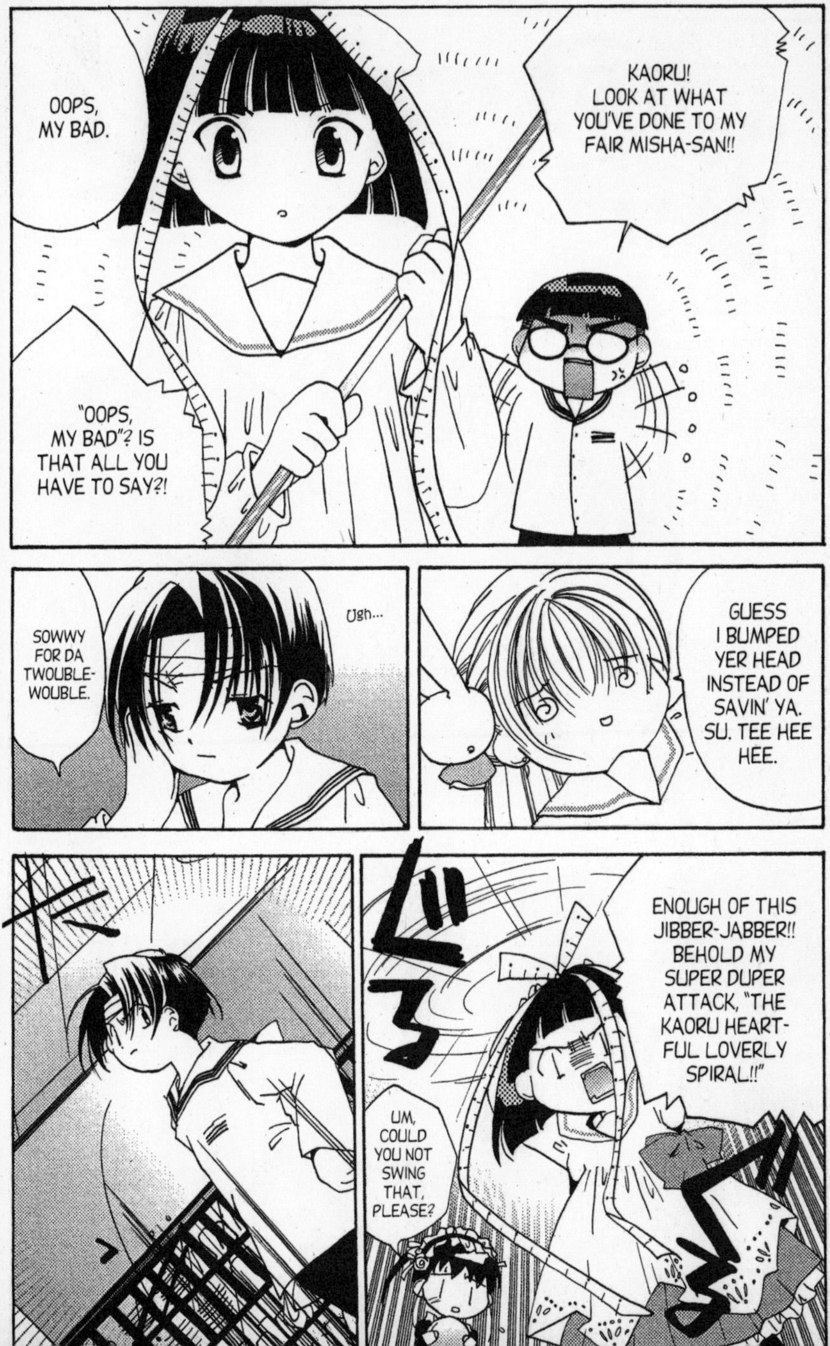
KAORU! LOOK AT WHAT YOU'VE DONE TO MY FAIR MISHA-SAN!!
OOPS, MY BAD.
"OOPS, MY BAD"? IS THAT ALL YOU HAVE TO SAY?!
GUESS I BUMPED YER HEAD INSTEAD OF SAVIN' YA. SU. TEE HEE HEE.
Ugh...
SOWWY FOR DA TWOUBLE-WOUBLE.
ENOUGH OF THIS JIBBER-JABBER!! BEHOLD MY SUPER DUPER ATTACK, "THE KAORU HEART-FUL LOVERLY SPIRAL!!"
UM, COULD YOU NOT SWING THAT, PLEASE?

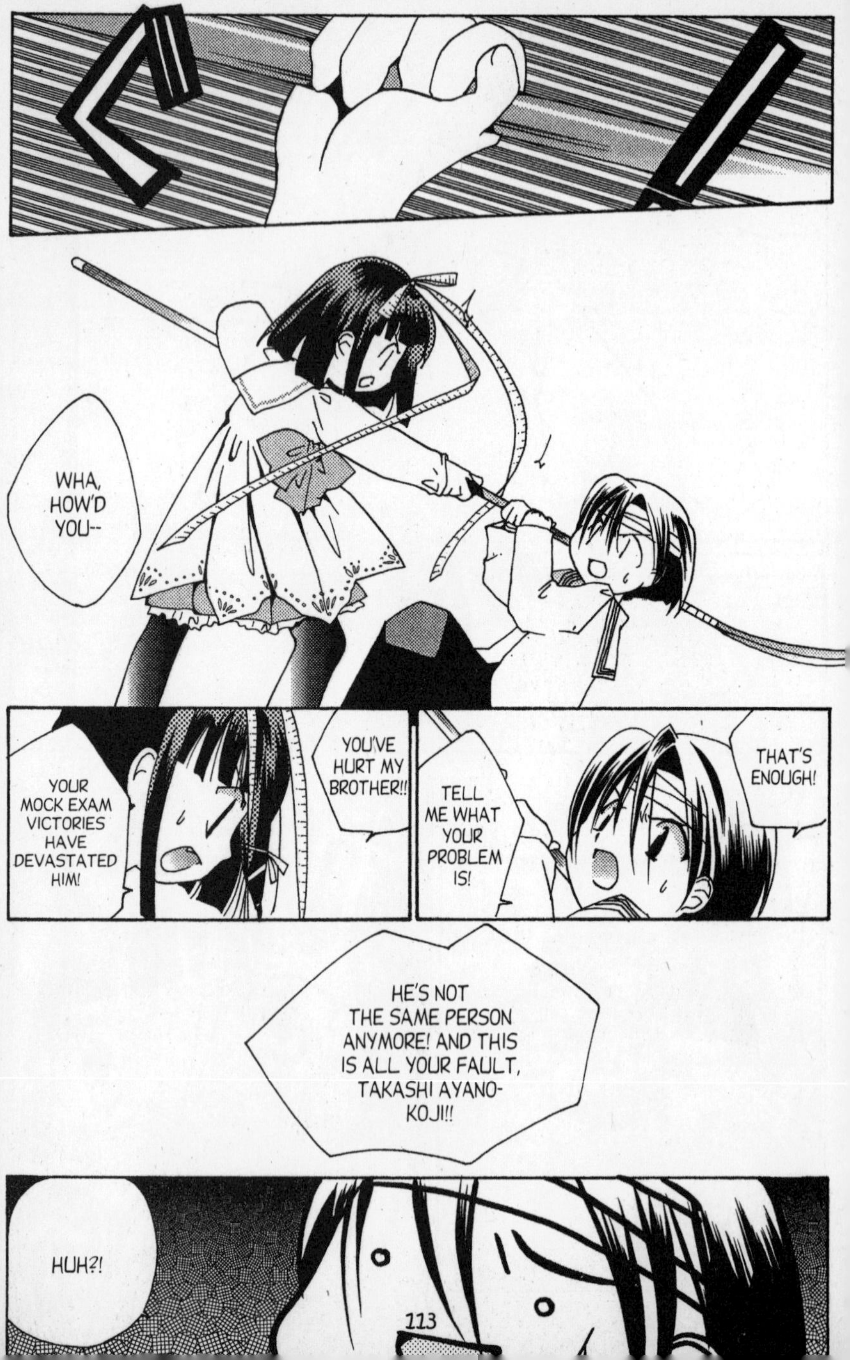
WHA, HOW'D YOU--
THAT'S ENOUGH!
TELL ME WHAT YOUR PROBLEM IS!
YOU'VE HURT MY BROTHER!!
YOUR MOCK EXAM VICTORIES HAVE DEVASTATED HIM!
HE'S NOT THE SAME PERSON ANYMORE! AND THIS IS ALL YOUR FAULT, TAKASHI AYANO-KOJI!!
HUH?!

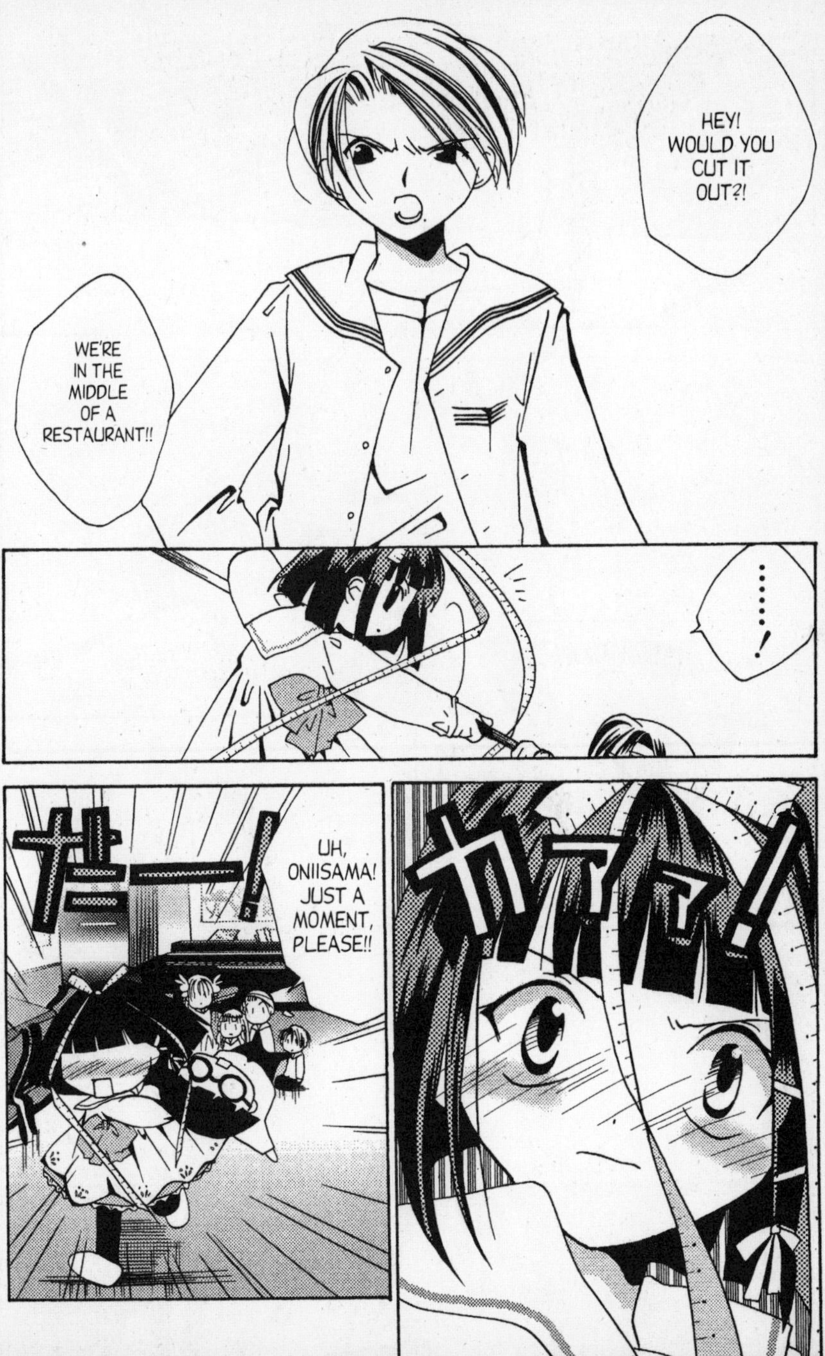
HEY! WOULD YOU CUT IT OUT?!
WE'RE IN THE MIDDLE OF A RESTAURANT!!
......!
UH, ONIISAMA! JUST A MOMENT, PLEASE!!

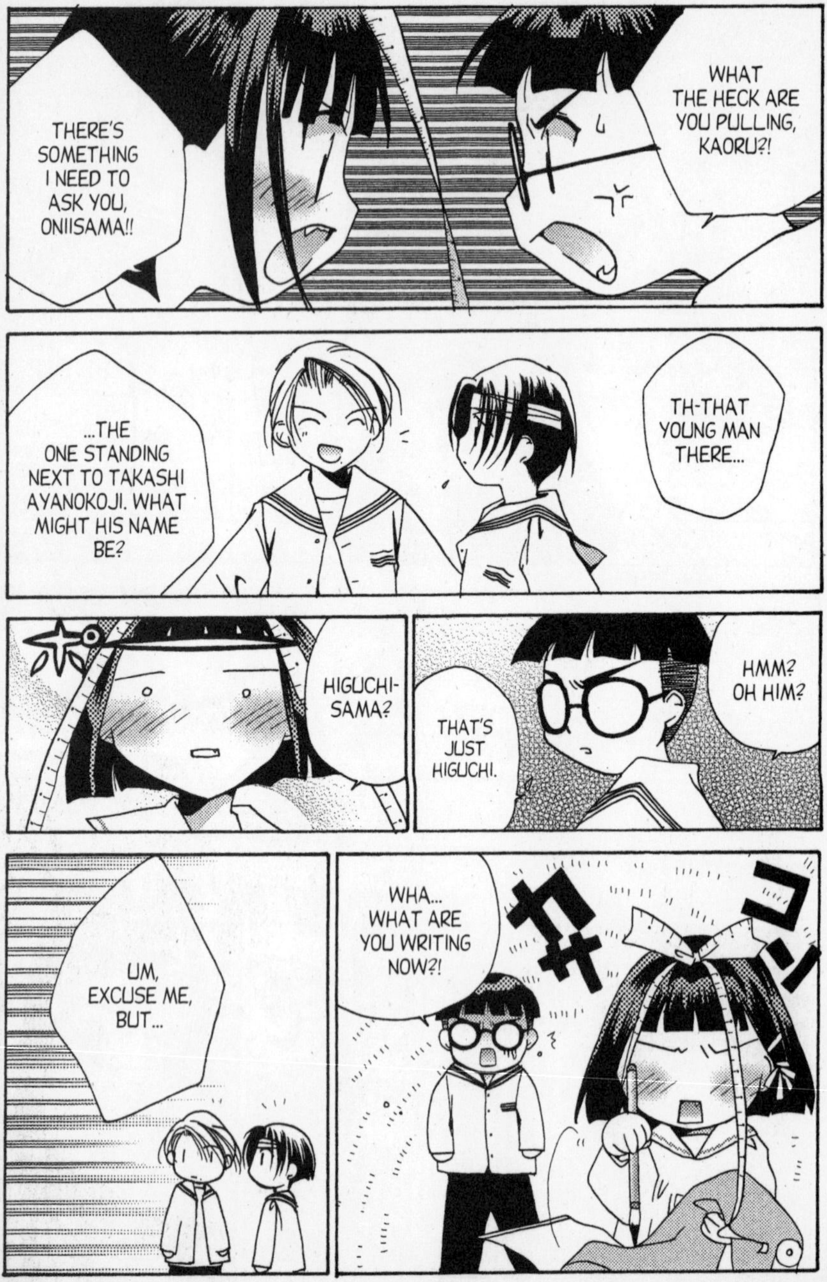
WHAT THE HECK ARE YOU PULLING, KAORU?!
THERE'S SOMETHING I NEED TO ASK YOU, ONIISAMA!!
TH-THAT YOUNG MAN THERE...
...THE ONE STANDING NEXT TO TAKASHI AYANOKOJI. WHAT MIGHT HIS NAME BE?
HMM? OH HIM?
THAT'S JUST HIGUCHI.
HIGUCHI-SAMA?
WHA... WHAT ARE YOU WRITING NOW?!
UM, EXCUSE ME, BUT...

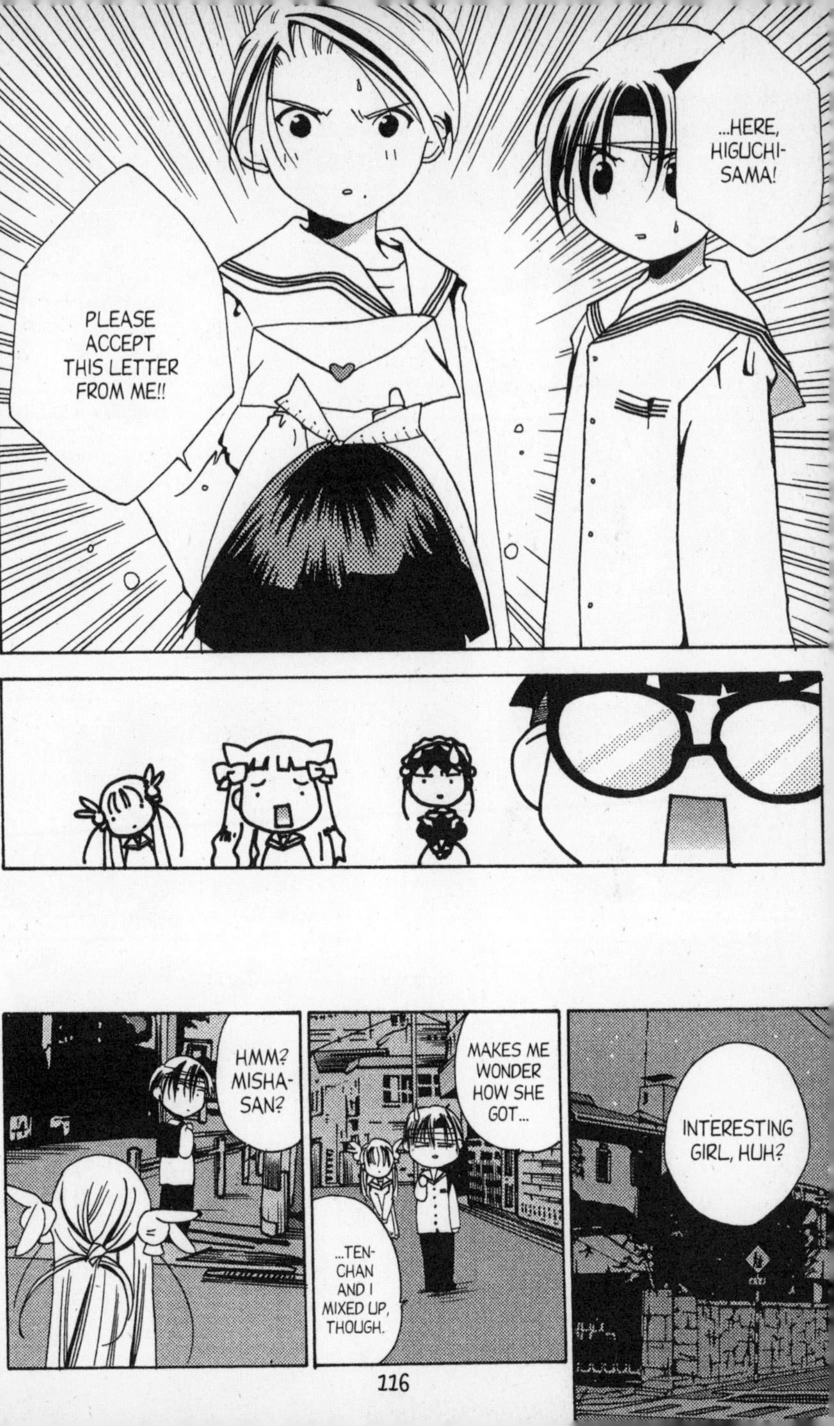
...HERE, HIGUCHI-SAMA!
PLEASE ACCEPT THIS LETTER FROM ME!!
INTERESTING GIRL, HUH?
MAKES ME WONDER HOW SHE GOT...
...TEN-CHAN AND I MIXED UP, THOUGH.
HMM? MISHA-SAN?

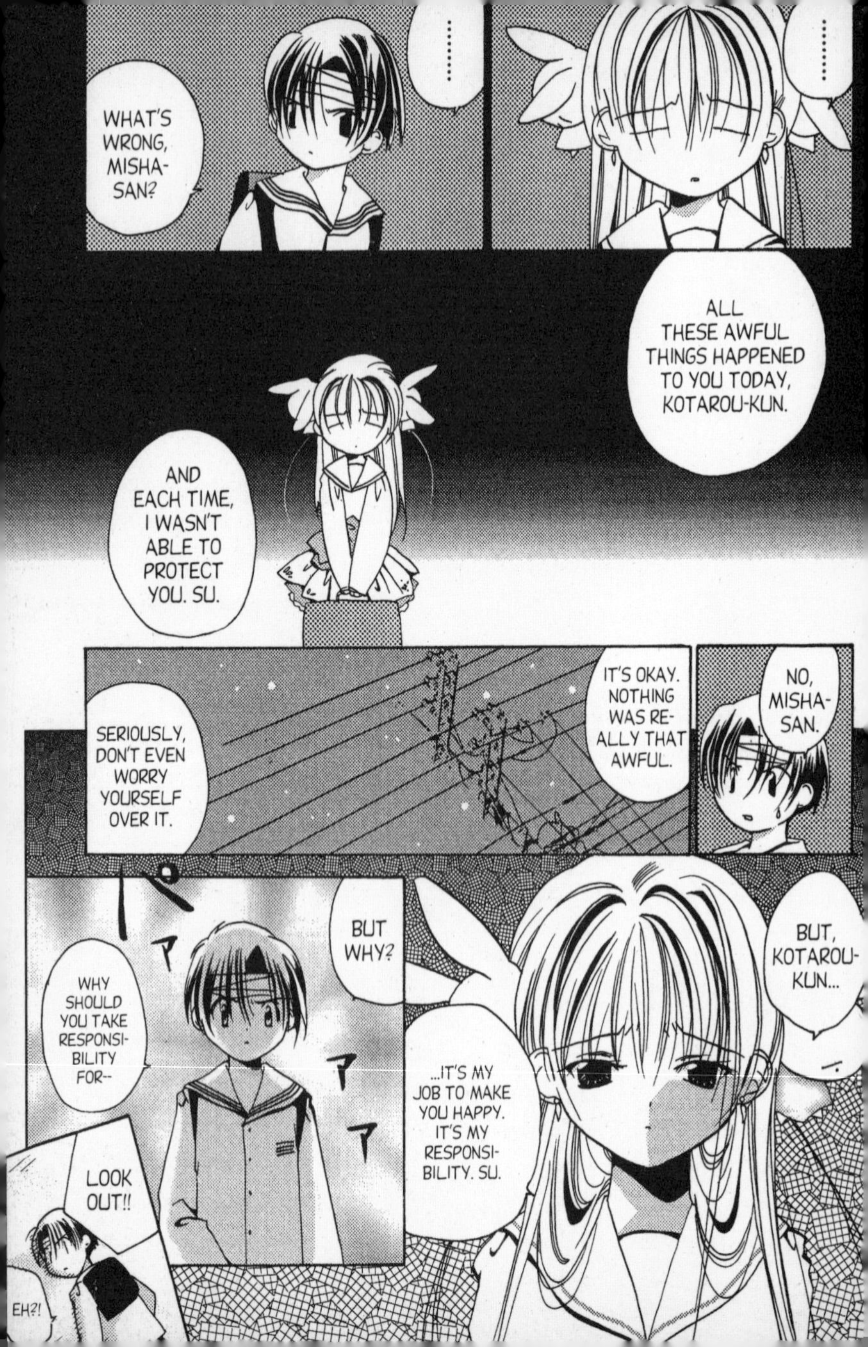
......
......
WHAT'S WRONG, MISHA-SAN?
ALL THESE AWFUL THINGS HAPPENED TO YOU TODAY, KOTAROU-KUN.
AND EACH TIME, I WASN'T ABLE TO PROTECT YOU. SU.
NO, MISHA-SAN.
IT'S OKAY. NOTHING WAS REALLY THAT AWFUL.
SERIOUSLY, DON'T EVEN WORRY YOURSELF OVER IT.
BUT, KOTAROU-KUN...
...IT'S MY JOB TO MAKE YOU HAPPY. IT'S MY RESPONSIBILITY. SU.
BUT WHY?
WHY SHOULD YOU TAKE RESPONSIBILITY FOR--
LOOK OUT!!
EH?!

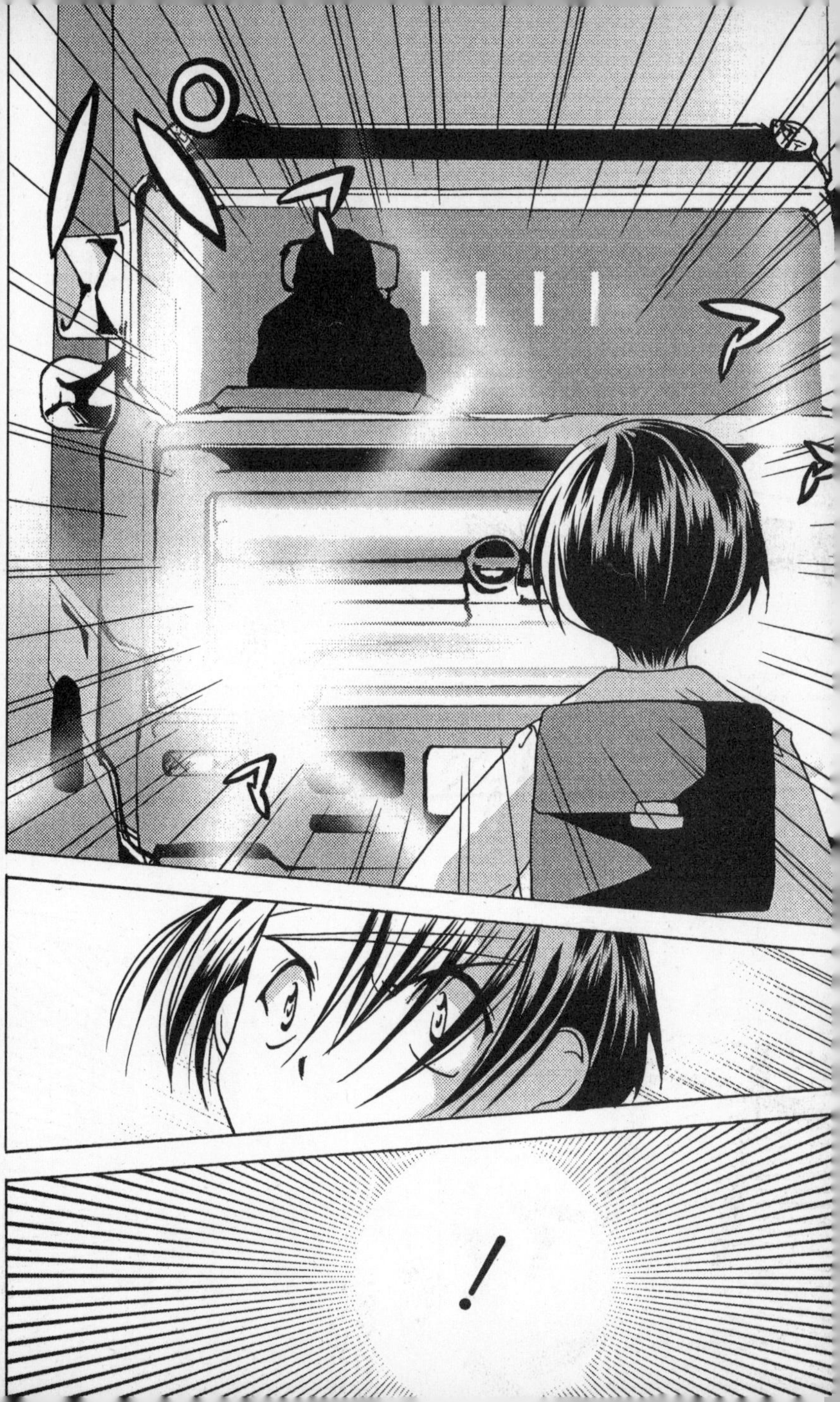
!

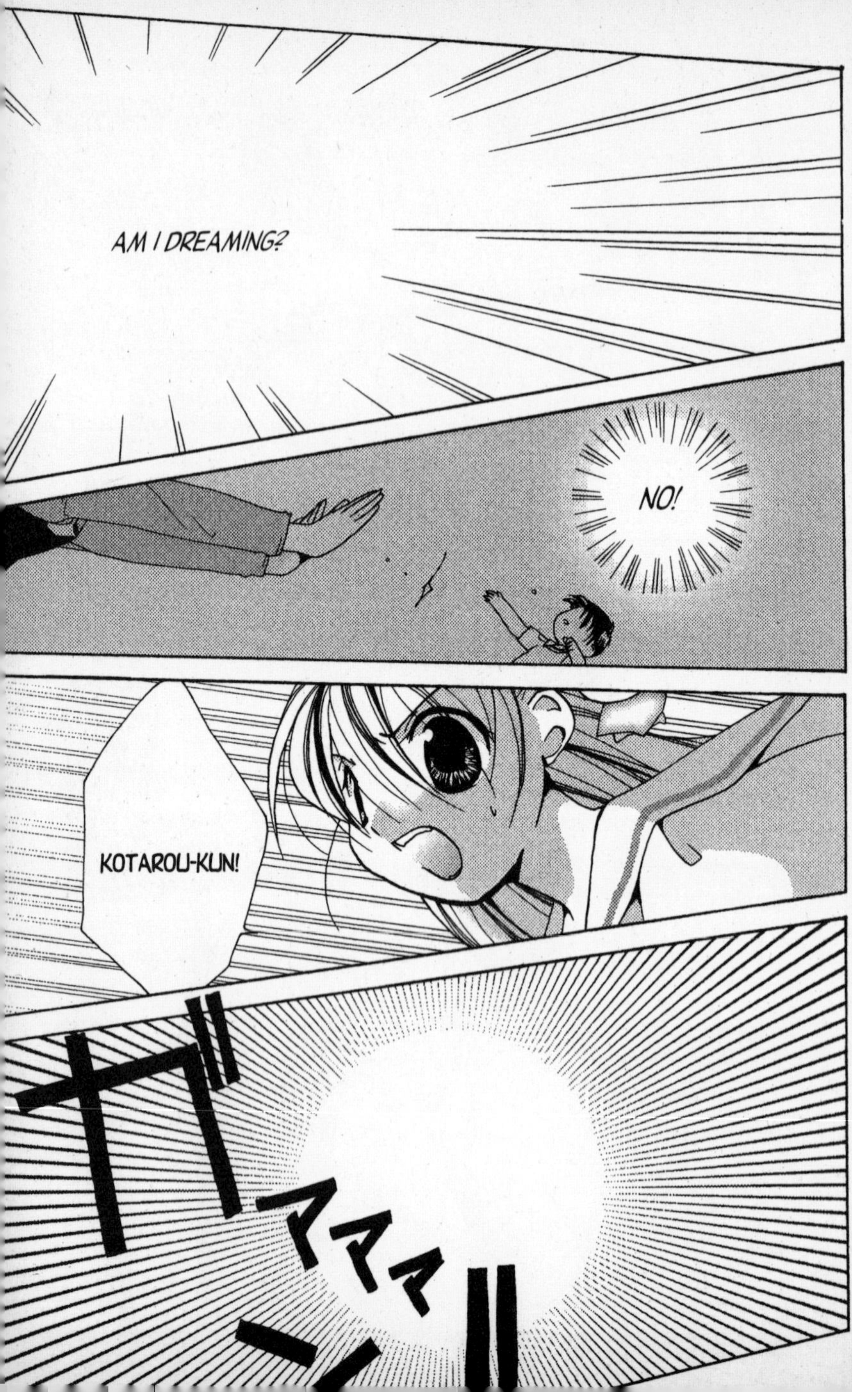
AM I DREAMING?
NO!
KOTAROU-KUN!

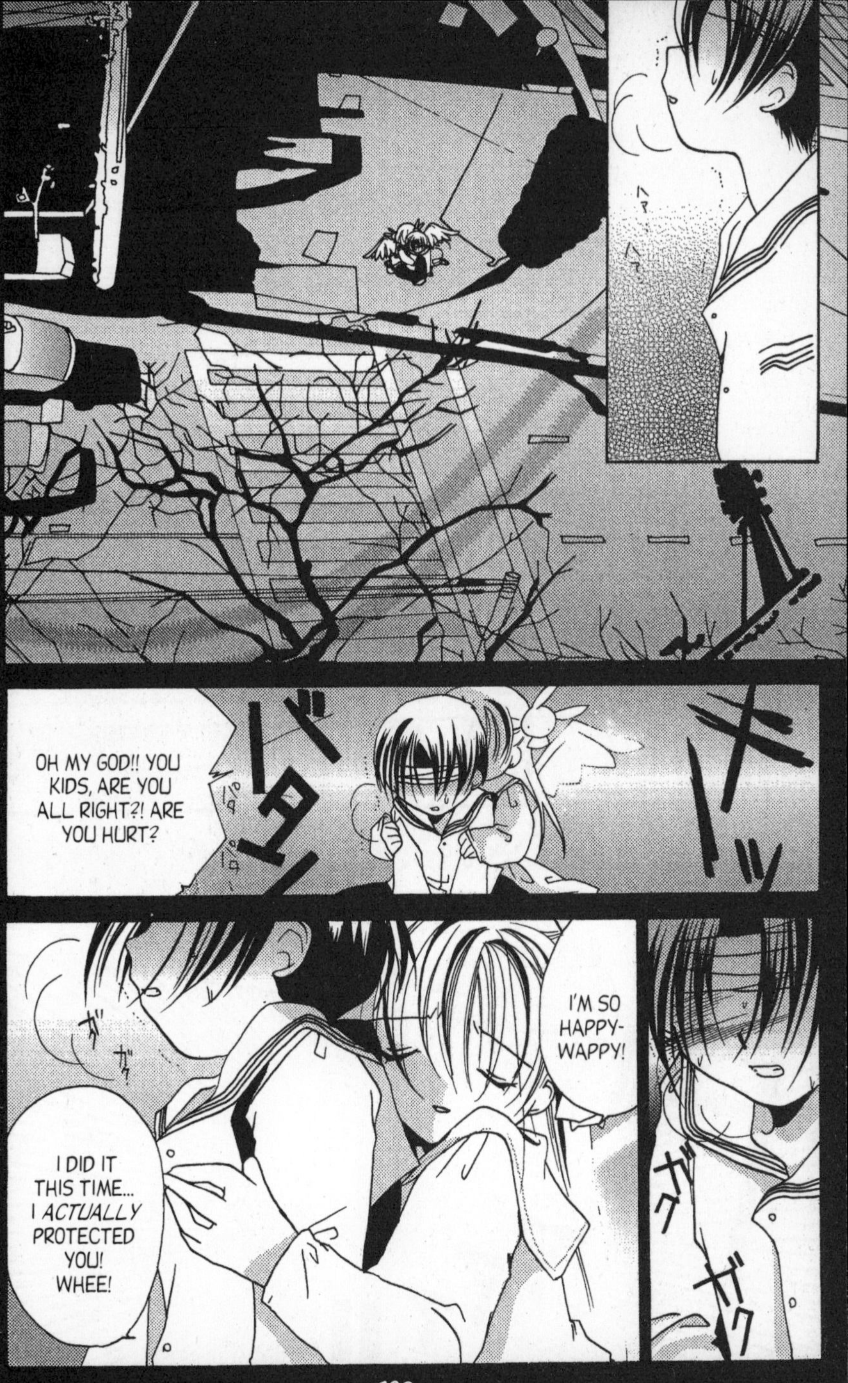
OH MY GOD!! YOU KIDS, ARE YOU ALL RIGHT?! ARE YOU HURT?
I'M SO HAPPY-WAPPY!
I DID IT THIS TIME... I *ACTUALLY* PROTECTED YOU! WHEE!

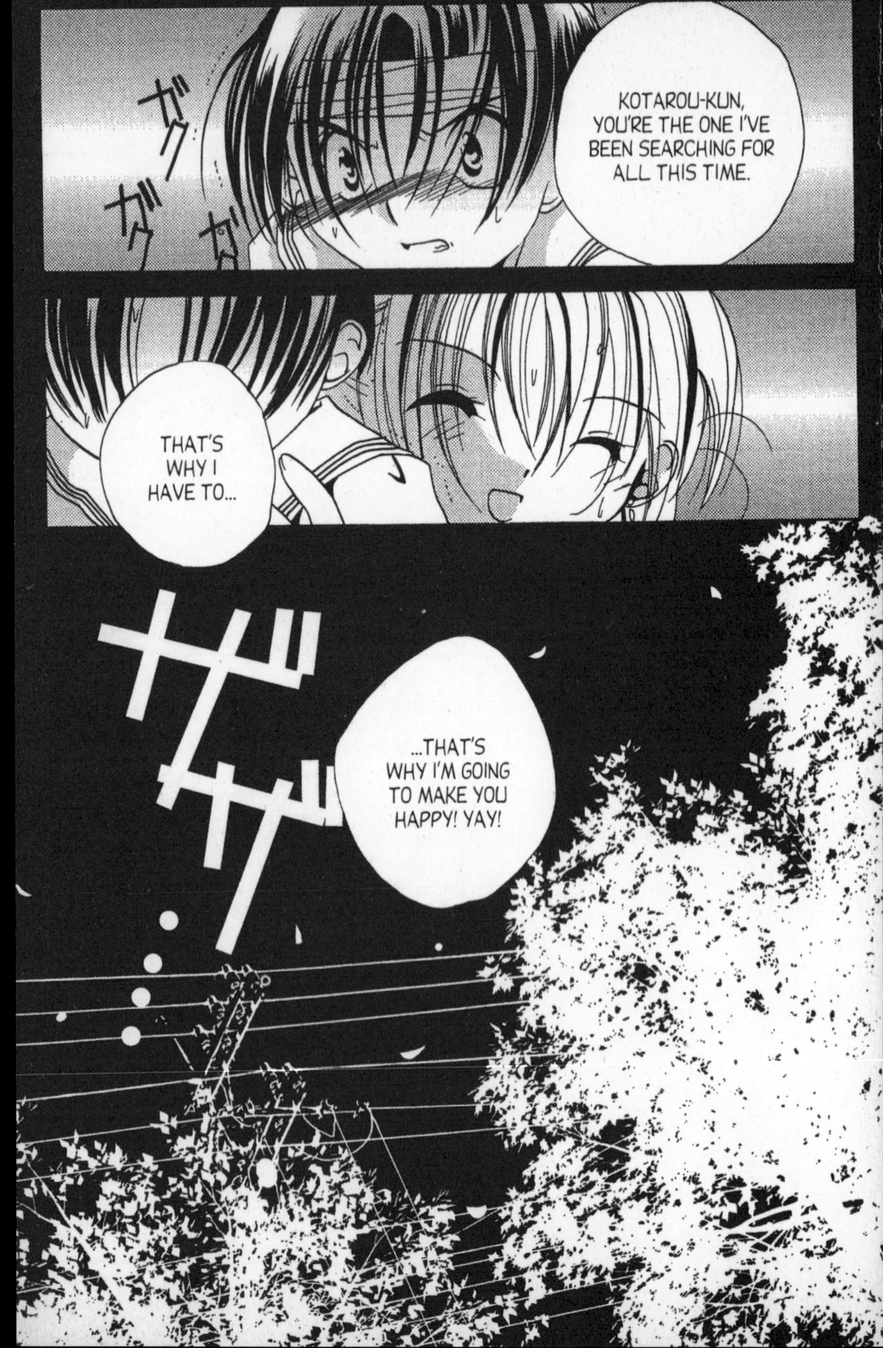
KOTAROU-KUN, YOU'RE THE ONE I'VE BEEN SEARCHING FOR ALL THIS TIME.
THAT'S WHY I HAVE TO...
...THAT'S WHY I'M GOING TO MAKE YOU HAPPY! YAY!

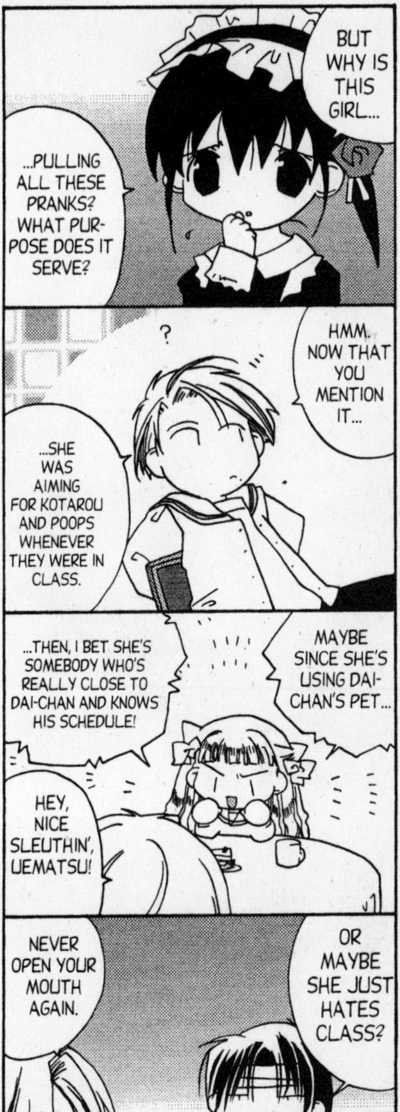

BUT WHY IS THIS GIRL...
...PULLING ALL THESE PRANKS? WHAT PURPOSE DOES IT SERVE?
HMM. NOW THAT YOU MENTION IT...
...SHE WAS AIMING FOR KOTAROU AND POOPS WHENEVER THEY WERE IN CLASS.
MAYBE SINCE SHE'S USING DAI-CHAN'S PET...
...THEN, I BET SHE'S SOMEBODY WHO'S REALLY CLOSE TO DAI-CHAN AND KNOWS HIS SCHEDULE!
HEY, NICE SLEUTHIN', UEMATSU!
OR MAYBE SHE JUST HATES CLASS?
NEVER OPEN YOUR MOUTH AGAIN.

Lesson 12

How to Cheer a Person Up

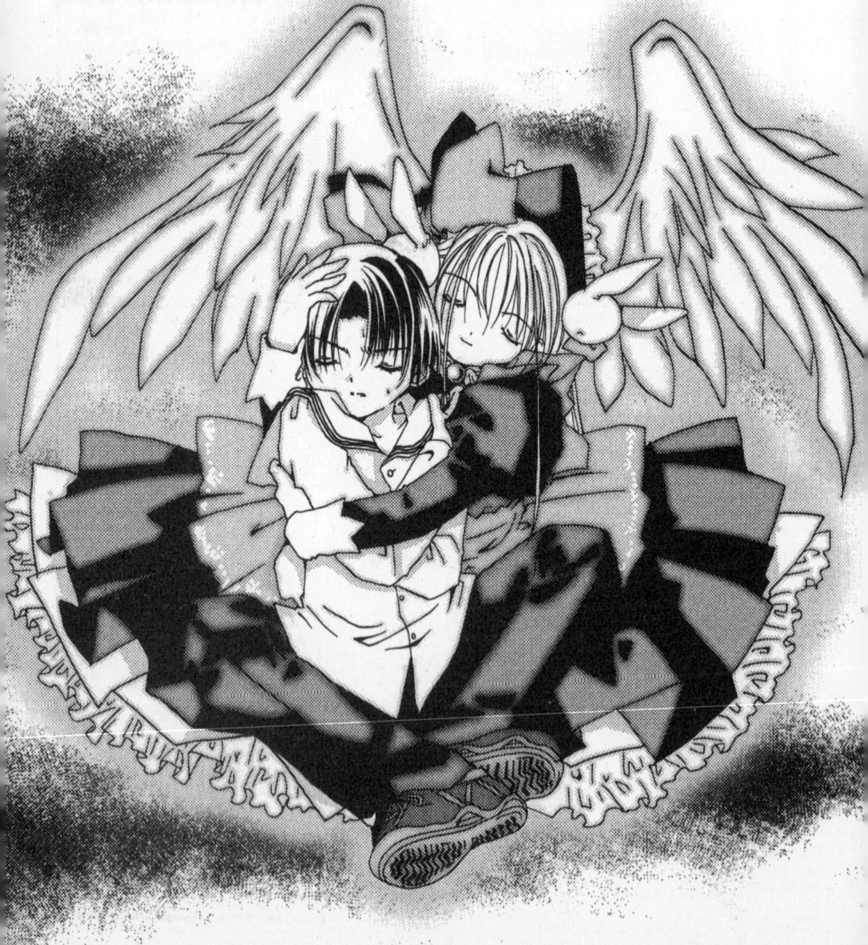

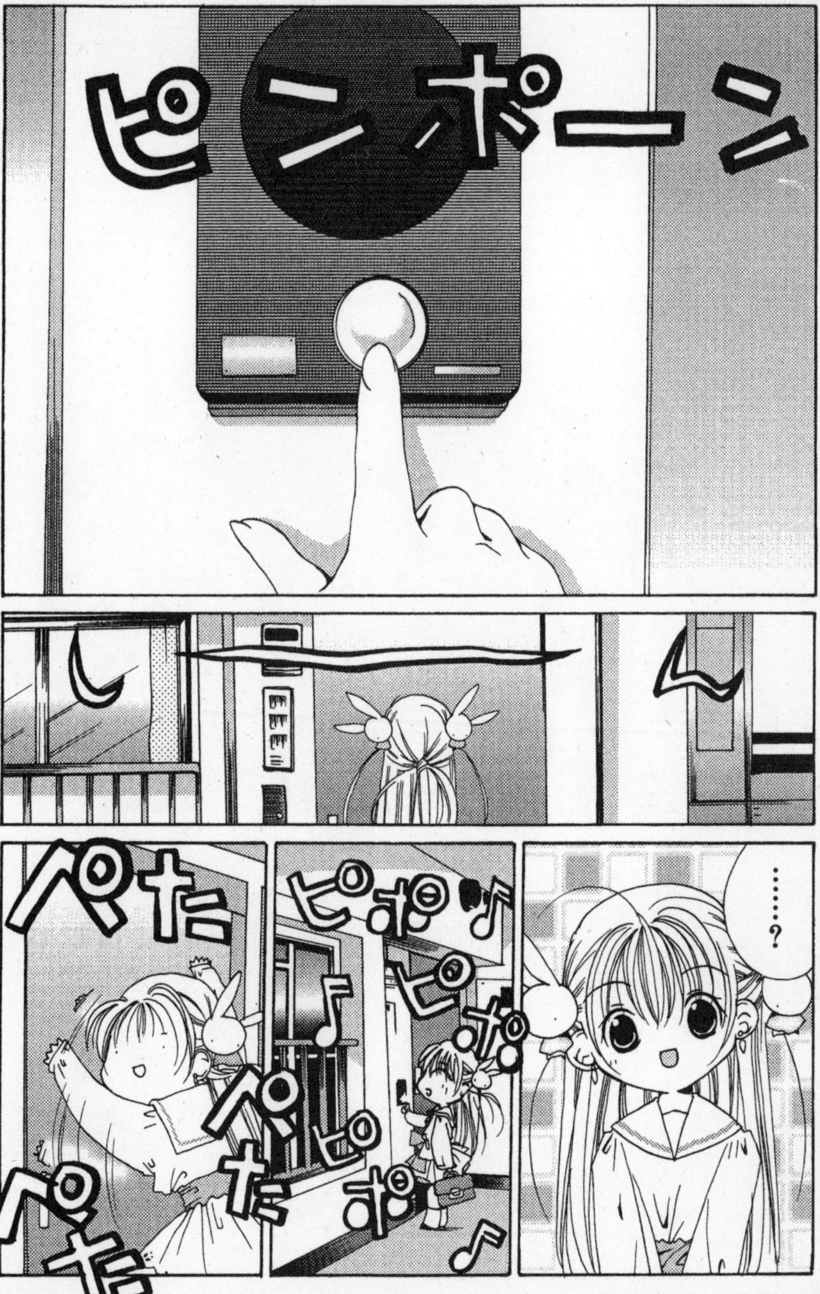
ピンポーン
し——ん
……?
ピポ♪
♪ピポ
ピポ♪
パた
パた
パた

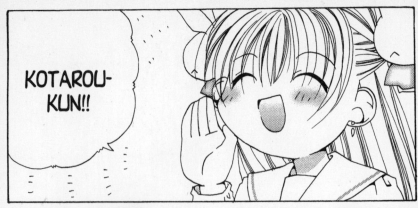

KOTAROU-
KUN!!

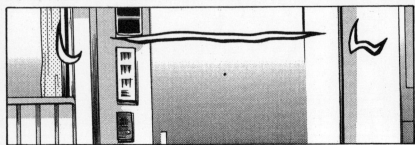

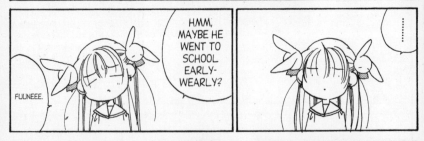

FUIINEEE.

HMM,
MAYBE HE
WENT TO
SCHOOL
EARLY-
WEARLY?

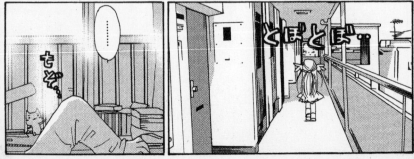

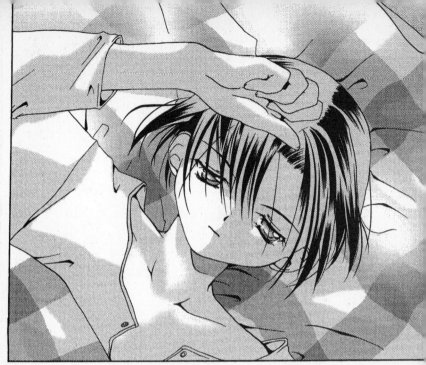

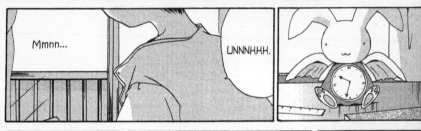

Mmnn...

UNNNHHH.

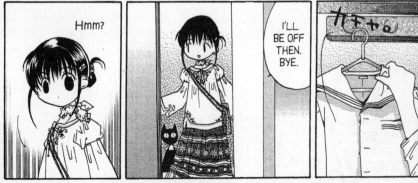

Hmm?

I'LL BE OFF THEN. BYE.

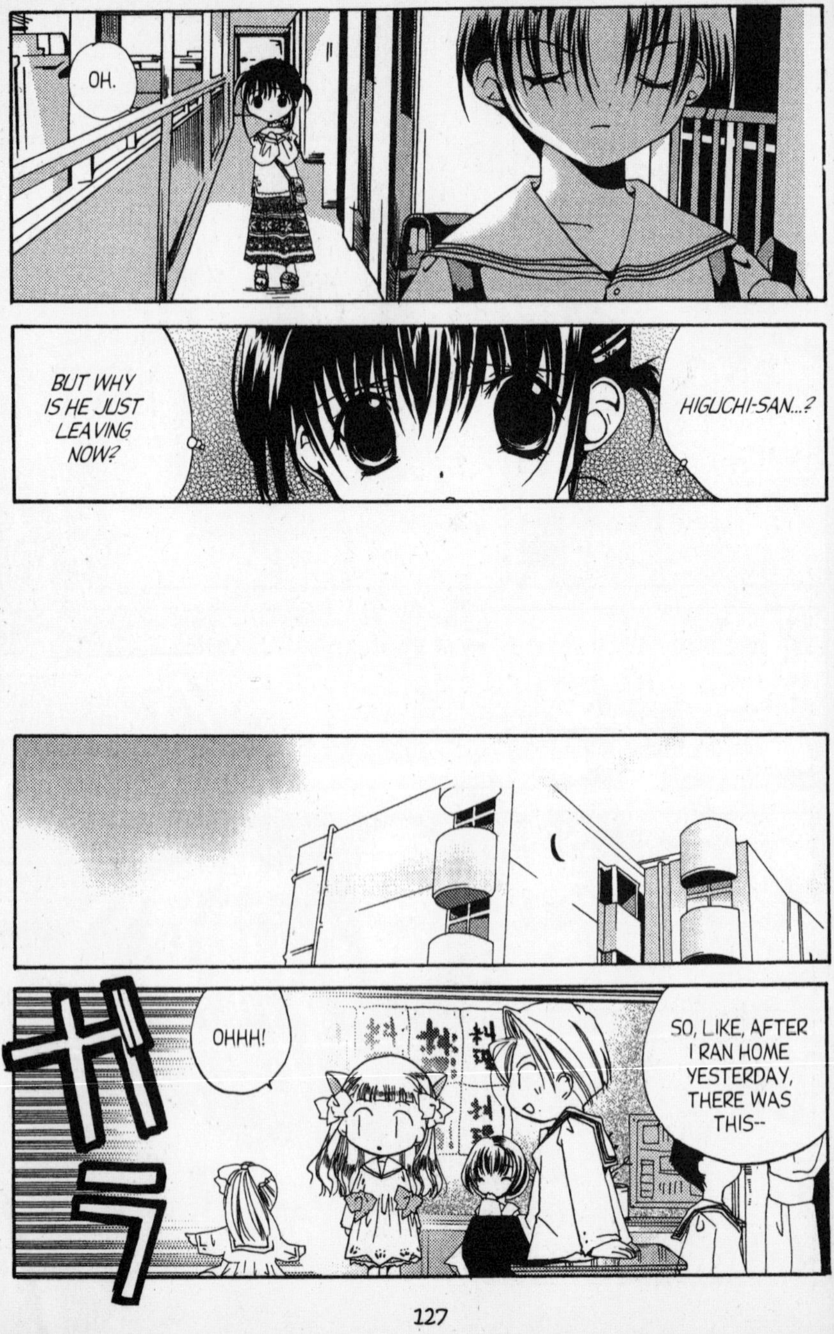
OH.
HIGUCHI-SAN...?
BUT WHY IS HE JUST LEAVING NOW?
SO, LIKE, AFTER I RAN HOME YESTERDAY, THERE WAS THIS--
OHHH!
ガラ

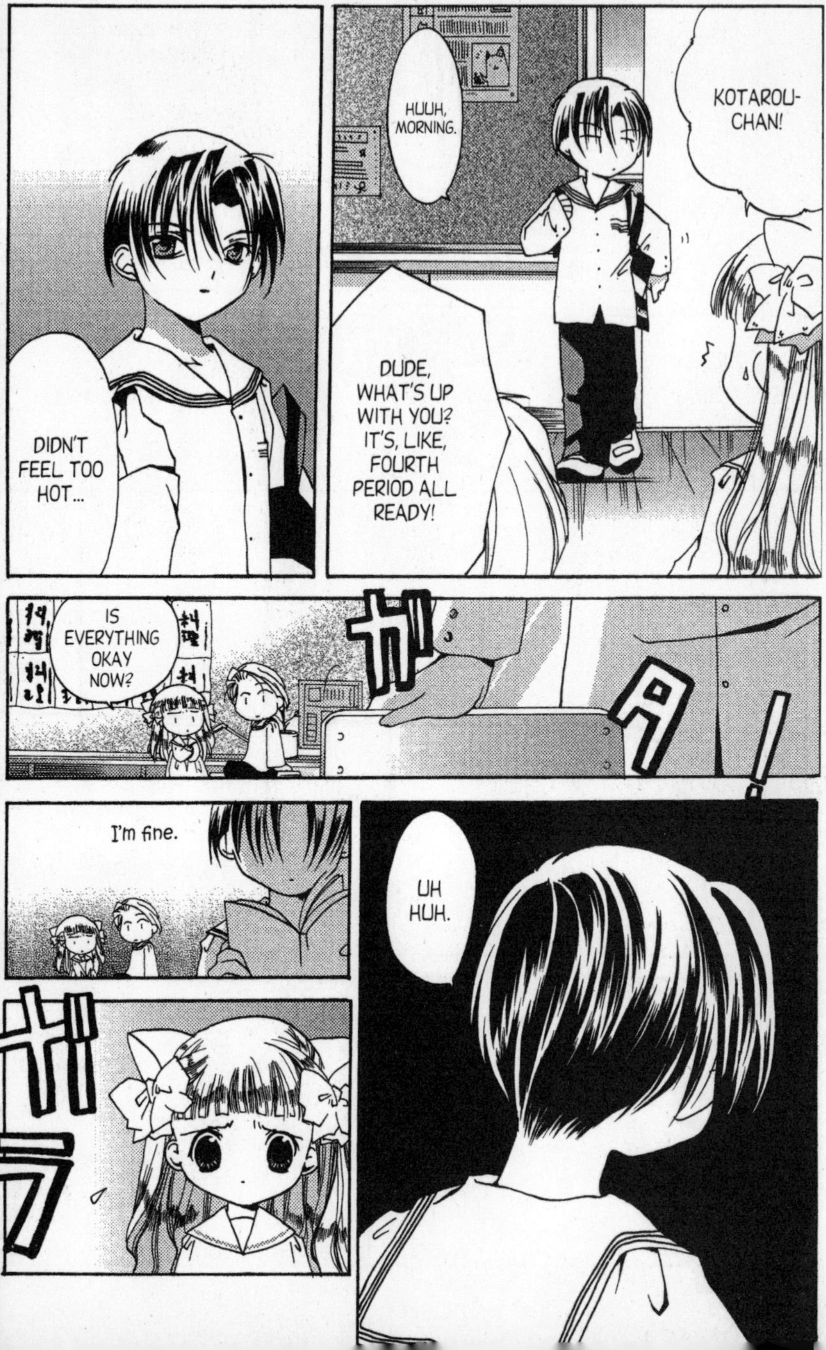
KOTAROU-CHAN!
HUUH, MORNING.
DUDE, WHAT'S UP WITH YOU? IT'S, LIKE, FOURTH PERIOD ALL READY!
DIDN'T FEEL TOO HOT...
ガタ!
IS EVERYTHING OKAY NOW?
UH HUH.
I'm fine.
ガラ

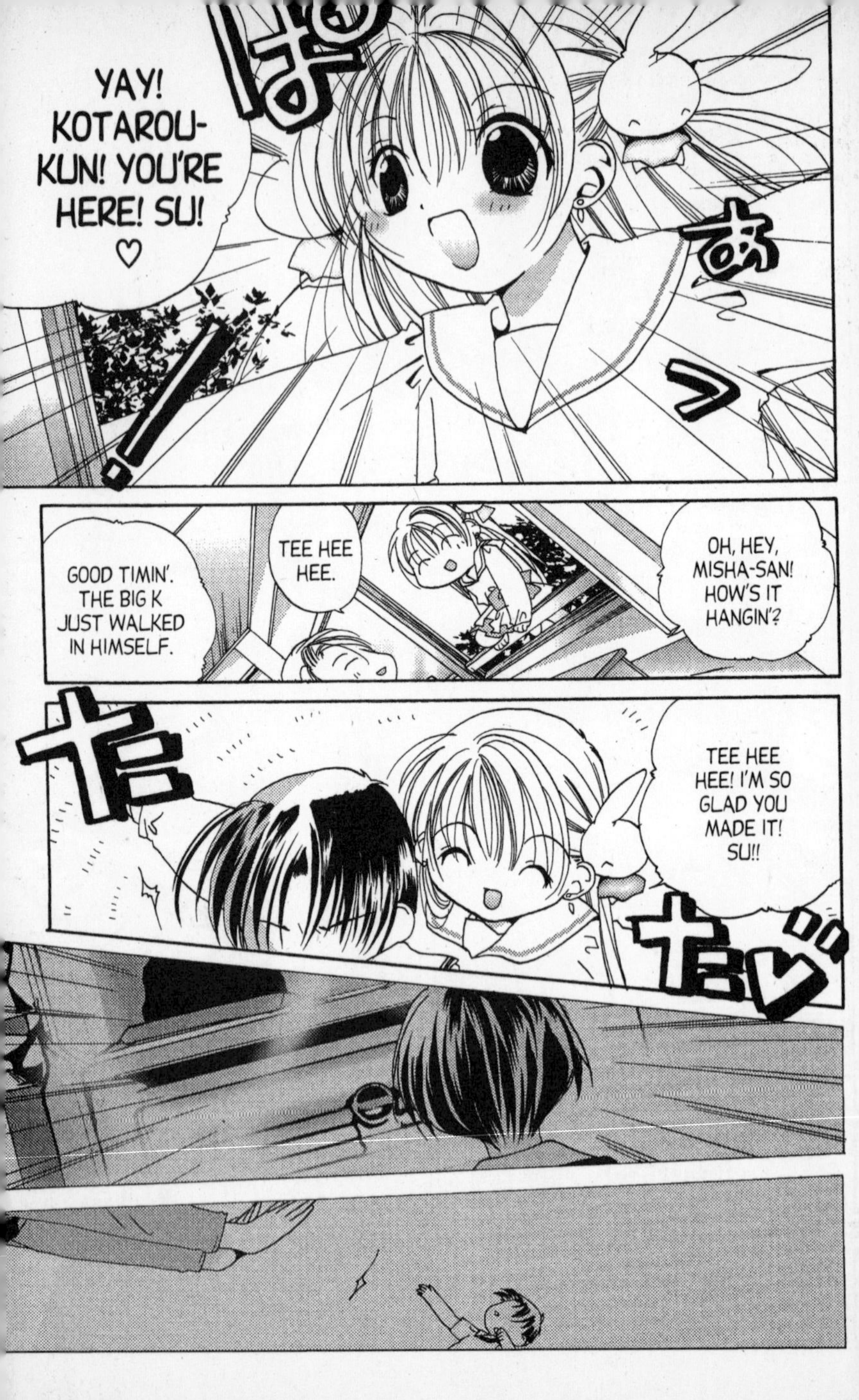
YAY! KOTAROU-KUN! YOU'RE HERE! SU! ♡
OH, HEY, MISHA-SAN! HOW'S IT HANGIN'?
TEE HEE HEE.
GOOD TIMIN'. THE BIG K JUST WALKED IN HIMSELF.
TEE HEE HEE! I'M SO GLAD YOU MADE IT! SU!!

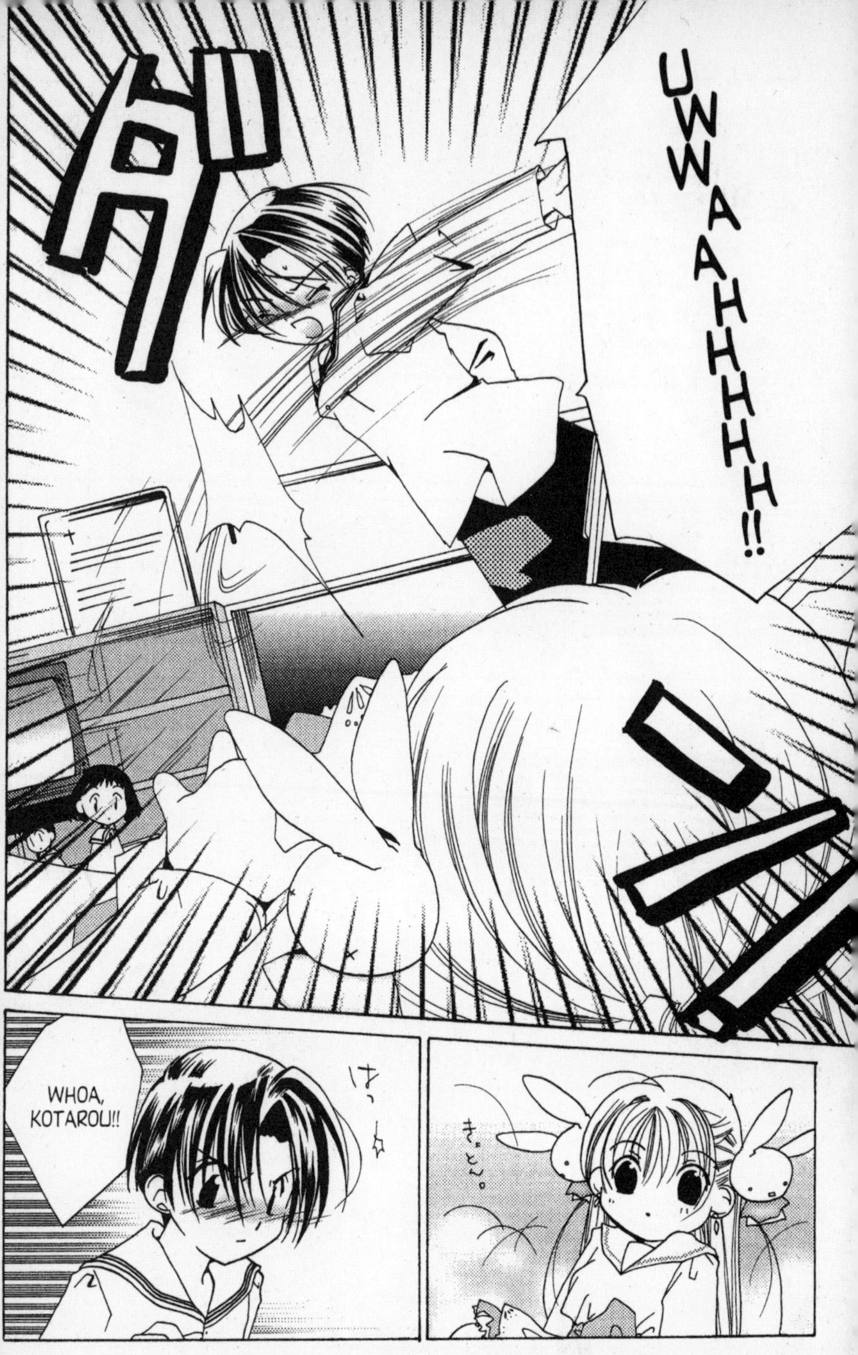

UWWAAHHHHH!!
きょとん。
はっ
WHOA, KOTAROU!!

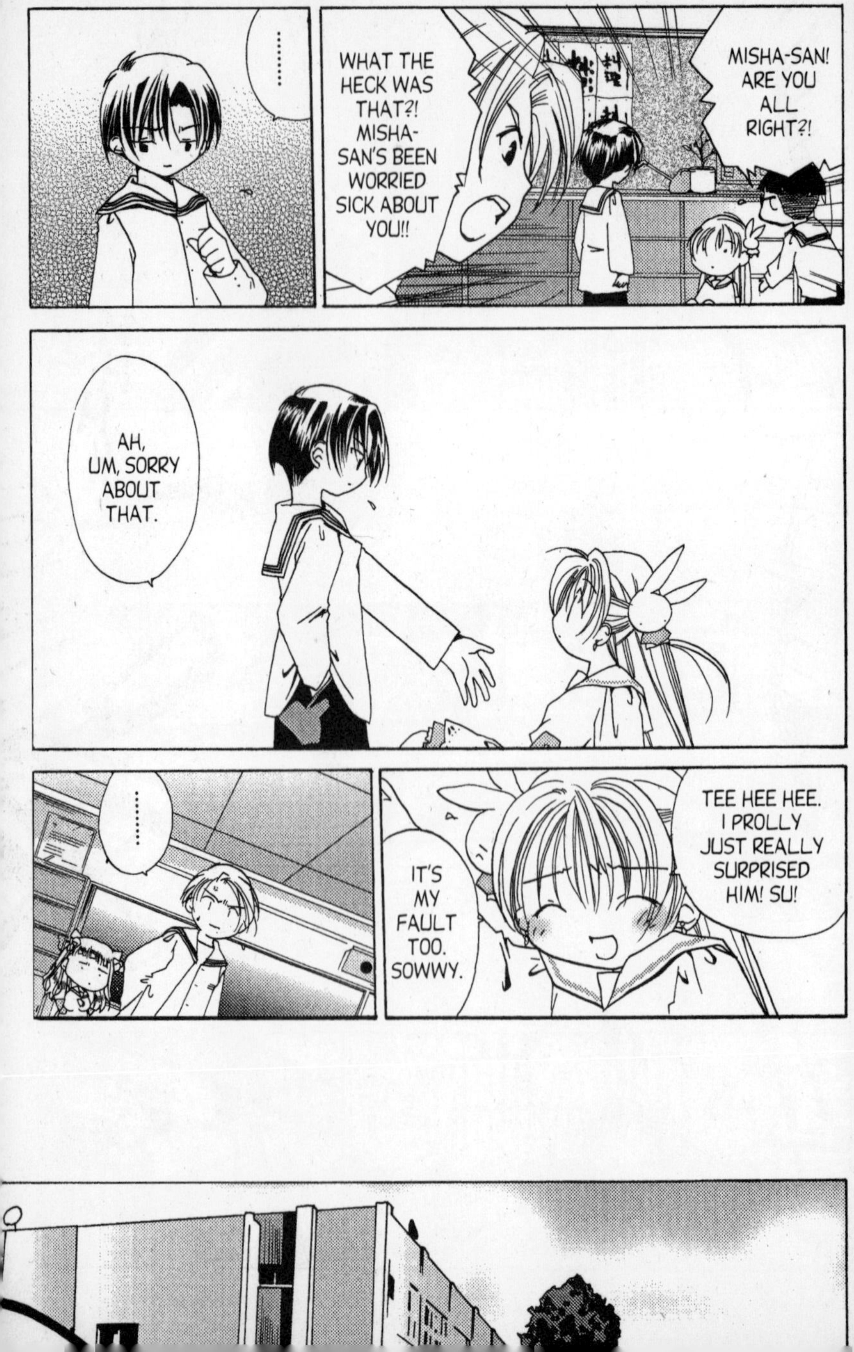
MISHA-SAN! ARE YOU ALL RIGHT?!
WHAT THE HECK WAS THAT?! MISHA-SAN'S BEEN WORRIED SICK ABOUT YOU!!
......
AH, UM, SORRY ABOUT THAT.
TEE HEE HEE. I PROLLY JUST REALLY SURPRISED HIM! SU!
IT'S MY FAULT TOO. SOWWY.
......

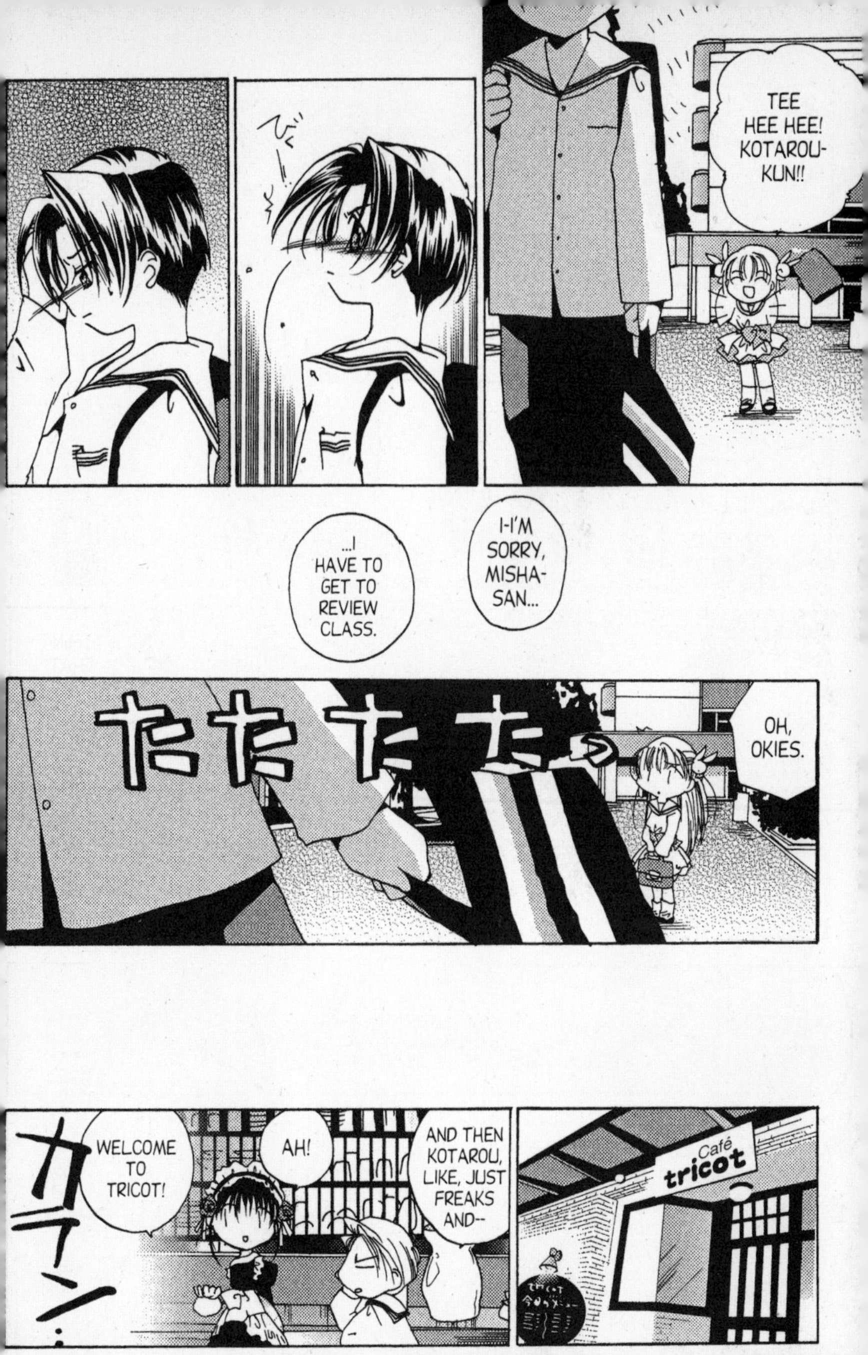
TEE HEE HEE! KOTAROU-KUN!!
I-I'M SORRY, MISHA-SAN...
...I HAVE TO GET TO REVIEW CLASS.
OH, OKIES.
たたたたっ
Café tricot
AND THEN KOTAROU, LIKE, JUST FREAKS AND--
AH!
WELCOME TO TRICOT!
カラン…

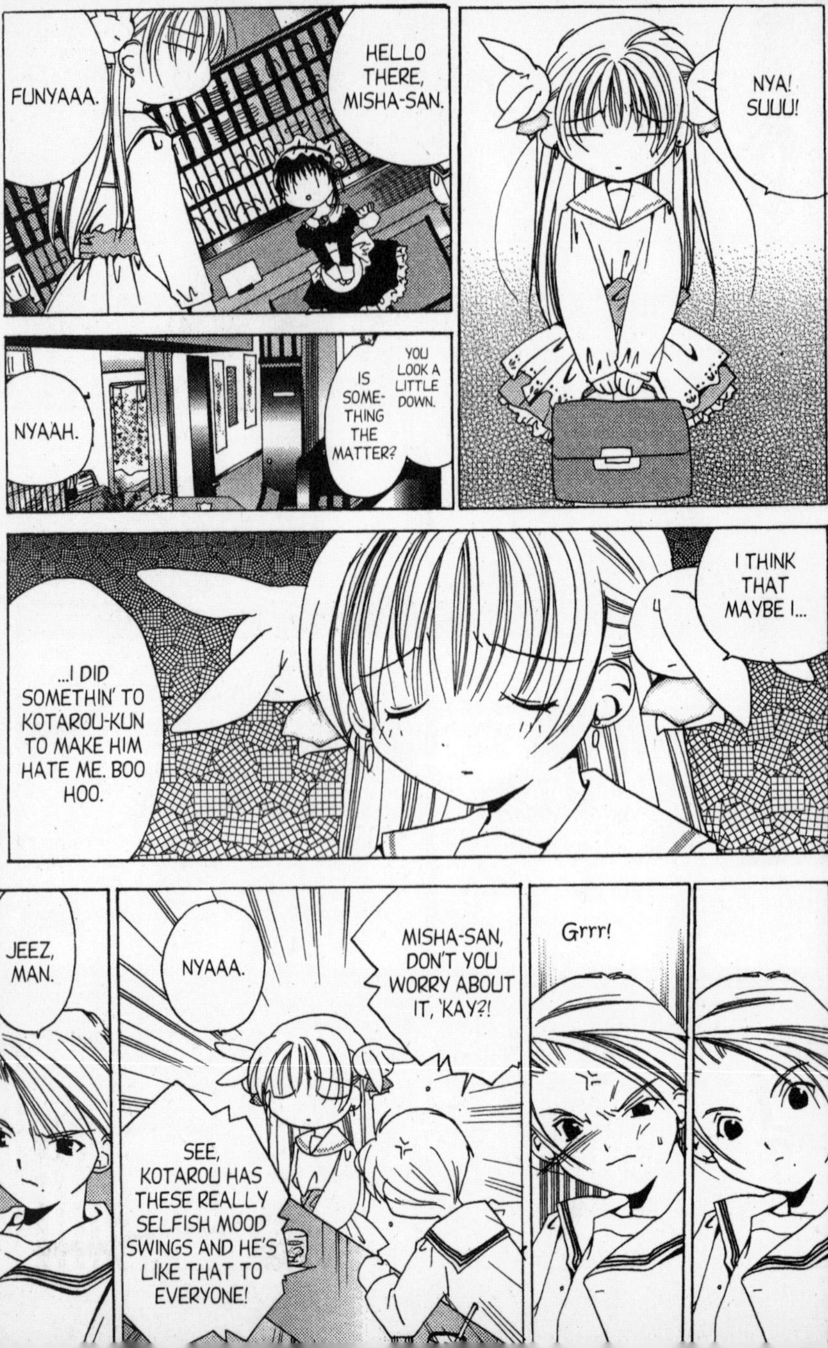
NYA! SUUU!
HELLO THERE, MISHA-SAN.
FUNYAAA.
YOU LOOK A LITTLE DOWN.
IS SOMETHING THE MATTER?
NYAAH.
I THINK THAT MAYBE I...
...I DID SOMETHIN' TO KOTAROU-KUN TO MAKE HIM HATE ME. BOO HOO.
Grrr!
MISHA-SAN, DON'T YOU WORRY ABOUT IT, 'KAY?!
NYAAA.
SEE, KOTAROU HAS THESE REALLY SELFISH MOOD SWINGS AND HE'S LIKE THAT TO EVERYONE!
JEEZ, MAN.

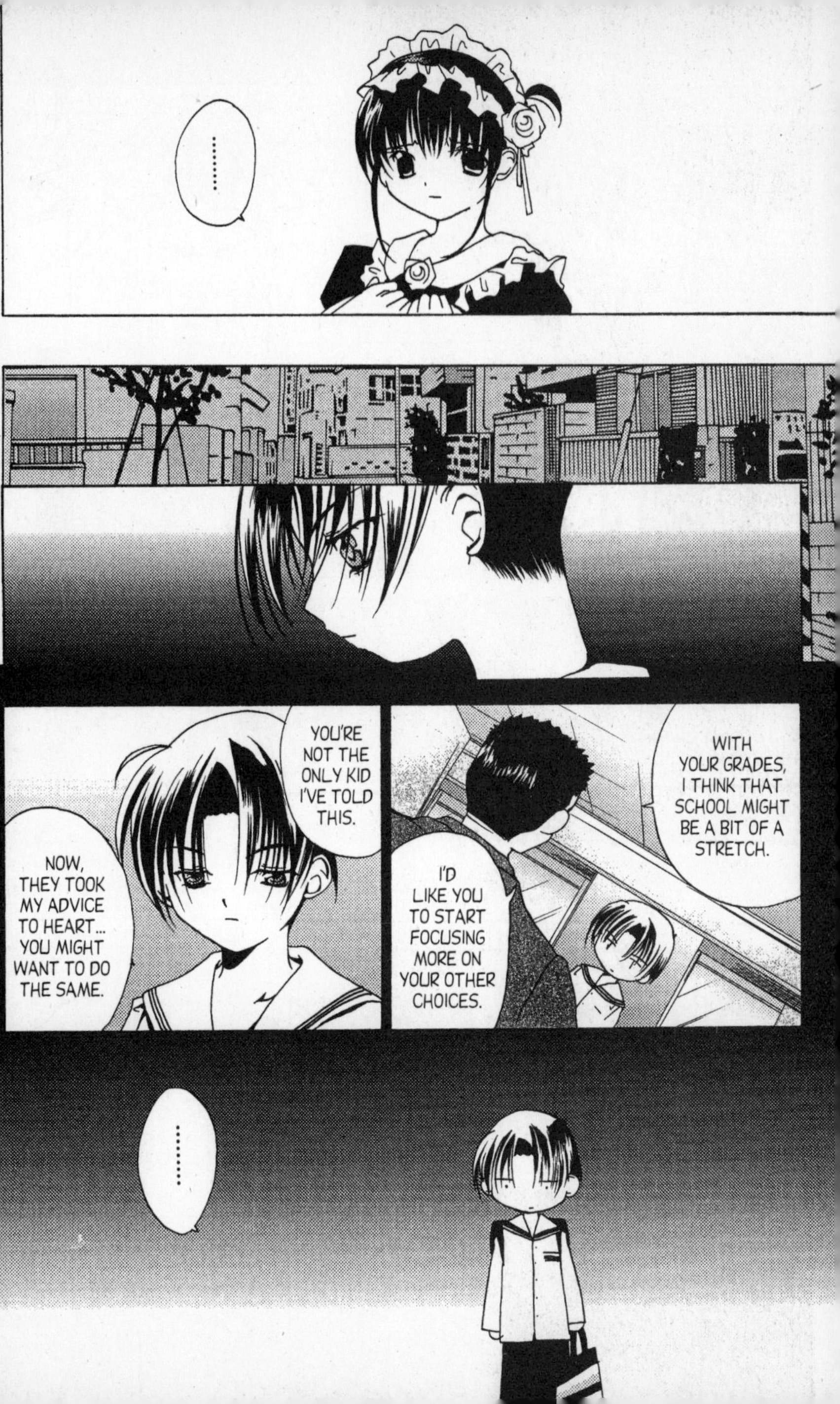
......
WITH YOUR GRADES, I THINK THAT SCHOOL MIGHT BE A BIT OF A STRETCH.
I'D LIKE YOU TO START FOCUSING MORE ON YOUR OTHER CHOICES.
YOU'RE NOT THE ONLY KID I'VE TOLD THIS.
NOW, THEY TOOK MY ADVICE TO HEART... YOU MIGHT WANT TO DO THE SAME.
......

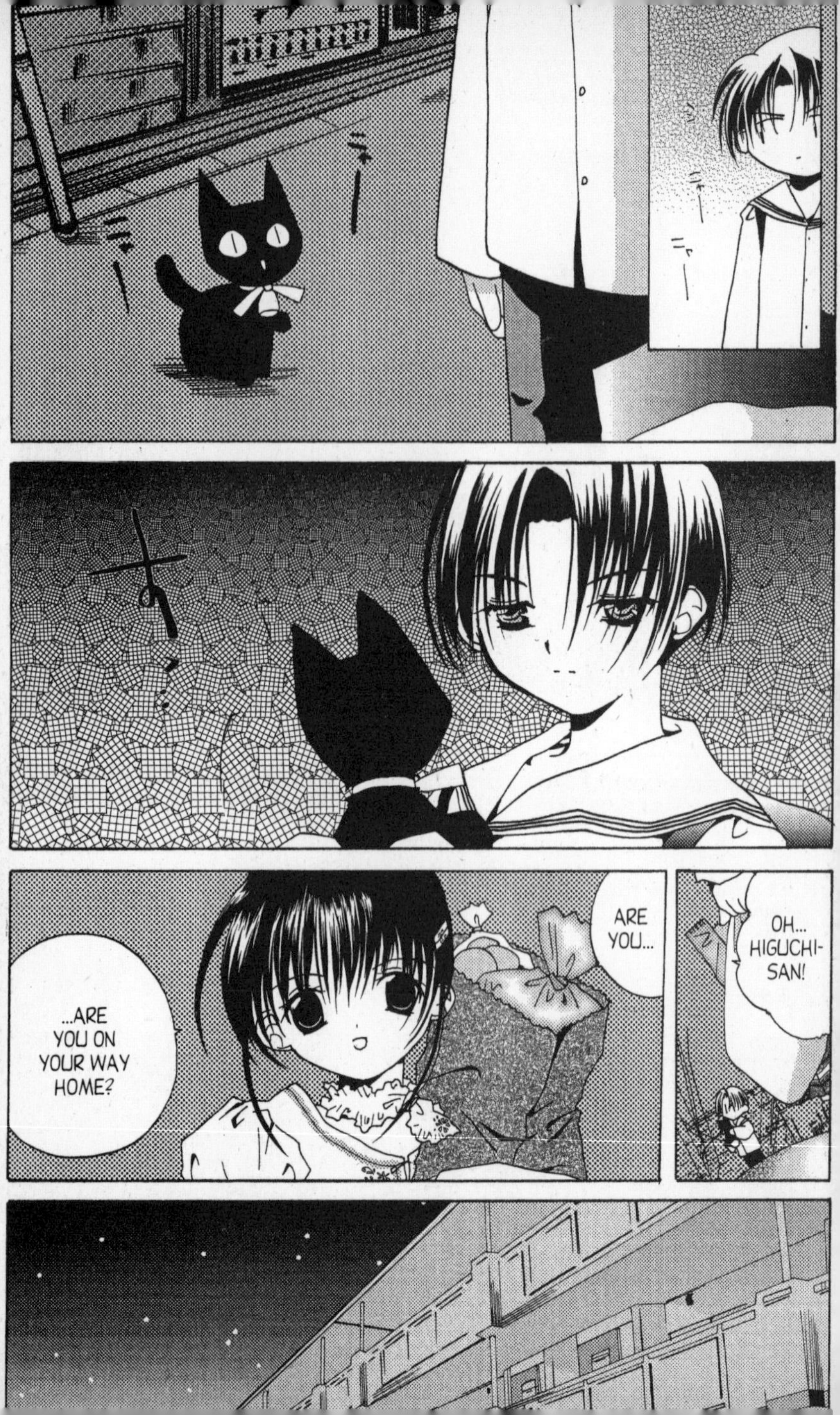
OH... HIGUCHI-SAN!
ARE YOU...
...ARE YOU ON YOUR WAY HOME?

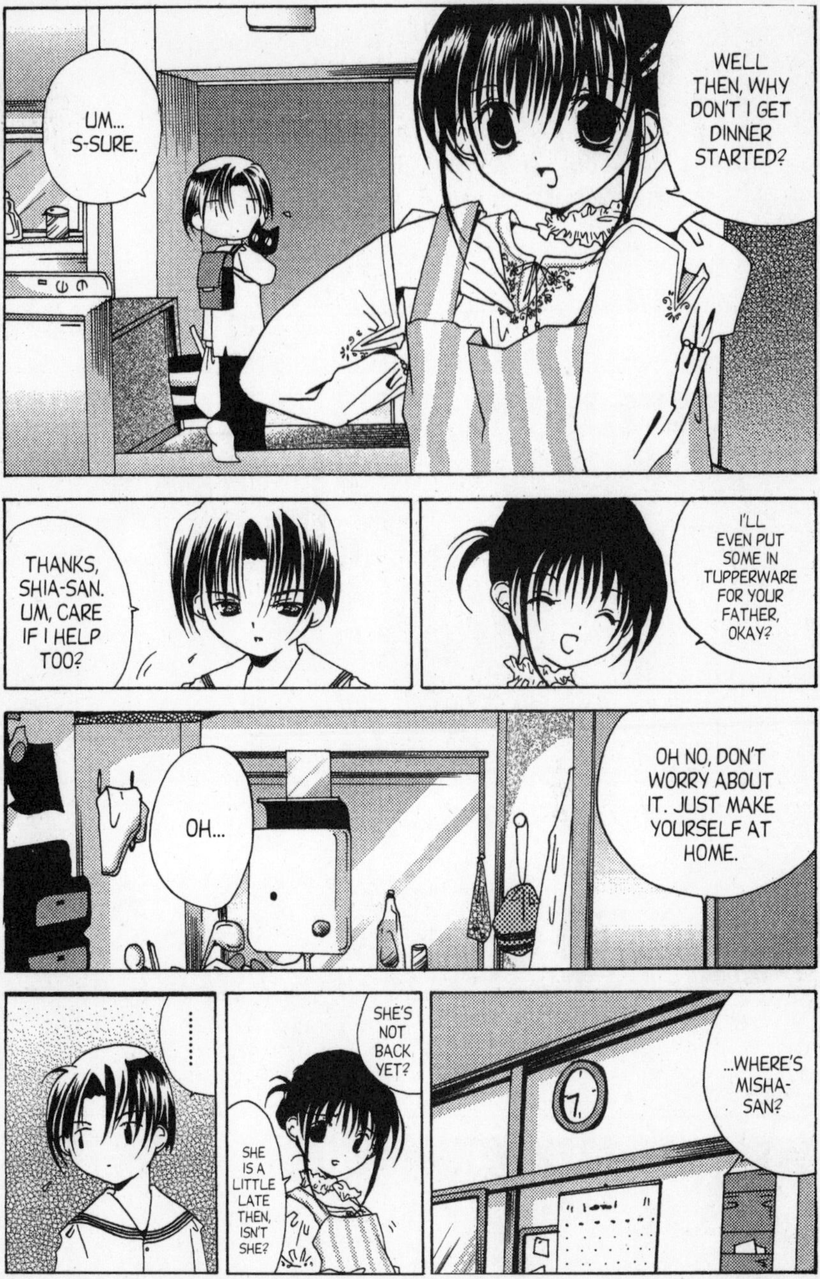
WELL THEN, WHY DON'T I GET DINNER STARTED?
UM... S-SURE.
I'LL EVEN PUT SOME IN TUPPERWARE FOR YOUR FATHER, OKAY?
THANKS, SHIA-SAN. UM, CARE IF I HELP TOO?
OH NO, DON'T WORRY ABOUT IT. JUST MAKE YOURSELF AT HOME.
OH...
...WHERE'S MISHA-SAN?
SHE'S NOT BACK YET?
SHE IS A LITTLE LATE THEN, ISN'T SHE?
....

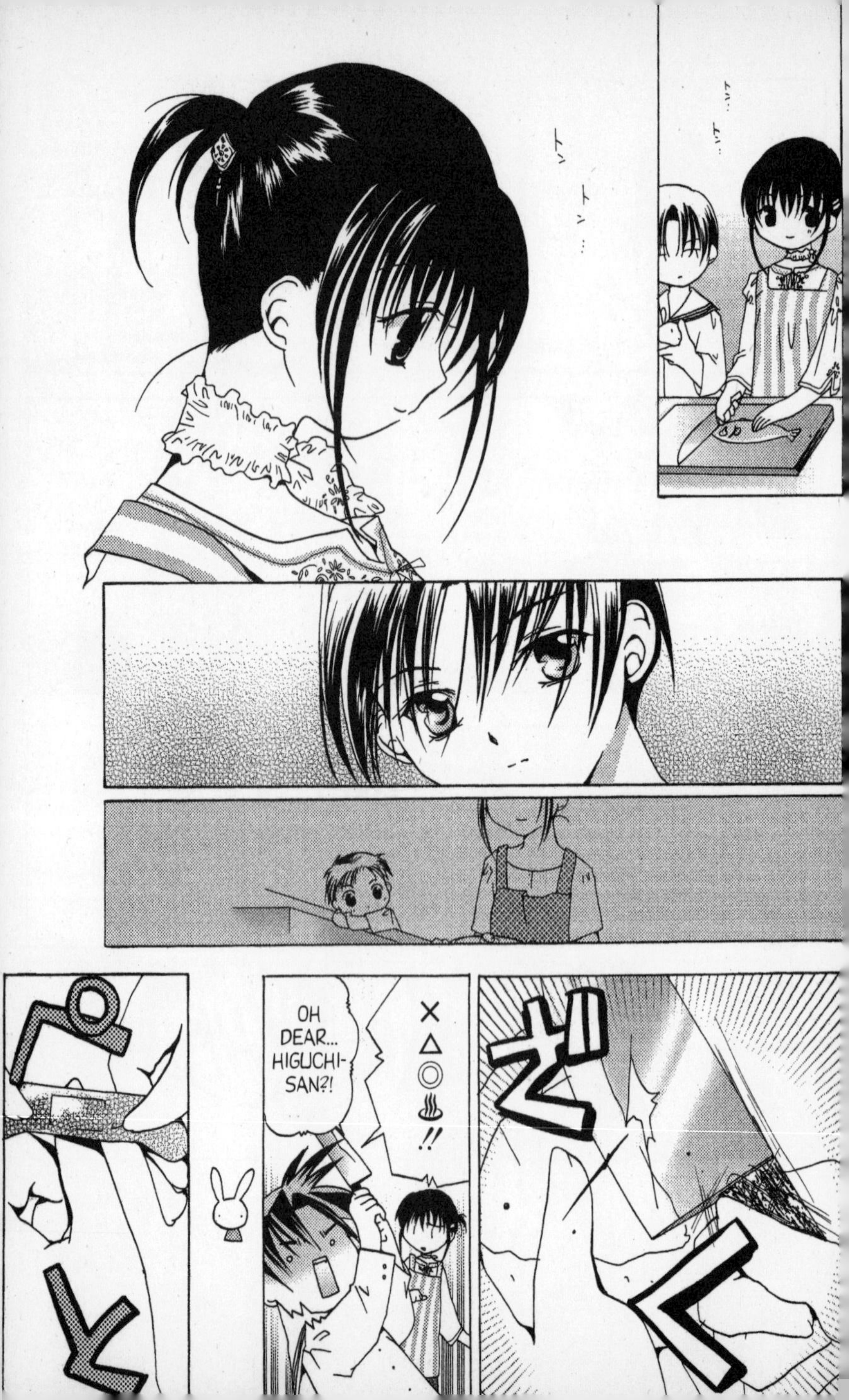
トントン…
ざく
OH DEAR... HIGUCHI-SAN?!
×△◎♨!!
ぺと

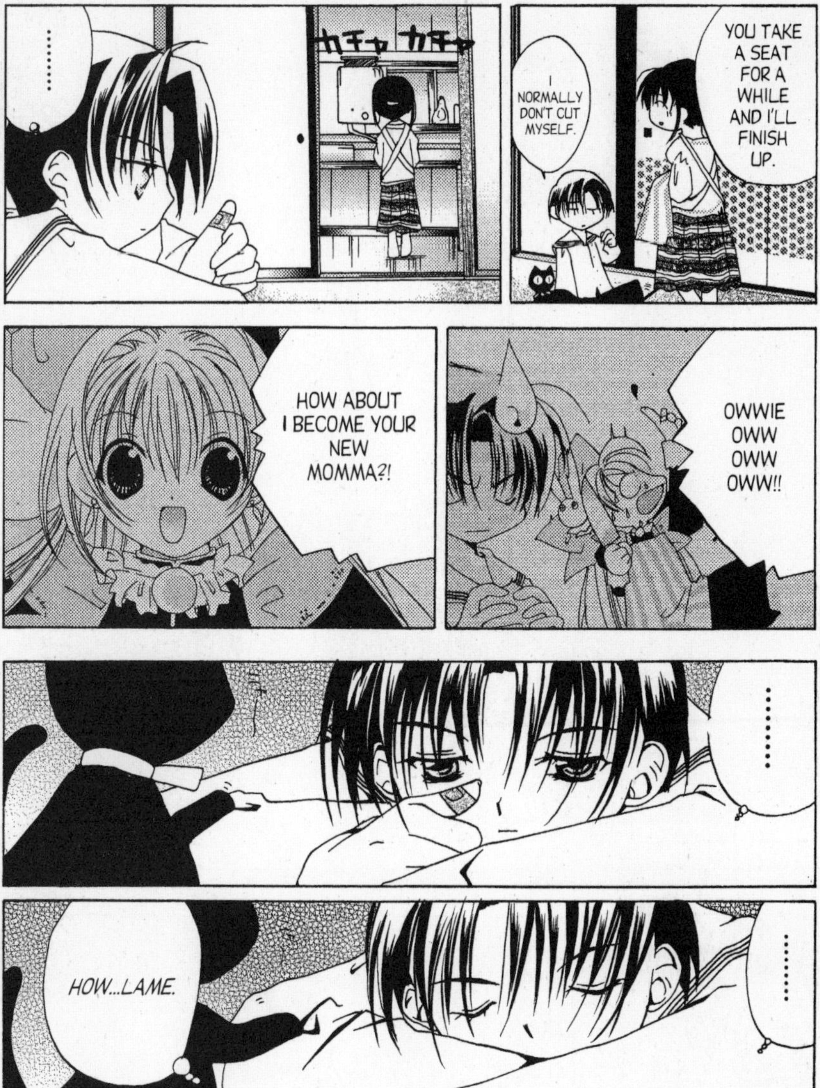
YOU TAKE A SEAT FOR A WHILE AND I'LL FINISH UP.
I NORMALLY DON'T CUT MYSELF.
カチャ カチャ
....
OWWIE OWW OWW OWW!!
HOW ABOUT I BECOME YOUR NEW MOMMA?!
....
....
HOW...LAME.

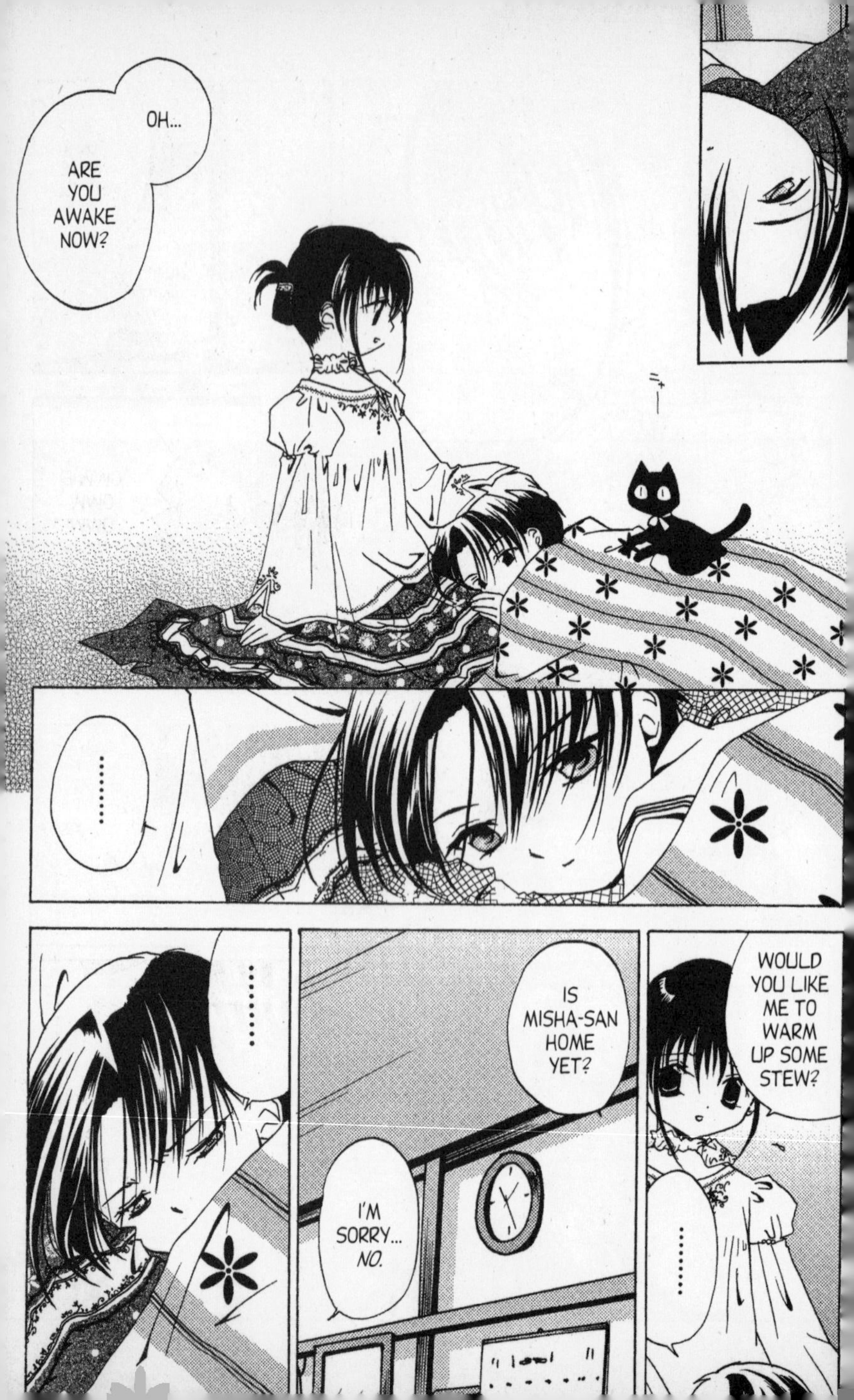
OH...
ARE YOU AWAKE NOW?
......
WOULD YOU LIKE ME TO WARM UP SOME STEW?
......
IS MISHA-SAN HOME YET?
I'M SORRY... NO.
......

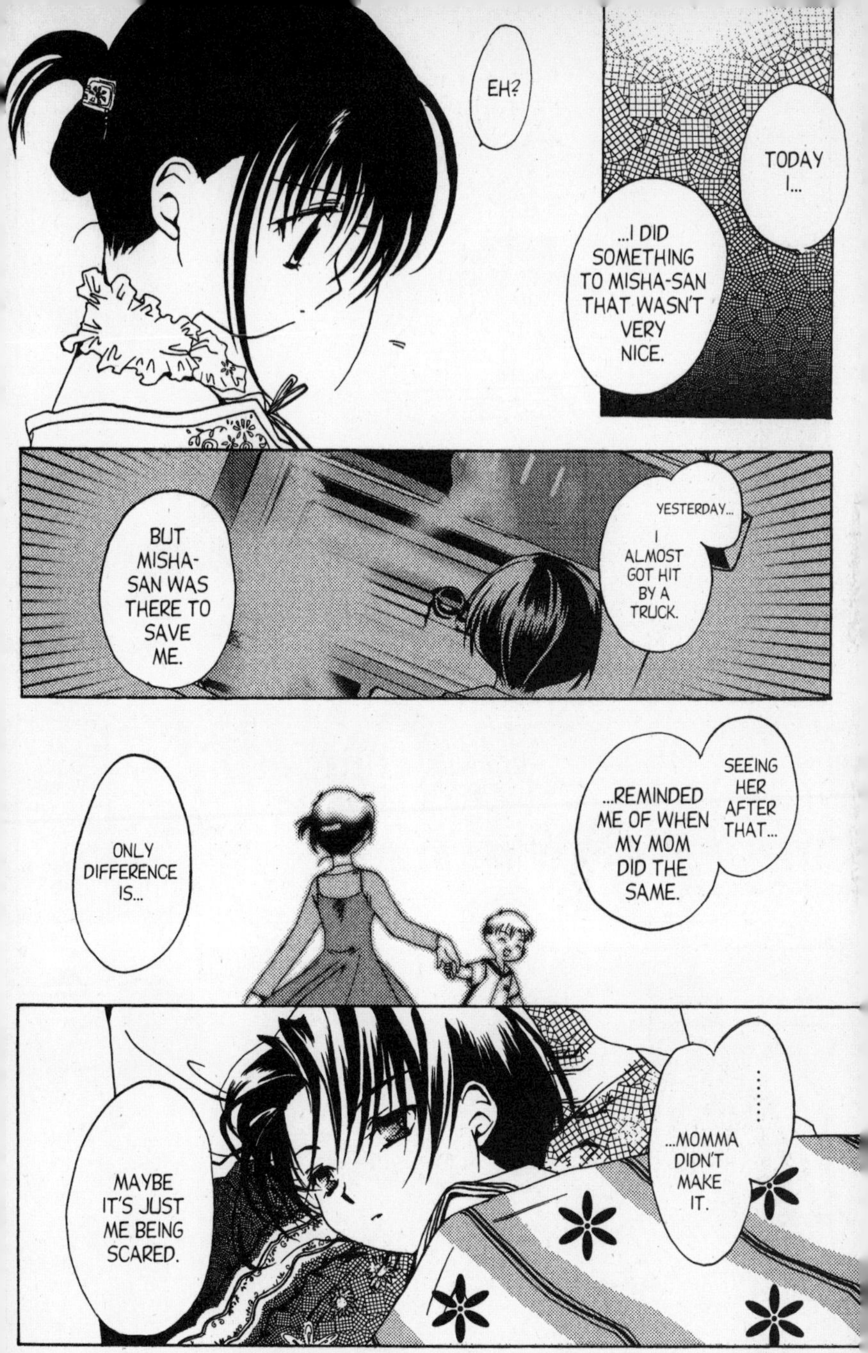
TODAY I...
...I DID SOMETHING TO MISHA-SAN THAT WASN'T VERY NICE.
EH?
YESTERDAY... I ALMOST GOT HIT BY A TRUCK.
BUT MISHA-SAN WAS THERE TO SAVE ME.
SEEING HER AFTER THAT...
...REMINDED ME OF WHEN MY MOM DID THE SAME.
ONLY DIFFERENCE IS...
......
...MOMMA DIDN'T MAKE IT.
MAYBE IT'S JUST ME BEING SCARED.

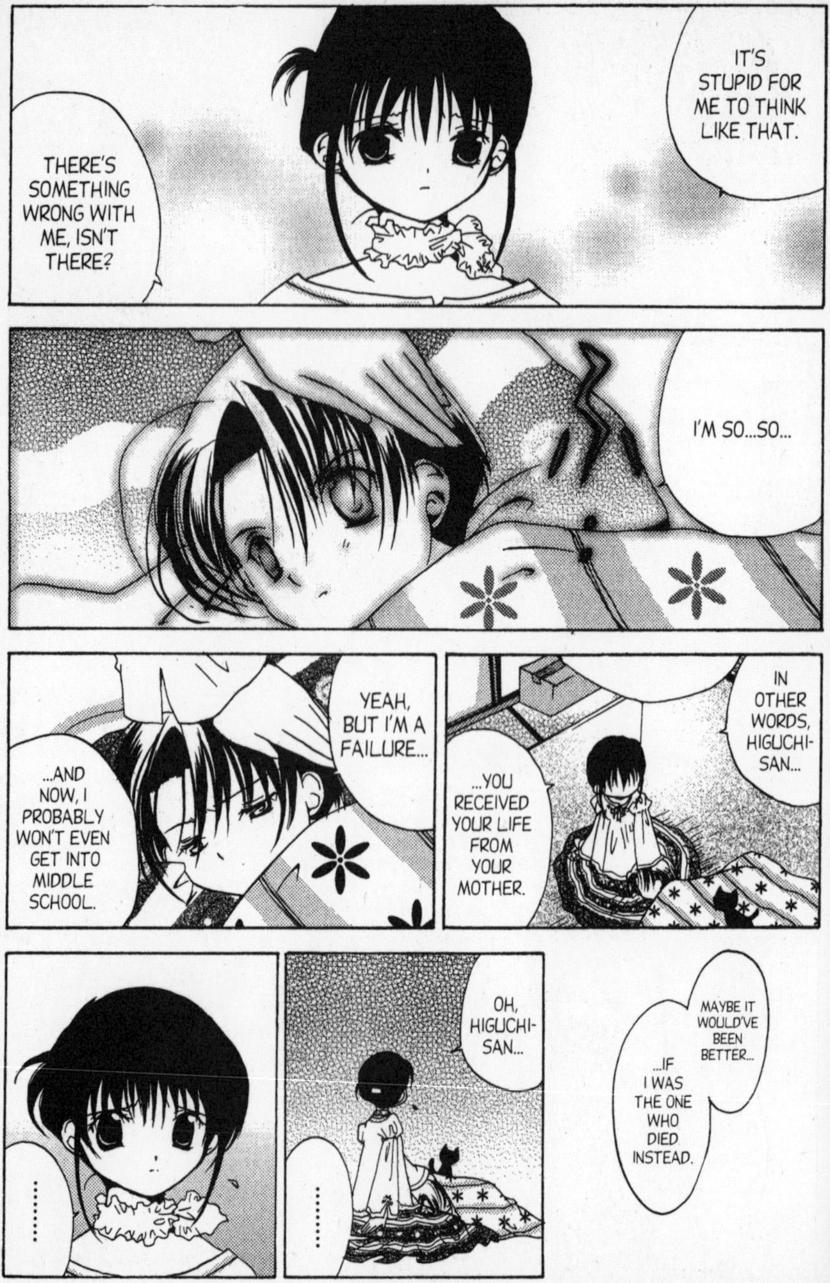
IT'S STUPID FOR ME TO THINK LIKE THAT.
THERE'S SOMETHING WRONG WITH ME, ISN'T THERE?
I'M SO...SO...
IN OTHER WORDS, HIGUCHI-SAN...
...YOU RECEIVED YOUR LIFE FROM YOUR MOTHER.
YEAH, BUT I'M A FAILURE...
...AND NOW, I PROBABLY WON'T EVEN GET INTO MIDDLE SCHOOL.
MAYBE IT WOULD'VE BEEN BETTER...
...IF I WAS THE ONE WHO DIED INSTEAD.
OH, HIGUCHI-SAN...
......
......

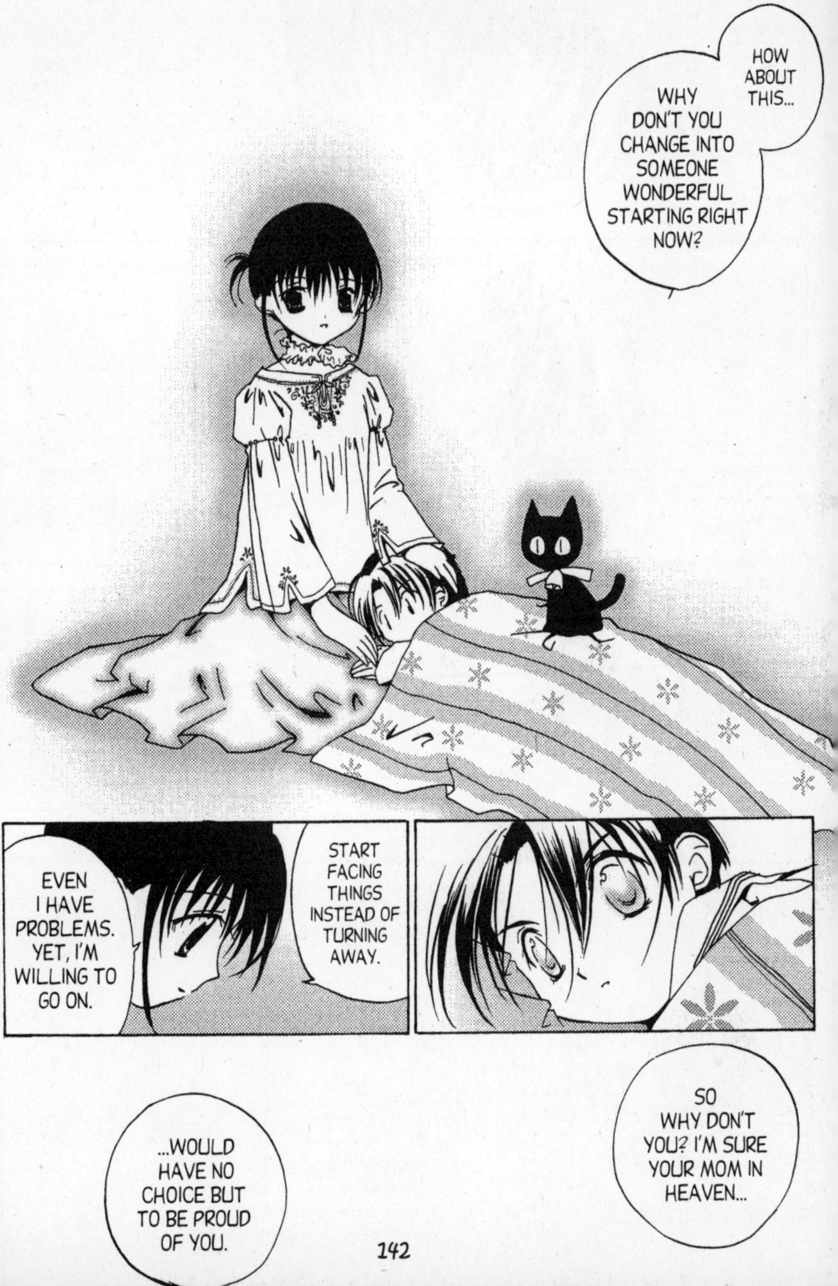
HOW ABOUT THIS...
WHY DON'T YOU CHANGE INTO SOMEONE WONDERFUL STARTING RIGHT NOW?
START FACING THINGS INSTEAD OF TURNING AWAY.
EVEN I HAVE PROBLEMS. YET, I'M WILLING TO GO ON.
SO WHY DON'T YOU? I'M SURE YOUR MOM IN HEAVEN...
...WOULD HAVE NO CHOICE BUT TO BE PROUD OF YOU.

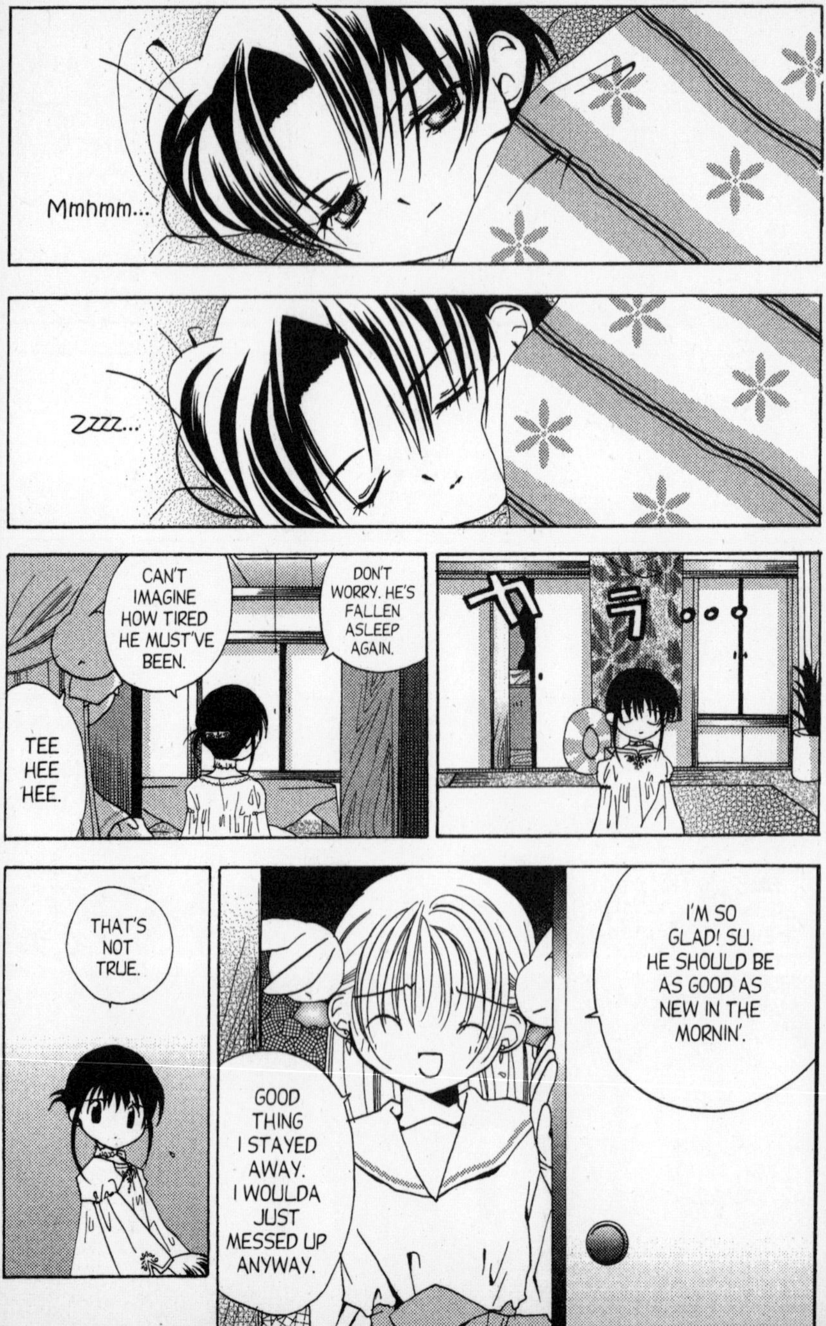
Mmhmm...
ZZZZ...
カラ
...
DON'T WORRY. HE'S FALLEN ASLEEP AGAIN.
CAN'T IMAGINE HOW TIRED HE MUST'VE BEEN.
TEE HEE HEE.
I'M SO GLAD! SU. HE SHOULD BE AS GOOD AS NEW IN THE MORNIN'.
GOOD THING I STAYED AWAY. I WOULDA JUST MESSED UP ANYWAY.
THAT'S NOT TRUE.

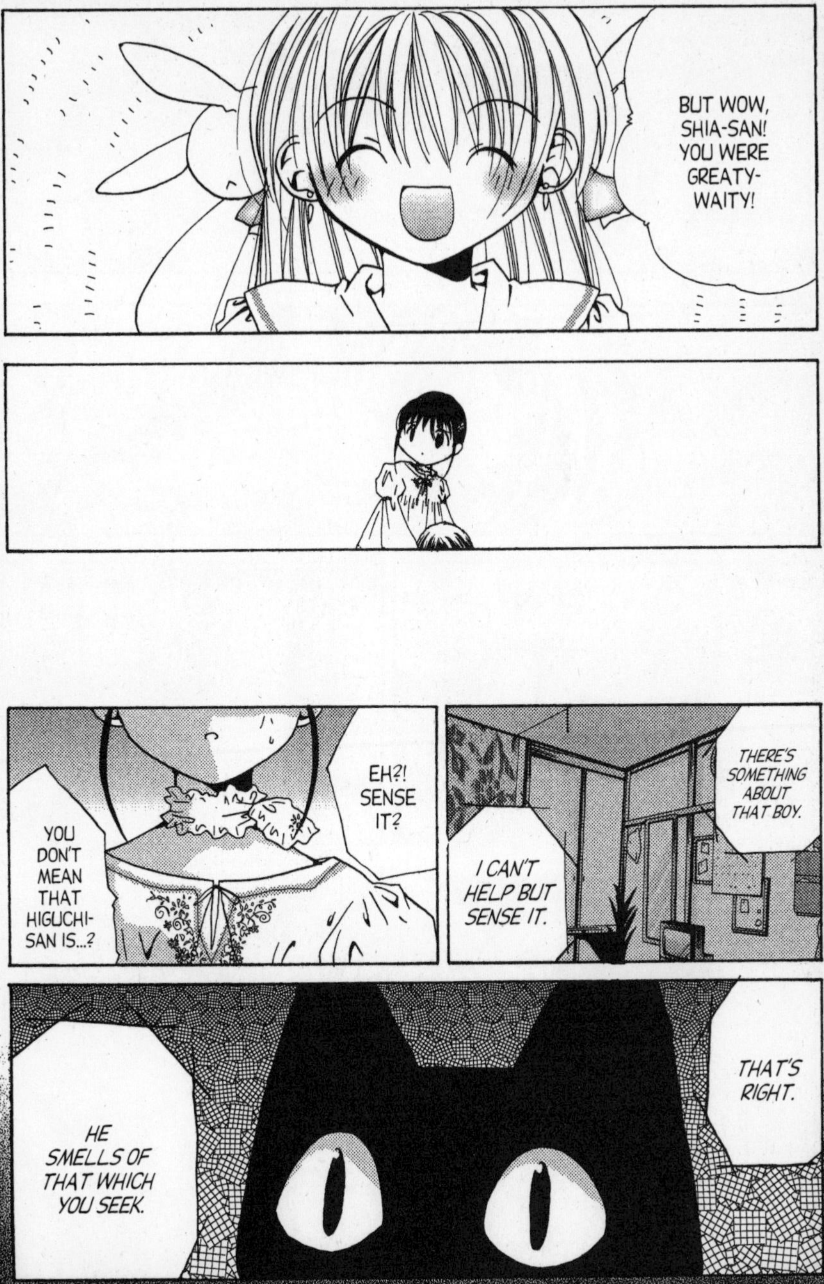
BUT WOW, SHIA-SAN! YOU WERE GREATY-WAITY!
THERE'S SOMETHING ABOUT THAT BOY.
I CAN'T HELP BUT SENSE IT.
EH?! SENSE IT?
YOU DON'T MEAN THAT HIGUCHI-SAN IS...?
THAT'S RIGHT.
HE SMELLS OF THAT WHICH YOU SEEK.

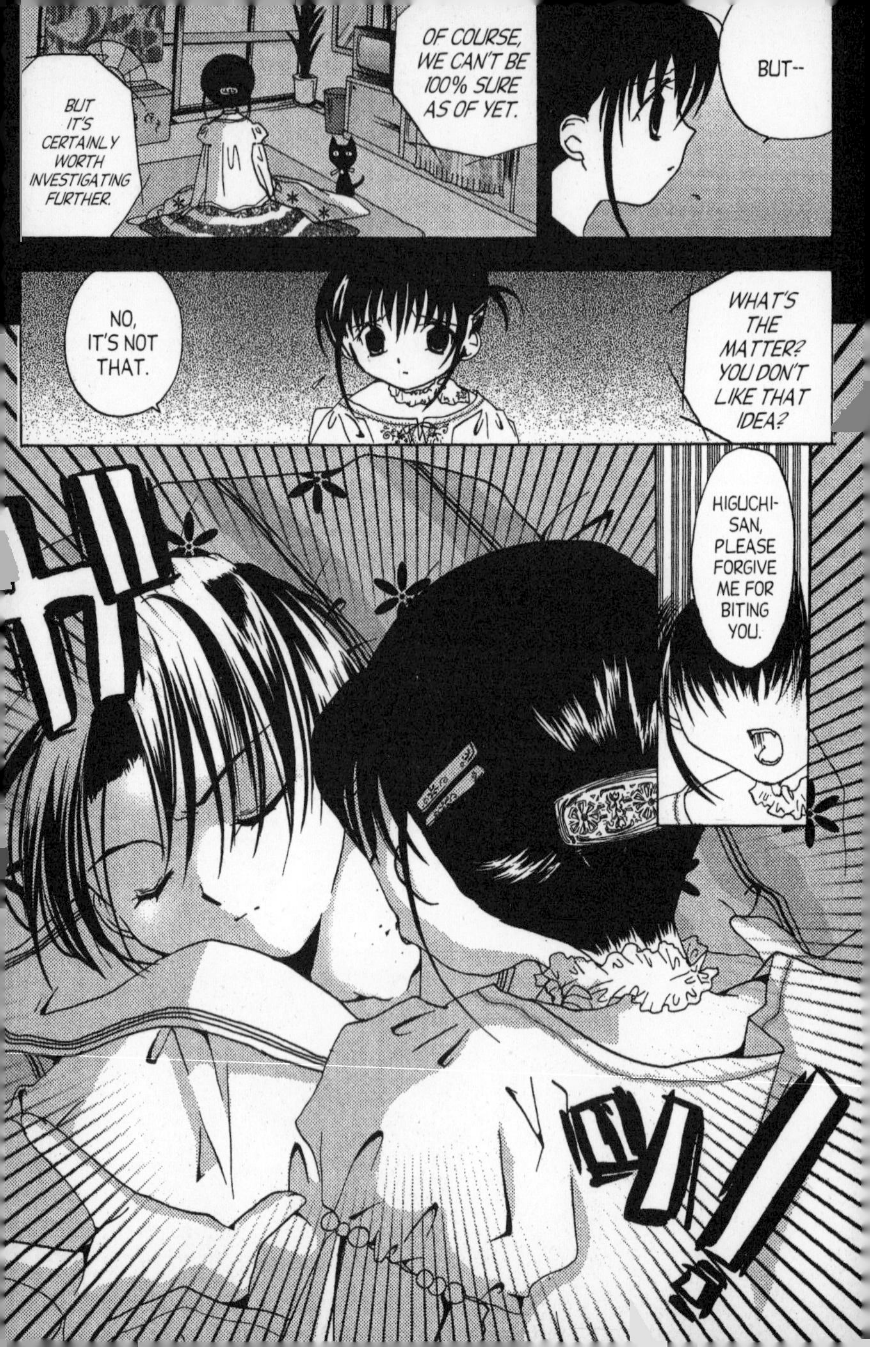
BUT--
OF COURSE, WE CAN'T BE 100% SURE AS OF YET.
BUT IT'S CERTAINLY WORTH INVESTIGATING FURTHER.
WHAT'S THE MATTER? YOU DON'T LIKE THAT IDEA?
NO, IT'S NOT THAT.
HIGUCHI-SAN, PLEASE FORGIVE ME FOR BITING YOU.

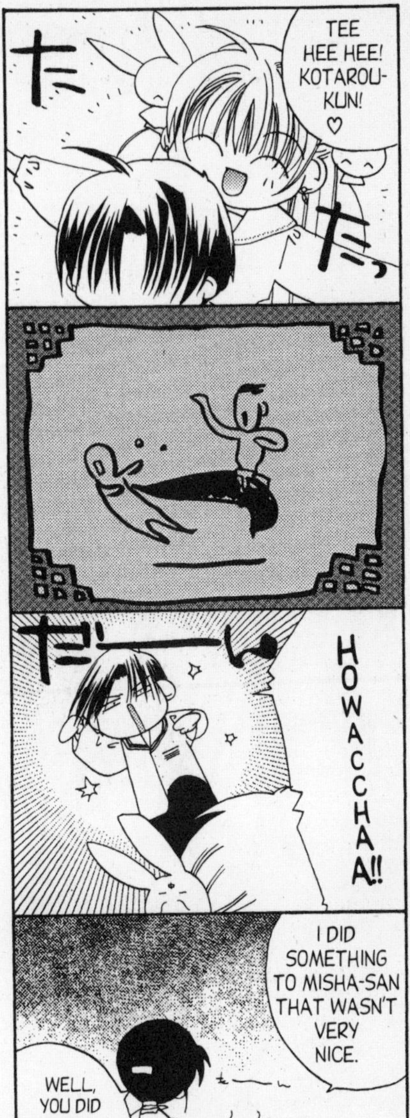
TEE HEE HEE! KOTAROU-KUN! ♡
HOWACCHAA!!
I DID SOMETHING TO MISHA-SAN THAT WASN'T VERY NICE.
WELL, YOU DID WATCH THAT KUNG FU MOVIE YESTERDAY.

Lesson 13

How to Elegantly Eat Apples

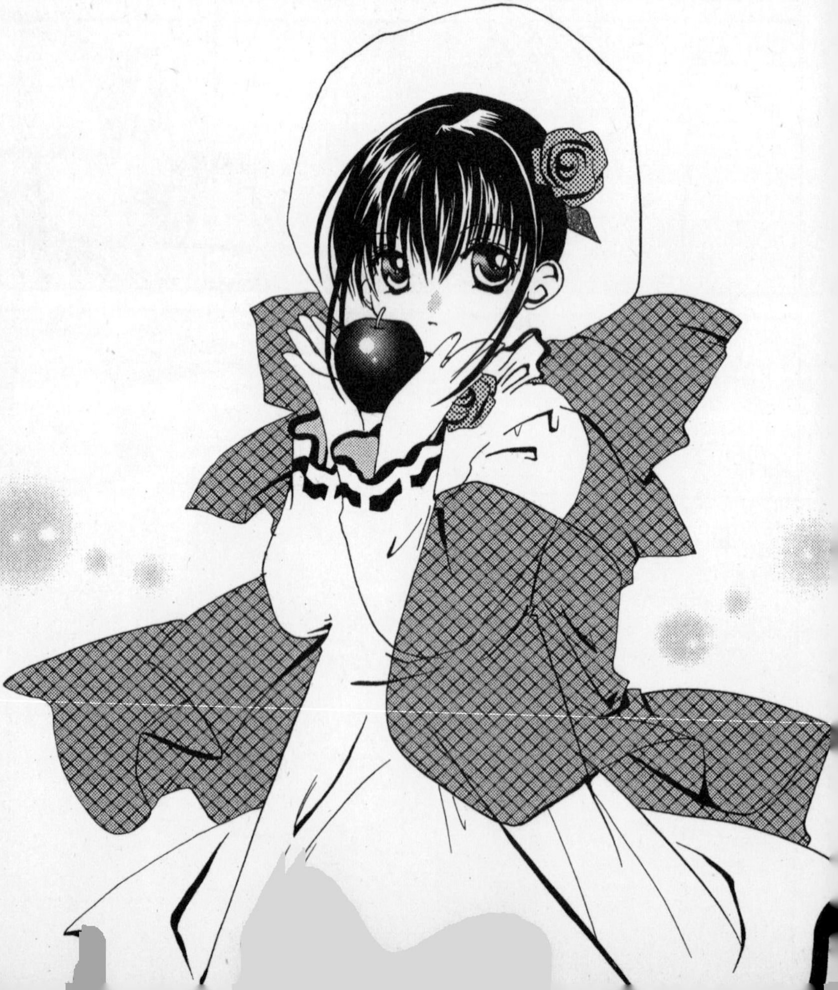

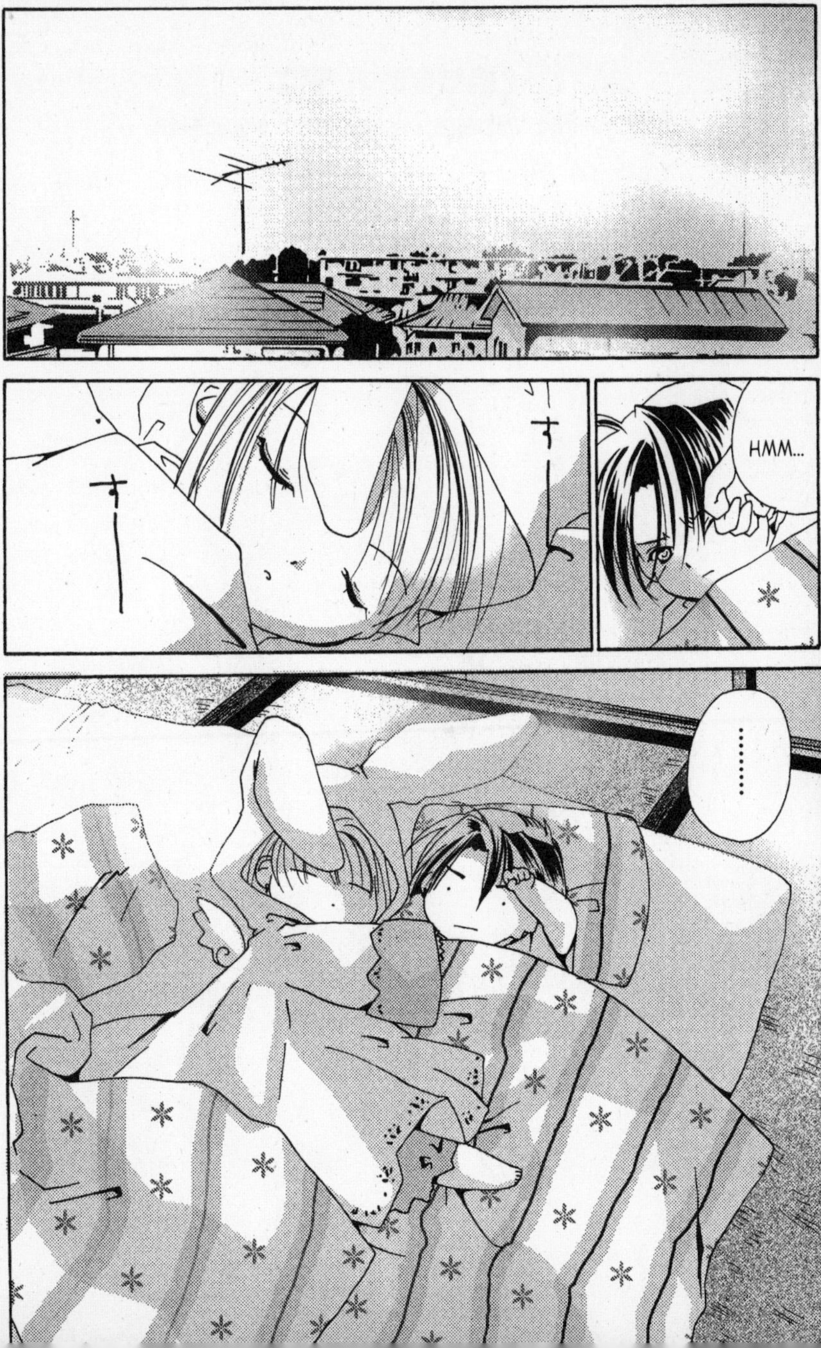
HMM...
すー
すー
......

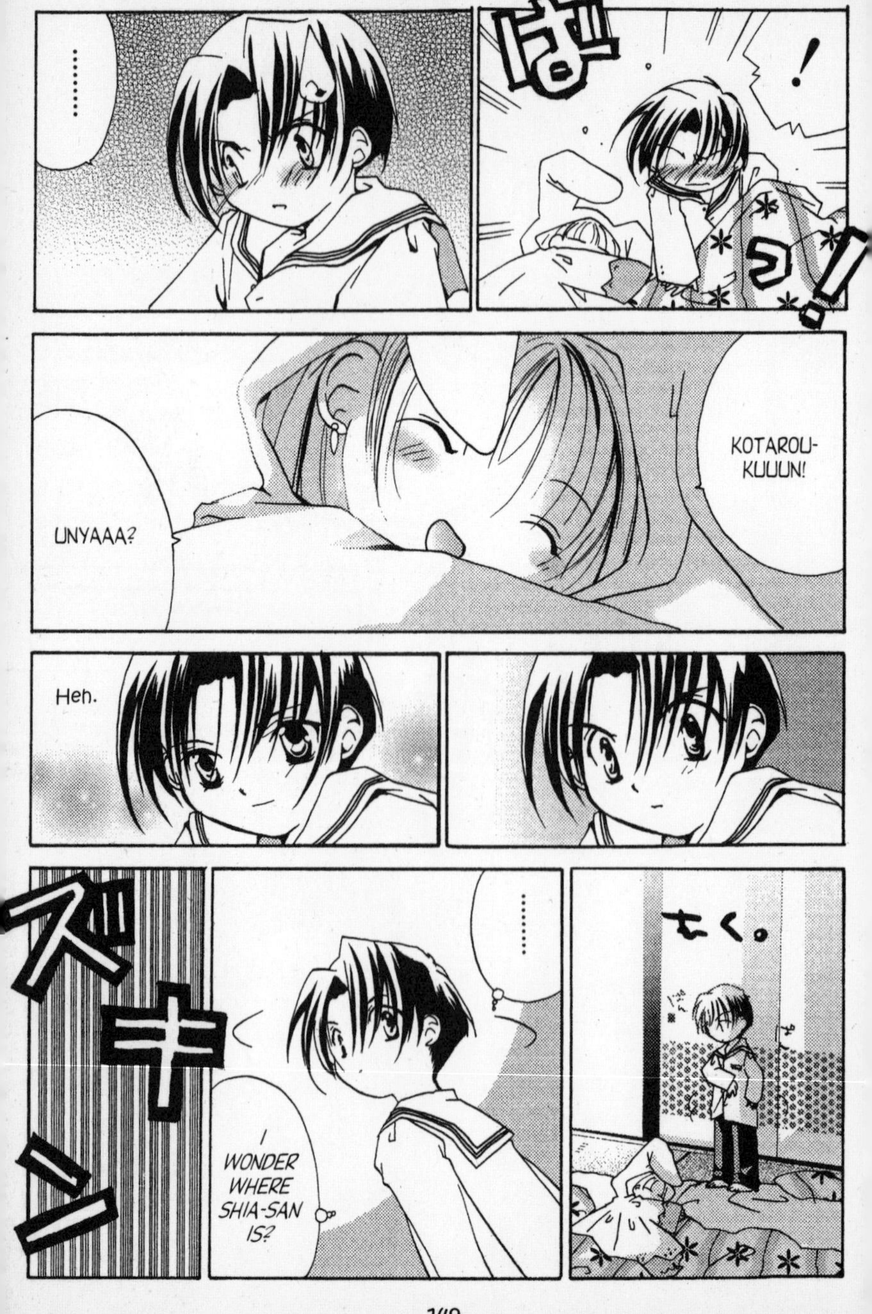
ぱ
!
っ!
……
KOTAROU-KUUUN!
UNYAAA?
Heh.
むく。
……
I WONDER WHERE SHIA-SAN IS?
ズキン

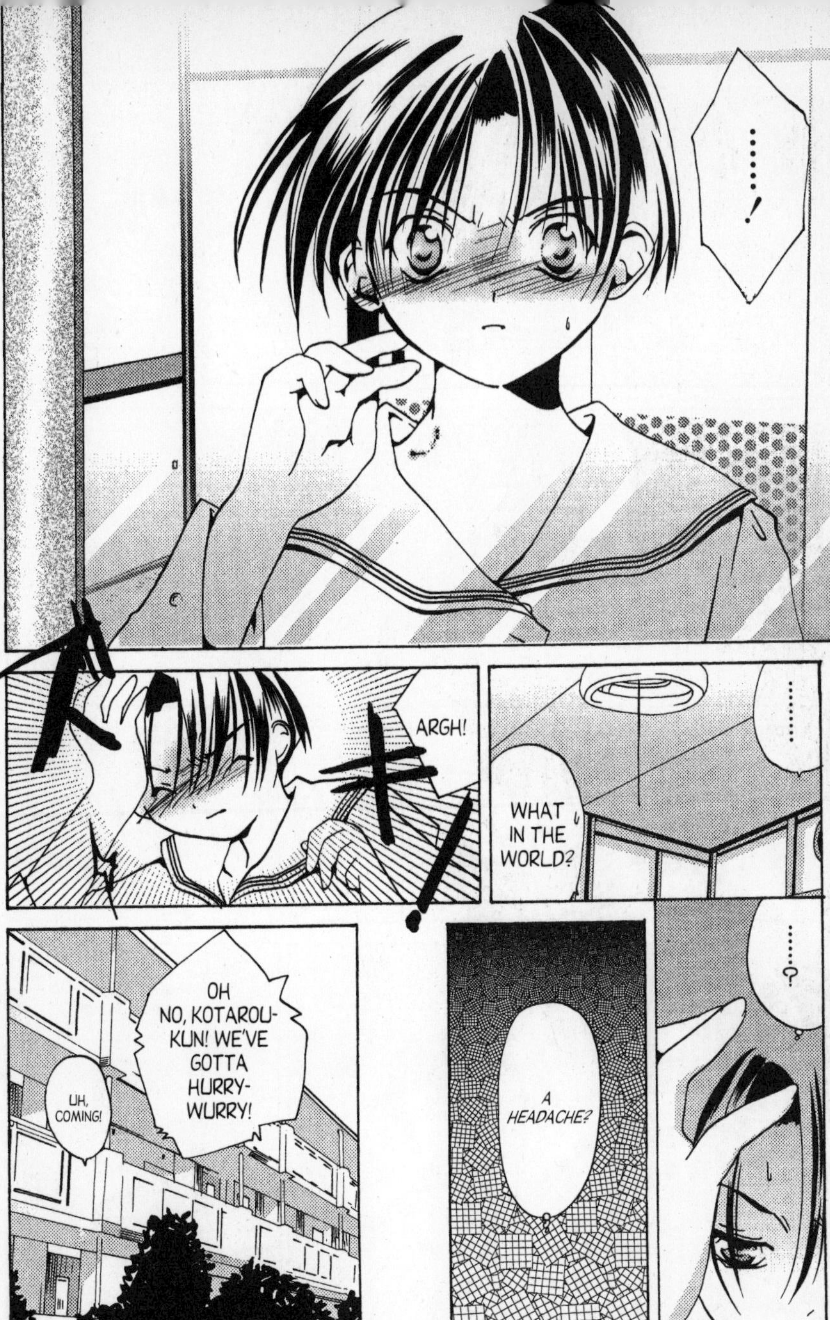
……!
……
WHAT IN THE WORLD?
ARGH!
……?
A HEADACHE?
OH NO, KOTAROU-KUN! WE'VE GOTTA HURRY-WURRY!
UH, COMING!

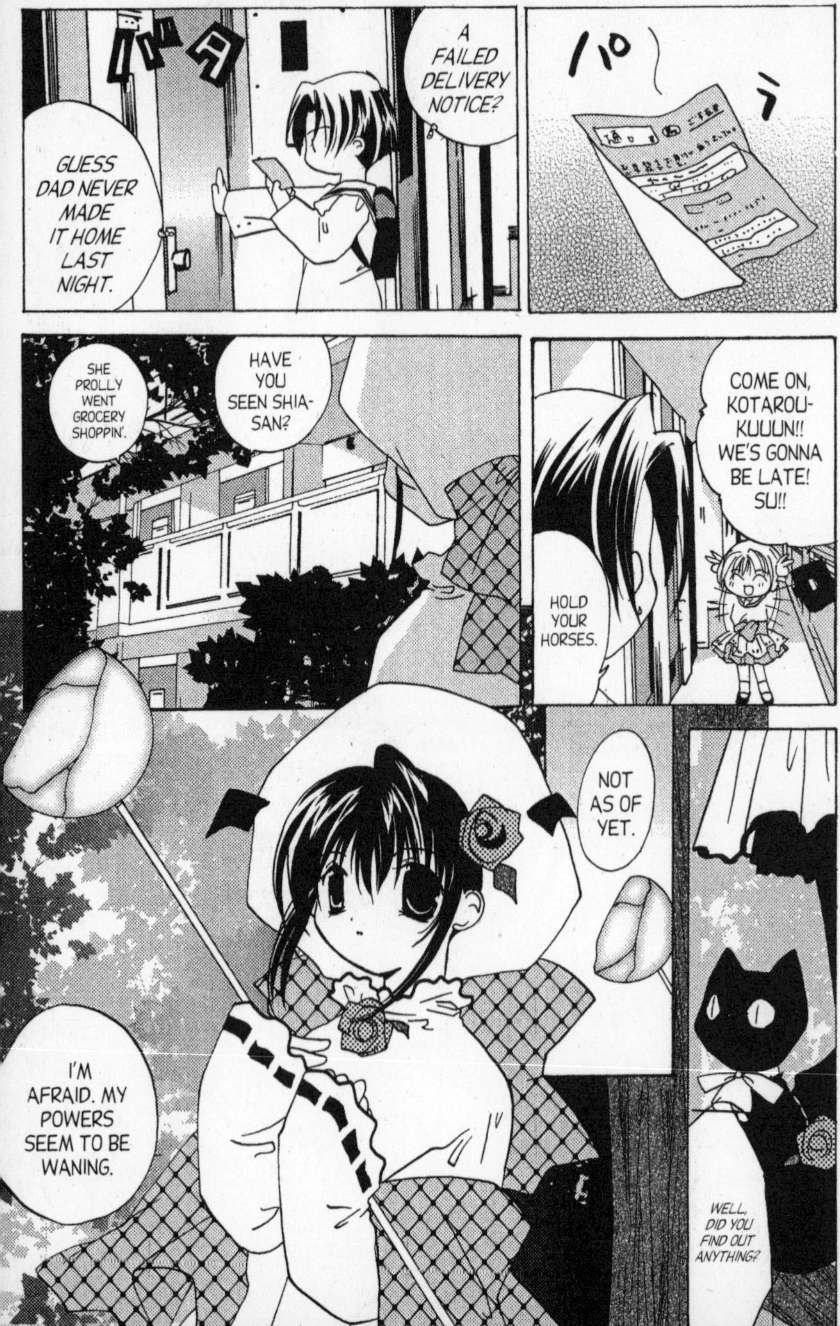
パラ
A FAILED DELIVERY NOTICE?
GUESS DAD NEVER MADE IT HOME LAST NIGHT.
COME ON, KOTAROU-KUUUN!! WE'S GONNA BE LATE! SU!!
HOLD YOUR HORSES.
HAVE YOU SEEN SHIA-SAN?
SHE PROLLY WENT GROCERY SHOPPIN'.
WELL, DID YOU FIND OUT ANYTHING?
NOT AS OF YET.
I'M AFRAID. MY POWERS SEEM TO BE WANING.

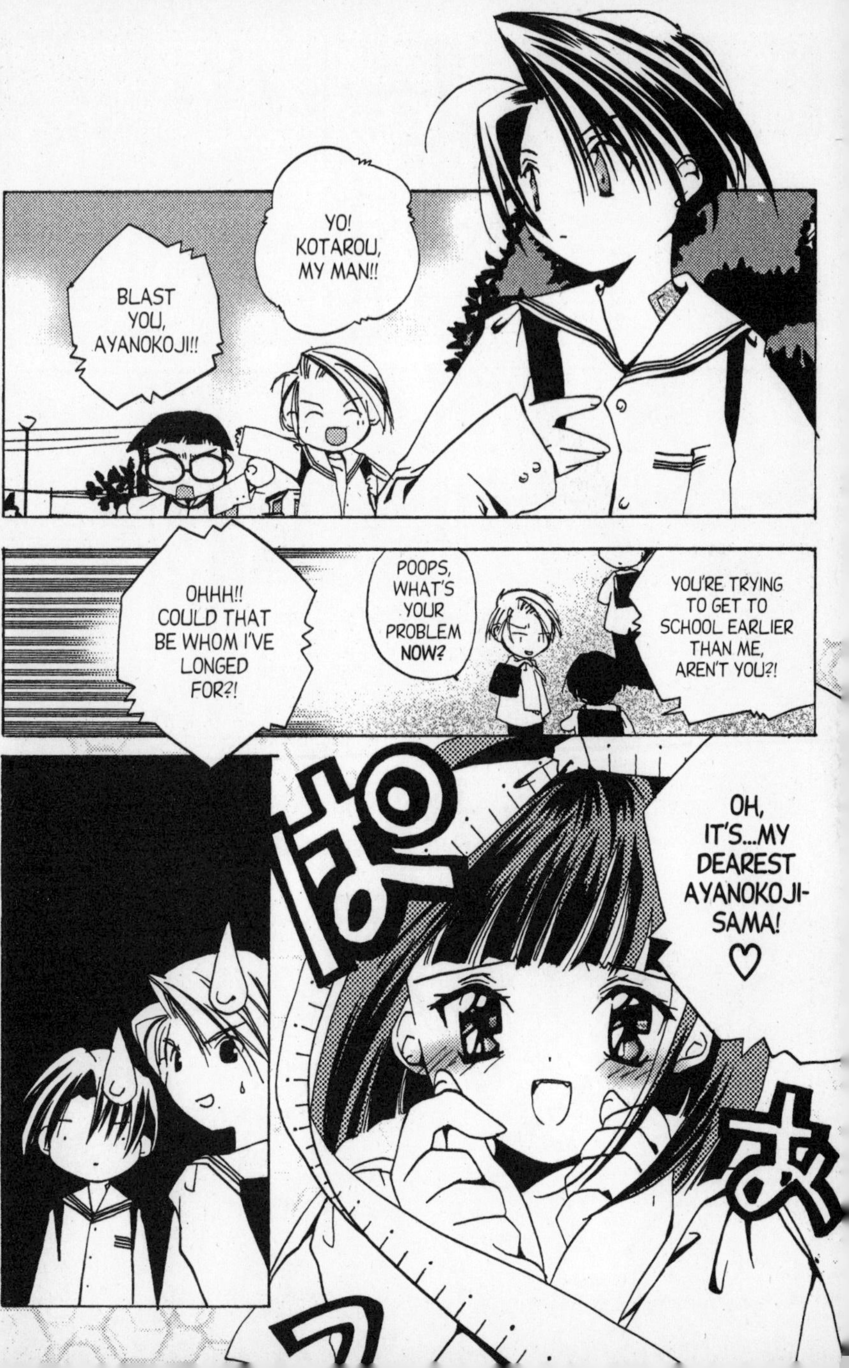
YO! KOTAROU, MY MAN!!
BLAST YOU, AYANOKOJI!!
YOU'RE TRYING TO GET TO SCHOOL EARLIER THAN ME, AREN'T YOU?!
POOPS, WHAT'S YOUR PROBLEM NOW?
OHHH!! COULD THAT BE WHOM I'VE LONGED FOR?!
OH, IT'S...MY DEAREST AYANOKOJI-SAMA! ♡

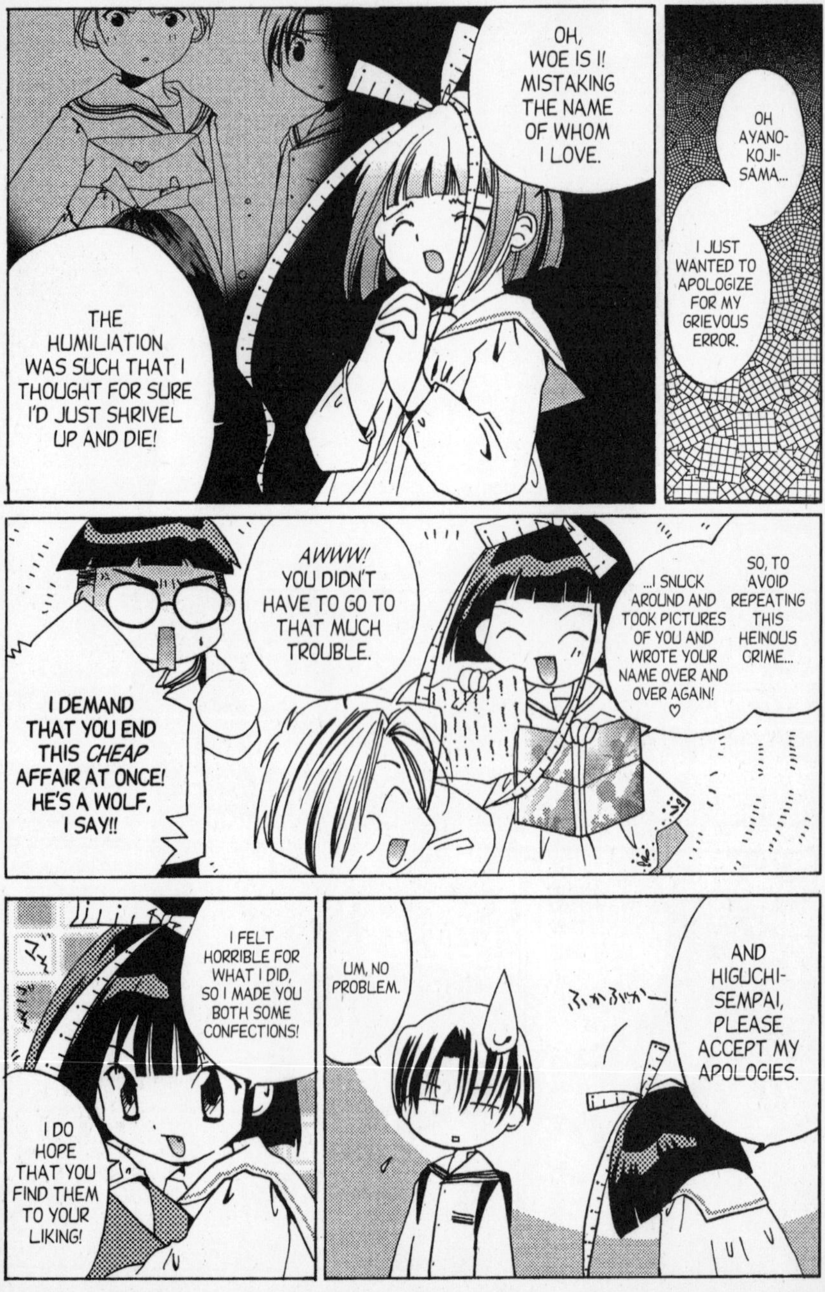
OH AYANO-KOJI-SAMA...
I JUST WANTED TO APOLOGIZE FOR MY GRIEVOUS ERROR.
OH, WOE IS I! MISTAKING THE NAME OF WHOM I LOVE.
THE HUMILIATION WAS SUCH THAT I THOUGHT FOR SURE I'D JUST SHRIVEL UP AND DIE!
SO, TO AVOID REPEATING THIS HEINOUS CRIME...
...I SNUCK AROUND AND TOOK PICTURES OF YOU AND WROTE YOUR NAME OVER AND OVER AGAIN! ♡
AWWW! YOU DIDN'T HAVE TO GO TO THAT MUCH TROUBLE.
I DEMAND THAT YOU END THIS *CHEAP* AFFAIR AT ONCE! HE'S A WOLF, I SAY!!
AND HIGUCHI-SEMPAI, PLEASE ACCEPT MY APOLOGIES.
ふかぶかー
UM, NO PROBLEM.
I FELT HORRIBLE FOR WHAT I DID, SO I MADE YOU BOTH SOME CONFECTIONS!
I DO HOPE THAT YOU FIND THEM TO YOUR LIKING!

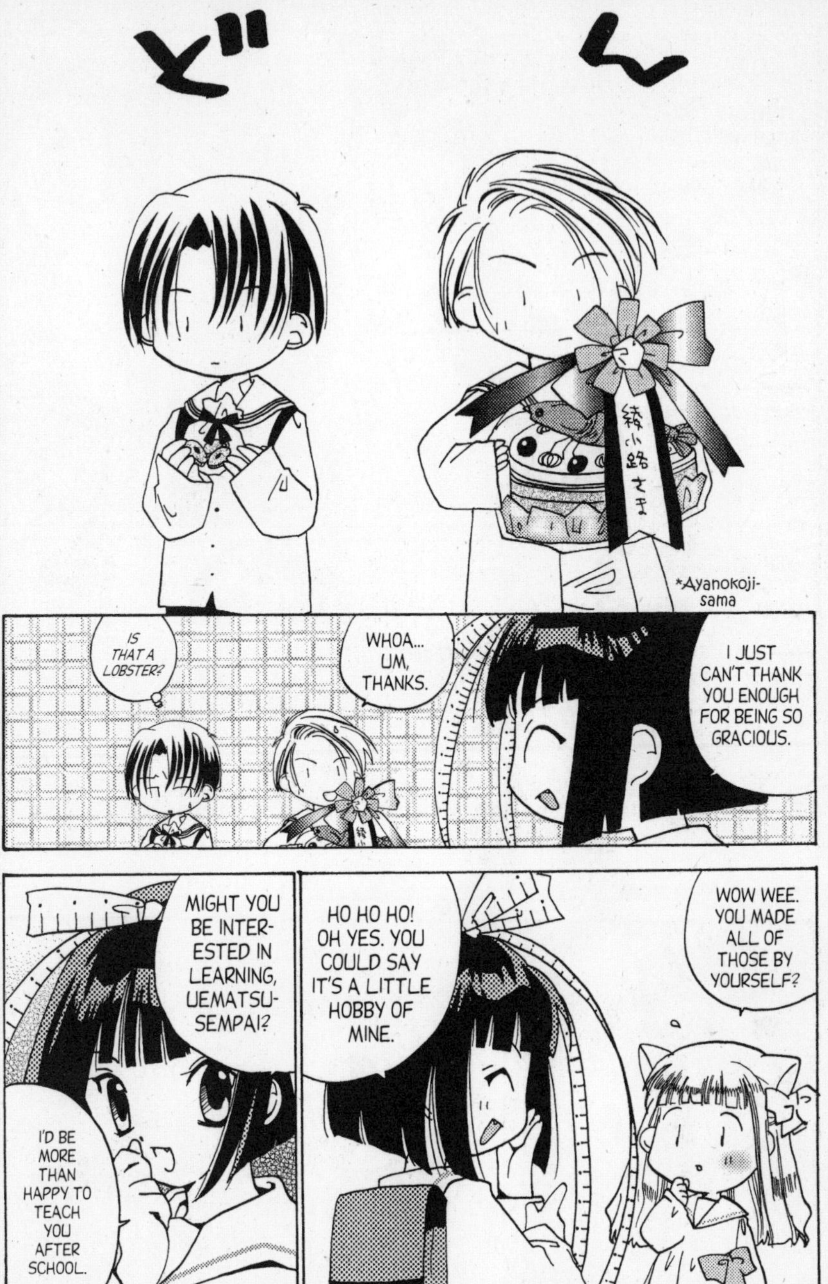
どん
綾小路さま
*Ayanokoji-sama
I JUST CAN'T THANK YOU ENOUGH FOR BEING SO GRACIOUS.
WHOA... UM, THANKS.
IS THAT A LOBSTER?
WOW WEE. YOU MADE ALL OF THOSE BY YOURSELF?
HO HO HO! OH YES. YOU COULD SAY IT'S A LITTLE HOBBY OF MINE.
MIGHT YOU BE INTERESTED IN LEARNING, UEMATSU-SEMPAI?
I'D BE MORE THAN HAPPY TO TEACH YOU AFTER SCHOOL.

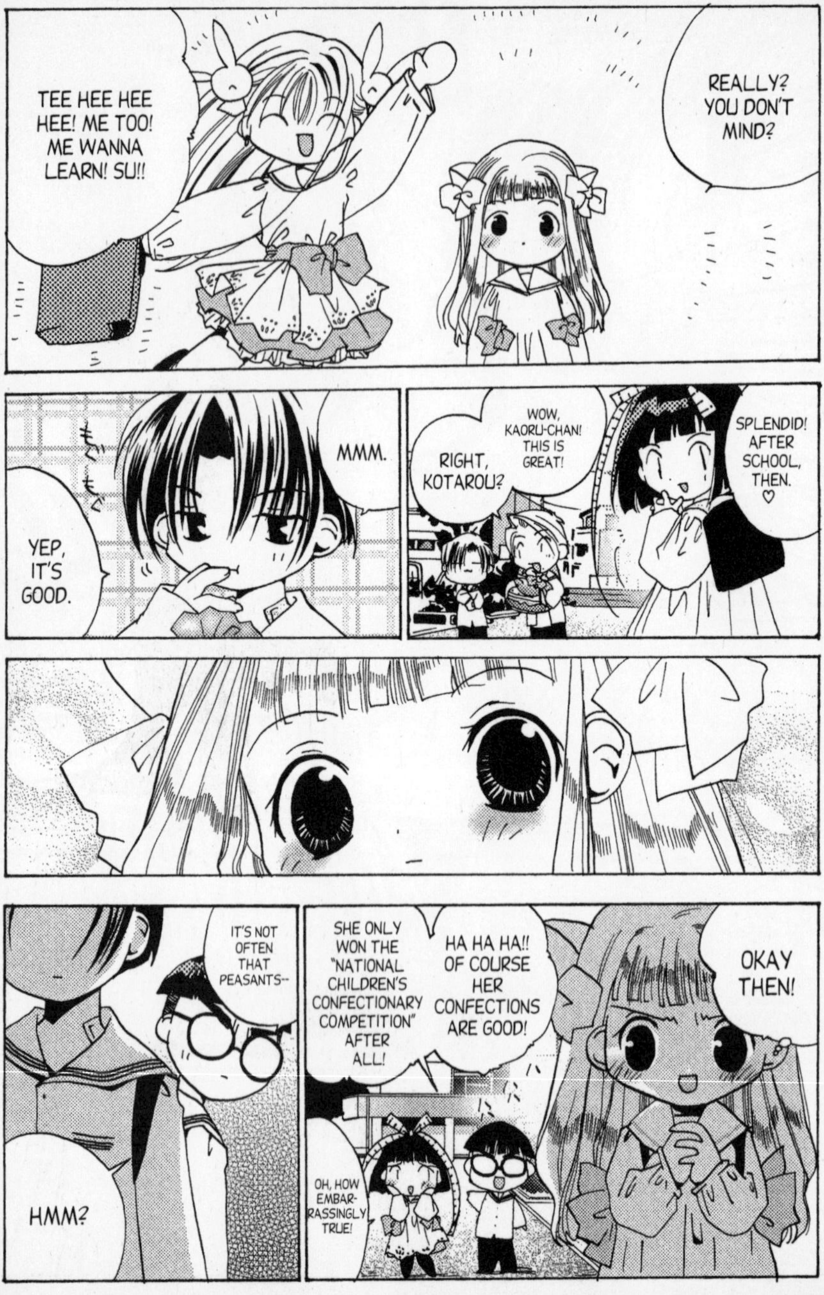
REALLY? YOU DON'T MIND?
TEE HEE HEE HEE! ME TOO! ME WANNA LEARN! SU!!
SPLENDID! AFTER SCHOOL, THEN. ♡
WOW, KAORU-CHAN! THIS IS GREAT!
RIGHT, KOTAROU?
MMM.
YEP, IT'S GOOD.
OKAY THEN!
HA HA HA!! OF COURSE HER CONFECTIONS ARE GOOD!
SHE ONLY WON THE "NATIONAL CHILDREN'S CONFECTIONARY COMPETITION" AFTER ALL!
OH, HOW EMBARRASSINGLY TRUE!
IT'S NOT OFTEN THAT PEASANTS--
HMM?

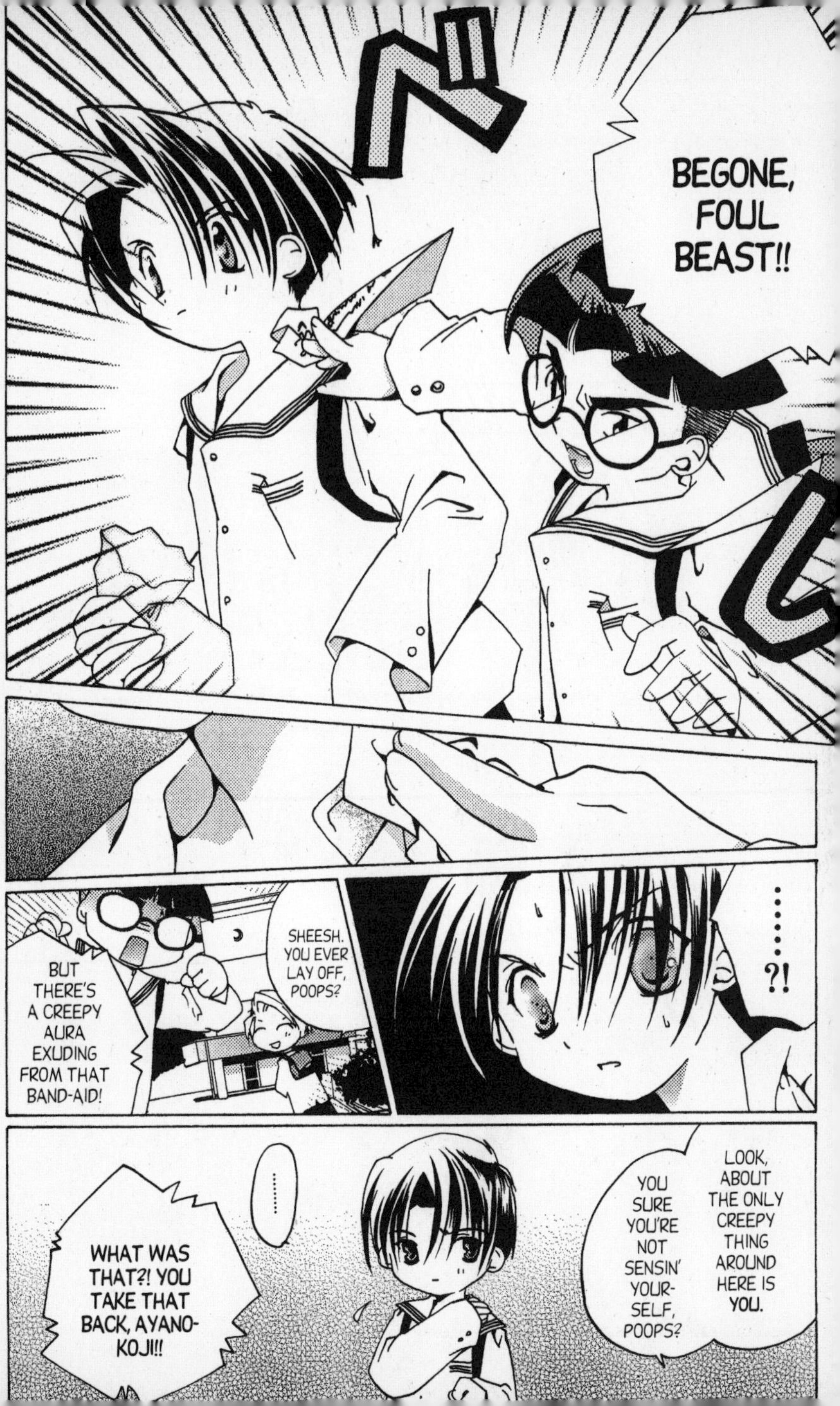
BEGONE, FOUL BEAST!!
......?!
SHEESH. YOU EVER LAY OFF, POOPS?
BUT THERE'S A CREEPY AURA EXUDING FROM THAT BAND-AID!
LOOK, ABOUT THE ONLY CREEPY THING AROUND HERE IS YOU.
YOU SURE YOU'RE NOT SENSIN' YOUR-SELF, POOPS?
......
WHAT WAS THAT?! YOU TAKE THAT BACK, AYANO-KOJI!!

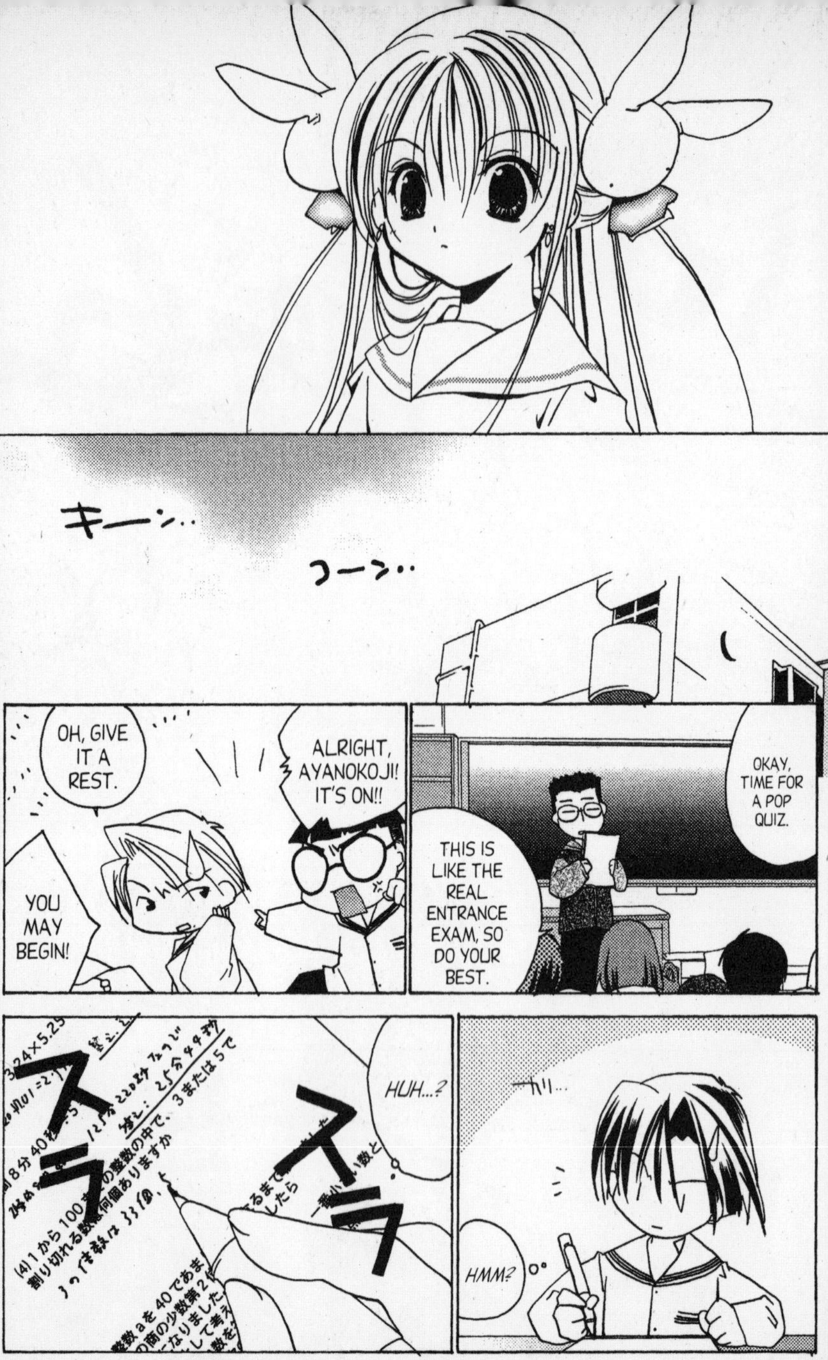
キーン…
コーン…
OKAY, TIME FOR A POP QUIZ.
THIS IS LIKE THE REAL ENTRANCE EXAM, SO DO YOUR BEST.
ALRIGHT, AYANOKOJI! IT'S ON!!
OH, GIVE IT A REST.
YOU MAY BEGIN!
カリ…
HMM?
HUH...?
スラ
スラ

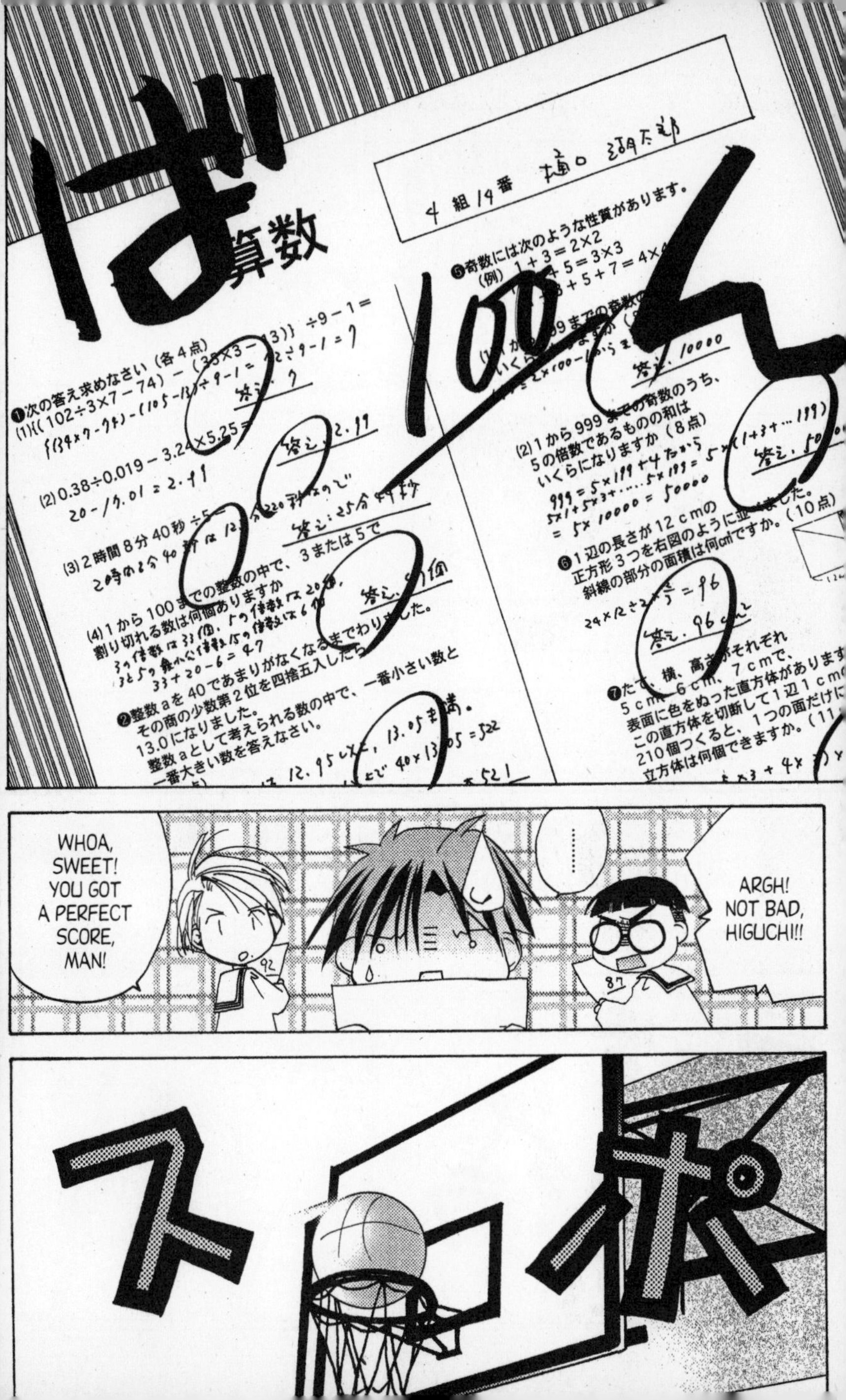
ぱ
100
ん
算数
4組14番
❶次の答え求めなさい（各4点）
(1){(102÷3×7−74)−(35×3−13)}÷9−1=
(2)0.38÷0.019−3.24×5.25=
(3)2時間8分40秒÷5=
(4)1から100までの整数の中で、3または5で割り切れる数は何個ありますか
❷整数aを40であまりがなくなるまでわりました。その商の少数第2位を四捨五入したら13.0になりました。整数aとして考えられる数の中で、一番小さい数と一番大きい数を答えなさい。
❺奇数には次のような性質があります。
（例）1+3=2×2
(2)1から999までの奇数のうち、5の倍数であるものの和はいくらになりますか（8点）
❻1辺の長さが12cmの正方形3つを右図のように並べました。斜線の部分の面積は何㎠ですか。（10点）
❼たて、横、高さがそれぞれ5cm、6cm、7cmで、
表面に色をぬった直方体があります
この直方体を切断して1辺1cm
210個つくると、1つの面だけに
立方体は何個できますか。
ARGH! NOT BAD, HIGUCHI!!!
……
WHOA, SWEET! YOU GOT A PERFECT SCORE, MAN!
スポ

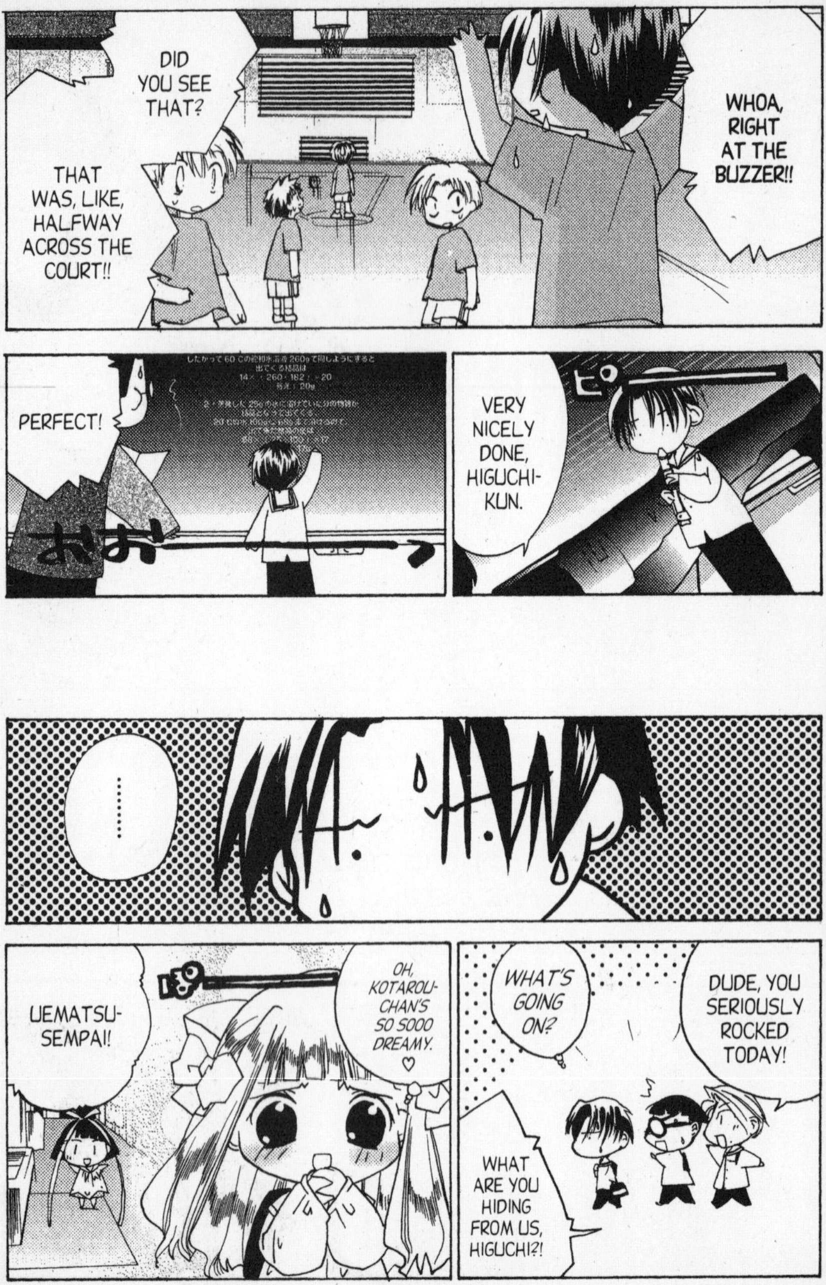
WHOA, RIGHT AT THE BUZZER!!
DID YOU SEE THAT?
THAT WAS, LIKE, HALFWAY ACROSS THE COURT!!
ピ
VERY NICELY DONE, HIGUCHI-KUN.
PERFECT!
おお
......
DUDE, YOU SERIOUSLY ROCKED TODAY!
WHAT'S GOING ON?
WHAT ARE YOU HIDING FROM US, HIGUCHI!?!
OH, KOTAROU-CHAN'S SO SOOO DREAMY. ♡
UEMATSU-SEMPAI!

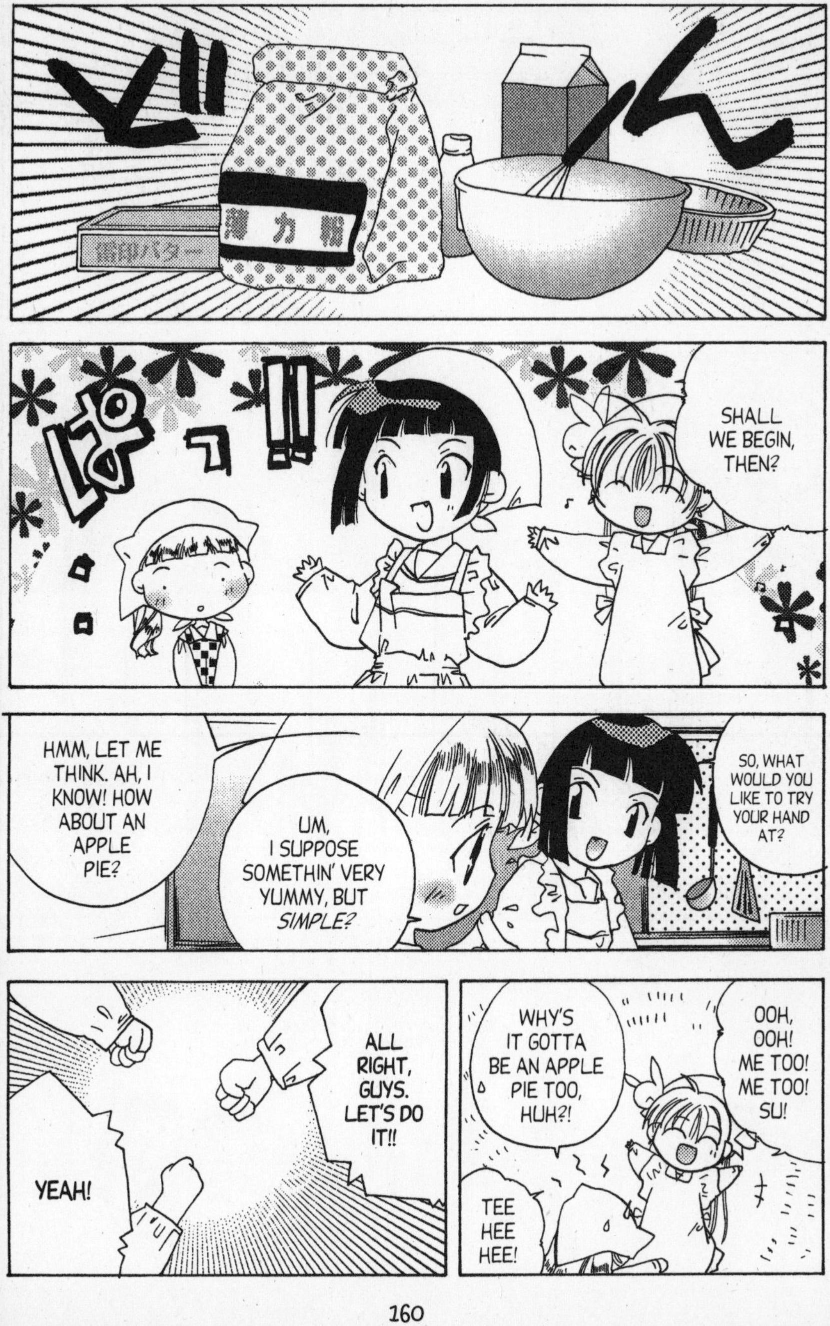
どーん
薄力粉
ぱっ!!
SHALL WE BEGIN, THEN?
SO, WHAT WOULD YOU LIKE TO TRY YOUR HAND AT?
UM, I SUPPOSE SOMETHIN' VERY YUMMY, BUT *SIMPLE?*
HMM, LET ME THINK. AH, I KNOW! HOW ABOUT AN APPLE PIE?
OOH, OOH! ME TOO! ME TOO! SU!
WHY'S IT GOTTA BE AN APPLE PIE TOO, HUH?!
TEE HEE HEE!
ALL RIGHT, GUYS. LET'S DO IT!!
YEAH!

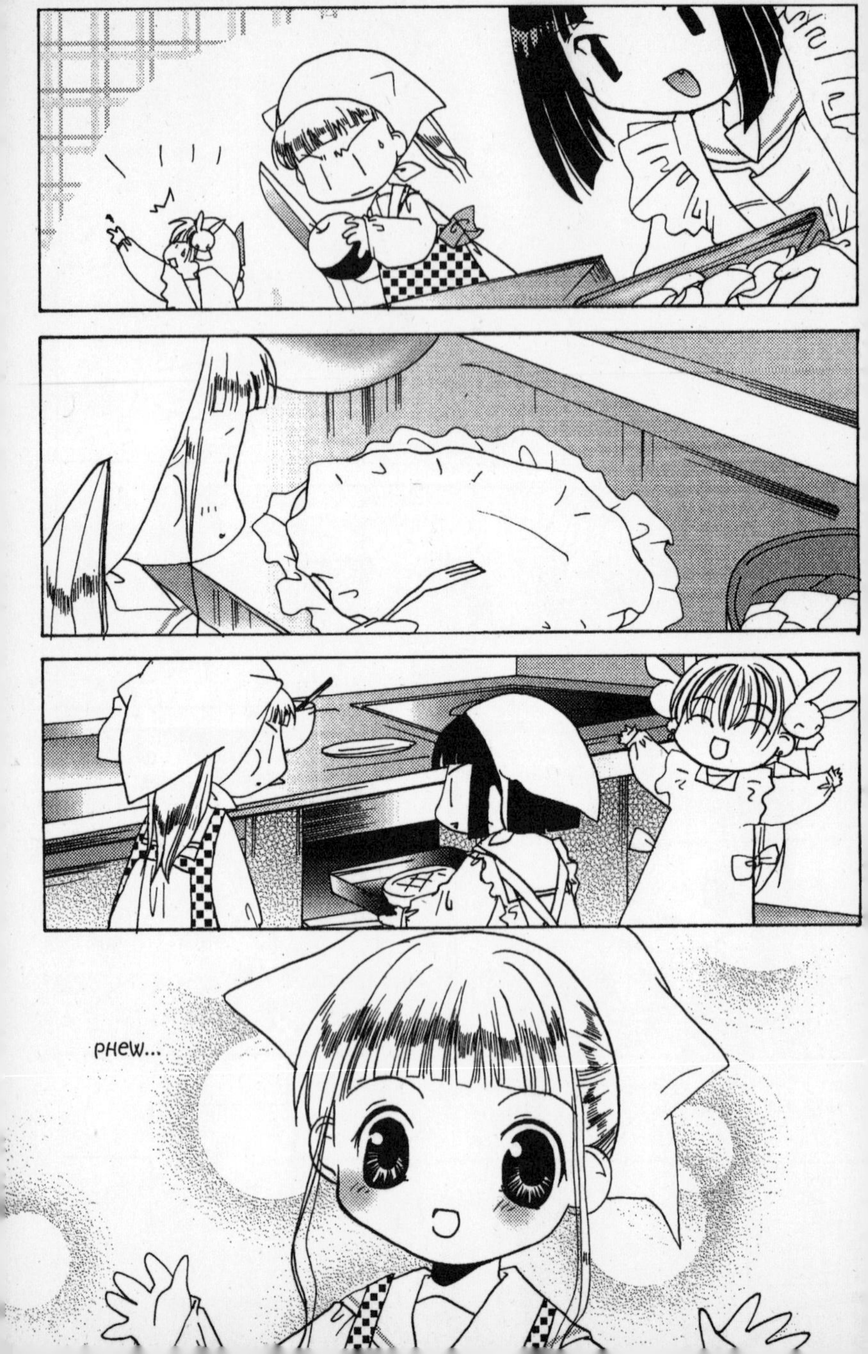
PHEW...

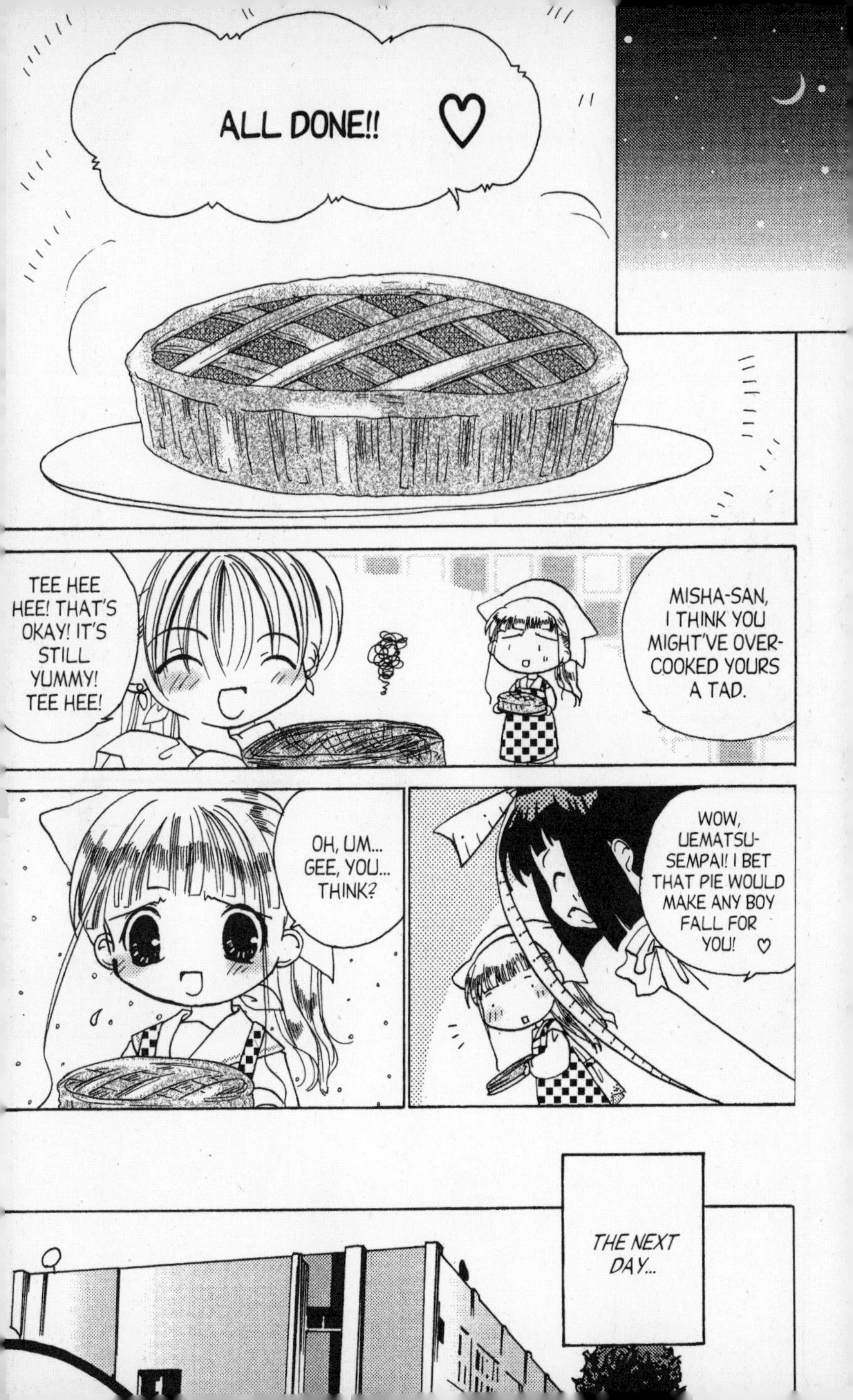
ALL DONE!! ♡
MISHA-SAN, I THINK YOU MIGHT'VE OVER-COOKED YOURS A TAD.
TEE HEE HEE! THAT'S OKAY! IT'S STILL YUMMY! TEE HEE!
WOW, UEMATSU-SEMPAI! I BET THAT PIE WOULD MAKE ANY BOY FALL FOR YOU! ♡
OH, UM... GEE, YOU... THINK?
THE NEXT DAY...

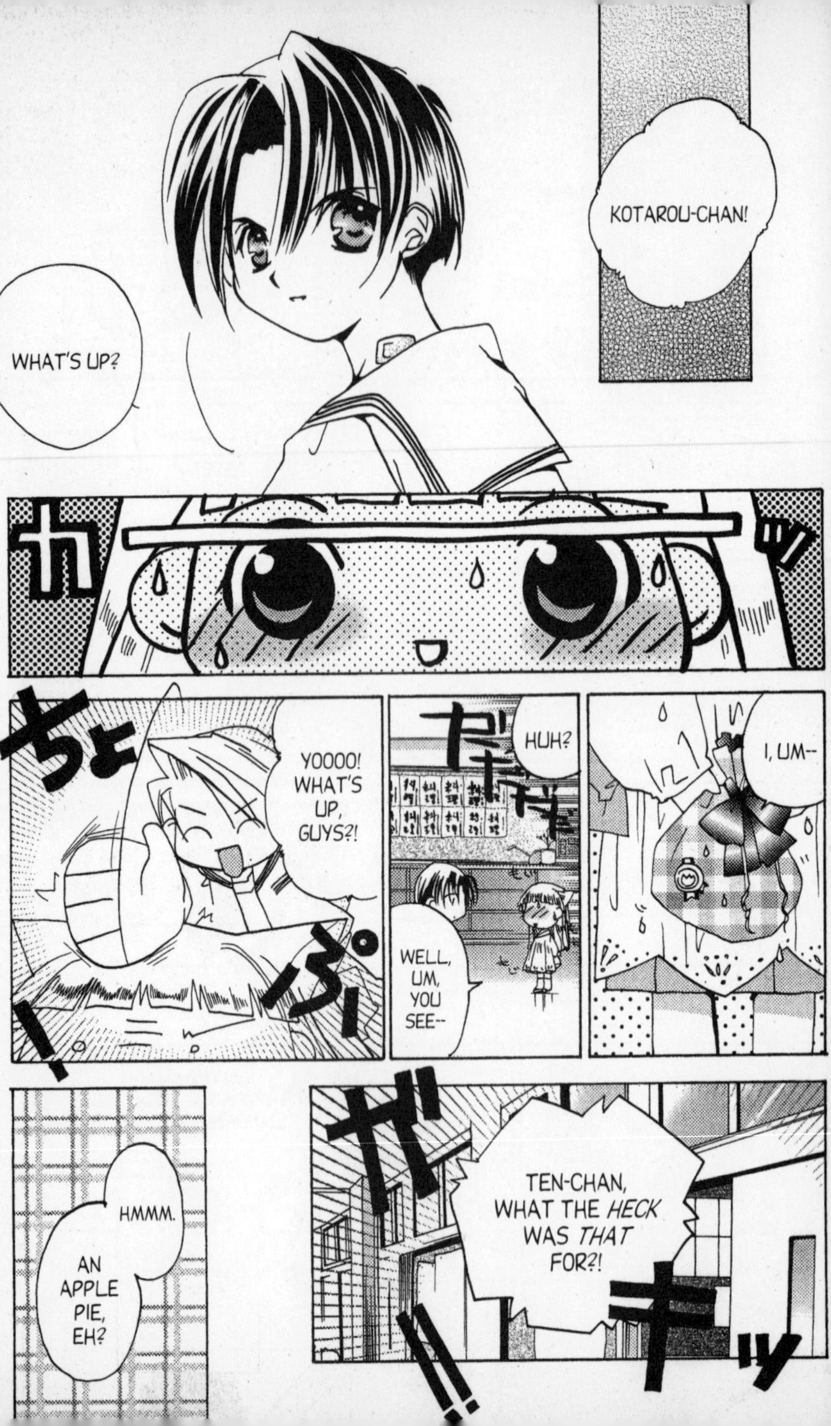
KOTAROU-CHAN!
WHAT'S UP?
I, UM--
HUH?
WELL, UM, YOU SEE--
YOOOO! WHAT'S UP, GUYS?!
TEN-CHAN, WHAT THE *HECK* WAS *THAT* FOR?!
HMMM.
AN APPLE PIE, EH?

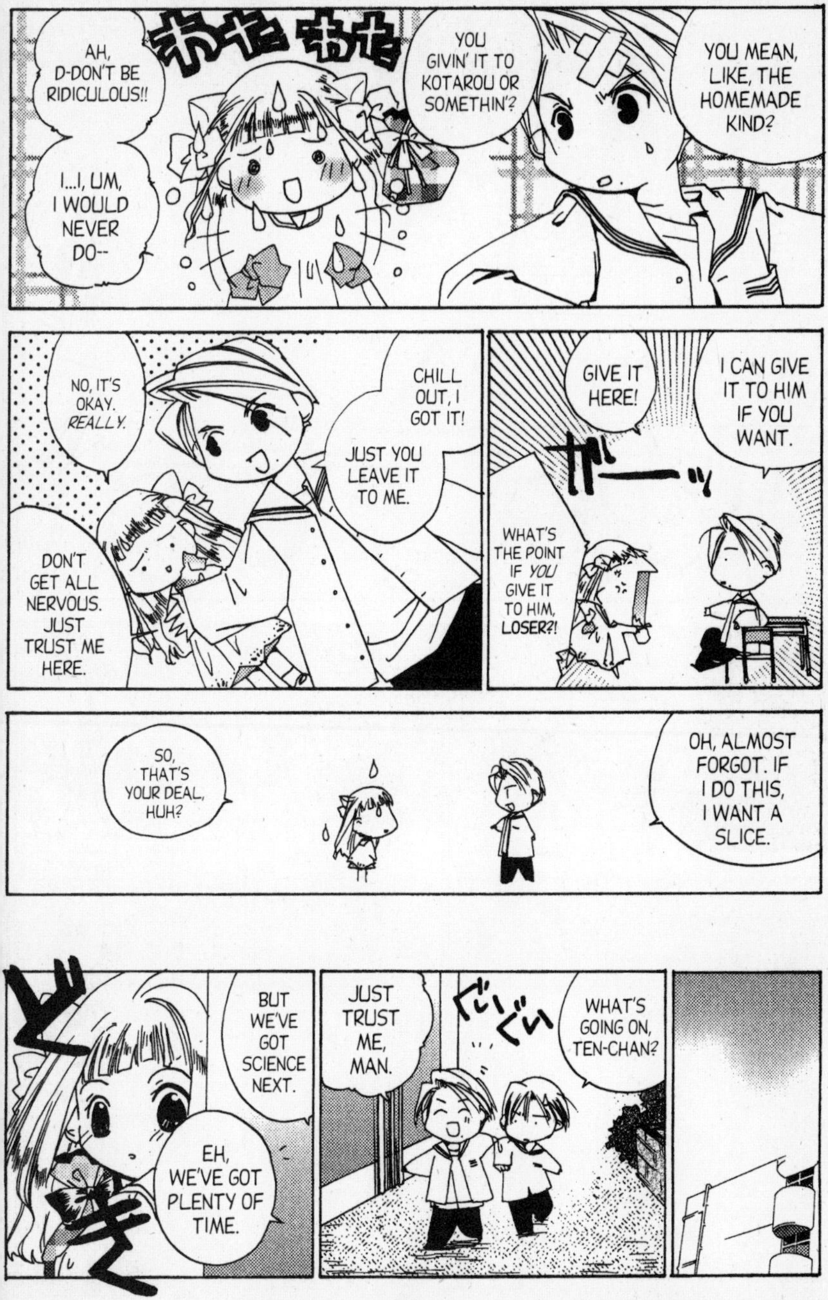
YOU MEAN, LIKE, THE HOMEMADE KIND?
YOU GIVIN' IT TO KOTAROU OR SOMETHIN'?
AH, D-DON'T BE RIDICULOUS!!
I...I, UM, I WOULD NEVER DO--
I CAN GIVE IT TO HIM IF YOU WANT.
GIVE IT HERE!
WHAT'S THE POINT IF *YOU* GIVE IT TO HIM, **LOSER?!**
CHILL OUT, I GOT IT!
JUST YOU LEAVE IT TO ME.
NO, IT'S OKAY. *REALLY.*
DON'T GET ALL NERVOUS. JUST TRUST ME HERE.
OH, ALMOST FORGOT. IF I DO THIS, I WANT A SLICE.
SO, THAT'S YOUR DEAL, HUH?
WHAT'S GOING ON, TEN-CHAN?
JUST TRUST ME, MAN.
BUT WE'VE GOT SCIENCE NEXT.
EH, WE'VE GOT PLENTY OF TIME.

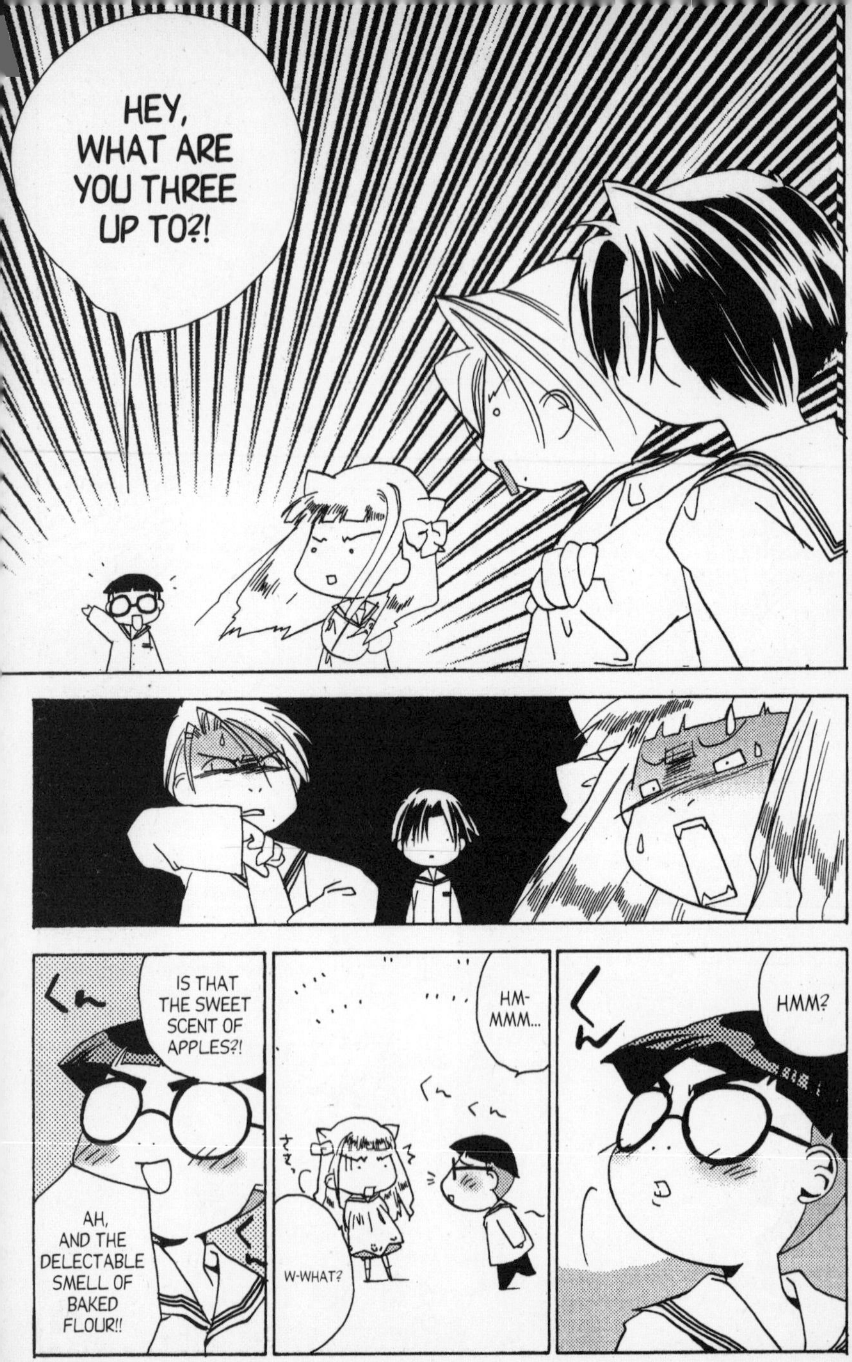
HEY, WHAT ARE YOU THREE UP TO?!
HMM?
HM-MMM...
W-WHAT?
IS THAT THE SWEET SCENT OF APPLES?!
AH, AND THE DELECTABLE SMELL OF BAKED FLOUR!!

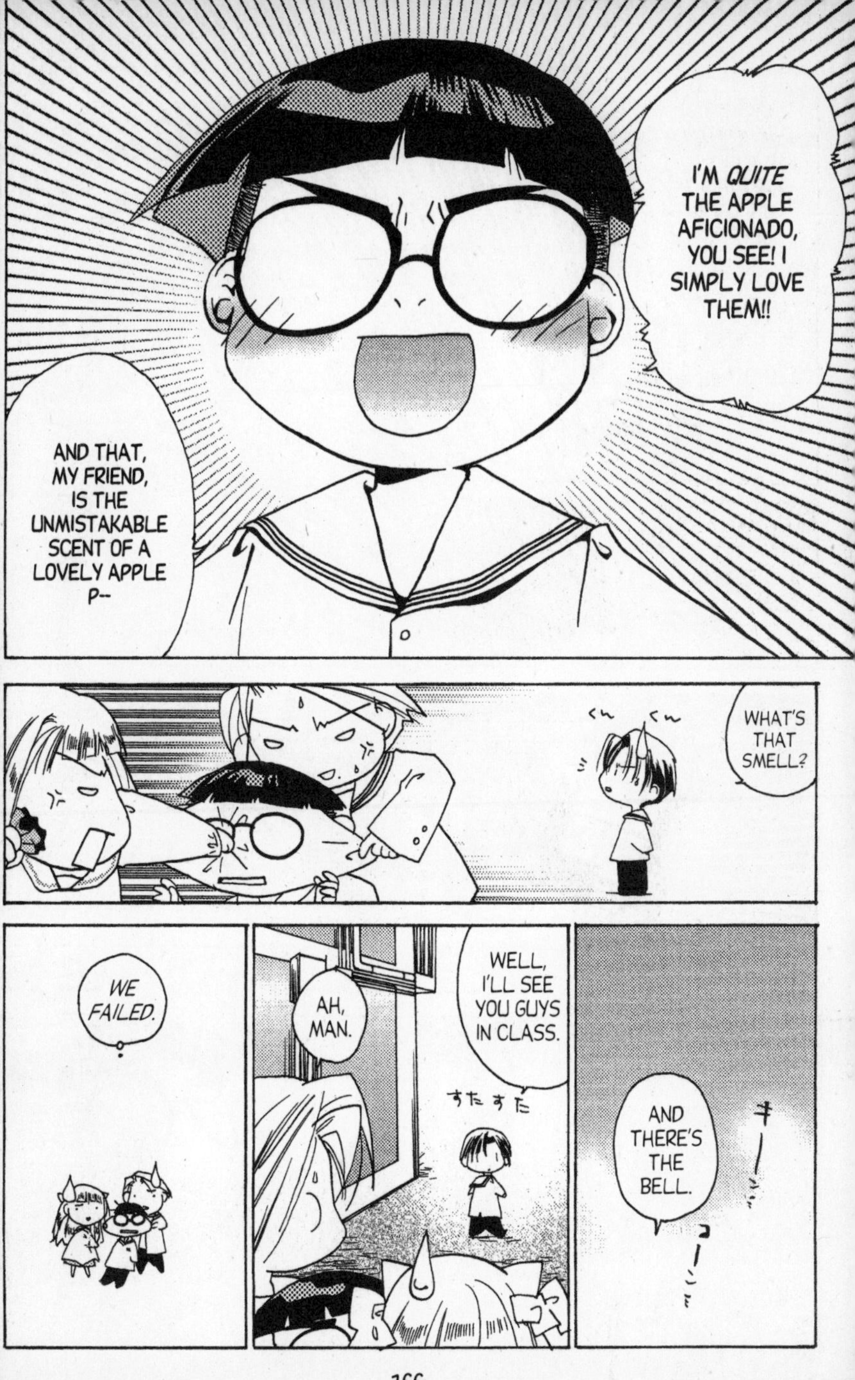
I'M *QUITE* THE APPLE AFICIONADO, YOU SEE! I SIMPLY LOVE THEM!!
AND THAT, MY FRIEND, IS THE UNMISTAKABLE SCENT OF A LOVELY APPLE P--
WHAT'S THAT SMELL?
くん くん
AND THERE'S THE BELL.
WELL, I'LL SEE YOU GUYS IN CLASS.
AH, MAN.
すた すた
WE FAILED.

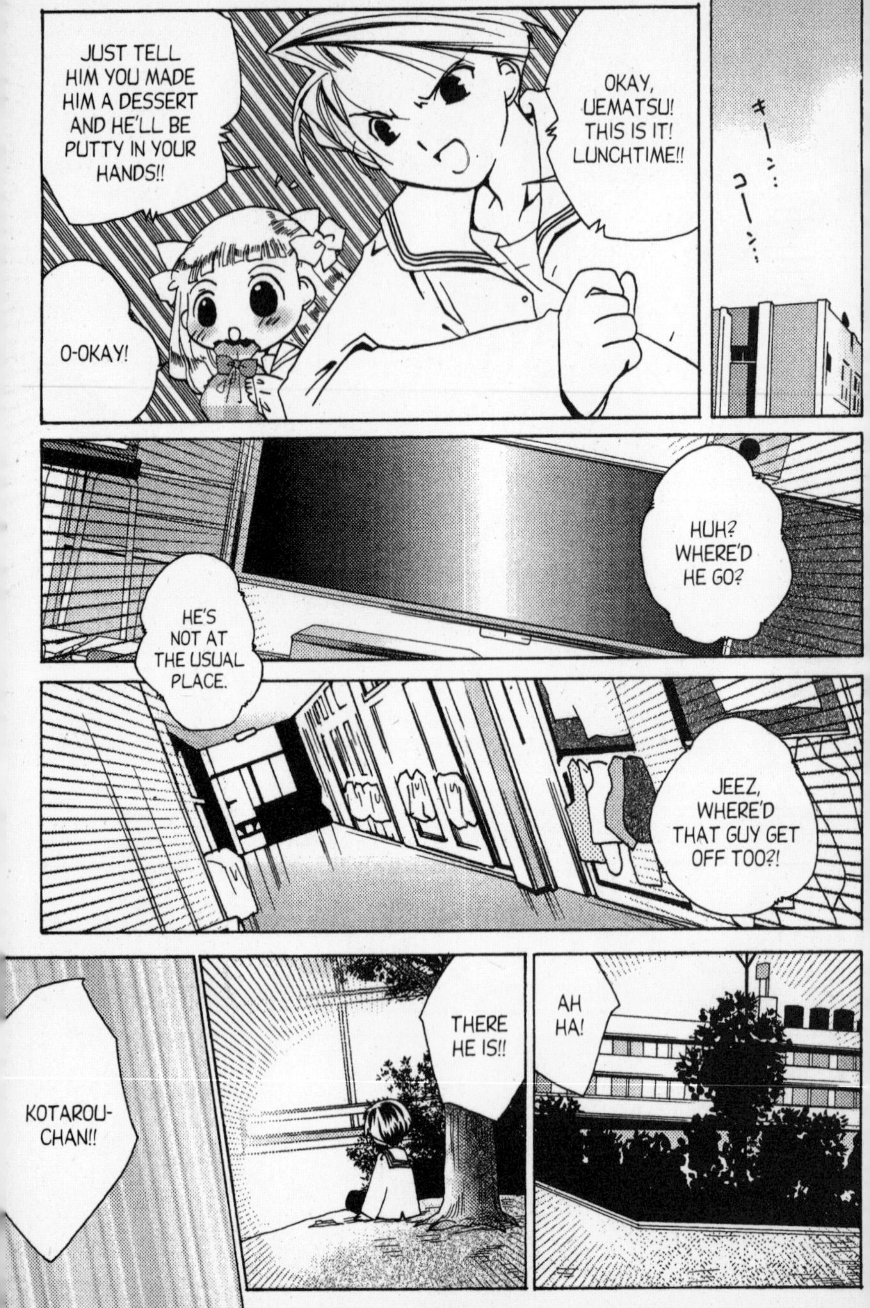
OKAY, UEMATSU! THIS IS IT! LUNCHTIME!!
JUST TELL HIM YOU MADE HIM A DESSERT AND HE'LL BE PUTTY IN YOUR HANDS!!
O-OKAY!
HUH? WHERE'D HE GO?
HE'S NOT AT THE USUAL PLACE.
JEEZ, WHERE'D THAT GUY GET OFF TOO?!
AH HA!
THERE HE IS!!
KOTAROU-CHAN!!

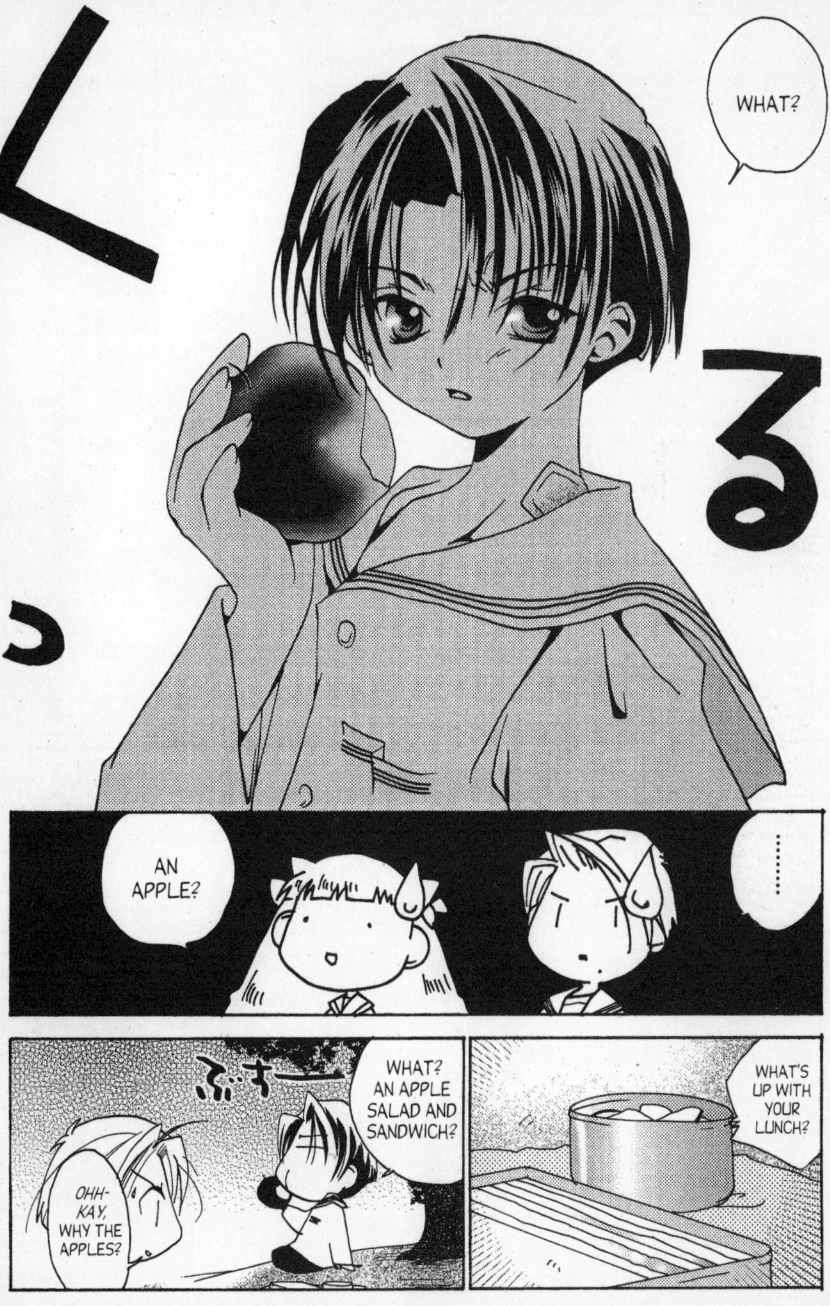
WHAT?
....
AN APPLE?
WHAT'S UP WITH YOUR LUNCH?
WHAT? AN APPLE SALAD AND SANDWICH?
ぶすー
OHH-KAY, WHY THE APPLES?

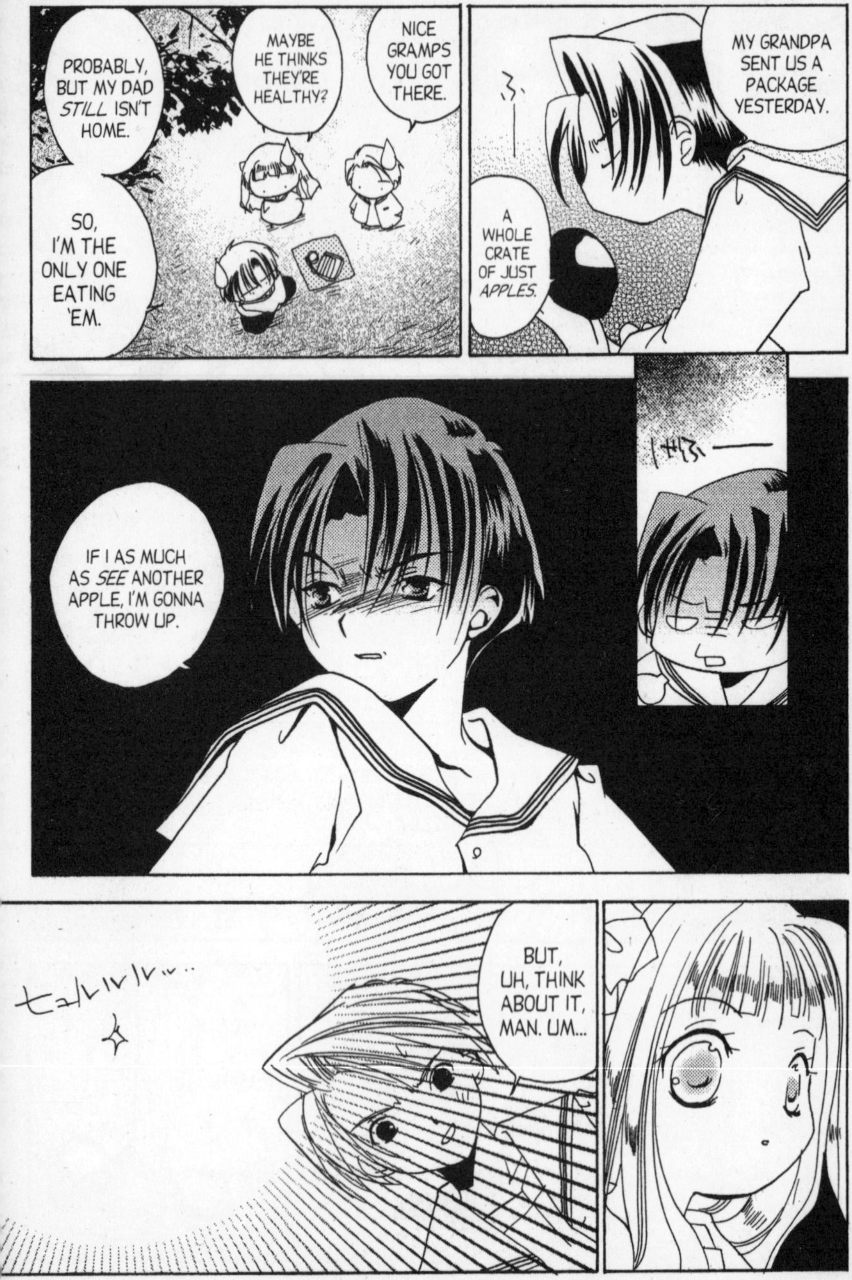
MY GRANDPA SENT US A PACKAGE YESTERDAY.
A WHOLE CRATE OF JUST *APPLES.*
NICE GRAMPS YOU GOT THERE.
MAYBE HE THINKS THEY'RE HEALTHY?
PROBABLY, BUT MY DAD *STILL* ISN'T HOME.
SO, I'M THE ONLY ONE EATING 'EM.
IF I AS MUCH AS *SEE* ANOTHER APPLE, I'M GONNA THROW UP.
BUT, UH, THINK ABOUT IT, MAN. UM...
ヒュルルルル…

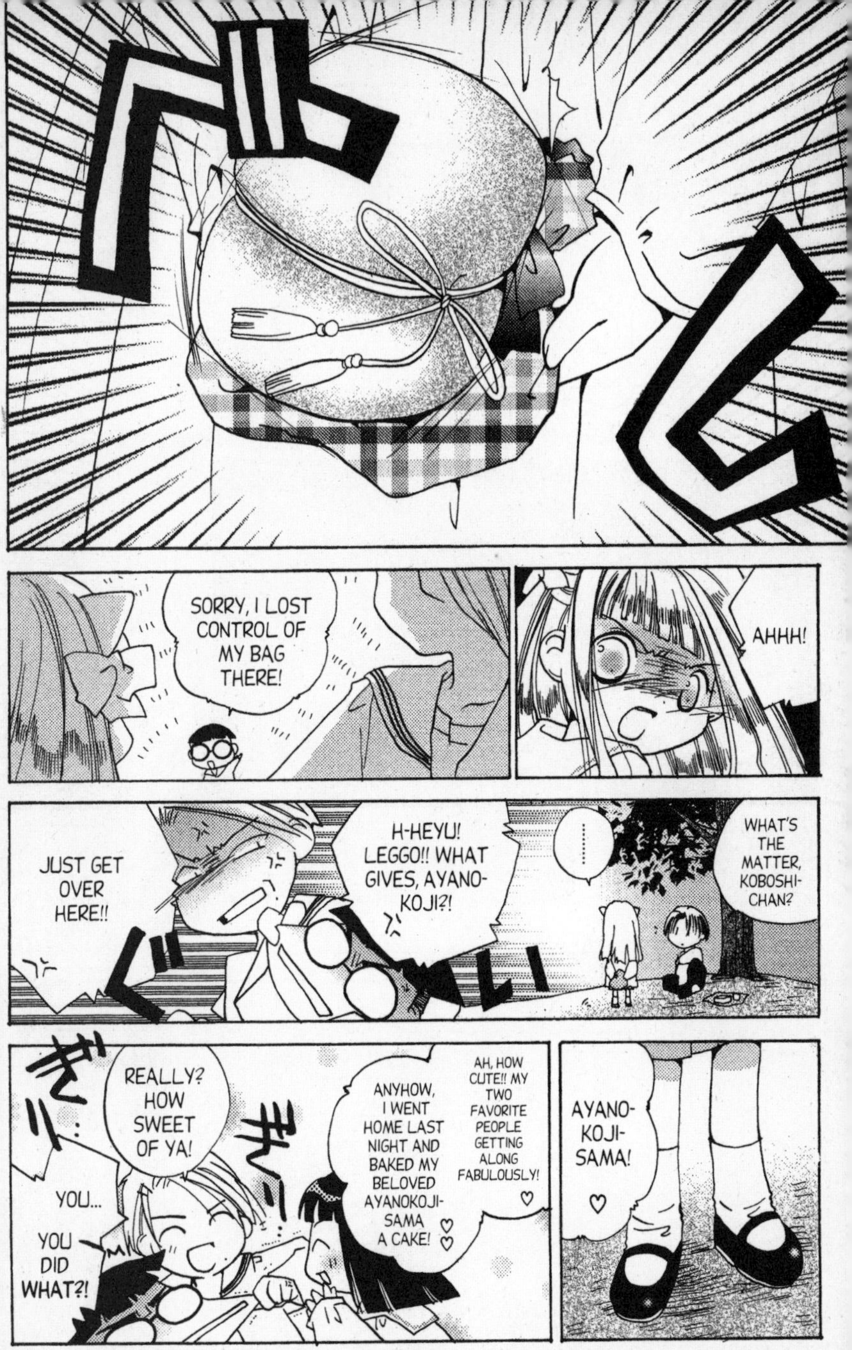
AHHH!
SORRY, I LOST CONTROL OF MY BAG THERE!
WHAT'S THE MATTER, KOBOSHI-CHAN?
......
H-HEYU! LEGGO!! WHAT GIVES, AYANO-KOJI?!
JUST GET OVER HERE!!
AYANO-KOJI-SAMA! ♡
AH, HOW CUTE!! MY TWO FAVORITE PEOPLE GETTING ALONG FABULOUSLY! ♡
ANYHOW, I WENT HOME LAST NIGHT AND BAKED MY BELOVED AYANOKOJI-SAMA A CAKE! ♡♡
REALLY? HOW SWEET OF YA!
YOU...
YOU DID WHAT?!

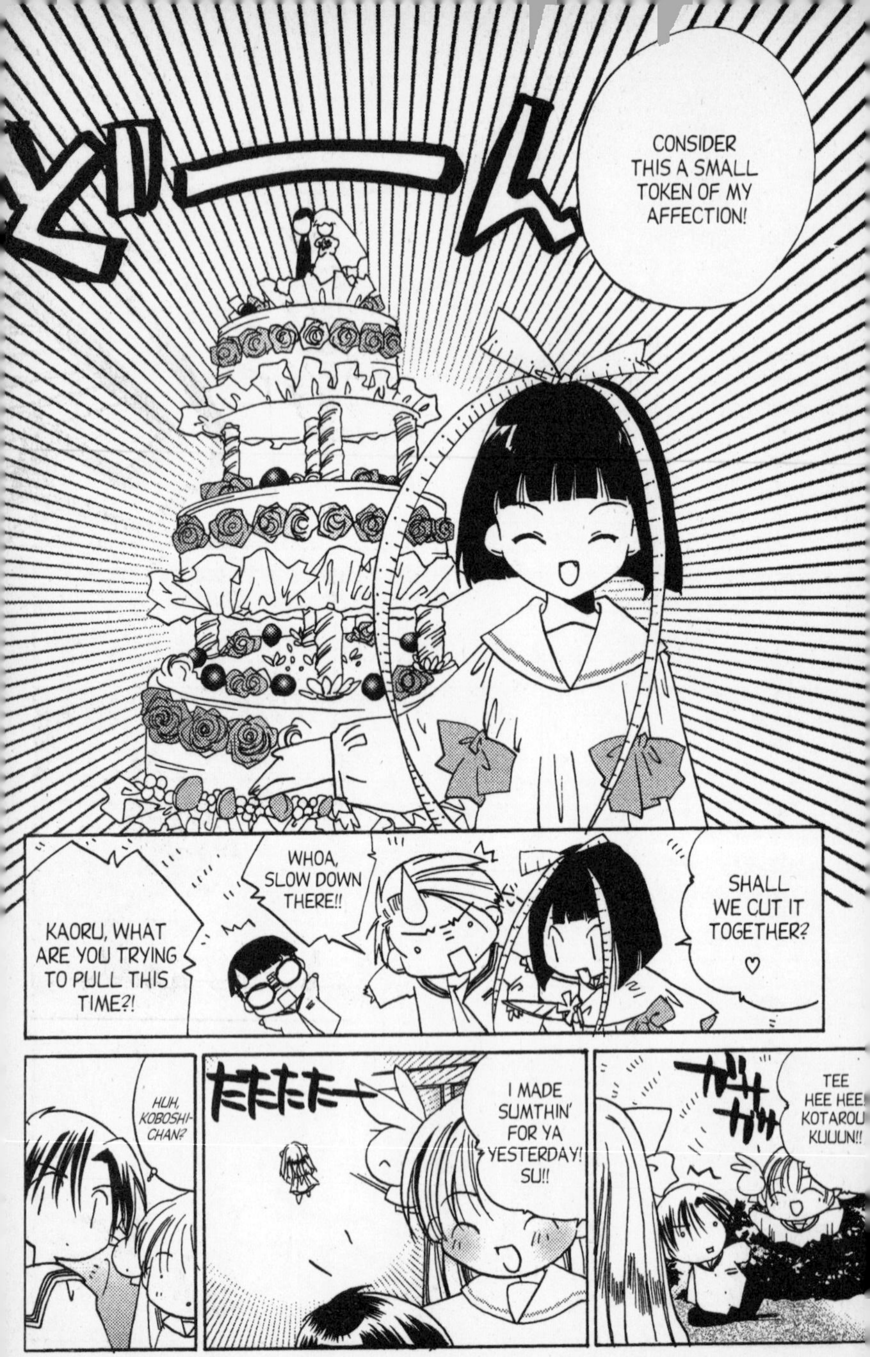
どーーん
CONSIDER THIS A SMALL TOKEN OF MY AFFECTION!
SHALL WE CUT IT TOGETHER? ♡
WHOA, SLOW DOWN THERE!!
KAORU, WHAT ARE YOU TRYING TO PULL THIS TIME?!
TEE HEE HEE! KOTAROU KUUUN!!
I MADE SUMTHIN' FOR YA YESTERDAY! SU!!
たたたたー
HUH, KOBOSHI-CHAN?

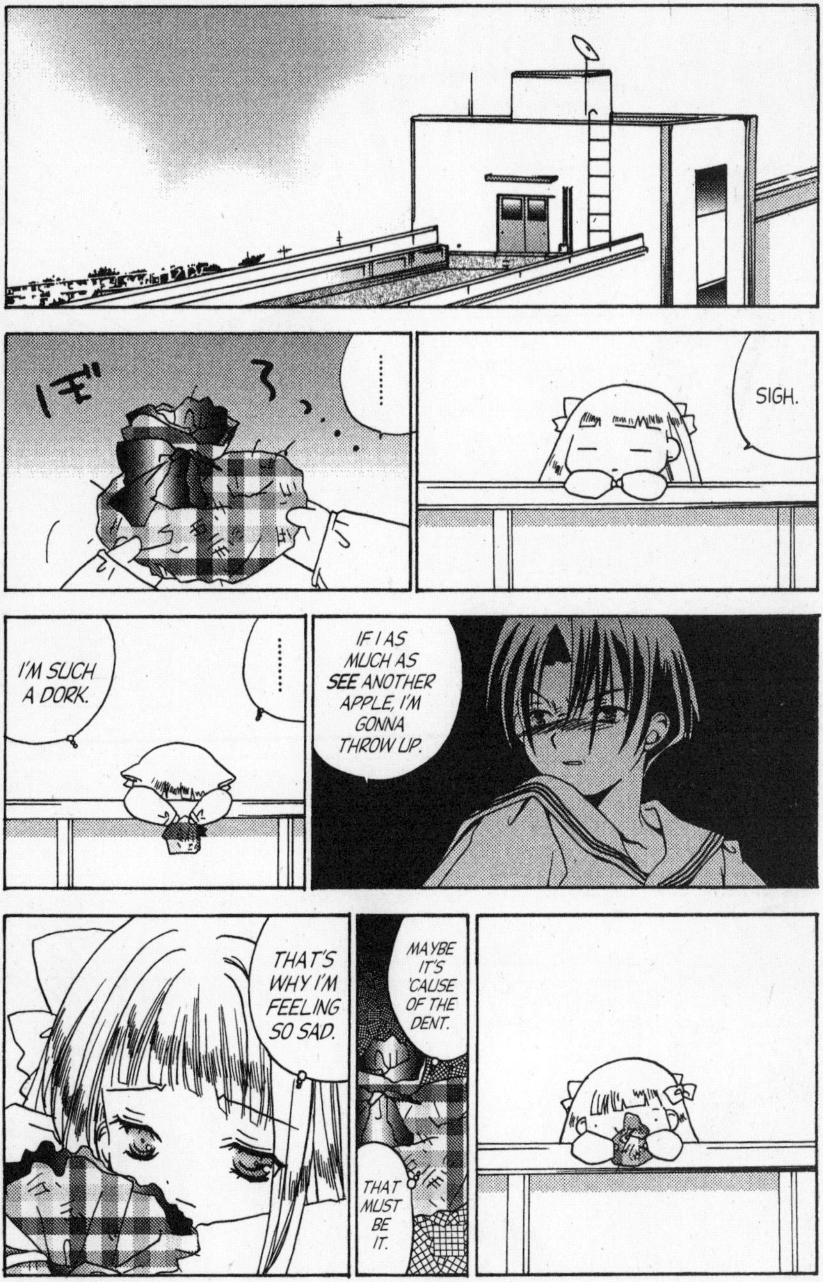

SIGH.
......
IF I AS MUCH AS **SEE** ANOTHER APPLE, I'M GONNA THROW UP.
......
I'M SUCH A DORK.
MAYBE IT'S 'CAUSE OF THE DENT.
THAT MUST BE IT.
THAT'S WHY I'M FEELING SO SAD.

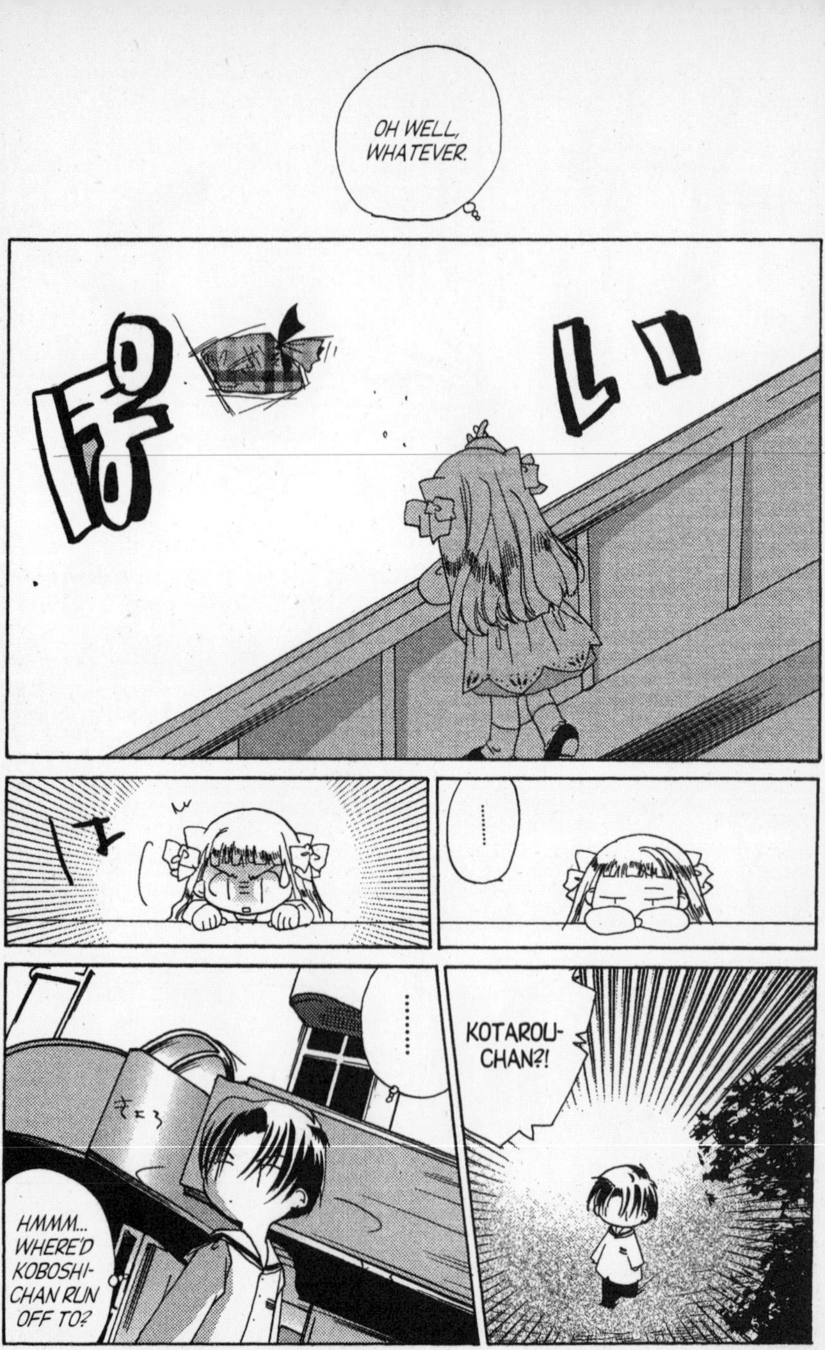
OH WELL, WHATEVER.
......
KOTAROU-CHAN?!
......
HMMM... WHERE'D KOBOSHI-CHAN RUN OFF TO?

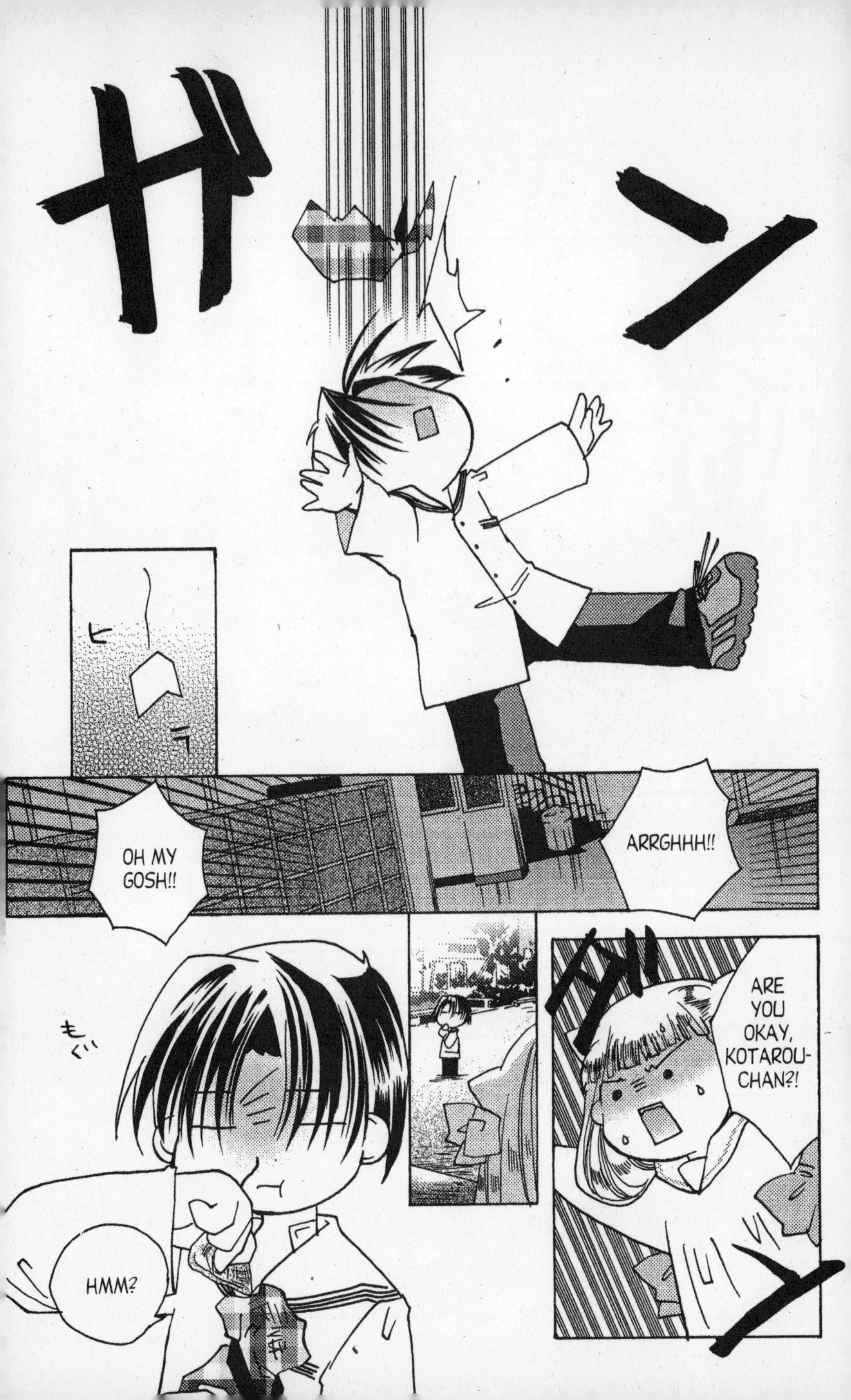
ガン
ARRGHHH!!
OH MY GOSH!!
ARE YOU OKAY, KOTAROU-CHAN?!
HMM?

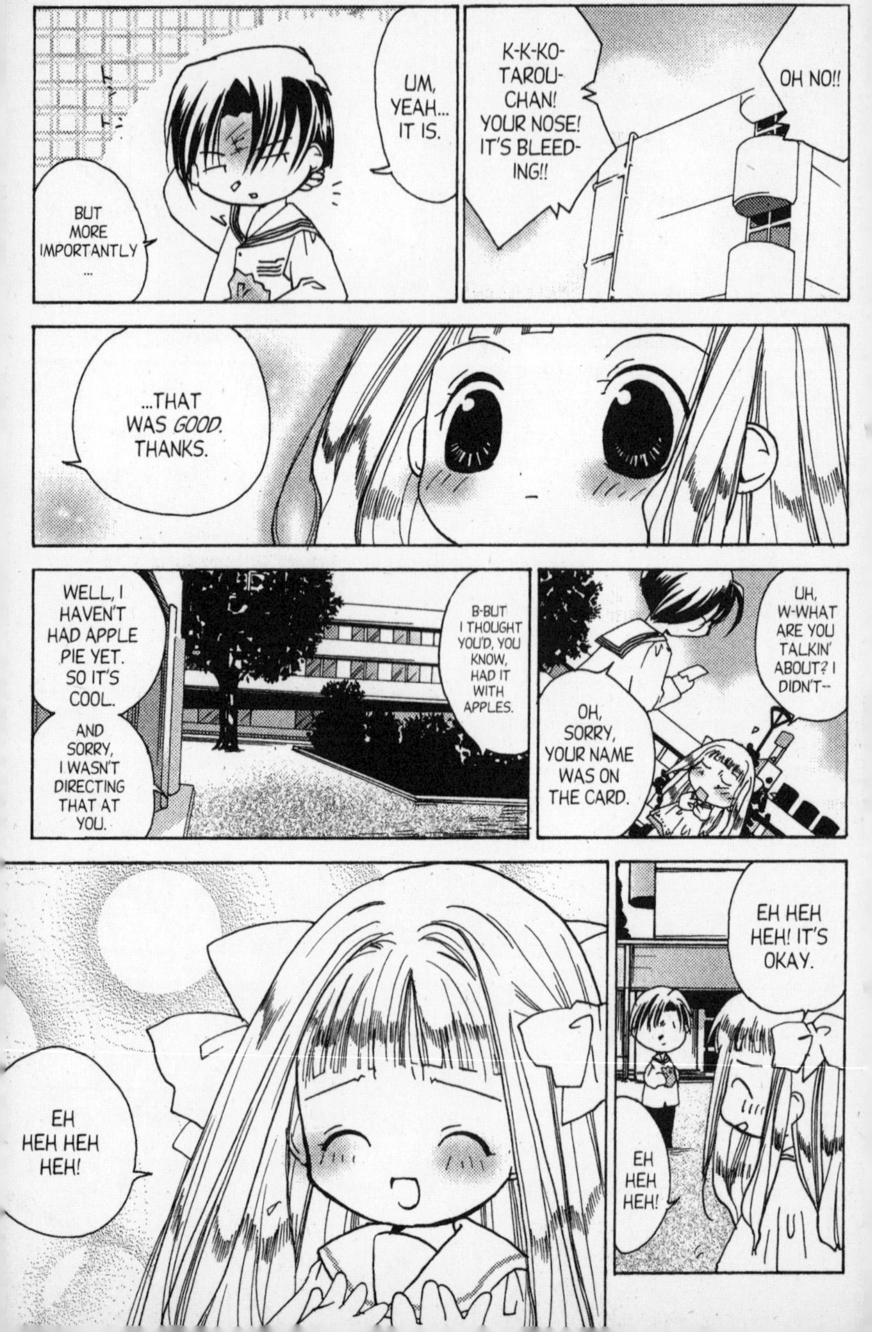
OH NO!!
K-K-KO-TAROU-CHAN! YOUR NOSE! IT'S BLEEDING!!
UM, YEAH... IT IS.
BUT MORE IMPORTANTLY ...
...THAT WAS *GOOD.* THANKS.
UH, W-WHAT ARE YOU TALKIN' ABOUT? I DIDN'T--
OH, SORRY, YOUR NAME WAS ON THE CARD.
B-BUT I THOUGHT YOU'D, YOU KNOW, HAD IT WITH APPLES.
WELL, I HAVEN'T HAD APPLE PIE YET. SO IT'S COOL.
AND SORRY, I WASN'T DIRECTING THAT AT YOU.
EH HEH HEH! IT'S OKAY.
EH HEH HEH!
EH HEH HEH HEH!

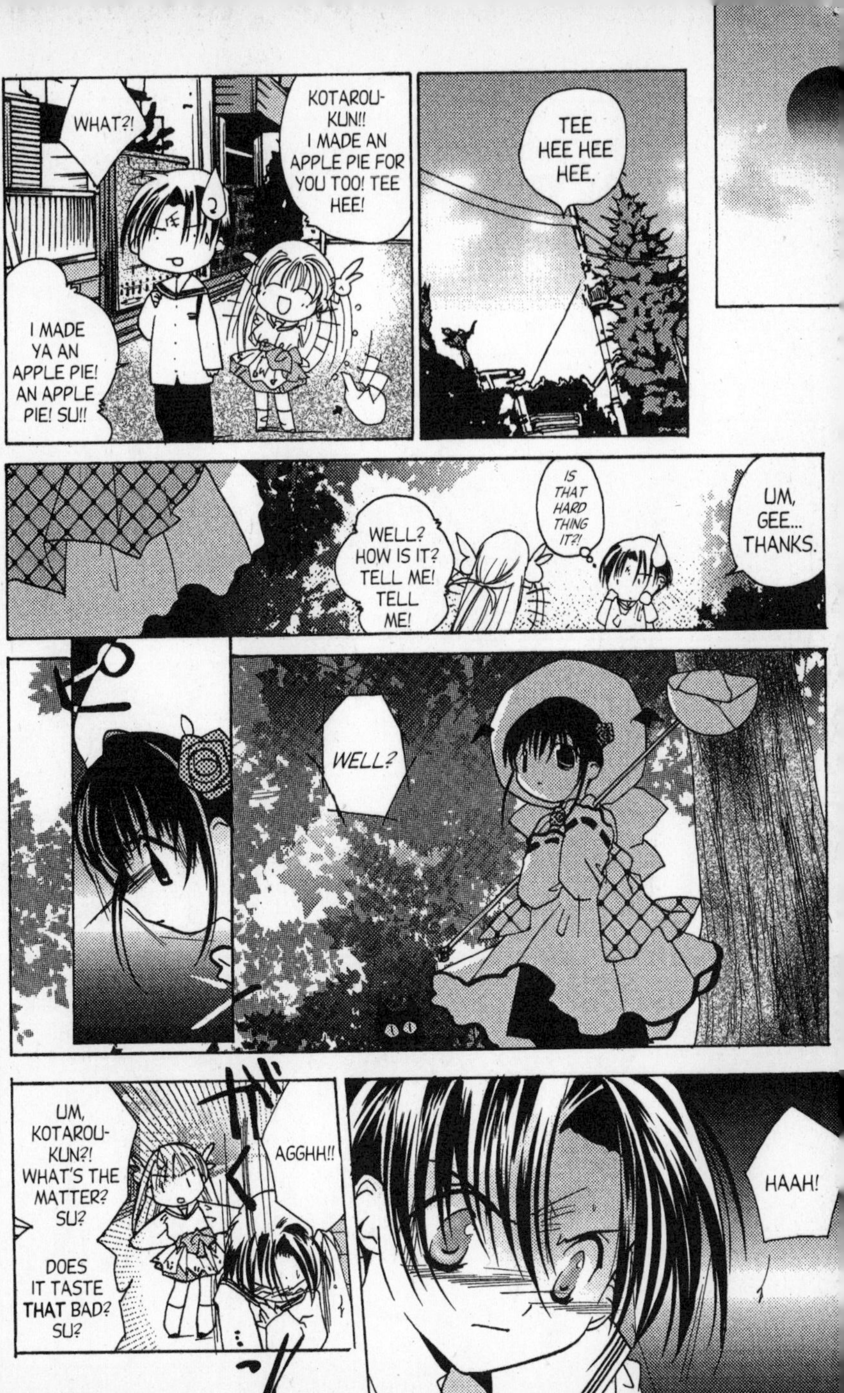

TEE HEE HEE HEE.
KOTAROU-KUN!! I MADE AN APPLE PIE FOR YOU TOO! TEE HEE!
WHAT?!
I MADE YA AN APPLE PIE! AN APPLE PIE! SU!!
UM, GEE... THANKS.
IS THAT HARD THING IT?!
WELL? HOW IS IT? TELL ME! TELL ME!
WELL?
HAAH!
AGGHH!!
UM, KOTAROU-KUN?! WHAT'S THE MATTER? SU?
DOES IT TASTE THAT BAD? SU?

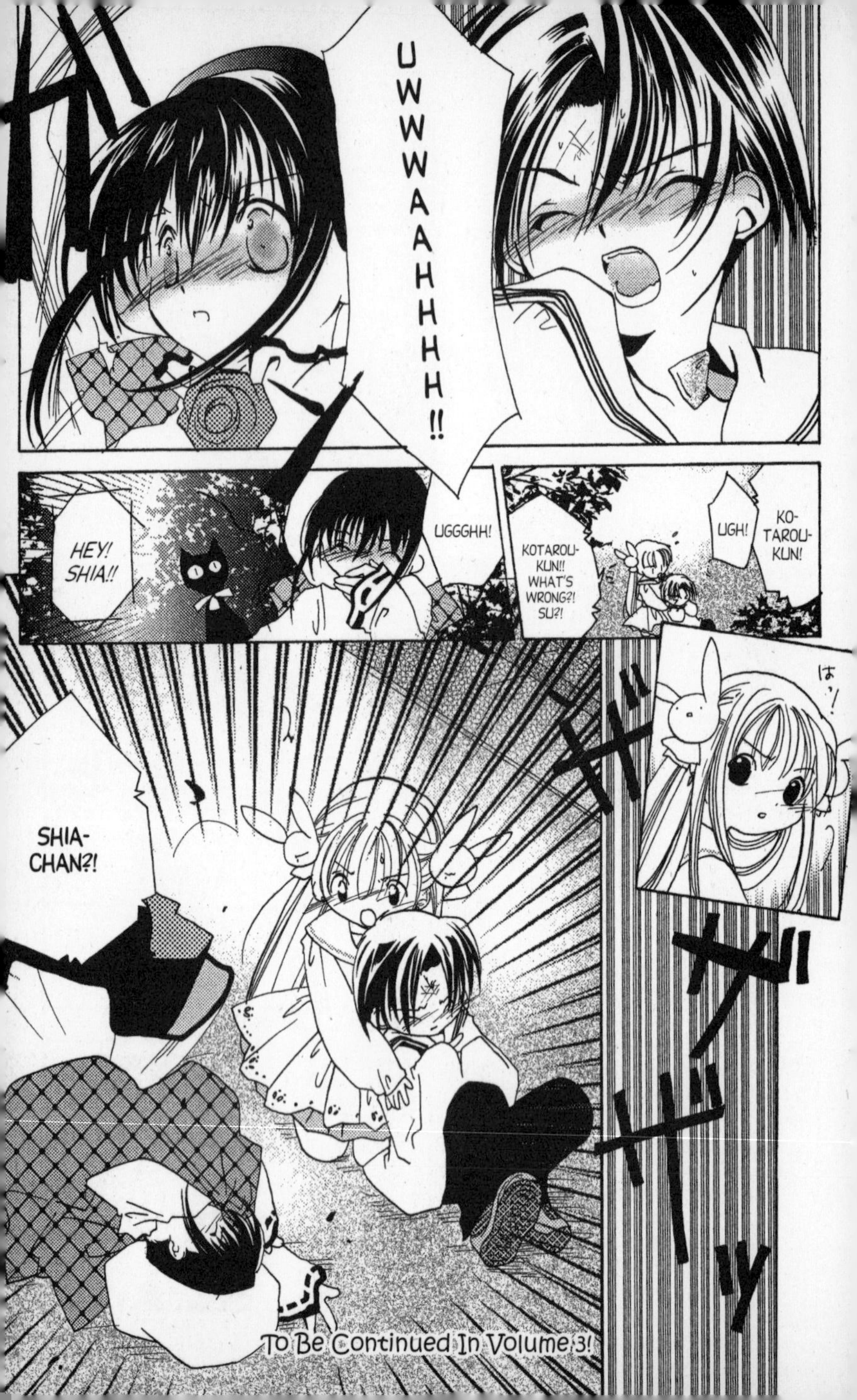
UWWWAAHHHHH!!
KO-TAROU-KUN!
UGH!
KOTAROU-KUN!! WHAT'S WRONG?! SU?!
UGGGHH!
HEY! SHIA!!
SHIA-CHAN?!
To Be Continued In Volume 3!

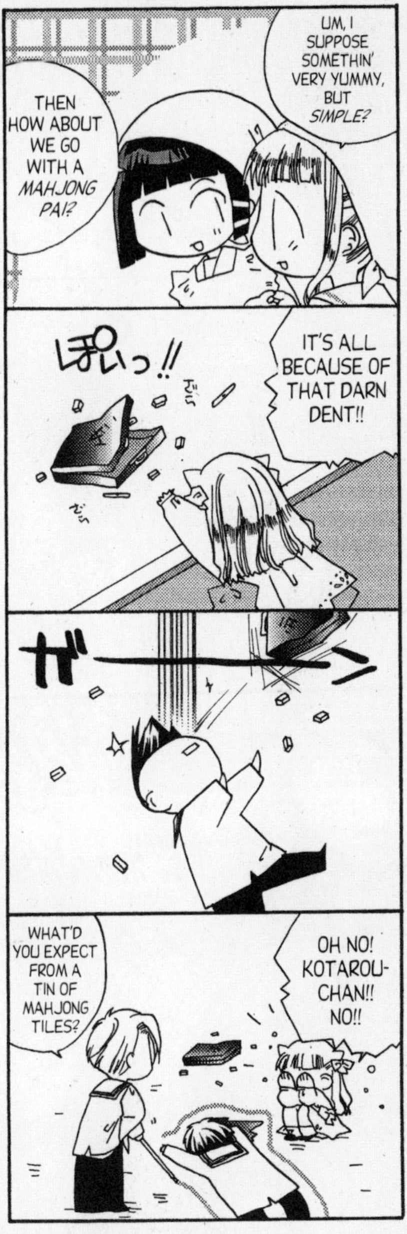
UM, I SUPPOSE SOMETHIN' VERY YUMMY, BUT *SIMPLE?*
THEN HOW ABOUT WE GO WITH A *MAHJONG PAI?*
IT'S ALL BECAUSE OF THAT DARN DENT!!
ぽいっ!!
ガーン
OH NO! KOTAROU-CHAN!! NO!!
WHAT'D YOU EXPECT FROM A TIN OF MAHJONG TILES?

* Afterword *

* Thank you, thank you so very much for reading this far into the series!

* The road to the making of this volume was chock full of horrors and heart-stopping trials and tribulations, but somehow it managed to make it to the press! Yay!

* And to everyone that continues to support me and my various projects...thank you so much! I truly appreciate it!!

* For everyone else, I promise I'll never stop trying! I'm going to continue learning how to perfect my craft so that I can one day make even better stories!!

Thanks for all your letters also!! I'm sorry I can't answer them all, but trust me; they are definitely helping to keep me going!! Thanks again!!

By the way, I received an e-mail that completely guessed the name of the actual school I used as the model for the one in the series. And yep, you're absolutely right. (Hee hee!) Very impressive...

(It's actually my alma mater, so one of my kohai also came up to me one day and asked, "Hey, isn't that our school?" Dohh!!♥
Weird thing is, it used to be a girl's academy and now it's co-ed. Wow, lucky them.)

I bet it has to do with the low birth rate.

Anyway, I hope that you'll stick around for Volume 3!♥

Until then...

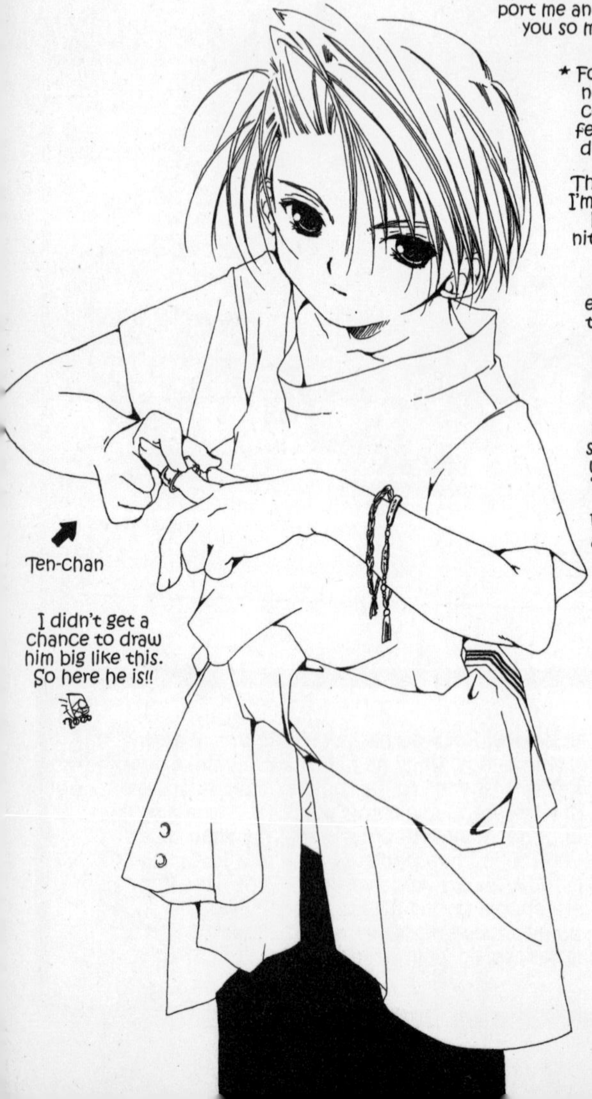

Ten-Chan

I didn't get a chance to draw him big like this. So here he is!!

In the Next Volume of...

PITA-TEN

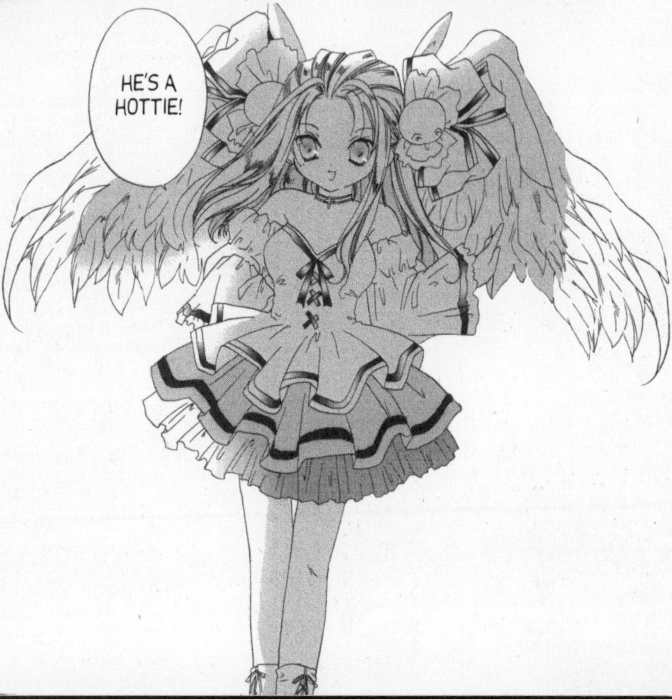
HE'S A HOTTIE!

Ever since he was a little boy, Kotarou has been able to see angels. This has certainly come in handy, since he has one living next door. But when the angel Sasha descends to Earth, she's a bit flustered by Kotarou's ability to sense her. How is this possible? Sasha also has suspicions about Shia. Indeed, what secrets does Shia keep safely tucked inside her raven-topped head? Why did she bite Kotarou? Is she a vampire? A demon? A ghost? Another angel? Why does her cat, Nya, dislike Misha with such a strong passion? In the midst of such contemplations, Sasha develops a massive crush on Takashi! But wait! Can it be? Does Takashi actually have feelings for...Shia?!

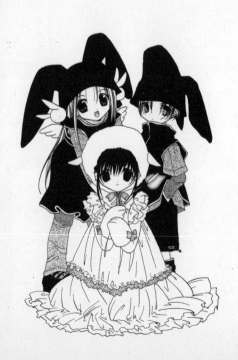

ALSO AVAILABLE FROM ☜☺ TOKYOPOP®

REBOUND
REMOTE
RISING STARS OF MANGA
SABER MARIONETTE J
SAILOR MOON
SAINT TAIL
SAMURAI DEEPER KYO
SAMURAI GIRL REAL BOUT HIGH SCHOOL
SCRYED
SEIKAI TRILOGY, THE CREST OF THE STARS
SGT. FROG
SHAOLIN SISTERS
SHIRAHIME-SYO: SNOW GODDESS TALES
SHUTTERBOX
SKULL MAN, THE
SNOW DROP
SORCERER HUNTERS
STONE
SUIKODEN III
SUKI
TOKYO BABYLON
TOKYO MEW MEW
UNDER THE GLASS MOON
VAMPIRE GAME
VISION OF ESCAFLOWNE, THE
WILD ACT
WISH
WORLD OF HARTZ
X-DAY
ZODIAC P.I.

NOVELS

KARMA CLUB
SAILOR MOON

ART BOOKS

CARDCAPTOR SAKURA
CLAMP NORTHSIDE
CLAMP SOUTHSIDE
MAGIC KNIGHT RAYEARTH
PEACH: MIWA UEDA ILLUSTRATIONS

ANIME GUIDES

COWBOY BEBOP ANIME GUIDES
GUNDAM TECHNICAL MANUALS
SAILOR MOON SCOUT GUIDES

TOKYOPOP KIDS

STRAY SHEEP

CINE-MANGA™

ASTRO BOY
CARDCAPTORS
DUEL MASTERS
FAIRLY ODDPARENTS, THE
FINDING NEMO
G.I. JOE SPY TROOPS
JACKIE CHAN ADVENTURES
JIMMY NEUTRON BOY GENIUS, THE ADVENTURES OF
KIM POSSIBLE
LILO & STITCH
LIZZIE MCGUIRE
LIZZIE MCGUIRE: THE MOVIE
MALCOLM IN THE MIDDLE
POWER RANGERS: NINJA STORM
SHREK 2
SPONGEBOB SQUAREPANTS
SPY KIDS 2
SPY KIDS 3-D: GAME OVER
TEENAGE MUTANT NINJA TURTLES
THAT'S SO RAVEN
TRANSFORMERS: ARMADA
TRANSFORMERS: ENERGON

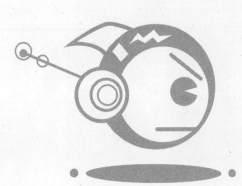

For more
information visit
www.TOKYOPOP.com

01.09.04T

ALSO AVAILABLE FROM TOKYOPOP®

MANGA

.HACK//LEGEND OF THE TWILIGHT
@LARGE
ABENOBASHI
A.I. LOVE YOU
AI YORI AOSHI
ANGELIC LAYER
ARM OF KANNON
BABY BIRTH
BATTLE ROYALE
BATTLE VIXENS
BRAIN POWERED
BRIGADOON
B'TX
CANDIDATE FOR GODDESS, THE
CARDCAPTOR SAKURA
CARDCAPTOR SAKURA - MASTER OF THE CLOW
CHOBITS
CHRONICLES OF THE CURSED SWORD
CLAMP SCHOOL DETECTIVES
CLOVER
COMIC PARTY
CONFIDENTIAL CONFESSIONS
CORRECTOR YUI
COWBOY BEBOP
COWBOY BEBOP: SHOOTING STAR
CRESCENT MOON
CULDCEPT
CYBORG 009
D.N. ANGEL
DEMON DIARY
DEMON ORORON, THE
DEUS VITAE
DIGIMON
DIGIMON ZERO TWO
DIGIMON TAMERS
DOLL
DRAGON HUNTER
DRAGON KNIGHTS
DREAM SAGA
DUKLYON: CLAMP SCHOOL DEFENDERS
ERICA SAKURAZAWA COLLECTED WORKS
EERIE QUEERIE!
ET CETERA
ETERNITY
EVIL'S RETURN
FAERIES' LANDING
FAKE
FLCL
FORBIDDEN DANCE
FRUITS BASKET
G GUNDAM
GATE KEEPERS

GETBACKERS
GIRL GOT GAME
GRAVITATION
GTO
GUNDAM SEED ASTRAY
GUNDAM WING
GUNDAM WING: BATTLEFIELD OF PACIFISTS
GUNDAM WING: ENDLESS WALTZ
GUNDAM WING: THE LAST OUTPOST (G-UNIT)
HAPPY MANIA
HARLEM BEAT
I.N.V.U.
IMMORTAL RAIN
INITIAL D
ISLAND
JING: KING OF BANDITS
JULINE
KARE KANO
KILL ME, KISS ME
KINDAICHI CASE FILES, THE
KING OF HELL
KODOCHA: SANA'S STAGE
LAMENT OF THE LAMB
LES BIJOUX
LEGEND OF CHUN HYANG, THE
LOVE HINA
LUPIN III
MAGIC KNIGHT RAYEARTH I
MAGIC KNIGHT RAYEARTH II
MAHOROMATIC: AUTOMATIC MAIDEN
MAN OF MANY FACES
MARMALADE BOY
MARS
MINK
MIRACLE GIRLS
MIYUKI-CHAN IN WONDERLAND
MODEL
ONE
PARADISE KISS
PARASYTE
PEACH GIRL
PEACH GIRL: CHANGE OF HEART
PET SHOP OF HORRORS
PITA-TEN
PLANET LADDER
PLANETES
PRIEST
PRINCESS AI
PSYCHIC ACADEMY
RAGNAROK
RAVE MASTER
REALITY CHECK
REBIRTH

01.09.04T

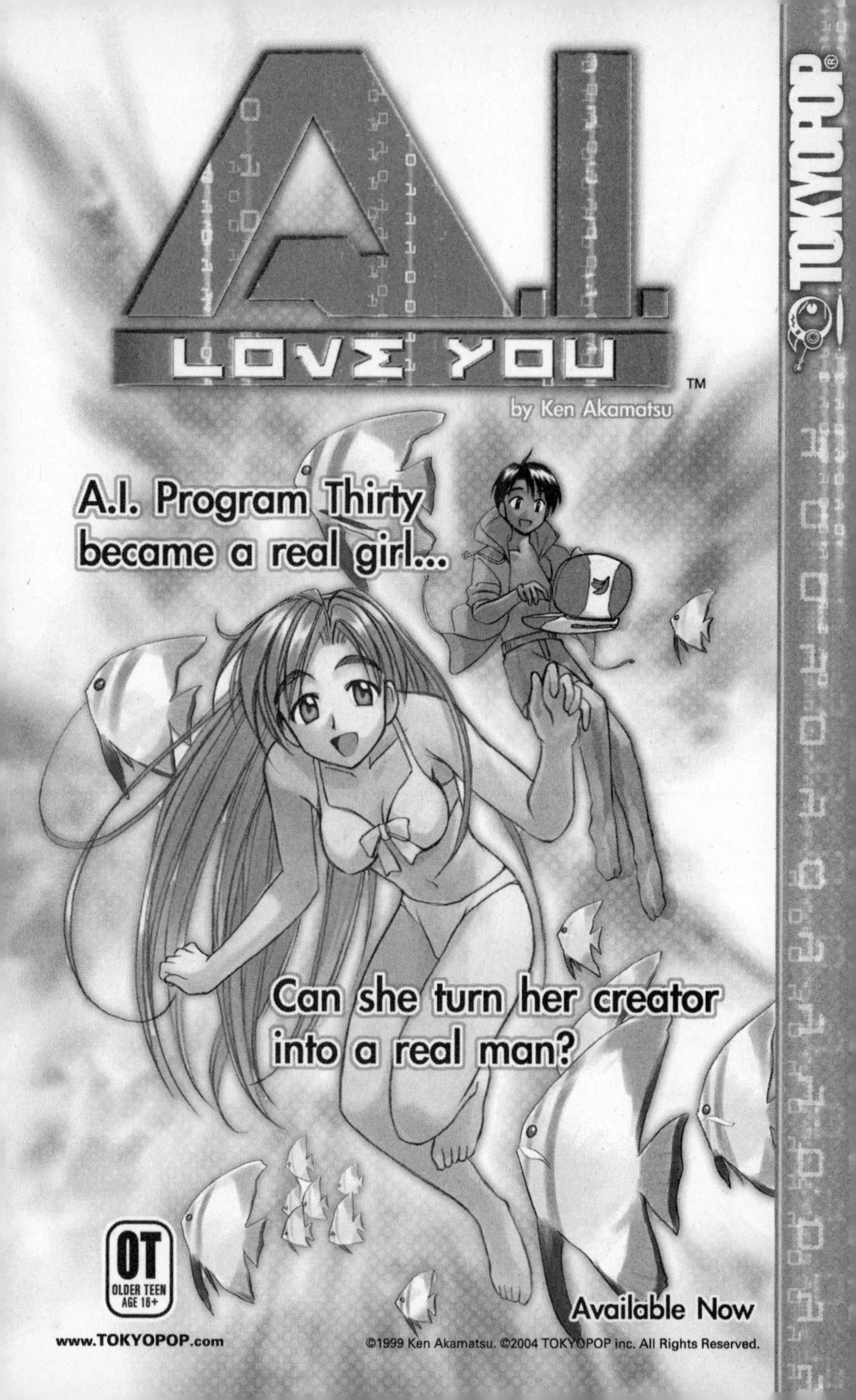
A.I. LOVE YOU™
by Ken Akamatsu
A.I. Program Thirty became a real girl...
Can she turn her creator into a real man?
OT OLDER TEEN AGE 16+
Available Now
TOKYOPOP®
www.TOKYOPOP.com
©1999 Ken Akamatsu. ©2004 TOKYOPOP inc. All Rights Reserved.

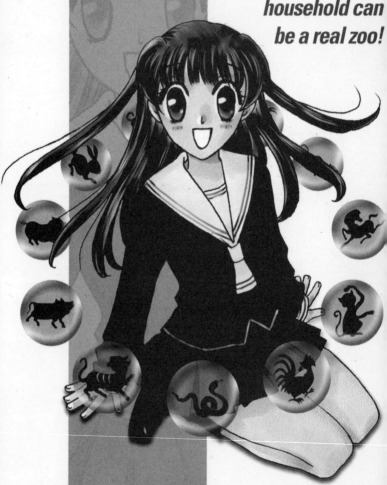

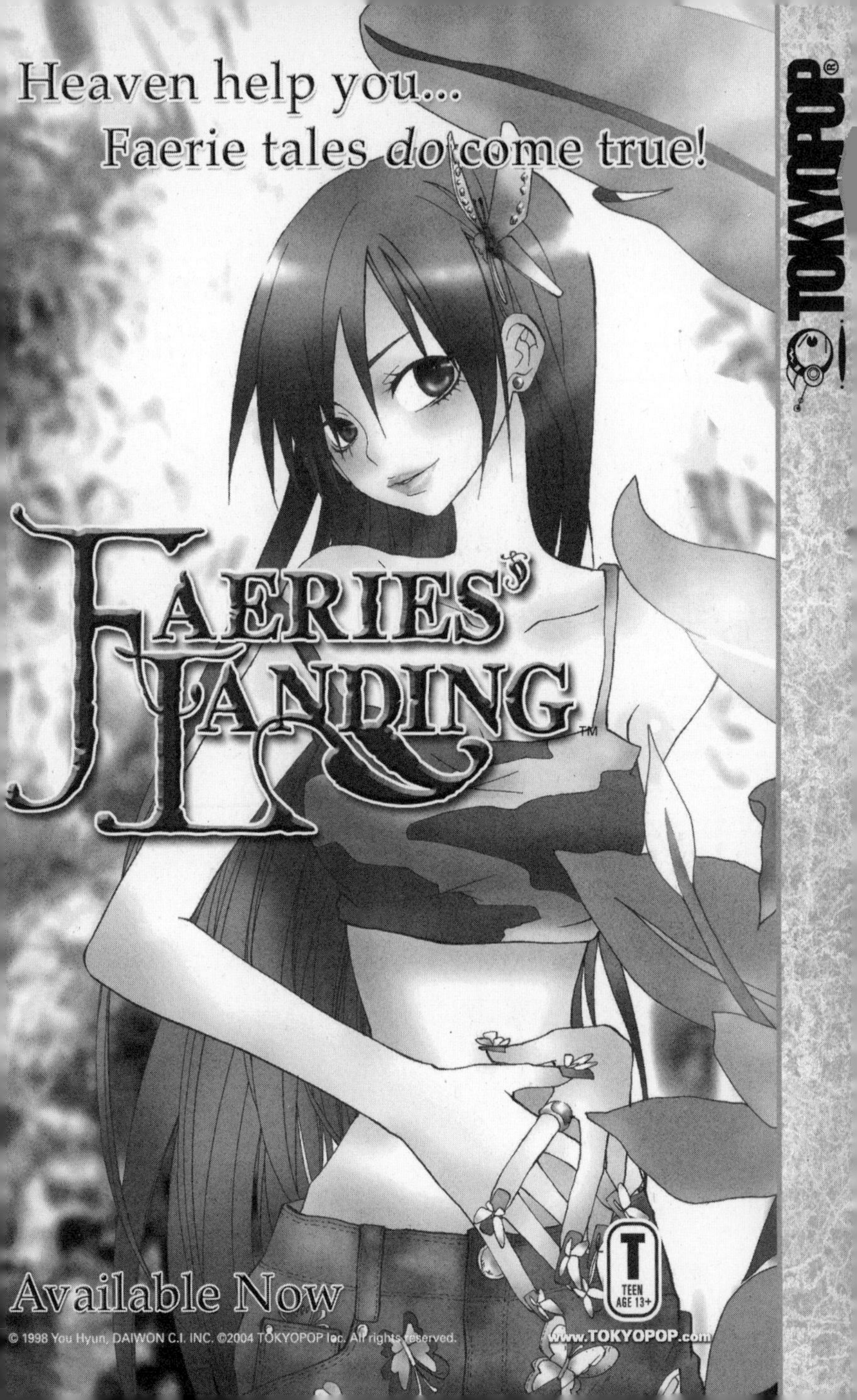
Heaven help you...
Faerie tales *do* come true!
TOKYOPOP®
FAERIES' LANDING™
Available Now
T
TEEN
AGE 13+
© 1998 You Hyun, DAIWON C.I. INC. ©2004 TOKYOPOP Inc. All rights reserved.
www.TOKYOPOP.com

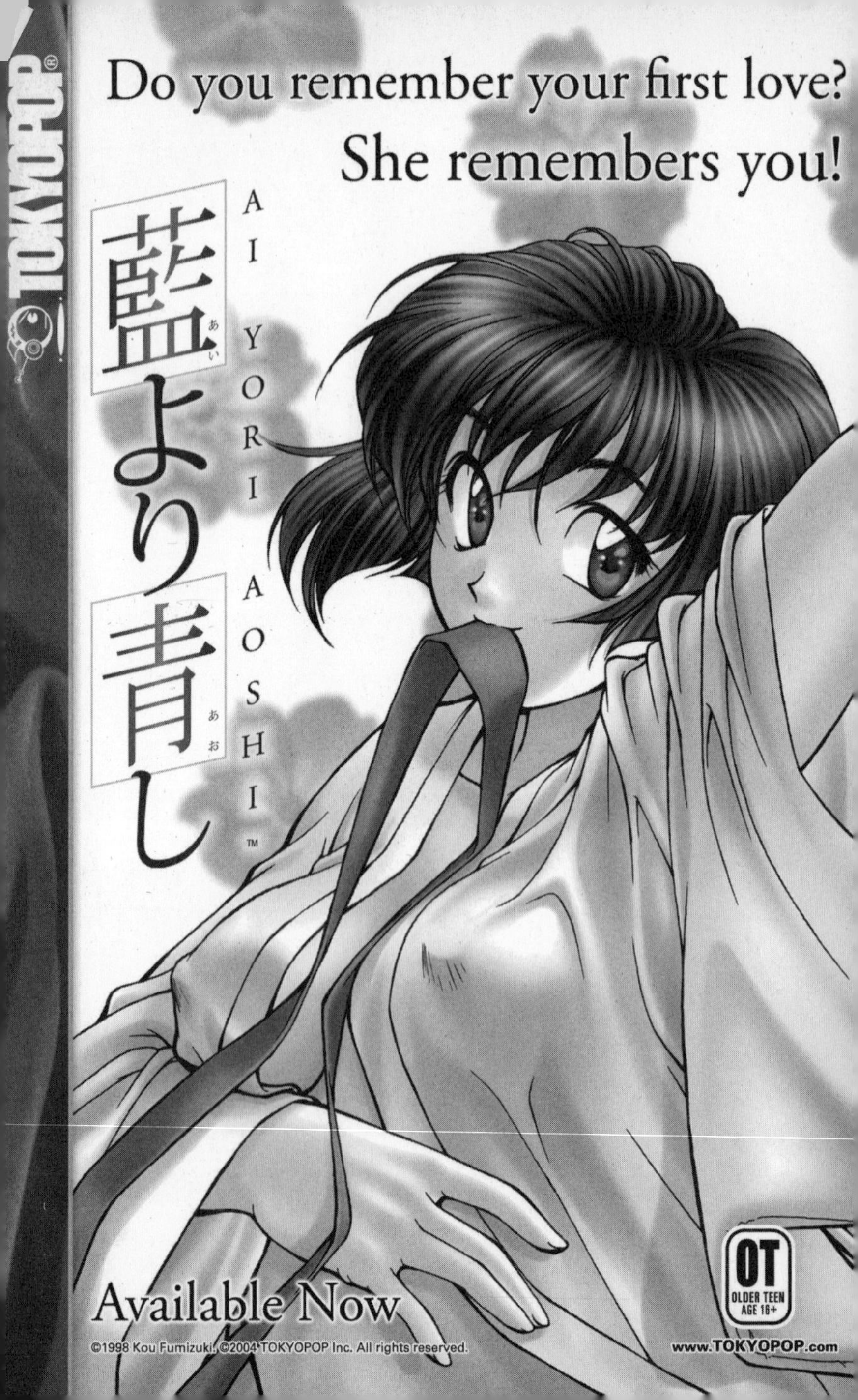
TOKYOPOP
Do you remember your first love?
She remembers you!
藍より青し
AI YORI AOSHI™
Available Now
OT
OLDER TEEN
AGE 16+
©1998 Kou Fumizuki. ©2004 TOKYOPOP Inc. All rights reserved.
www.TOKYOPOP.com

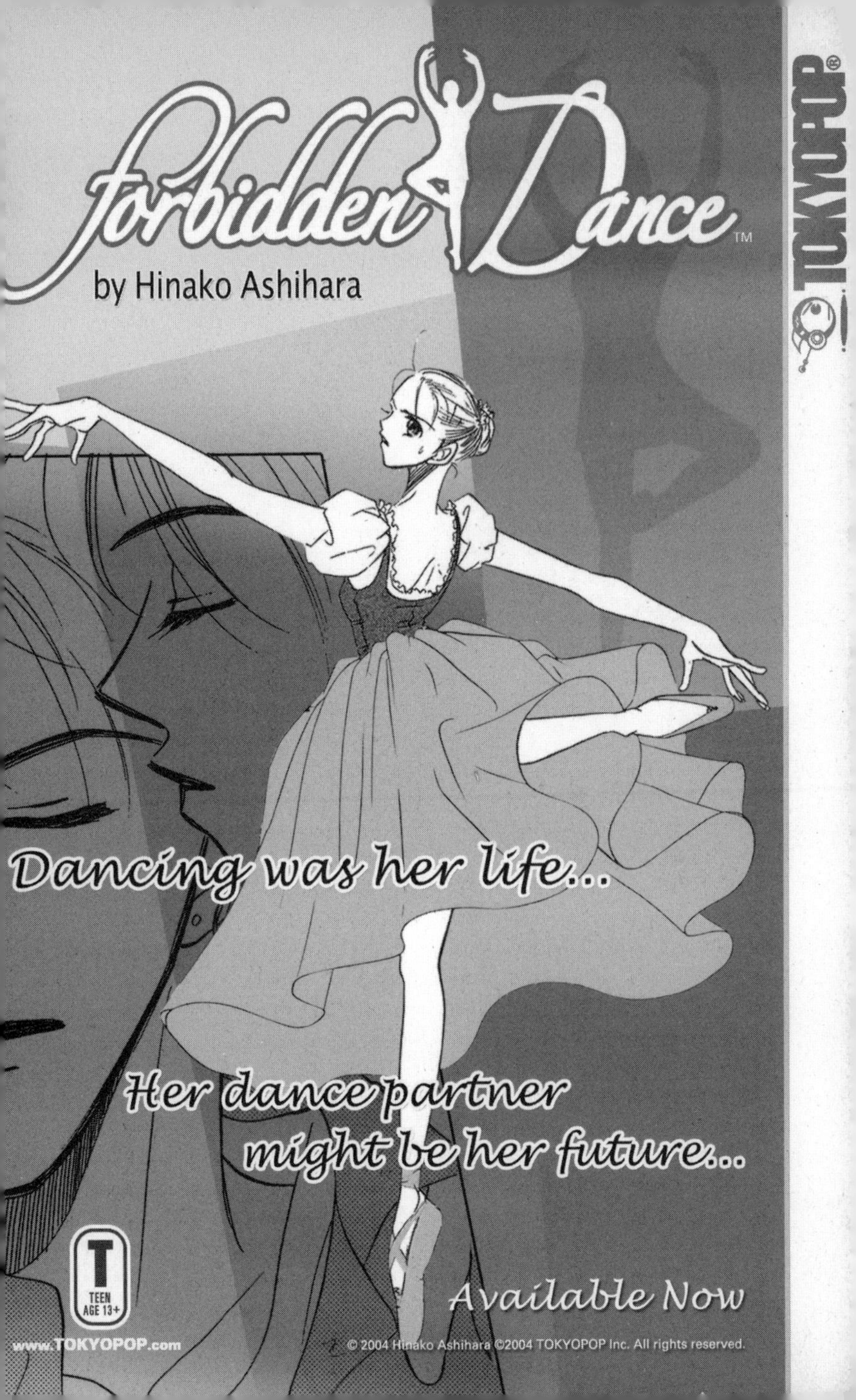
forbidden Dance™
by Hinako Ashihara
TOKYOPOP®
Dancing was her life...
Her dance partner
might be her future...
T
TEEN
AGE 13+
Available Now
www.TOKYOPOP.com
© 2004 Hinako Ashihara ©2004 TOKYOPOP Inc. All rights reserved.

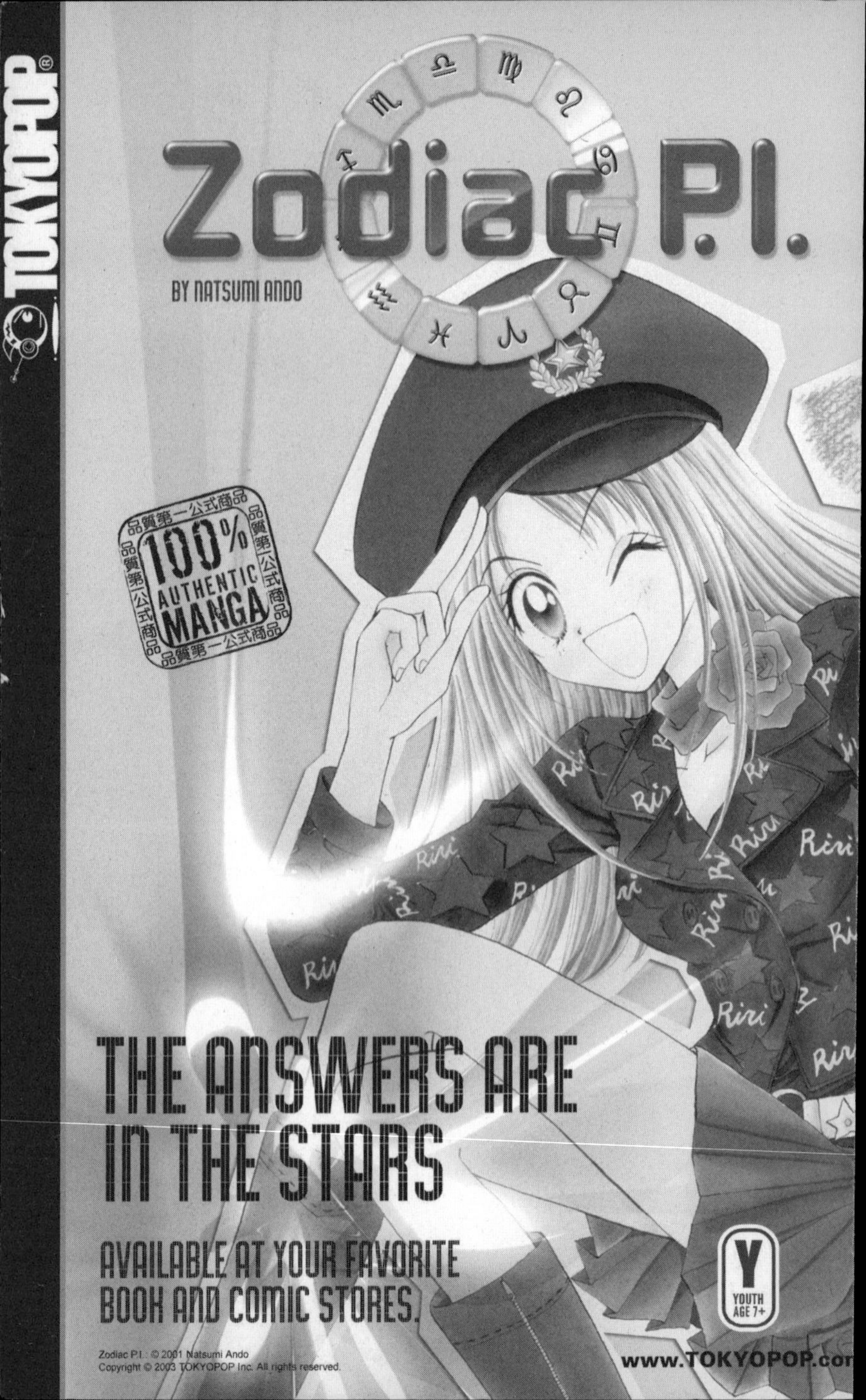

Zodiac P.I.

BY NATSUMI ANDO

100% AUTHENTIC MANGA

THE ANSWERS ARE IN THE STARS

AVAILABLE AT YOUR FAVORITE
BOOK AND COMIC STORES.

www.TOKYOPOP.com

Y YOUTH AGE 7+

TOKYOPOP®

kare kano

his and her circumstances

Story by Masami Tsuda

Life Was A Popularity Contest For Yukino.
Somebody Is About To Steal Her Crown.

Available Now At Your Favorite Book And Comic Stores!

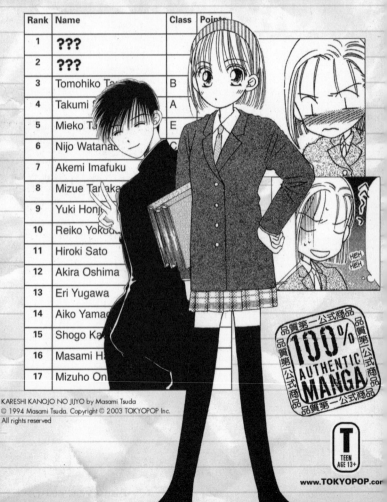

Rank	Name	Class	Points
1	???		
2	???		
3	Tomohiko Ta	B	
4	Takumi S	A	
5	Mieko Ta	E	
6	Nijo Watanab	C	
7	Akemi Imafuku		
8	Mizue Tanaka		
9	Yuki Honj		
10	Reiko Yokod		
11	Hiroki Sato		
12	Akira Oshima		
13	Eri Yugawa		
14	Aiko Yamag		
15	Shogo Ka		
16	Masami Ha		
17	Mizuho On		

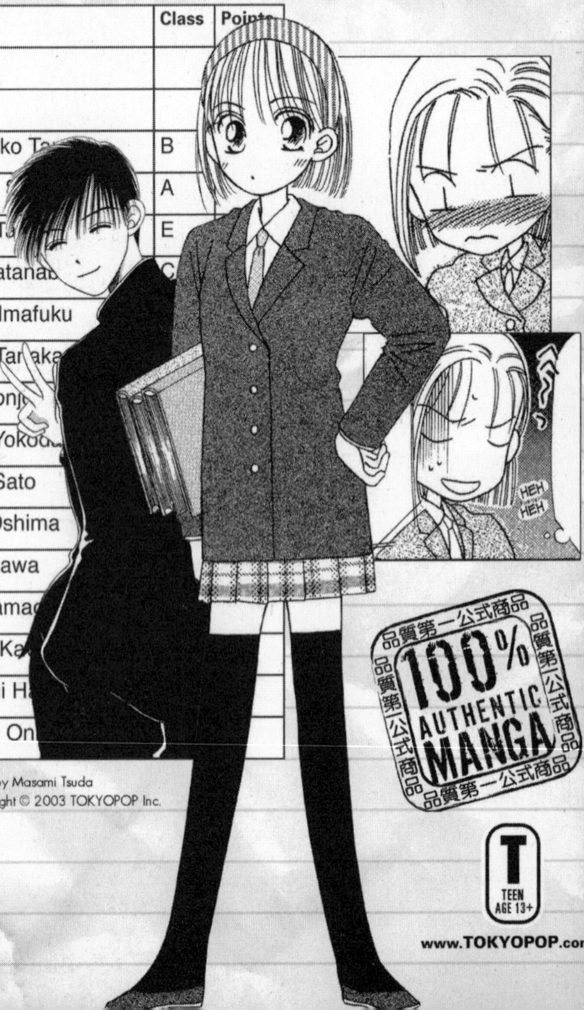
HEH
HEH

品質第一公式商品 100% AUTHENTIC MANGA

T TEEN AGE 13+

www.TOKYOPOP.com

S0-AVE-524

STOP!

This is the back of the book.
You wouldn't want to spoil a great ending!

This book is printed "manga-style," in the authentic Japanese right-to-left format. Since none of the artwork has been flipped or altered, readers get to experience the story just as the creator intended. You've been asking for it, so TOKYOPOP® delivered: authentic, hot-off-the-press, and far more fun!

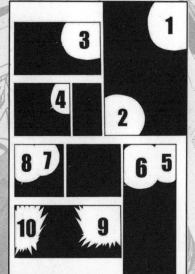

DIRECTIONS

If this is your first time reading manga-style, here's a quick guide to help you understand how it works.

It's easy... just start in the top right panel and follow the numbers. Have fun, and look for more 100% authentic manga from TOKYOPOP®!

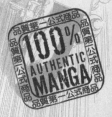